THE TRAVELS OF MARCO POLO

THE TRAVELS
OF
MARCO POLO

TRANSLATED INTO ENGLISH FROM THE TEXT OF
L. F. BENEDETTO

BY
ALDO RICCI

WITH AN INTRODUCTION AND INDEX BY
E. DENISON ROSS

GYAN

Published by

Gyan Publishing House
5, Ansari Road
Daryaganj, New Delhi-110002
Phone: 011-47034999, 9811692060
E-mail: books@gyanbooks.com

Distribution Network
gyanbooks.com
India, USA, Canada, UK, Australia, France

ISBN : 978-81-212-4567-8 (HB)
First Published, London, 1931

2nd Impression 2020

Printed at: Gyan Press, Delhi.

THE BROADWAY TRAVELLERS

EDITED BY SIR E. DENISON ROSS
AND EILEEN POWER

THE TRAVELS OF MARCO POLO

Translated into English from the text of
L. F. BENEDETTO

by

PROFESSOR ALDO RICCI

With an Introduction and Index by
SIR E. DENISON ROSS

Published by
GEORGE ROUTLEDGE & SONS, LTD.
BROADWAY HOUSE, CARTER LANE, LONDON

PLATE I

MINIATURE IN THREE COMPARTMENTS

(a) The Emperor Baldwin and the Brothers Niccolò and Matteo Polo in Constantinople

(b) The Brothers Polo before the Legate Tebaldo de Vicenza

(c) The Brothers Polo set sail for the Black sea

From the French manuscript containing the recension used by Pauthier and Yule, dating from the middle of the Fourteenth Century

[*B.M. Royal Manuscript* 19. *D. I. fol.* 58(*a*)]

[*front*

ILLUSTRATIONS

PAGE

I. MINIATURE IN THREE COMPARTMENTS *Frontispiece*
(*a*) The Emperor Baldwin and the Brothers Niccolò and Matteo in Constantinople.
(*b*) The Brothers Polo before the Legate Tebaldo de Vicenza.
(*c*) The Brothers Polo set sail for the Black Sea.
From the French Manuscript containing the recension used by Pauthier and Yule dating from the middle of the Fourteenth Century.
(*Royal Manuscript* 19 D. I, *fol.* 58 (*a*)) .

II. KUBILAI GIVES THE GOLDEN TABLET (PAÏZAH) TO THE BROTHERS POLO.
(*Royal Manuscript* 19 D. I, *fol.* 59 (*b*)) 6

III. CA' POLO, VENICE 18

IV. CHINESE BANK NOTE OF THE REIGN OF HUNG-WU (1368–1398) 148

IN THE TEXT

SEAL OF KUBILAI KAAN (Hu-pi-lieh).
This seal has the form of a rat in bronze . . . *on page* vi

SEAL OF CHINGIZ KHAN (Ch'êng-chi-ssŭ-han).
This seal has the form of a tortoise in black jade . *on page* vi

THE GREAT MAGNIFICENCE OF PRESTER JOHN, LORD OF GREATER INDIA AND OF ETHIOPIA . . . . *on page* xviii

MAPS

THE BROTHERS POLO STARTING OUT WITH THEIR CARAVAN.
Detail from the *Atlas Catalan* de la Bibliothèque Nationale de Paris 96

MAP OF HENRICUS MARTELLUS 208

MAP FROM RAMUSIO'S "NAVIGATIONI ET VIAGGI" . . . 284

MAP OF PTOLEMÆUS BY BERNARDUS SYLVANUS 336

忽必烈

SEAL OF KUBILAI KAAN [Hu-pi-lieh]

This seal has the form of a rat in bronze

成吉思汗

SEAL OF CHINGIZ KHAN [Ch'êng-chi-ssŭ-han]

This seal has the form of a tortoise in black jade

TWO SEALS BEARING THE NAMES OF CHINGIZ KHAN AND KUBILAI KAAN RECENTLY BROUGHT FROM CHINA

INTRODUCTION

MARCO POLO, the son of Niccolò Polo, was born in Venice in 1254. Soon after this date Niccolò Polo and his brother Matteo set out on a journey for the purposes of trade in the East which eventually led them via Bukhara to the court of the Great Kaan Kubilai in Cathay. Kubilai was so well pleased with these Venetians that he despatched them on a mission to the Pope with letters inviting His Holiness to send one hundred educated missionaries who might convert his people to Christianity.

When the brothers, on their return journey, reached Acre in April 1269, they learnt that there was no Pope: for Clement IV had died in the previous year (29th November 1268) and no new Pope had been elected. When, in the middle of 1271, the cardinals had still not made their choice of Pope, the Polos set out again for Cathay, taking the seventeen-year-old Marco with them. They had not gone far when news came that a new Pope had at last been elected (1st September 1271). The new Pope, Gregory X, instead of complying with Kubilai's request for one hundred missionaries, sent only two Dominicans, who, losing heart, turned back when they had gone only a very short distance.

The first objective of the Polos was Hormuz, whence they intended to proceed by sea. On reaching the Persian Gulf they changed their plans and set out overland for China, via Kerman, Khurasan, Balkh, Badakhshan, Kashghar, Yarkand, Khotan, and Lop Nor, eventually arriving about May 1275 in the presence of

Kubilai Kaan, who was in his summer retreat at K'ai-p'ing-fu or Chandu (Coleridge's Xanadu).

During the long residence of the Polos in China, Marco was employed in various capacities (none probably as exalted as he would have us believe) and was sent on several distant missions, including one to Yün-nan and Burma and another to the Eastern provinces of China.

Kubilai became so attached to the Polos that it was only by chance that, at the end of seventeen years, they were able to leave the court, where they were virtual prisoners. It so happened that about the year 1289 envoys arrived from Arghun Khan, the Il-Khan or provincial ruler of Persia (A.D. 1284–1291), reporting the death of his favourite wife, Bolgana, and requesting the Great Kaan to send to Persia another lady of her kin. A suitable bride was found in the person of the seventeen-year-old Princess Cocachin, and the question was how to convey her in safety to Persia. It was a choice of evils. The long sea route naturally involved risks for the clumsy Chinese junks, while the land route presented no less serious dangers on account of the disturbed state of the provinces which lay on the route to Persia.

When at length the sea route was chosen, the envoys requested that they might be accompanied by the three Venetians, whose maritime experience would minimise the dangers of the voyage. Kubilai, though most reluctant to part with the Polos, set the safety of the Princess Cocachin above his own personal feelings and consented to let them go. Early in 1292 the little fleet, composed of 14 ships and carrying 600 passengers in addition to the crews, set sail from the port of Zayton.

The whole journey to Hormuz lasted over two years. The course followed is fairly well-established, and included Champa, Java, Sondur and Condur, the Straits of Singapore, the Straits of Malacca, the Nicobar

Islands, Ceylon, Malabar, Makran, and so on to Hormuz in the Persian Gulf. It seems evident that if Marco Polo visited the Western littoral of India, it was during one of his missions and not on this particular journey to Persia.

By the time the Polos reached Hormuz their numbers had been sadly depleted, for according to Marco Polo only eighteen passengers had survived the hardships of the journey, though this is probably an exaggeration. He tells us that Arghun had already died—as a matter of fact he had died before they left China in 1291. Princess Cocachin was placed under the protection of Kaikhatu who had succeeded his brother, and she was eventually given in marriage to Ghazan Khan, the son of Arghun, who in 1295 became Il-Khan of Persia.

The Polos after spending nine months at the court of Kaikhatu proceeded homewards via Trebizond, Constantinople and Negropont, finally reaching Venice some time in 1295, after 25 years absence.

Ramusio tells us how the three Polos on arrival at their house found it occupied by relatives, who having supposed them long since dead refused to recognise them. Indeed their appearance was much changed and they had, we are told, "a certain indescribable smack of the Tartar both in air and accent" (*che rappresentava un non so che del Tartaro nel volto, e nel parlare*).

Not many months after their arrival in Venice news came that Lamba Doria, captain of the Genoese fleet, had arrived with 70 galleys at the Island of Curzola, and in the expedition now sent out from Venice to attack them, Marco Polo, according to Ramusio, commanded a galley. A battle took place in September in which the Venetian fleet was defeated and Marco Polo, while displaying the greatest courage in an attempt to save the situation, was wounded and taken prisoner. He was sent to Genoa where Ramusio tells us how, the fame of his rare qualities and his wonderful journey having been spread abroad, all the city assembled to see and speak to him, treating him not as a prisoner, but as a dear friend and a highly honoured gentleman. He grew so tired of telling his adventures that he was advised to put them into writing. In order to refresh his memory he sent a letter asking his father in Venice to send him the notes and memoranda which he had brought with him from the East. The narrative thus dictated was put into literary form by a man of letters from Pisa called Rustichello, who was one of Marco's fellow-prisoners. It seems to be definitely proved that none of the manuscripts which have come down to us represent the original form of the narrative, but that certain texts show a greater nearness to this lost original than others.

Almost all the MSS. and early printed editions known to us may be grouped in one or other of two main categories; namely, Group A, those resembling the so-called Paris Geographic text, and Group B, those related to the Italian version prepared by Ramusio and printed in 1559—two years after his death.

Group A includes almost all the known remodellings, translations and editions, especially important being the MS. fr. 116 of the Bibliothèque Nationale. But they all descend from a prototype which was already far removed from the original as we know from the many lacunae and errors.

Group B is represented by Ramusio, by certain Venetian MSS. and by a Latin MS. recently discovered in the Ambrosian Library, Milan, by Professor Benedetto, now known as Codex Z. This MS. is a copy made in 1795 of a manuscript written in the XIV-XVth centuries and belonging to Cardinal Zelada. It is obviously derived from a Franco-Italian version infinitely superior to Group A but it is not complete, for about one-third of the text consists of arbitrary abridgements, though the remaining two-thirds reproduce faithfully the text of fr. 1116 where they coincide. It contains no less than 200 passages not met with in Group A and three-fifths of these are found in Ramusio, who obviously had a "brother" of "Z" before him. But Codex Z is certainly not the Latin manuscript "di maravigliosà antichità" belonging to the family of Ghisi which Ramusio said he had seen and thought *might* be a copy of the *original*, for there is still much in Ramusio which is to be found neither in the other known versions nor in "Z." The original of "Z" is said to be in Toledo, but Professor Benedetto has been unable to obtain any news of it, and until this MS. is forthcoming the Milan copy must be received with a certain amount of caution.

With reference to the discovery of Codex "Z" it should be mentioned that some years ago Professor Benedetto was entrusted by the Comitato Geografico Nazionale Italiano in Florence with the task of preparing a new national edition of Marco Polo. He travelled all over Europe in order to study the known MSS. and if possible to discover others; and in the course of his visits to about fifty libraries he discovered many hitherto unknown MSS. of Marco Polo.

It has been Benedetto's difficult task to reconsider the whole question of Marco Polo texts in the light of newly-discovered manuscripts, and the result of his labours is given in a magnificent edition of the most famous of all manuscripts, namely the Geographic text (fr. 1116) carefully edited for the first time and collated with all the best known texts. To this text he has added at the foot of the page in their original form all those passages occurring in Ramusio, in "Z" and in other texts which seem to furnish valuable additions, and in some cases important variants.

Those who are unable to consult Benedetto's great edition, which was limited to 300 copies, are recommended to turn to the excellent introduction prefixed by Mr Penzer to his reprint of John Frampton's translation.[1] Here will be found, set out in very clear detail, a resumé of Benedetto's conclusions. In this place I have only given the briefest summary of this strange story.

The famous Gregoire group based on a lost Franco-Italian prototype and known as FG which formed the basis of both Pauthier's and Yule's versions was little utilized by Benedetto in his edition for reasons which at the time seemed to him sufficient.

Since the publication of his fine edition Benedetto has made a translation of the Geographic text and embodied in it the most important additional passages from the other texts. While making his Italian translation he has frequently had recourse to readings in the FG family of MSS. not noted in his edition. The present volume represents in the main the English translation of his Modern Italian version made by the late Signor Aldo Ricci whose untimely death occurred shortly after he had completed it. This English rendering has since been checked with the original texts by myself in consultation with Professor Benedetto.

Among the more important additions to Marco Polo's narrative furnished by MS. "Z" mav be mentioned the following:—

1. On p. 72 there is a new chapter on the province of Icoguristan with its capital Carachoco. These are the old kingdom of the Uighurs and the ruined city of Qara Khoja.

2. On pp. 261–263 there will be found translated a long passage from MS. "Z" (see Benedetto's edition, p. 158) describing "a race of people" living

[1] The Most Noble and Famous Travels of Marco Polo, together with the Travels of Nicolo de' Conti. Edited from the Elizabethan Translation of John Frampton, with Introduction, Notes, and Appendixes, by N. M. Penzer. pp. lx, 381, London, The Argonaut Press, 1929.

in Fu-chien, who professed what Marco Polo believed to be a peculiar kind of Christianity. Monsieur Pelliot in a notice of Benedetto's edition (*Journal des Savants*, January 1929, p. 42) points out that this passage undoubtedly refers to the Manichaeans who were very numerous in this province, and did not altogether disappear till the beginning of the seventeenth century.

3. On pp. 301, 302 there is a passage in connection with Malabar, derived from MS. "Z" (Benedetto's edition, p. 183), which constitutes a fresh tribute to the accuracy of Marco Polo's notes: "Again, in every day in the week they say there is an unlucky hour, that they call *choiach*; thus, for example, they say on Monday it is the hour of half-tierce; on Tuesday the hour of tierce; on Wednesday the hour of none; and so on for each day, the whole year through." I have not been able to trace the origin of the word *choiach*, but the superstition is still preserved in Malabar to-day under the name of *Ragu Kalam*, and the various times of the day correspond exactly with Marco Polo's description. They are, as I have learnt from a Malabari gentleman, as follows: Monday, 7.30 a.m. to 9 a.m.; Tuesday, 3 p.m. to 4.30 p.m.; Wednesday, 12 noon to 1.30 p.m.; Thursday, 1.30 p.m. to 3 p.m.; Friday, 10.30 a.m. to 12 noon; Saturday, 9 a.m. to 10.30 a.m.; Sunday, 4.30 p.m. to 6 p.m. The passage in "Z" begins: "Item pro qualibet die in ebdomada dicunt esse unam horam infelicem que uciacham (sic) quam appellant choiach. . . ." In Ramusio the passage begins: "Item per ciascun giorno della settimana hanno un'hora infelice, qual chiamano Choiach. . . ." It is therefore possible that the original word resembles *uciacham* rather than *choiach*. Mr Moule suggests that *que uciacham* represents an insufficiently erased lapse into some modern language occurring in some progenitor of "Z." The Dravidian expression for the evil hour is *Karippu Kal* which would be pronounced

Kachukka by a low-caste Tamil or Malayalim. *Karippu* means the act of propitiating malignant deities.

4. A passage beginning on p. 389, line 18, " I wish, however, to tell you first . . ." and continuing down to p. 392, line 18, ". . . martens' heads." (Benedetto's edition, pp. 233, 234) constitutes a curious addition to the chapter on Russia found in the Geographic text.

I have not myself seen the Italian version from which Signor Ricci made his translation, but from my correspondence with Professor Benedetto I gather that certain differences will be found to exist between that version and the English translation as it now stands. This is especially the case in regard to obvious errors in matters of fact, for whereas Professor Benedetto has corrected these in his translation with a view to accuracy in the narrative, I have persuaded him to allow me in such cases to adhere to the original readings, however faulty, with a view to accuracy in the text. I have, however, agreed to change the date on p. 8 from 1260 as given in fr. 1116 to 1269, as the former date is historically absurd. The date on p. 3, 1250, though probably a mistake for 1260, has been allowed to stand. Many such errors occur in connection with the names and genealogies of the Mongol Khans. On p. 83, for example, the list of the successors of Chingiz Khan to the overlordship of the Mongol Empire is full of errors. The correct list down to Kubilai should run as follows: Chingiz 1206–1227, Ögödei 1227–1241, Küyük 1246–1248, Möngkä 1248–1259, Kubilai 1260–1294. Between 1241 and 1246 there was an interregnum during which the lady Turakina acted as regent for her eldest son Küyük. Ögödei is omitted altogether, and neither Batu nor Hulagu (here represented by Alton, *see* Index) were Great Kaans.

On p. 116 Marco Polo says the eldest son of Kubilai was " called Chingis in memory of the good Chingis

Kaan." This is an error of which Marco Polo was obviously not aware, for if we change the name of this prince to Chinkim, his correct name, the sentence loses its meaning. In Yule (third edition, Vol. I, p. 359) we read: "The Emperor hath, by these four wives of his, twenty-two male children; the eldest of whom was called *Chinkin* for the love of the good Chinghis Kaan." A note on the following page says: "Marco was probably wrong in connecting the name of the latter (*i.e.* Chinkim) with that of Chinghiz." Of course Marco did nothing of the kind, he mistook the prince's name and thinking it was Chingiz naturally thought he received it in memory of his illustrious ancestor. Charignon (Vol. II, p. 41) says that the Polo MSS. always give the two names Chinkim and Chingiz with identical spelling, and presumes that Marco Polo was too well informed to take these names as identical. Ramusio has *Cingis* in both cases. I think it is evident that these represent not errors of the MSS. but rather errors made in his notes on the spot by Marco Polo and as such are worth preserving.

The four outstanding editions of the nineteenth century are the Geographic Text published in 1814 and the translations of Marsden (1818), or Pauthier (1865), and of Henry Yule (First edition 1871). The most comprehensive edition is the second edition of Yule revised by Cordier and published in 1903, and as far as regards the elucidation of the narrative this is likely long to remain the standard work on Marco Polo, although fresh light is constantly being thrown by scholars on some particular identification or difficulty. Most valuable notes of this kind have, for example, been contributed recently by Monsieur Paul Pelliot, the Rev. A. C. Moule, and Sir Aurel Stein, to mention only a few. It may now be claimed that most of the places mentioned by Marco Polo have been identified, in spite of peculiar spellings and of apparent inconsistencies. The difficulty of following him on his many journeys has been much simplified by the process of distinguishing whenever possible between those places which lay on his main route to China and his return journey by sea to Persia, and those which he visited during his stay in China and those which he never visited at all.

It will be observed that I have not added annotations to this translation. I have, however, with the aid of Miss Stella Buchanan, prepared a full index in which will be found all the identifications which have been made with some degree of certainty by Yule and his successors in the field of Poliana.

Had Signor Aldo Ricci been alive he would no doubt have contributed a preface describing the methods by which he was guided in his translation. In default of this I may be permitted to quote from a letter he wrote me dated from Florence the 31st August 1929:—

> "Please allow me now to take this opportunity of submitting a small matter to you in connection with the translation. Quite apart from the question of the texts Yule used for his version, his style of translating does not seem to me perfectly satisfactory, alternating as it does between archaisms and forms and expressions redolent of the fairy tale. Doubtless Yule intended by means of the latter to reproduce the ingenuousness of the author, but surely the ingenuousness of Marco Polo is not that of the child, and still less that of the grown-up telling a tale to children, which is the impression Yule so often leaves on one. It is, of course, a purely literary ingenuousness, so to speak, the inability to express oneself clearly at a time when a vernacular prose style did not yet exist, and on the part of a person who was by no means a "clerk." But the mentality is naturally far from being that of the child, except perhaps in the sense in which the middle ages are popularly considered childish.

" After making several experiments, I have come to the conclusion that the only really legitimate way of translating Polo is to be as literal as the difference between the two languages will allow. In this way his mentality, if I may say so, is allowed to speak for itself, and his constant visible effort to express his meaning—which is extremely interesting from so many points of view, both literary and psychological—is in no way disguised. For this same reason I also believe that Yule was ill-advised in compressing and even suppressing so many passages and sentences of repetitions, not to mention the " formulae " at the end of chapters which he often passes over."

In conclusion I desire to thank Monsieur Pelliot, the Rev. A. C. Moule, and Mr W. Perceval Yetts, for the help and advice they were kind enough to give me while this book was passing through the press.

E. Denison Ross.

¶ La gran Magnificentia del Prete Ianni Signore dellIndia Maggiore e della Ethiopia

THE GREAT MAGNIFICENCE OF PRESTER JOHN, LORD OF GREATER INDIA AND OF ETHIOPIA

Frontispiece to a popular Italian poem on Prester John written by Giuliano Dati (1445–1524), Bishop of Saint-Leon in Calabria.

This poem, containing fifty-nine verses of eight lines, was printed in Florence at the end of the Fifteenth Century, but bears no date.

The Copy in the British Museum is numbered C20.C23.

The Travels of Marco Polo

EMPERORS and Kings, dukes and marquesses, counts, knights and burgesses, and all ye, whoever ye be, who wish to know of the various races of men, and of the diversities of the different regions of the world, take this book and have it read to you. You shall find in it all the mighty wonders all the great singularities of the vast regions of the East—of the Greater Armenia, of Persia, of Tartary, and of India, and of many a country besides—set down by us clearly and in due order, as they were recounted by Messer Marco Polo, called *Milione*, wise and noble citizen of Venice, who saw them with his own eyes. Some things there will, in truth, be that he did not see, but only heard tell of by men worthy of credit. And we will set down the things seen as seen, and those heard as heard, that our book may be correct and truthful, without any falsehood.

And all who read this book or hear it read, must believe it, as all the things contained in it are true. For I tell you that ever since the Lord our God did with his own hands mould our first Father Adam, there never was up to the present day any man, Christian or Pagan, Tartar or Indian or of any other race whatsoever, who knew and explored so great a part of the various regions of the world and of its great marvels, as this Messer Marco knew and explored. Hence, it seemed to him, it were too great a pity, did he not cause to be written down all the great marvels he had seen or heard tell of as true, that others also, who had neither seen nor heard of them, might acquire knowledge of them by means of this book.

And you must know that, to learn so many things, he lived no less than twenty-six years in those regions and provinces. When afterwards he was a captive in the prison of Genoa, he had all these things recorded in writing by Master Rustichello of Pisa, who was in the same prison, in the year 1298 from the birth of Jesus. And he only set down a small part of the things he had learnt—namely those that he could remember.

How Messer Niccolò and Messer Matteo left Constantinople to explore the world

YOU must know that, in the year 1250 after Christ's Incarnation, when Baldwin was emperor of Constantinople, and Messer Ponte the Venetian Podestà in that city, there were two brothers there, Messer Niccolò Polo, the father of Messer Marco, and Messer Matteo, brother to Messer Niccolò, who had gone thither from Venice with their merchandise. They were in truth most noble and wise and prudent men. They took counsel together, and decided to go to the Greater Sea with a view to their own gains and profits. Therefore they purchased a quantity of jewels, and sailed from Constantinople in a ship, and went to Soldaia.

How Messer Niccolò and Messer Matteo left Soldaia

After remaining some time at Soldaia, they decided to proceed yet further. What more shall I tell you? They left Soldaia and set out, riding until, without encountering any adventure worthy of mention, they reached the Court of Barca Khan, Lord of a part of the Tartars, who resided at that time at Bolgara and Sarai. This Barca treated Messer Niccolò and Messer Matteo with great honour, and greatly rejoiced at their arrival. The two brothers gave him all the jewels they had brought. Barca accepted them willingly, being immeasurably pleased with them, and had twice their value given to the brothers. He sent the jewels to be set in various places, and they were very well set.

When they had been a year in the land of Barca, war broke out between him and Alau, Lord of the

Tartars of the Levant; and each marched against the other with all his men. They came to grips, and there was great slaughter on both sides, but Alau ended by remaining victorious. And on account of that battle and of the war, no one could travel along the roads without being taken. But this was in the direction whence the brothers had come, whereas forward they could go. Hence the two brothers reasoned among themselves: "As we cannot return to Constantinople with our wares, let us go forward by way of the east; we may be able to return by an indirect route." They made ready and left Bolgara, proceeding to a city called Ucaca, where the Kingdom of Barca, Lord of the Ponent, came to an end. Departing from Ucaca, and crossing the river Tigris, they traversed a desert which extended for seventeen days' journey. They found neither cities nor towns, but only Tartars living in tents on the produce of their cattle.

How the two brothers crossed a desert and arrived at the city of Bucara

Having crossed the desert, they reached a very noble and large city, called Bucara. The province, also called Bucara, was ruled by a King called Barac. The city was the finest in the whole of Persia. The two brothers, once they had reached it, could proceed no further, nor could they turn back, and so they remained there three years.

And while they were living there, an envoy arrived, sent by Alau, Lord of the Levant, to the Lord of all the Tartars, namely Cublai, who lived at the extremity of the earth between east and north-east. When the envoy saw Messer Niccolò and Messer Matteo, he marvelled greatly, no Latin having ever been seen in those parts. He said to the two brothers: "Gentlemen, if you but place trust in me, you will receive great profit and honour thereby." The two brothers said they would willingly place trust in him; as long as what was to be done lay in their power. And the envoy said: "Gentlemen, know that the Great Lord of the Tartars has never seen any Latins, and is filled with the greatest desire of seeing some; hence if you will come to him with me, I assure you that he will see you with great pleasure, and will treat you most honourably and generously. And with me you can travel in safety and without difficulty."

How the two brothers followed the advice of the envoy to the Great Kaan

On hearing the envoy's words, the two brothers rejoiced and declared they would willingly go with him. Hence they set out together with the envoy, and journeyed for one year to the north and north-east before reaching the land where the Lord lived. They met with great marvels and many novelties, that we shall not deal with here, because Messer Marco, the son of Messer Niccolò, who also saw all these things, will relate them to you at length further on in this book.

How the brothers reached the Court of the Great Kaan

When Messer Niccolò and Messer Matteo reached the Court of the Great Lord, he received them honourably; and gave them a joyful and hospitable welcome. He was greatly pleased by their arrival. Many questions he asked them: first about their emperors, how they governed their lands according to justice, and how they went out to battle, and about all their other actions. After that, he asked them about their kings and princes and other lords.

How the Great Kaan questioned the two brothers concerning the Christians

After that, he questioned them concerning the Lord Pope and all the affairs of the Roman Church, and all the customs of the Latins. And Messer Niccolò and Messer Matteo told him the whole truth about everything, in an orderly fashion and well and wisely, as befits wise men like them, who well knew the Tartar and Turkish languages.

How the Great Kaan sent the two brothers as envoys to the Roman Pontiff

When the Great King called Cublai Kaan, who was Lord of all the Tartars of the world, and of all the provinces and kingdoms and territories of that immense region of the earth, had heard about all the affairs of the Latins, even as the two brothers had excellently and clearly explained them to him, he was greatly pleased. He decided to send envoys to the Pope; and so he begged the two brothers to go on this mission together with one of his barons. They answered that they would execute all his commands as those of their liege Lord. Then the Great Lord summoned to his presence one of his barons, who was called Cogatal, and said to him that he wished him to go to the Pope, together with the two brothers. And the baron answered: "Sire, I am your servant, and am ready to carry out all your commands to the best of my ability." After this, the Great Lord had letters written out in the Turkish language from himself to the Pope, and entrusted them to the two brothers and to his baron, whom he charged with what he wished them to say to the Pope on his behalf. Know, then, that the purport of the letters and of the embassy he sent was as you shall hear: he made his request to

KUBILAI GIVES THE GOLDEN TABLET (PAÏZAH) TO THE BROTHERS POLO

[*B.M. Royal Manuscript* 19. *D. I. fol.* 59(*b*)]

[*face p.* 6

the Pope that he should send him some hundred wise men, learned in the law of Christ, conversant in the Seven Arts, and fully capable of entering into discussions, and clearly proving to idolaters and to people of other persuasions that their laws were anything but divinely inspired, and that all the idols they kept in their houses, and worshipped, were things of the devil; in a word, he desired that the Pope should send him men able to show clearly, in the light of reason, that the Christian Law was better than their own. The Great Lord further bade the two brothers bring him some oil from the lamp that burns above God's Sepulchre in Jerusalem. This, even as you have heard, was the purport of the embassy sent by the Great Lord to the Pope by means of the two brothers.

How the Great Kaan gave the two brothers the Golden Tablet of Authority

When the Great Lord had duly instructed the two brothers and his baron as to the message he was sending to the Pope, he caused a golden tablet to be given them, the purport of which was that, wheresoever they went, they were to be furnished with all the necessary quarters, and with horses and men to escort them from one town to another. And when Messer Niccolò and Messer Matteo, together with the other envoy, duly provided themselves with all that was needful to them, they took leave of the Great Lord, and, mounting their horses, set out on their journey. When they had ridden some distance, the Tartar baron who was going with them fell sick, and, being unable to continue the journey, remained behind in a certain city. When Messer Niccolò and Messer Matteo saw that he was ill, they left him, and proceeded on their way. And I assure you that, wherever they went, they were honoured and furnished with all they wished to command. What more shall I tell you? They rode so long, day after day, that they reached Laias. And I tell you that they toiled three years on the way. And this was due to the fact that they could not always ride on account of foul weather or snow or rivers that were big.

How the two brothers reached the city of Acre

They left Laias and went to Acre, reaching it in the month of April, in the year 1269 after Christ's Incarnation. And they found that the Lord Pope was dead. And when Messer Niccolò and Messer Matteo found that the Pope (Clement by name) was dead, they went to a wise clerk who was Legate of the Church of Rome for the whole kingdom of Egypt. He was a man of great authority and his name was Tebaldo of Piacenza. They told him of the mission upon which the Great Lord of the Tartars had sent them to the Pope. And when the Legate had heard what the two brothers told him, he marvelled greatly, and thought that it was very much to the honour and advantage of Christendom. He said to the two brothers: "Gentlemen, ye see that the Pope is dead; ye must therefore needs wait until there be another. And when there is a Pope, ye shall then be able to execute your mission." The two brothers, seeing that what the Legate said was right, declared that, while waiting for the election of the Pope, they would proceed to Venice to see their family. So they left Acre and went to Negropont. From Negropont they departed in a ship, and sailed until they reached Venice. Messer Niccolò found that his wife was dead, and had left a son of fifteen years of age, whose name was Marco; and this is the Marco of whom the present book relates. Messer Niccolò and Messer Matteo remained at Venice about two years, waiting until there should be a Pope.

How the two brothers left Venice to return to the Great Kaan, and took with them Marco, the son of Messer Niccolò.

When the two brothers had waited as long as you have heard, seeing that no Pope was being made, they thought they should delay no longer in returning to the Great Kaan. So they departed from Venice, taking with them the boy Marco, and went straight to Acre, where they found the Legate of whom I have told you above. They spoke at length of these matters with him, and asked him leave to go to Jerusalem to fetch some of the oil from the lamp of Christ's Sepulchre, that the Great Kaan had asked them for, being desirous of having it because his mother was a Christian. The Legate gave them leave to go. So the brothers left Acre and proceeded to Jerusalem, and took of the oil of the lamp of Christ's Sepulchre. They returned to the Legate at Acre, and said to him: "Sir, as we see that no Pope is being elected, we wish to return to the Great Lord, for we have tarried too long." And the Lord Legate, who was one of the greatest lords of the Church of Rome, said to them: "Since you wish to return to the Great Lord, I am content." So he prepared his letters and his message to send to the Great Kaan, witnessing that Messer Niccolò and Messer Matteo had come to perform their commission, but that, as there was no Pope, they had been unable to do so.

How the two brothers and Marco left Acre

When the two brothers had received the Legate's letters, they departed from Acre and set out on their journey to return to the Great Lord; and they journeyed until they reached Laias. They had hardly arrived there, when that same Legate was elected Pope, assuming the name of Gregory. The two brothers were greatly pleased. And a short time after, a messenger reached Laias, sent by the Legate who had been elected Pope, to Messer Niccolò and Messer Matteo, to tell them, should they not have already left, to return to him. The two brothers were still in that city because at that time the roads along which they were to travel were closed and ravaged by a nephew of the Great Kaan, who had been a Christian, and having fought against the Great Kaan had taken flight. They greatly rejoiced at this message and said they would return willingly. What more shall I tell you? The King of Armenia had a galley armed for the two brothers, and sent them with all due honours to the Legate.

How the two brothers went to the Roman Pontiff

When they had come to Acre, they went to the Lord Pope, and most humbly paid him their respects. The Lord Pope received them honourably, and gave them his blessing, welcoming them with joyful hospitality. Then he caused new letters to be prepared for the Great Lord, in which, among other things, he requested that the Great Lord's nephew Abaga, namely the Lord of the Tartars of the Levant, might vouchsafe his aid and favour to the Christians, so as to make their passage overseas possible. The Pope further appointed many splendid gifts of crystal and of other substances for the Great Kaan. Then he gave Messer Niccolò and Messer Matteo two preaching friars, the wisest that were to be found in the whole province. The one was called Fra Niccolò of Vicenza, and the other Fra Guglielmo of Tripoli. He endowed the two friars with the necessary authority, that they might do everything in those countries with full powers, ordain priests and consecrate bishops, and bind and unbind even as he himself. He gave them their written credentials and letters, and entrusted them with the message he wished to send to the Great Kaan. And when Messer Niccolò and Messer Matteo and the two preaching friars had received the credentials and letters and the message of the Lord Pope, they asked him to give them his blessing; then all four set out, and with them went Marco, the son of Messer Niccolò. They went straight to Laias. When they had arrived there, Bondocdaire, who was the Soldan of Babylon, came to Armenia with a large host, doing great damage throughout the country. And the messengers ran the risk of being killed. When the two preaching friars saw this, they were greatly afraid to proceed further. So they said that they would not go. They consigned to Messer Niccolò and Messer Matteo all the credentials and letters that they had, and left them, going away with the Master of the Temple.

How the two brothers and Marco reached the city of Kemenfu, where the Great Kaan was

And Messer Niccolò and Messer Matteo, with Marco, the son of Niccolò, set out on their journey, riding so long, winter and summer, that they reached the Court of the Great Kaan, who at that moment was in a large and wealthy city, called Kemenfu. Of what they found on their journey we will make no mention at present, because we shall tell you about it further on in this book, all in due order. But you must know that they toiled no less than three and a half years on the way, on account of the snows, and the rains, and the vast rivers and the furious winds, and because they could not ride in winter as in summer. And I assure you that when the Great Kaan heard that Messer Niccolò and Messer Matteo were coming, he sent messengers to meet them at the distance of forty days' journey, so that they were excellently honoured and provided with everything.

How the two brothers and Marco came to the presence of the Great Kaan in his palace

And what more shall I tell you? When Messer Niccolò and Messer Matteo, together with Marco, had come to that great city, they went to the Royal Palace, where they found the Great Kaan surrounded by a large company of barons. So they kneeled before him and paid him their respects in the humblest possible manner. The Great Kaan made them rise, and received them honourably, giving them a joyful and hospitable welcome. And much did he question them concerning their condition and how they had fared. The two brothers told him that they had fared very well, seeing that they had found him in good health and prosperous. Then they presented the credentials and letters the Pope sent him, which pleased him exceedingly. They then consigned the holy oil, over which he rejoiced very much, setting great store by it. When the Great Kaan saw Marco, who was a young man, he asked who he was. "Sire," said Messer Niccolò, "he is my son and your servant." "He is welcome," said the Great Kaan. But why should I make a long story of it? Know that truly there was great rejoicing and good cheer made by the Great Kaan and all his Court over the arrival of these envoys. And they were much honoured, and furnished with everything. They remained at the Court, and received marks of honour above the other barons.

How the Great Kaan sent Marco as an envoy

Now it happened that Marco, the son of Messer Niccolò, learnt so well the customs, languages and manners of writing of the Tartars, that it was truly a wonder, for I tell you in sooth that, not long after he had reached the Court of the Great Lord, he knew four languages, and their alphabets, and manner of writing. He was exceedingly wise and prudent, and the Great Kaan loved him very much for the goodness and the worth that he saw in him. And when the Great Kaan saw that Marco was so wise, he sent him as envoy to a land called Carajan, on the way to which he toiled no less than six months. The young man performed his mission well and wisely. Now, he was aware, because he had often seen and heard it, that, when the envoys sent to the various parts of the world returned and spoke of the mission upon which they had been sent, without being able to give other information about the countries to which they had gone, the Great Kaan used to call them fools and ignorant men, asserting that he preferred to hear of the novelties, and customs, and habits of those foreign countries, than of the mission upon which he had sent them. So Marco, knowing this full well, when he went upon this mission, paid attention to all the novelties and strange things he came across, in order to be able to repeat them to the Great Kaan. He further collected sundry wonderful things to present them to the Great Kaan, who appreciated them greatly.

How Marco returned from his mission, and reported upon it to the Great Kaan

On his return from his mission, Marco presented himself before the Great Kaan, and reported on the mission on which he had been sent, and which he had accomplished excellently well; then he told of all the novelties and strange things that he had seen on this journey, and he did so in such a pleasant and wise manner that the Great Kaan and all the others that were listening, marvelled greatly, and said to one another: " If this young man lives, in sooth he cannot but become a man of great discretion and worth." What more shall I tell you? From the time of this mission, the young man was called *Messer* Marco Polo, and so he shall henceforward be called in this book. And this was most just, for he was so wise and courteous.

But why should I make a long story of it? Know in truth that Messer Marco lived with the Great Kaan no less than seventeen years, and during all that time never ceased going upon missions. For, seeing that Messer Marco brought so much news from every country and accomplished so well all the tasks he was charged with, the Great Kaan entrusted him with all the important and distant missions. And Messer Marco carried out his missions very well, and knew how to relate many novelties and strange things. And the Great Kaan was so delighted with Messer Marco's ways, that he loved him dearly, and did him such great honour, keeping him so near him, that the other barons were aggrieved thereat.

The reason why Messer Marco came to know as no one ever knew, the features of these regions, was because he explored more of those strange lands than any man that was ever born, and because he paid greater attention to the acquisition of this knowledge.

How Messer Niccolò, Messer Matteo, and Messer Marco asked leave of the Great Kaan to depart.

When Messer Niccolò, Messer Matteo, and Messer Marco had lived with the Great Kaan for all the time that you have heard, they decided among themselves to return to their own country. More than once they asked leave of the Great Kaan and, with the kindest words, begged him grant it. But the Great Kaan loved them so much, and kept them about him so willingly, that he would not give them leave, for anything on earth.

Now it happened that Queen Bolgana, who was wife to Argon, Lord of the Levant, died, and this queen left it stated in her will that no lady should sit on her throne or be the wife of Argon, unless she were of her own lineage. So Argon took three of his barons, who were called, the first Oulatai, the second Apusca, and the third Coja. He sent them, with a splendid retinue, to the Great Kaan, begging him to send him a lady of the lineage of his wife, Queen Bolgana, who had died. When these three barons reached the Court of the Great Kaan, they told him the reason of their coming. The Great Kaan received them honourably, and gave them a joyful and hospitable welcome. Then he summoned a lady called Cocachin, who was of the lineage of Queen Bolgana, and was seventeen years old, and most beautiful and charming. He said to the three barons that this was the lady whom they sought. They replied that they were content. The Great Kaan then gave them a large and splendid retinue to accompany the bride to King Argon. And when all the necessary preparations had been made, the three envoys took leave of the Great Kaan and set out in the same direction whence they had come. They rode for eight months, when a war broke out between certain Tartar Kings, so that the roads were closed. As it was no longer possible to proceed, the three envoys were obliged against their will to return to the Great Kaan, to whom they related all that had happened to them.

At that time, Messer Marco had returned from India, after traversing many strange seas, and had told many novelties of those lands. The three barons, when they saw that Messer Niccolò, Messer Matteo, and Messer Marco were Latins and wise men, said among themselves that they wished that they might accompany them by sea. They went to the Great Kaan and begged him, of his grace, to be sent back by sea and to have the three Latins as companions. The Great Kaan who had so great an affection for these three, as I have told you, granted this request most unwillingly, and allowed the three Latins to accompany the lady together with the three barons.

Here is told how Messer Niccolò, Messer Matteo, and Messer Marco left the Great Kaan

And when the Great Kaan saw Messer Niccolò, Messer Matteo, and Messer Marco about to depart, he summoned all three to his presence and gave them two Tablets of Authority, containing orders that they should be free from all restraint throughout the whole of his domains, and should receive, whithersoever they went, victuals for themselves and for their company. He charged them with missions to the Pope, to the King of France, the King of Spain and other Kings of Christendom. Then he had fourteen ships prepared, each of which had four masts, and often spread twelve sails. (Well could we explain to you how, but, as the subject is too vast, I will say nothing of it at present.) And I also tell you that among those ships there were at least four or five that were manned by 250 to 260 sailors.

When the ships were ready, the three barons and the Lady, together with Messer Niccolò, Messer Matteo, and Messer Marco, took leave of the Great Kaan, and went on board the ships with a large following. And the Kaan furnished them with food for two years. What more shall I tell you? They put out to sea, and sailed for no less than three months, until they reached an island called Java, lying to the south: in this island there are sundry marvellous things, of which I will tell you in this book. Then they left this island; and you must know that they sailed across the Sea of India for as many as eighteen months before they arrived at the place they wished to reach. (And they came across many great marvels which we will also tell you of in this book.) And when they had arrived, they found that Argon was dead.

And I assure you, in very truth, that when they went on board the ships, they were no less than six hundred, without counting the sailors. And all died except eighteen. Of Argon's three envoys, only one survived, he whose name was Coja; of all the ladies and damsels of the retinue, one alone was left.

As, after the death of Argon, the lordship was held by one Kiacatu, the lady was placed under his protection, and the mission was executed to him. He ordered the lady to be given to Casan, son of Argon, who at that time was in the region of the Arbre Sol on the confines of Persia, garrisoning certain passes with sixty thousand men. Thus it was done. After this, Messer Niccolò, Messer Matteo, and Messer Marco returned to Kiacatu, as their road lay through his city. Here they remained nine months. And when Messer Niccolò, Messer Matteo, and Messer Marco had accomplished all their mission in regard to the lady and delivered all the messages entrusted to them by the Great Kaan, they took leave and left, setting out on their journey. And you must also know that Kiacatu gave them four gold Tablets of Authority, each of which was a cubit long and five fingers in breadth, and weighed three or four pounds; and they bore an inscription ordering that, by virtue of the Eternal God, the name of the Great Kaan should be honoured and praised, and if anyone disobeyed, he should be put to death, and his property confiscated. Of the four gold tablets, two bore gerfalcons, one a lion, and the fourth was smooth; and the purport of their inscription was that the same honour and service should be rendered to the three envoys throughout the Kaan's lands as to the Kaan himself, and that the envoys should be provided with horses and all the necessary victuals and escorts.

And truly so it was done, for throughout the Kaan's states they were freely supplied with horses and victuals and all that was needful. For I assure you, in truth, that they were often given two hundred horsemen, or more or less, according to their needs, to escort them, that they might journey in safety from one town to another. And this was most necessary for, as Kiacatu was no rightful lord, the people did not hesitate to do mischief, as would have been the case had they had a legitimate prince.

One thing should, I think, be particularly mentioned to the honour of the three envoys. For in truth the Great Kaan placed so much confidence in Messer Niccolò, Messer Matteo, and Messer Marco, and so dearly did he love them, that he conferred upon them such great authority as to entrust them with Queen Cocachin, and also with the daughter of the King of Manji that they might conduct them to Argon, the Lord of all the Levant. And they did so. They conducted them by sea, as I related above, with all that retinue and that immense amount of provisions. And those two great ladies were at the mercy of the three envoys. The latter watched over their safety, as if the ladies had been their daughters, and the two ladies, both very young and most beautiful, looked upon them as fathers, and obeyed them as such. And the three envoys gave them into the hands of their lord. I tell you in very truth that Queen Cocachin, wife to Casan, now reigning, was so attached to the three envoys (and her husband Casan no less than she), that there is nothing she would not have done for them, as if they had been her fathers. And you must know that when these three envoys left her to return to their country, she wept for sorrow at their departure.

Honourable indeed is this that I have just told you, namely that two such ladies should have been entrusted to these three envoys, to be conducted to their lord from so distant a land. Now we will leave this, and

PLATE II

CA' POLO, VENICE

[face p. 18

proceed with our narrative. What more shall I tell you? When the three envoys had left Kiacatu, they set out on their way, and rode so long day after day, that they reached Trebizond; from Trebizond they passed to Constantinople; from Constantinople to Negropont; and from Negropont to Venice. And this was in the year 1295 after Christ's Incarnation.

And now that I have told you all the prologue, even as you have heard, let us pass to the book, to the description of the wonderful things seen by Messer Niccolò, Messer Matteo, and Messer Marco in the various countries in which they have been.

Here is told of Lesser Armenia

You must know that there are two Armenias: the Greater and the Lesser. The Lord of Lesser Armenia is a king who governs his state wisely, and is subject to the Tartar. There are many cities and towns. There is great abundance of everything. It is further a land that offers much sport in every kind of chase, both of beasts and of birds. But I tell you that it is no healthy country; on the contrary it is most harmful to the health. Once its nobles were valiant men, full of prowess, but nowadays they are weak and vile, and have no other quality than that of being good drinkers. On the sea-shore, there is a city called Laias, which is a great centre of trade; for you must know in sooth that all spices, and cloths of silk and gold, and all manner of precious goods of the interior are brought thither; and the merchants of Venice, and Genoa, and other countries, flock there, and buy them and distribute them all over the world. And all the merchants and others who would go into the interior begin their journey from this city.

Bordering on this Kingdom of Lesser Armenia, there is, to the south, the Promised Land, which is in the hands of the Saracens; to the north, that part of Turcomania called Caramania; to the east and north-east, Turcomania, with Cæsaria Sevasta and many other cities, all subject to the Tartars; to the west, the sea, by which one goes to the countries of the Christians.

We have now told you of Lesser Armenia, and we will next tell you of Turcomania.

Here is told of the province of Turcomania

In Turcomania, there are people of three races. In the first place there are the Turcomans, worshippers of Mahomet and followers of his Law. They are simple folk, speaking an uncouth language. They inhabit mountains and prairies, where they know there is good pasture, because they live by breeding cattle. Good Turcoman horses and excellent mules of great value are produced in the country. The other races are Armenians and, mixed with them, Greeks, who inhabit the cities and towns, living by trade and handicrafts. For you must know that the finest carpets in the world, and the most beautiful, are manufactured there. Most splendid and rich silk cloths, both crimson and of other colours, are also made there, together with many other things. The most important cities are Conia, Cæsaria, and Sevasta. There are also many other cities and towns, of which I shall make no mention, for it were too long a matter to go into. They are subject to the Tartar of the Levant, who governs them by means of lords of his own choice.

We will now cease speaking of this province, and tell of Greater Armenia.

Here is told of Greater Armenia

Greater Armenia is a large country. It begins at a city called Arzingan, in which the best buckram in the world is made, and all kinds of other crafts flourish.

There are the finest and best spring-water baths to be found on earth. The people are Armenians, and subject to the Tartar. There are many cities and towns. The finest is Arzingan, which is the seat of an Archbishop. Then there is Arziron — a large city where silver is mined in abundance—and Arzizi. An important silver mine is also found in a village called Paipurth, on the way from Trebizond to Toris. It is a very vast province. And you must know that in summer the whole host of the Tartars of the Levant sojourns in it, for, at that season, there is excellent pasture for animals in the province; on this account the Tartars live there in summer, but in winter they do not, for the cattle would have nothing to live on by reason of the cold, due to the snow that falls there in immense quantities; hence in winter the Tartars leave this country and go to warmer lands where they find abundant grass and good pasture for their cattle. And I will tell you, too, that, in the centre of Greater Armenia, there is a very great and high cup-shaped mountain, on which it is said that Noah's Ark rested; for which reason it is called the Mountain of Noah's Ark. It is so broad and vast that one cannot go round it in two days; and the summit is everlastingly covered with so much snow that no one can climb it. But on account of the water that flows from this snow, the mountain is so rich in grass on its lower slopes, that from all the neighbouring districts cattle are brought to graze there in summer.

On the south, towards the east, Greater Armenia borders on a kingdom called Mosul, inhabited by Christians, namely by Nestorians and Jacobites, of whom I shall tell you more later on; on the south, too, are the lands of Mus and Meridin, of which we shall speak afterwards, and many others, with which it were too long to deal. On the north, the country borders on Georgiania, of which I shall also tell presently. On this frontier towards Georgiania, there is a spring from which flows oil in such abundance that a hundred ships at a time may be loaded with it. The oil is not good to eat, but it is good to burn and to anoint camels with, against mange and dandruff. People come from great distances to fetch this oil, and in the whole district no other oil is burnt but this.

We will now cease speaking of Greater Armenia, and tell you of the province of Georgiania.

Here is told of the Georgians, of their King, and of other things concerning them

The Georgians have a king whose name is always David Melik, that is, in our language, David King. He is subject to the Tartar. In ancient days, all the kings of that province were born with the mark of an eagle on the right shoulder. They are a handsome people, brave, good archers, and excellent soldiers in battle. They are Christians, and follow the Greek rite. They wear their hair cropped like clerks. This is the province Alexander was unable to traverse when he wished to go to the Ponent, because the road was narrow and dangerous. For on the one side there is the sea, and on the other vast mountains and forests, impassable to horsemen. The road between the mountain and the sea is exceedingly narrow and stretches for over four leagues, so that a few men could hold the pass against the whole world. This was the reason why Alexander could not pass. And you must know that Alexander raised a tower there and built a fortress, in order to prevent those people from passing and attacking him; this was called the Iron Gate, and is the place the *Book of Alexander* means, when it tells how Alexander shut up the Tartars between two mountains. (It is not, however, true that they were Tartars, but a people called Comanians and others besides, for there were no Tartars in those days.)

There are very many cities and towns. They have great abundance of silk, and make cloths of silk and gold, the most beautiful that were ever seen. There are also the best goshawks in the world, called *avigi*. There is plenty of everything, and the people live by trade and handicrafts. The province is full of great mountains and narrow and strong defiles, so that the Tartars never could enforce their authority completely over it. The forests are all of box-wood.

There is here a convent of monks, called St. Leonard's, where occurs a strange wonder that I will tell you. You must know that near the church of St. Leonard's there is a great lake formed by a stream that flows from a mountain. In the water which flows from that mountain, no fish, great or small, are to be found during the whole year, except from the first day in Lent; then they begin to come and continue doing so every day in Lent until Easter Saturday, namely Easter Eve. During all that time, fish are found in great quantities; during the rest of the year there is no trace of them.

The province is watered by two seas. On the one side there is the Greater Sea, and on the other the sea of which we spoke, which comes up to the mountain, and is called the Sea of Ghelukelan or Abaco. It has a circuit of about 2800 miles, and is like a lake, for it communicates with no other sea, the nearest being at twelve days' journey. The Euphrates, the Tigris, the Jon and many other rivers flow into it. All round it are mountains and towns. Recently Genoese merchants have taken to sailing on it, having placed thereon ships of their own. From here comes the silk called *ghelle*.

In that sea there are many populous islands, with fine cities. They are inhabited by those who fled before the Great Tartar when the latter was conquering the province of Persia, where, at that time, the cities and districts were governed municipally; in their flight they took refuge in the said islands and in the mountains, where they hoped to live more securely. Thus it was that these islands came to be inhabited. There is abundance of fish in that sea, and especially sturgeon, salmon (at the river-mouths), and other big fish.

Near this province there is a fine and very large city called Tiflis. Round it are many towns and cities dependent upon it. It is inhabited by Christians, that is by Armenians and Georgians; there are also some Saracens and Jews, but not many. Cloths of silk and of many other kinds are manufactured there. The people live by their handicrafts, and are subject to the Great King of the Tartars.

We have told you of the lands with which Armenia marches on the north. We will now speak of the other countries, on which it borders between south and east.

And observe that we only speak of the principal cities of each province, two or three at most; but there are many others which it were too long to mention in detail, especially if they have nothing very remarkable about them.

Here is told of the Kingdom of Mosul

Mosul is a large kingdom, inhabited by peoples of different races, of which I will now tell you. There is one kind of people called Arabi, who worship Mahomet. There is another kind who follow the Christian Law, but not as the Church of Rome bids, for they err in many things: they are called Nestorians, Jacobites, and Armenians. They have a Patriarch, whom they call Jatolic; this Patriarch creates archbishops, bishops, abbots, and every kind of prelate, sending them into every quarter, to India, to Cathay and to Baudac [*sic*] after the manner of the Pope of Rome. I must add, moreover, that all the Christians you find in the countries I mention are Nestorians and Jacobites.

All the cloths of silk and gold called *mosulins* are

made there. And to this kingdom too belong all those great merchants called *mosulins* that bring us those immense quantities of every kind of precious spices, and pearls, and cloths of silk and gold.

And in the mountains of this kingdom there lives yet another people, the Curds; for the most part they are Nestorian and Jacobite Christians, but some of them are Saracens, worshipping Mahomet. They are a bold and wicked people, and delight in plundering merchants.

Near this is another province named after the cities of Mus and Meridin. It produces an immense quantity of cotton, from which is made a great deal of buckram and other things. The people are craftsmen and traders; and are subject to the King of the Tartars.

Now we will cease speaking of the Kingdom of Mosul, and tell you of the great city of Baudac.

Here is told how the great city of Baudac was taken

Baudac is a great city, where the Calif of all the Saracens in the world resides, just as in Rome is the head of all the Christians in the world. Through the city, passes a very large river, down which one can go to the Sea of India. Up and down it, merchants come and go with their wares. You must know that the length of the river from Baudac to the Sea of India is eighteen days' journey. The merchants who wish to go to India descend the river as far as a city called Kisi, and there enter the Sea of India. I will add, too, that on this river, between Baudac and Kisi, there is a great city called Bastra, and in the woods all round the city grow the finest dates in the world. In Baudac, there are made many different kinds of gold and silk cloths, as, for example, *nasich*, and *nac*, and cramoisy, and other kinds yet, very richly worked with figures of animals and birds. And almost all the pearls that are brought from India to Christian countries, are pierced in Baudac. It is an important place of study for all sciences, and especially for the Law of Mahomet, for necromancy, physics, astronomy, geomancy, and physiognomy. It is the noblest and largest city in those parts.

And you must know, in truth, that the Calif of Baudac was found in possession of the greatest treasure of gold, silver and precious stones that any man was ever found possessed of; and I will tell you how.

In the days when they began to exercise their sway, the Lords of the Tartars were four brothers, the eldest of whom, called Mongu, was the Great Kaan. They had already, with their great might, subdued Cathay and other neighbouring lands. But they were not content with this, desiring on the contrary to have much more; so they purposed subduing the whole world. Hence they divided it into four parts, so that one of them should set out to conquer lands to the east, another to the south, and the other two in the remaining directions. The south fell by lot to the share of that one of them that was called Alau. He, the Great Lord of the Tartars, and brother to the Great King who is now reigning, gathered together a very great army, and boldly undertook the conquest of those lands, marching against Baudac in the year of Christ 1255. Well knowing the great strength of the city, and the multitude of folk within it, he decided to take it rather by cunning than by force. He had a hundred thousand horsemen, besides foot-soldiers, and in order that the Calif and his men within the city should suppose his host less numerous, he secretly concealed the greater part of his troops in the woods on either side of the city, before attacking the latter. With the rest he charged up to the very gates. Seeing that the enemy were few, the Calif made light of them, and, trusting in the standard of Mahomet, thought that he would be able to destroy them easily. Thus he sallied forth from the city without delay. When Alau saw this, he pretended to flee, and enticed the Calif beyond the woods where his men lay concealed. Having thus surrounded them, he destroyed them. The Calif himself was captured together with the city—truly a most wonderful enterprise, for in Baudac there were a hundred thousand horsemen, besides the foot-soldiers. Once he had taken the town, Alau found that the Calif possessed a tower all full of gold, silver, and other treasures, such as had never before been seen collected in a single place. When he saw this great treasure, he marvelled greatly, and, sending for the Calif, summoned him to his presence. Then he said: "Calif, why hast thou gathered together such a great treasure? What didst thou intend to do with it? Didst thou not know that I was thy enemy, and that I was coming against thee with so great an army to dispossess thee? And knowing this, why didst thou not take thy treasure, and give it to thy knights and soldiers to defend thee and thy city?" The Calif answered nothing, for he knew not what to say. Then Alau added: "Calif, as I see thou lovest thy treasure so greatly, I will give it to thee to eat." Then he had the Calif taken, and put into the tower of the treasure, commanding that nothing should be given him to eat or drink. Then he said: "Calif, eat now of thy treasure as much as thou wilt, for never shalt thou have anything else to eat but it." After this, he left him in the tower, where he died four days later. And certainly it would have been better for the Calif to have given his treasure to his soldiers that they might defend his dominion and his folk, than to be put to death with all his people, and dispossessed. And since the days of that Calif, there has never been another.

We will next tell you of Toris. Still, it is true that I might have told you more of the people of Baudac and of their affairs and customs, and indeed have shortened my account as the matter is too vast to be dealt with fully. So I will now add another great and wonderful circumstance, as you shall hear.

Of the great miracle of the mountain that occurred at Baudac

We will tell you of a great marvel that occurred between Baudac and Mosul.

You must know that in the year 1225 after Christ's Incarnation, there was a Calif in Baudac, who detested the Christians, and ever thought, day and night, how he might make all the Christians in his lands turn Saracens, or, failing that, how he might have them all killed. And every day he took counsel on this matter with his priests and wise men; for they all greatly detested the Christians. It is, indeed, an indisputable fact, that all the Saracens of the world detest all the Christians. Now, the Calif and his councillors chanced to come across a passage such as you shall hear. They found it written in one of the Gospels that if a Christian's faith were as great as a grain of mustard-seed, he could, by prayer to the Lord God, make two mountains come together. When they had found this, they were delighted, for they said that here was the thing whereby they could make the Christians turn Saracens, or have them all put to death. The Calif thus summoned all the Christians, both Nestorians and Jacobites, who were in his kingdom, and they were a great multitude. When they had come into the Calif's presence, the latter showed them that Gospel, and bade them read it. When they had done so, he asked them whether it were true. The Christians replied that it was indeed true. "Therefore you assert," said the Calif, "that if a Christian's faith be as great as a grain of mustard-seed, he may, by means of his prayer to his God, make two mountains come together?" "We do truly assert it," replied the Christians. "Here then is the choice I lay before you," said the Calif, "for seeing that you are so many, there must be some one amongst you who possesses a little faith. I say then to you: either you make yonder mountain move"—and he pointed out to them a mountain near-by—"or I will make you all die an evil death. For if you do not make it move, you will show that you have no faith. Then I will have you all killed, unless you turn to our good Law, that Mahomet our Prophet gave us; and, possessing sound faith, you shall be saved. And to do this, I give you ten days' time. If by then you have not done it, I will have you all put to death." He said no more and dismissed the Christians.

How the Christians were greatly dismayed by the words of the Calif

When the Christians had heard the Calif's words, they were sorely dismayed, and greatly afraid of being put to death. Still, they trusted in their Creator, that He would aid them in these straits. All their wise men, namely their prelates, took counsel together, for there were Bishops, and Archbishops, and priests in great numbers. No other counsel could they find, than that of praying to their Lord God that out of His pity and mercy, He might advise them in this emergency, and save them from the cruel death to which the Calif would put them, if they did not do what he bade them. What more shall I tell you? Know in very truth that the Christians remained in prayer day and night, and devoutly besought the Saviour, Lord of Heaven and earth, that, out of His great pity, He might help them in the terrible danger in which they were.

For eight days and eight nights, all of them, men and women, old and young, were gathered together raising this prayer. Now, it happened that while they were thus praying, the angel, God's messenger, came in a vision to a Bishop, who was a man of very saintly life. And he said: "Bishop, go to such and such a cobbler, who has only one eye, and tell him to pray that the mountain may move, and the mountain shall move straightaway."

Now I will tell you what kind of a man this cobbler was, and what was his life. You must know in very truth that he was a most honest and chaste man; he fasted and committed no sins; every day he went to Church and to Mass, and gave away in charity a part of his bread. He was a man of such good customs and such saintly life, that one could find none better, either near or far. And I will tell you of a thing he did, whereby he obtained the fame of being a good man, of sound faith, and holy life. You must know that he had frequently heard that passage of the Holy Gospel read, which says that if thy eye offend thee, and lead thee into sin, thou must pluck it out or blind it, so that it may not make thee sin. One day it chanced that a beautiful woman went to this cobbler's to buy shoes. The cobbler desired to see her leg and foot in order to judge which shoes would fit her. So he asked her to show her leg and foot, and the woman showed them at once—and in very truth, both the leg and the foot were so beautiful, that you need not seek for their equal. And when the cobbler, who was as good as I have told you, saw this woman's leg and foot, he straightway fell into temptation, for his eyes looked on them with pleasure. He let the woman go away and would not sell her the shoes. When she had gone, he said to himself: "Ah! faithless traitor! What art thou thinking of? Truly I will take great vengeance on my eyes that have offended me." So he at once took a little stick, and made it very sharp, and stuck it into one of his eyes so that it burst within his head, and saw no more. Thus, even as you have heard, that cobbler destroyed one of the eyes of his head. Truly he was a very saintly and righteous man.

Let us now return to our subject.

How the Bishop had the vision that the prayer of a cobbler would make the mountain move

Now, you must know that when this Bishop had several times had this vision, namely that he should send for this cobbler, who with his prayers should make the mountain move, he recounted to the other Christians all the details of the vision that had appeared to him so often. And the Christians were all agreed that they should summon the cobbler before them. And so they did. When he had come, they told him that they wished him to pray the Lord God to make the mountain move. Hearing what the Bishop and the other Christians requested of him, the cobbler declared that he was not so righteous a man that the Lord God would accomplish such a great deed in answer to a prayer of his. But the Christians implored him with great sweetness that he should offer this prayer to God. What more shall I tell you? They begged with such insistence that he promised to do what they desired, and offer up the prayer to his Creator.

How the Christian's prayer caused the mountain to move

When the appointed day came round, the Christians rose very early in the morning, and all, men and women, old and young, went to their Church and sang the Holy Mass. When they had done this, and performed all the service to Our Lord God, they all set out together and went to the plain at the foot of the mountain, the Cross of the Saviour being borne before them. When all the Christians—who were not less than a hundred thousand—had reached the plain, they assembled before the Cross of Our Lord. The Calif was there, with such an immense multitude of Saracens that it was indeed a wonder; and they had all come there to kill the Christians, for they did not think that the mountain would move. The Christians, all of them, both old and young, were filled with fear and dismay, though they still rested their hopes in their Creator. When all those people, Christians and Saracens, were gathered together in the plain, the cobbler knelt before the Cross, raised his hands to Heaven, and earnestly prayed his Saviour that the mountain might move, and that so many Christians as were there, might not be put to an ill death. When he had ended his prayer, he said: " In the name of the Father, of the Son, and of the Holy Ghost, I bid thee, O mountain, by virtue of the Holy Ghost, to move yonder from where thou art." And the mountain at once began to crumble, and advanced one mile.

On seeing this, the Calif and the Saracens were greatly amazed, and many of them were converted to the Christian Law. The Calif himself turned Christian, though secretly; but when he died, a cross was found hanging round his neck, so that the Saracens did not bury him with the other Califs, but put him elsewhere.

Thus took place this miracle, even as you have heard. And in honour of that cobbler, and of the grace there obtained, every year the Christians, both Nestorians and Jacobites, solemnly celebrate the anniversary of the miracle, fasting completely on the eve of the feast. They agree in this celebration, but for the most part, as their faiths differ in many points, those Christian (Armenians, Nestorians, and Jacobites), are greatly inimical to one another.

Here is told of the noble city of Toris

Toris is a great city, situated in a province called Yrac, in which there are many other cities and towns. Still, Toris is the noblest city of the whole province and so I will speak of it.

The inhabitants of Toris live by trade and handicrafts, for they make many kinds of cloths of gold and silk, of great value. The city is excellently situated, so that wares are brought thither from India, Baudac, Mosul, and Cormos, and from many other regions besides, and Latin merchants, especially Genoese, go there to buy the goods that come from foreign lands. One can also buy there precious stones, of which there is great abundance. It is a city in which travelling merchants make great profits.

The people are insignificant, and there is a great mixture of different faiths. There are Armenians, Nestorians, Jacobites, Georgians, and Persians; there are also worshippers of Mahomet ; these latter are the inhabitants of the city, and are called Torisins. The city is surrounded by beautiful and pleasant gardens, full of abundant and excellent fruit. The Saracens of Toris are most evil and treacherous. This is because the Law that Mahomet their prophet gave them, says that there is no sin in doing any amount of evil to all those who are not of their faith, or in depriving them of their property. And if one of them is killed, or in any way injured by a Christian, he is considered a martyr to the faith. For this reason their ill-deeds would be very great, were it not for the authorities that restrain them. Such indeed is the habit of all the Saracens in the world. For, when they are on the point of death, it is enough for them, in order to obtain salvation, that a priest of theirs should go to them and ask them whether they believe that Mahomet is the true prophet of God, and that they should answer that they do. For this reason, namely on account of the ease with which they grant absolution and allow ill deeds, they have converted the Tartars, and many other peoples to their Law.

Toris is at twelve days' journey from Persia.

Here is told of the Monastery of St Barsamo

In the territory of Toris there exists a monastery, called after the Blessed Barsamo, a saint greatly venerated in those parts. There is an abbot in it, with many monks, who wear a habit after the manner of the Carmelites. In order not to remain in idleness, they are ever knitting woollen girdles, which they lay on the altar of the Blessed Barsamo during the celebration of the offices. When they go begging about the country (like the Brethren of the Holy Ghost), they give these girdles away to their friends and to the nobles, because they are good for removing any bodily pain one may have. This is why every one wishes to have one of these girdles for piety's sake.

Here the book begins to tell of the great province of Persia

Persia is a very large province, that in ancient times was most noble and important; but now the Tartars have destroyed it and laid it waste.

In Persia is the city of Sava, whence the three Magi set out when they came to adore Jesus Christ. In the city there are three very large and most beautiful tombs, in which the three Magi are buried. Above each tomb there is a square edifice, surmounted by a round structure, of excellent workmanship. The three Magi lie one beside the other, and their bodies are still whole, with hair and beard. One of them was called Beltasar, another Gaspar, and the third Melchior. Messer Marco Polo questioned many people of the city concerning these three Magi, but there was no one who could tell him anything; all they said was that they were three kings, buried there in ancient times. But he ultimately got to know what I will now tell you.

At three days' journey from Sava, he found a town called Cala Ataperistan, which, in our language, means the town of the fire-worshippers. And it is quite rightly named, for the people there do worship fire. And I will tell you why they do so. The inhabitants relate that once, in the days of old, three Kings of that country went to adore a Prophet who had just been born, and took with them three offerings—gold, frankincense, and myrrh—to ascertain whether that Prophet were God or an earthly king or a physician. For, they said, if he takes the gold, he is an earthly king; if he takes the frankincense, he is God; if he takes the myrrh, he is a physician. When they reached the birth-place of the Child, the youngest of the three Kings went in alone to see it; and it seemed to him the Child was like him, seemingly of the same age and aspect; whereat he came away marvelling greatly. After him, the one of middle age entered; and the Child appeared to him, as to the first, of his age and aspect; he too came away all amazed. Then the third and oldest went in, and the same happened to him as to the others; he too came away all pensive. When the three Kings were all together again, they told one another what they had seen. They marvelled very much, and decided to go in all three together. Thus they all entered at the same time into the presence of the Child, and found it with the aspect of its real age, namely but thirteen days. Then they adored the Child, and offered it the gold and the frankincense and the myrrh. The Child took all three offerings, and then gave them a closed box. Whereupon the three Kings went away to return to their own land.

Here is told of the three Magi who came to adore God

After riding several days, they resolved to see what the Child had given them. So they opened the box, and found a stone in it. They wondered greatly what it might be. The Child had given it to them as a token that they should abide firm as a rock in the faith that they had just accepted. For, when they had seen the Child take all three offerings, they had concluded that he was God and earthly king and physician, and the Child, knowing well that this faith was born in them, had given them the stone to signify that they should remain firm and constant in their faith. The three Kings took the stone and threw it into a well, for they knew not wherefore it had been given to them. As soon as the stone was thrown into the well, a flame descended from Heaven and came straight to the well into which the stone had been thrown. Seeing this great marvel, the three Kings were all amazed, and repented having thrown the stone into the well, fully realizing now that it had a great and excellent meaning. They straightway took some of that fire and carried it to their country, placing it in a very fine and rich Church of theirs. And they ever keep that fire alight, and adore it as a God; and all the sacrifices and holocausts that they offer, they burn with that fire. If at any time the fire should by chance go out, they have recourse to others of the same faith, who are also fire-worshippers, and, obtaining from them some of the fire that burns in their Church, they return to kindle their own; nor would they ever rekindle it with any other fire than that I have told you of. Often, in order to find it, they have to go on a ten days' journey.

This is why the inhabitants of this country worship fire. And I assure you that they are very numerous.

All these things were told Messer Marco Polo by the people of the town. And they are all truth. I will add, too, that one of the three Magi came from Sava, another from Ava, and the third from Cashan.

Having told you this story in detail, I will now tell you of many other cities of Persia, of their affairs, and of their customs.

Here is told of the eight Kingdoms of Persia

Know, then, that Persia—for it is a very large country—contains eight kingdoms; I will tell you their names one by one. The first, that is to say the first one reaches when coming from Toris, is called Casvin; the second, lying to the south, is called Curdistan; the third, Lor; the fourth, Sulistan; the fifth, Isfaan; the sixth, Serazi; the seventh, Soncara; the eighth, which is at the extremity of Persia, Tunocain. All these kingdoms lie towards the south, except one, Tunocain, which is near the region of the Arbre Sol.

In these kingdoms abound splendid horses, many of which are taken to India to be sold. For you must know that they are very valuable, selling at as much as 200 livres tournois each, which is the value of the majority. Here too there are asses the finest in the world, worth 30 silver marks each, for they run very fast and are excellent for ambling. Further they take little food, carry great burdens, and cover a great distance in one day; neither horses nor mules could endure so great an effort. For the merchants of those parts, when they travel from one region to another, have to cross great deserts, that is to say, arid and sandy tracts, without grass, or anything else wherewith to feed the horses; moreover, wells and fresh springs are at such great intervals that long marches have to be undertaken before the animals can have anything to drink. As no horse would be able to endure this, so the merchants prefer these asses, buying them at a higher price. They also use camels, which carry great burdens too and are cheap to keep, but they are not so swift as the asses.

The inhabitants of these kingdoms take the horses I have mentioned as far as Kisi and Cormos, which are two cities situated on the shores of the Sea of India. Here they find dealers who buy them, and take them to India, where they then sell them at the high price

I mentioned. It should be noticed that the heat in India is so intense that they can in no way keep horses alive there, and none are born, or, if any happen to be born, they are abortions, that is they have deformed or monstrous limbs, and are of no value.

These kingdoms are full of cruel and bloodthirsty people, for they are constantly at one another's throats, and would do great mischief to travelling merchants, were fear not instilled into them by the sovereign, namely the Tartar of the Levant. The latter has them punished severely, and has further ordained that in all the dangerous passes the inhabitants be obliged, at the merchants' request, to supply them with good and trusty guides to escort them safely from one district to another. He has also ordained that the guides be given two or three Venetian *grossi* for each load, according to the length of the journey. Yet, in spite of the force of authority, they do not hesitate to do frequent mischief, for, if the merchants are not well provided with weapons and bows, they kill and ill-treat them. And you may be sure they all follow the Law of Mahomet, their Prophet.

In the cities there are many merchants and craftsmen, who live by trade and handicrafts; for they make cloths of gold and silk of all kinds. Much cotton grows there. They have plenty of wheat, barley, millet, panic-grass, and every variety of corn and also wine, and all kinds of fruits. Some might object that the Saracens drink no wine, as their Law forbids it. We answer that they gloss the text of their Law as follows: if the wine be made to boil a little on the fire, until some of it is consumed, and it turns sweet, they may drink it without violating their commandment; for then they no longer call it wine, and so, by changing its taste, it changes its name.

We will now cease speaking of these kingdoms, and tell you of the great city of Yasdi, and of all its affairs and customs.

Here is told of the city of Yasdi

Yasdi is also in Persia, and it is a very fine and noble city, with considerable trade. A great quantity of silk cloths called *yasdi* are manufactured there, and carried thence by merchants, with great profit, to one or another foreign land. They worship Mahomet.

When one leaves this region to journey further, one travels for seven days over plains, passing only three inhabited places where one can find accommodation. There are many fine palm-groves, which one can ride through. They are rich in game. There is abundance of partridges and quails, that furnish much sport to the merchants who ride through. There are also very fine wild asses.

At the end of the seven days' journey, one reaches a kingdom called Kerman.

Here is told of the Kingdom of Kerman

Kerman is also a kingdom of Persia, and in former times had a hereditary sovereign. Ever since the Tartars conquered it, however, it has no longer had a hereditary dynasty, the Tartar sending a sovereign of his own choice. In this kingdom are born the stones called turquoises, which exist in great abundance, for they are found in the mountains, where they are extracted from the rocks. There are also plentiful seams of steel and *ondanique*. The people make excellently all kinds of harness for horsemen, namely bridles, saddles, spurs, swords, bows, quivers, and all sorts of weapons after the fashion of those parts. The women and girls do exquisite needlework in silks of all colours, embroidering it with beasts, and birds, and other figures. For the noblemen and great gentry they work curtains so ably and richly, that they are a wonder to see; they also make most dainty quilts, cushions, and pillows.

In the mountains of this land are found the best and swiftest falcons in the world. They are smaller than the peregrine, and are red on the breast and beneath the tail, between the thighs. I assure you that their flight is so incredibly swift, that there is no bird that can escape them by flying.

On leaving the city of Kerman, one rides seven days over a plain, ever coming across cities, and towns, and dwellings in great numbers. Riding there is very pleasant and enjoyable, for there is any amount of game, and quantities of partridges.

When one has ridden seven days across this plain, one reaches a very great mountain. After that, begins a great descent, and for two days one continues going down, ever finding great abundance and variety of fruits. Formerly there were dwellings, but now there is none, the district being inhabited by people who graze their cattle there. During the winter, it is so cold from the city of Kerman to this descent, that one can hardly survive by wearing many clothes and furs.

I will also tell you of an experiment that has been made in this kingdom of Kerman.

The people of Kerman, then, are good, very humble, peaceful, and as helpful to one another as possible. For this reason, one day that the King of Kerman was surrounded by his wise men, he said to them: " Gentlemen, I am greatly astonished at not knowing the reason of the following fact: namely that, whereas in the kingdoms of Persia, so near to our land, the people are so wicked and treacherous that they constantly kill one another, with us, who yet are almost one with them, there hardly ever occur outbursts of wrath or disorder." The wise men answered him that the cause lay in the soil. Then the King sent some of his men into Persia, and particularly to the Kingdom of Isfaan above mentioned, whose inhabitants surpassed all the others in wickedness. Here, on the advice of his wise men, he had seven ships loaded with earth, and brought to his kingdom. When the earth arrived, he had it sprinkled, after the manner of pitch, on the floor of certain much frequented rooms; and had it covered with carpets, in order that its softness should not soil those present. There they then sat down to a banquet, and straightway, at the very first course, they began offending one another with words and deeds, and wounding one another mortally. Then the king declared that truly the cause of the fact lay in the soil.

Here is told of the city of Camadi

After the two days' descent of which I have told you, one comes to a very vast plain, at the beginning of which stands a city called Camadi, which erstwhile was wonderfully noble and great, but which now is such no longer, for the Tartar invaders have sacked it several times. That plain, I assure you, is exceedingly hot.

The province with which we are now beginning to deal is called Reobar. It produces dates, apples of Paradise, pistachios, and other fruit that we do not possess in our cold countries. Wheat and other corns also grow there. There are numberless turtle-doves on account of the abundance of berries they find to feed on; they are truly without number because the Saracens hold them in abomination as food. There are also pheasants. There is a special variety of francolins in that plain, differing from those of other countries, for they are of a mixed black and white colour, with red legs and bill. No less do the animals differ; and first I will tell you of their oxen. They are very large, and all white as snow; the hair is short and smooth, and this is due to the heat of the country; the horns are short and thick, and not pointed: between the shoulders they have a round hump, no less than two palms high. They are the handsomest creatures in the world. When you want to load them, they kneel down like camels; then, when they are loaded, they get up and carry their burden very well, for they are most remarkably strong. There are sheep as big as asses, with tails so long and broad as to weigh as much as thirty pounds. They are fine fat beasts, and excellent food.

In this plain there are many towns and cities surrounded by high and thick ramparts to defend them against the Caraunas, who are brigands that infest that country. Why are they called Caraunas? It is because they are born of Indian mothers and Tartar fathers. When they want to overrun the country plundering it, these brigands are able, by certain spells of a devilish nature, to make the day dark, so that one can only see at a short distance: they can make this darkness extend over the space of seven days' journey. They are very well acquainted with the lie of the land, and, once they have made darkness around them, they ride one beside the other (sometimes up to the number of ten thousand, sometimes more, sometimes less), in such wise as to stretch across the whole of the plain they intend to plunder. Thus nothing that they find in the open can escape, and men, animals, and things become their prey. Of the men they capture, they kill the old, and the young they take away to sell as serfs and slaves. Their king is called Nogodar. He had gone to the court of Chagatai, own brother to the Great Kaan, with ten thousand of his men, and took up his abode with him, for Chagatai was his uncle and a most powerful Lord. While living with him, he planned and committed a great infamy, and I will tell you how.

Leaving his uncle, Chagatai, who was then in Greater Armenia, he fled with ten thousand of his men, most cruel and ribald fellows; he passed through Balashan, then through a province called Pashai, and then through another called Keshimur, where he lost many of his men and animals, because the roads were narrow and bad. Once they had passed through all those provinces, they entered India from the direction of a province called Dilivar. They captured a noble city, also called Dilivar, where Nogodar settled, taking the sovereignty away from a king called Asidin Soldan, who was very rich and powerful. There lives Nogodar with his men, fearing nobody, and waging war on all the other Tartars that live round about his kingdom. His men, who were Tartars, and hence white, mixed with the Indian women, who were black, and begot children who were called Caraunas, which in their language means "mixed." They are the Caraunas that overrun the plain of Reobar and other districts. And you must know that they learnt from the people of Maabar the magic and devilish arts whereby they make darkness come and obscure the light of day. On their plundering forays they ride sometimes thirty and sometimes forty days, but for the most part they resort to the region of Reobar. This is because all the merchants who go to Cormos for the purpose of trading, while waiting for the arrival of those who come from the direction of India, send their mules and camels during the winter to the plains of Reobar, in order to fatten them on the abundant grass, after they have grown thin during the long journey. The Caraunas keep a watch for this, plundering everything, and killing or selling all those who do not possess wherewith to ransom themselves.

I have now told you of the plain of Reobar and of the people who make darkness in order to plunder. I now add that Messer Marco Polo himself was almost caught by these people in even such a darkness; but he made his escape to a town called Canosalmi. But of his companions many were taken and sold, and some were killed.

We will now go on telling you of other things.

Here is told of the great descent

You must know that the plain of which I have told you, stretches to the south for the space of five days' journey. At the end of the five days, one reaches another descent, and for the space of twenty miles one must continue going down. The road is exceedingly bad and infested by robbers, and hence perilous. When one reaches the bottom of this descent, one finds another very beautiful plain, called the plain of Cormos. It stretches for two days' journey. There are fine rivers, with plenty of dates and other fruit. There are also francolins and parrots and other kinds of birds, different from ours.

After two more days' riding, one reaches the Ocean Sea. On the shore there is a city called Cormos, which possesses a harbour. You must know that here arrive the traders from India with their ships, bringing all kinds of spices, precious stones, pearls, gold and silk cloths, elephants' teeth, and many other wares. In that city they sell them to other merchants, who then take them all over the world, selling them to others again. It is indeed a city of very considerable trade. There are many other cities and towns subject to it. It is the capital of the kingdom. The name of its king is Maimodi Acomat. The heat there is very great because the sun burns exceedingly. It is an unhealthy country. If a foreign merchant dies there, the king takes possession of all his goods.

In this land they make wine with dates and a quantity of spices; it is very good. If those who drink it are not accustomed to it, it acts as a laxative, and purges violently; but afterwards it is good for one, and makes one put on flesh. The people do not use our foods, because, if they ate wheat-bread or meat, they would fall ill. To keep healthy, they eat dates and salt fish, namely tunny; they also eat onions. Such are the foods they eat to keep healthy.

Their ships are very bad, and many of them are wrecked, because they are not put together with iron nails, but sewn with twine made from the husk of Indian nuts. They steep the husk in water until it becomes like the hairs of a horse's mane; then they make twine of it, with which they stitch their ships. The salt sea-water does not spoil it; and indeed it holds out very well. The ships have one mast, one sail, and one rudder, but no deck. After they are loaded, however, the cargo is covered with a piece of hide, and on the top of the cargo thus covered are placed the horses that are taken to India to be sold. They possess no iron to make nails, and so have recourse to wooden treenails, and to stitching with twine. It is hence a matter of no little peril to sail in those ships. I assure you that many are lost, for violent storms are frequent in the Sea of India.

The people are black, and worship Mahomet. In summer they do not live in the cities, for the heat is such that they would all die. They go outside, to their gardens, wherever there is abundance of rivers and water. They are wont to make platforms on the water, with hurdles, one end of which rests on the bank, and the other is lashed to poles sunk into the river-bed; above, they entwine branches to protect themselves from the sun. Nor would this be enough to save them, if they did not have recourse to yet another expedient which I will now tell you of. You must know that during summer, from the direction of the sandy wastes surrounding that plain, there often blows a wind of such intolerable heat that it would be mortal, did not the people, on feeling it approach, enter the water up to the neck. Thus they escape the effects of that burning wind.

To show how hot that wind was, Messer Marco Polo told of the following case that occurred when he was in those parts.

As the King of Cormos had not paid his tribute to the King of Kerman, the latter got ready 1600 horse and 5000 foot, sending them across the region of Reobar, to attack the others by surprise. This he did at the time when the people of Cormos were living outside the city in the country. One day, the assailants, being wrongly guided, were unable to reach the place appointed for passing the night, and rested in a wood not very far from Cormos. When, on the next morning, they were about to set out again, that wind caught them, and suffocated them all, so that none survived to bring the news to their Lord. When the people of Cormos heard of this, they went to bury them in order that all those corpses should not infect the air. But the corpses were so baked by the immense heat, that when they took them by the arms to put them into the pits, the arms parted from the bodies. It was hence necessary to make the pits next to the bodies and to throw them in.

They sow their wheat, barley, and other cereals in the month of November, and reap them already everywhere in March; the same applies to all their products, for they are perfectly ripe by March. Nor would you find anything green on the ground after that, except dates, which last till May. This is due to the great heat which dries everything up.

As for their ships, I shall add that they are not pitched, but greased with a fish-oil.

Moreover, I will tell you that when some one dies, man or woman, they make great lamentations, and the widows mourn their husbands for no less than four years, and at least once a day. For this purpose they come together with their kinsfolk and neighbours, and make great weeping, and lamenting, and moaning invocations to the dead man. And as there is no lack of people dying, the lamentations are constant. In that country there are women, experts in mourning, who may be hired at a price to weep for the dead of others, on any day.

Now we will cease speaking of this town. I will

not tell you of India at this point, for I wish to do so further on in this book, in due time and place. At present, we will turn northwards, to tell you of the countries there, returning by another road to the city of Kerman, of which I have already spoken, for you cannot reach the countries of which I wish to tell you, except through that city of Kerman. And I will add that King Maimodi Acomat, whom we have just left, is subject to the King of Kerman.

The return journey from Cormos to Kerman passes through most beautiful plains, rich in food-stuffs. There are, too, many hot baths. There is also abundance of partridges, which are very cheap. There are plenty of dates and other fruit. The wheaten bread, in these places, is so bitter that it is impossible to eat it, unless one is accustomed to it. This is due to the fact that the water is bitter. The baths I mentioned above are of very hot spring water and are most beneficial for many diseases, especially of the skin.

Now I wish to begin speaking of the northern countries of which my book is to tell you. Let us start.

How one traverses a very wild and poor country

On leaving the city of Kerman, one has seven days of most wearisome riding; and I will tell you why.

During the first three days, one finds no water, or practically none, and what one does find is brackish and as green as meadow grass, and so bitter that no one could possibly drink it; a single drop of it, if you drink it, will open your bowels at least ten times. The same applies to the salt produced from this water: the least grain of it will purge a man violently. For this reason those who pass this way take drinking-water with them. Animals drink of the local water with great difficulty, and only when driven to it by thirst, and I assure you that it has a remarkable purgative effect on them. During these three days' journey you meet no habitation, all being desert and extreme drought. There are no animals, for they would have nothing to feed on.

On the fourth day, one reaches a fresh-water river flowing underground; in certain places, however, there are as it were caverns and holes made by the running water, where the river may be seen flowing before it disappears again under the ground. But there is plenty of water near which travellers, weary with the hardships of the desert, rest to refresh themselves and their animals.

For the next three days you are once more in an arid desert; the water is bitter as before, and there are no plants or animals, except wild asses.

At the end of these three days, one reaches the boundary of the kingdom of Kerman, and finds the city of Cobinan.

Here is told of the great and noble city of Cobinan

Cobinan is a great city. The inhabitants worship Mahomet. There is abundance of iron, steel, and *ondanique*. Very fine large steel mirrors are manufactured there. They also make *tutia* which is very good for the eyes. They prepare *spodium*, too, and I will tell you how. They take earth from a suitable vein; they then pile it up in a flaming furnace, above which is an iron grating. The smoke and moisture that issue from the earth stick to the grating and form *tutia*; what remains of the earth in the fire is *spodium*.

Let us now cease speaking of this city and proceed further.

How another desert is crossed

On leaving this city of Cobinan, one rides no less than eight days across a very arid desert, without fruits or trees, and with water as bitter and bad as in the other. One must therefore take all necessary food and drink with one, except the drink for the animals, which can, with some difficulty, be made to drink the water by mixing it with flour in order to attract them to it.

At the end of the eight days one comes to a province called Tunocain. It possesses many cities and towns. It is situated on the northern borders of Persia. It comprises a great plain, where is situated the Arbre Sol, which the Christians call Arbre Sec. I will tell you what it is like. It is very tall and thick, and its leaves are green on one side, and white on the other. It produces husks like those of the chestnut, but without anything inside. Its wood is hard and yellow like that of box-wood. All around it, to a distance of over a hundred miles, there are no trees, except in one direction only, where trees are found at ten miles' distance. This is the place where, according to the inhabitants, took place the battle between Alexander and Darius. The cities and towns are amply provided with all good and fine things, for the country has a splendid climate, neither too hot nor too cold. The inhabitants all worship Mahomet. They are handsome people, and the women especially are surpassingly beautiful.

We will now leave this place and tell you of a country called Mulehet, where once lived the Old Man of the Mountain.

Here is told of the Old Man of the Mountain and of his Assassins

Mulehet is a country where in ancient days lived the Old Man of the Mountain. Mulehet is also the name of the heretics of the Saracen Law. I will now tell you the whole story of this Old Man as it was told by many people to me, Messer Marco Polo.

In their language, the Old Man was called Alaodin.

In a valley between two mountains he had had made the largest and finest garden that ever was seen. In it there were all the good fruits in the world. Here he had had built the fairest houses and the most beautiful palaces that any man ever saw, for they were covered with gilding, and adorned with the pictures of all the beautiful things of the earth. Further, he had had conduits made, and down one flowed wine, down another milk, down a third honey, and down a fourth water. There were also ladies and damsels there, the fairest on earth, who could play on all kinds of instruments, and sang and danced better than other women. And the Old Man made his people believe that this garden was Paradise. He had, in fact, built it just this way, because Mahomet told the Saracens that those who go to Paradise will have at their disposal beautiful women to their heart's content, and will find there rivers of wine and milk and honey and water. This is why he had had the garden made like the Paradise that Mahomet had described to the Saracens; and the Saracens in those parts really believed that the garden was Paradise.

Into that garden no man ever entered except those he wished to make Assassins. At the entrance of the garden was a castle so strong as to fear no man in the world; and there was no other way into the garden but that.

The Old Man kept with him at his court all the young men of the district, from twelve to twenty years of age, such as seemed capable of bearing arms. And they knew well, because they had heard it told, that according to what Mahomet, their Prophet, had said, Paradise was made just as I have described it; and they truly believed it.

What more shall I tell you? The Old Man used to have these youths put in the garden, four, ten or twenty at a time, as he pleased. And he did it in the following way: he had a potion given them, as a result of which they straightway fell asleep; then he had them taken up and put into the garden, and then awaked.

When they awoke, they found themselves inside, and saw all the things that I have told you, and so believed that they were really in Paradise. And the ladies and damsels remained with them all day, playing music and singing and making excellent cheer; and the young men had their pleasure of them. So these youths had all they could desire, and would never have left the place of their own free will.

How the Old Man of the Mountain trained his Assassins, and made them obedient to himself

The Old Man kept a fine and splendid court, and led a grand life, making those simple mountain-folk about him believe that he was a prophet; and such they firmly believed him to be.

When the Old Man wanted to send any of his men anywhere to kill some person, he would order the potion to be given to a certain number of them, and once they were asleep, he would have them taken up and brought into his palace. When the youths awoke and found themselves in the castle in the Old Man's palace, they would be greatly amazed and by no means pleased, for never would they, of their own accord, have left the paradise in which they had been. They would now go into the presence of the Old Man, and humble themselves before him, believing that they were in the presence of a great Prophet. The Old Man would then ask them whence they came, and they would answer they came from Paradise. They would assert that it was indeed the Paradise promised by Mahomet to their fathers, and they would relate to him all the things they had found there. The other youths, who had not been there and were present at the narrative, would then be consumed by the desire to go to the Paradise, feeling ready to die in order to be able to do so, and longing for the day when it would come about.

So when the Old Man wished to have some great person murdered, he first of all tested his Assassins, to see which were the best. He sent many of them not very far off in the neighbouring region, and ordered them to kill a given man. They went at once, and carried out their Lord's command, and then, after killing the man, returned to the court—those of them at least, who survived, for some were taken and killed. Once the survivors had returned to their Lord, they told him that their task was performed, and he gave them a joyous welcome. And he knew very well which of them had borne himself most valiantly, for behind each he had sent men to watch them, in order to inform him afterwards which was the boldest and ablest in killing.

So, when the Old Man desired to have some great person or any other man killed, he made use of some of these Assassins of his, sending them where he wished. And he told them that he did so to send them back to Paradise: let them but go and kill such and such a one, and if they died they would straightway go to Paradise. Those who received such orders from the Old Man were delighted by them more than by anything else, and went and performed all that the Old Man commanded. Thus no man could escape death, if such was the will of the Old Man. And I assure you that many kings and many barons paid him tribute and kept on good terms with him, fearing lest he might have them killed. And this was due to the fact that then those peoples had no unity of dominion, but were divided in their allegiance and interests.

How the Old Man of the Mountain was suppressed

I have now told you what were the Old Man of the Mountain and his Assassins; I will now tell you how he was suppressed, and by whom.

But first of all I wish to add another thing that I had omitted about him. I tell you, then, that this Old Man had made two more Old Men, who were his subordinates, and in every way followed his practice and procedure. One he had sent into the province of Damascus, and the other into Curdistan. But enough of this: let us come to his suppression.

Know then, that about the year 1262 after Christ's Incarnation, Alau, Lord of the Tartars of the Levant, who was informed of all the wicked deeds of the Old Man, resolved to have him suppressed. He therefore took one of his barons and sent him to that castle with a great army. They besieged the castle for no less than three years without being able to take it. Nor would they ever have taken it, if the besieged had had food; but at the end of three years, they had no victuals left. Then the castle was taken, and the Old Man of the Mountain, Alaodin by name, was killed, together with all his men. And ever since the days of that Old Man there has never been any other Old Man, nor any Assassin. With him ended the infamous Lordship exercised in past times by the Old Men of the Mountain.

We will now leave this subject and proceed further.

Here is told of the city of Sapurgan

When you leave this castle, you ride across beautiful plains and valleys and charming hill-slopes, rich in fine grass and excellent pasture, and with abundance of fruits, and all other good things. Armies are glad to stop there on account of the great plenty. This country extends for a distance of no less than six days' journey; there are cities and towns in it, and the inhabitants worship Mahomet. At times one comes across a desert, some fifty or sixty miles in length, where no water is to be found; here it is necessary for travellers to bring water with them; the animals have to do without drinking until they have got across the desert, and reached places where water is to be found.

After riding six days as I have told you, one reaches a city called Sapurgan. It is a city where everything is to be found in great abundance. And I assure you that they have the finest melons in the world, and in vast quantities, and this is how they dry them: they pare them round and round into something like strips of leather; then they put them in the sun and thus dry them, so that they become sweeter than honey. And I will add that there is a great trade in them, and they are sold in large quantities in all the neighbourhood. There is also an incredible amount of game, both beasts and birds.

We will now cease speaking of this city, and tell of another called Balc.

Here is told of the great and noble city of Balc

Balc is a great and noble city, but once it was still more noble and great, for the Tartars and other peoples have ravaged and destroyed it. For I assure you that once there were many beautiful palaces and splendid marble houses in it: and they can still be seen, damaged and ruined. And I will add that, according to what the inhabitants say, this is the city in which Alexander married the daughter of Darius. The people worship Mahomet. And you must know too that the dominions of the Lord of the Tartars of the Levant extend as far as this city, which is on the borders of Persia between north-east and east.

We will now cease speaking of this city and pass on to tell of another country, called Taican.

Here is told of a land called Taican, where the mountains are of salt

Leaving the city of which I have spoken, one rides for as many as twelve days between north-east and east without coming across a single dwelling, for the inhabitants have all taken refuge among the mountains, in fortresses, on account of brigands and armies that cruelly harassed them. There is plenty of water, and there is plenty of game, and there are lions too. One can procure no provisions during those twelve days, and so travellers must take with them food for themselves and for their horses.

At the end of the twelve days' journey, one reaches a town called Taican, where there is a great corn market. It is a very fine district, and the mountains to the south of it are very large, and all made of salt. (Other mountains in the district abound in almonds and pistachios, in which there is also a great trade.) People come from all the country around, to the distance of thirty days' journey, to fetch that salt, which is the best in the world. It is so hard that it can only be gathered by using great iron picks. And I assure you there is so much of it that the whole world would have enough till the Day of Doom.

Leaving this city, one journeys for three days between north-east and east, always traversing fine lands with numerous habitations, and rich in fruits and corn and vines. The people worship Mahomet. They are wicked and blood-thirsty. They indulge in prolonged drinking-bouts, for they are fond of drinking, and have excellent boiled wine. They wear nothing on their heads, save a cord, some ten palms long, which they coil round it. They are excellent hunters, and take a great deal of game. They have no other clothes than the skins of the animals they take in the chase, which they tan and use to make clothes and foot-wear. All of them know how to tan the skins of the animals they catch.

After three days' journey, one reaches a city called Scasem, which belongs to a count, whose other cities and towns are on the mountains. Through the city flows quite a large river. There are quantities of porcupines. When the hunters wish to catch them, and set their dogs on them, the porcupines curl up, and shoot out the quills on their back and sides at the dogs, wounding them in many places.

This city of Scasem is in a large province also called Scasem. They have a language of their own. The peasants who have cattle live in the mountains, and build fine large dwellings for themselves. They make them in the form of caves, which is not difficult, as the mountains are all composed of earth.

When one leaves the city I have just told you of, one journeys three days without finding habitations, or anything to eat or drink. Travellers take everything with them, except for their animals, which find grass enough.

At the end of three days one comes to the province of Balashan, and I will now tell you about it.

Here is told of the great province of Balashan

Balashan is a great province, whose inhabitants worship Mahomet, and have a language of their own. It is a vast kingdom, stretching to the extent of twelve days' journey. The kingship is hereditary, and the royal line descends from King Alexander and the daughter of Darius, the great Lord of Persia. In memory of the great Alexander, all their kings still call themselves, in their Saracen language, Zulcarnein, which is the equivalent of our Alexander.

In this country are born the precious stones called *Balas* rubies, which are so beautiful and of such great value. They are born within the rocks of the mountains. You must know that the people dig great caves into the mountains, and go very deep, just like those who work silver-mines. This is done more precisely in a mountain called Sighinan. But you must also know that the King has them dug up on his own account, and no one else could go to that mountain to dig for *Balas* rubies without being immediately put to death; moreover, should anyone take them out of the kingdom, he would forfeit both his life and his goods. For the King sends them by means of his own men to other kings and princes and great lords, to some as tribute and to others as gifts; some too he has sold for gold and silver. This the King does in order that the *Balas* rubies may remain costly and valuable, even as they are. For if he were to allow others to dig for them and carry them about the world, so many would be extracted that they would no longer be so costly and valuable. This is why he has established so great a punishment to prevent people from digging for them without his permission.

In this province, in another mountain are also born sapphires, which are mined like the *Balas* rubies. And you must also know that in another mountain of the same region is found the stone of which azure is made—the finest and best azure in the world. Of this stone of which azure is made veins are formed in the mountains, as with other stones. And I will add that in yet other mountains are found veins of silver, copper, and lead, mined in large quantities.

It is a very cold country. You must also know that excellent horses are bred there, which are very good runners, and are not shod, though they constantly go on the mountains. Once there were in this country horses descended from the breed of Alexander's horse, Bucephalus; they were all born with a horn on their head, like their ancestor, Bucephalus. The only one to possess the breed was an uncle of the King's who refused to let the King have one, so that the latter had him killed. The widow then, in despite, destroyed the whole breed, so that now it is extinct.

In the same mountains there are saker falcons, which are very good and swift. There are also lanner falcons. There is great abundance of game, too, both beasts and birds. They have excellent wheat but their barley is huskless. They have no olive-oil, but they make oil from sesame and walnuts.

In this kingdom there are many narrow passes and many fastnesses, so that the people have no fear of invaders coming to ravage the country. Their cities and towns are situated on great mountains, in very strong positions. And this is the nature of these mountains: they are very high, so that one must walk from dawn till sunset to get from the foot to the top of them; on the summit, however, there are broad plateaus, rich in grass and trees, where very copious and pure spring-waters flow like rivers down over the rocks; in these streams are found grayling and other kinds of delicate fish. On those heights the air is so pure and healthy, that if an inhabitant of the cities and dwellings situated in the valleys at the foot of the mountains falls sick of fever, be it tertian or quartan ague, or continuous, or of any other kind soever, it is enough for him to rest two or three days on those plateaus to shake off the malady and recover his health. And Messer Marco said that he had had personal experience of this. When he was in those regions, in fact, he lay ill for about a year, but as soon as he took the advice of going to that mountain, he recovered. There are also two or three mountains abounding in sulphur, and sulphurous waters constantly flow from them. There is also an enormous number of wild sheep, in flocks of four, five and six hundred; and though many are taken, they never grow the scarcer.

They are excellent archers and hunters. They dress for the most part in the skins of animals, for cloth is scarce with them. The great ladies of the nobility wear trousers such as I will describe. For a pair of trousers, or rather drawers, those ladies use as much as sixty, eighty, or one hundred ells of cotton cloth, which they pleat. This they do to make their buttocks appear big, for their men delight in fat women.

We have now told you about this kingdom. We will now leave the subject, and tell you of a strange people that lives to the south, at ten days' journey from this province.

Here is told of the province of Pashai

You must know, then, that at ten days' journey to the south of Balashan there is a province called Pashai. They have a language of their own. The people are idolaters, and worship idols. They are dark-skinned. They are very expert in sorcery and in diabolical arts. The men wear little rings in their ears, and many brooches of gold and silver, with pearls and precious stones. They are a very cunning people, and, after their fashion, clever. The country is very hot. Their food consists of meat and rice.

We will now cease speaking of this province, and tell you of another, situated at seven days' journey from this, towards the south-east. It is called Keshimur.

Here is told of the province of Keshimur

Keshimur is also a province where the people are idolaters and have a language of their own. As devil-charmers, they are wonderfully clever, for they make their idols speak. By means of charms they make the weather change, and a thick darkness descend. With their charms and their talents they perform such marvels as no one can believe who has not seen them.

I will add, indeed, that they are the principal idolaters, and that idolatry was born amongst them.

From this place one could go to the Sea of India.

The men are dark-skinned and lean; the women are as beautiful as dark women can be. Their diet consists of meat, milk and rice. The climate is temperate, without excess of heat or cold. There are many cities and towns, and also forests and deserts and such formidable passes that they are afraid of no one. They are independent, and have a king of their own, who governs them according to justice.

They have hermits, after a fashion, who live in hermitages, and practise great abstinence in eating and drinking; they also remain surpassingly chaste, and are exceedingly scrupulous about committing sins forbidden by their Law. By their fellow-countrymen they are considered very holy. And you must know that they live to a very advanced age. And it is for love of their idols that they practise such strict abstinence. They also have numerous abbeys and monasteries of their faith, where the brethren lead very strict lives, and wear a tonsure like our Dominicans and Minorites. The people of this province kill no animals, nor spill blood. There are, however, Saracens living among them who slaughter the animals for them, that they may have food.

The coral exported from our countries finds a better market there than anywhere else.

If you were to proceed for twelve more days' journey, you would reach the lands where pepper grows, namely near the country of the Brahmins. But we will not proceed, and we will cease speaking of this province and district, for we should otherwise enter India, and I do not wish to do so now; we will tell you everything about India, in the proper order, on our return journey. At present we shall therefore return to our provinces, in the direction of Balashan, as we cannot proceed in any other direction.

Here is told of a province called Vocan

On leaving Balashan, one journeys twelve days between east and north-east, along a great river. The country belongs to the brother of the Lord of Balashan, and there are towns and habitations in great numbers. The people are chivalrous, and worship Mahomet.

At the end of the twelve days' journey, one reaches a fairly small province (for it extends only three days' journey in each direction), called Vocan. The people worship Mahomet, and have a language of their own. They are valiant in war. They have no Lord of their own, but are governed by one whom they call None (which is the equivalent of our count), and are subject to the Lord of Balashan. There is any amount of wild animals, and all kinds of game, both beasts and birds.

Here is told of a country called Pamier

Leaving this region, one travels three days to the north-east, always through mountains. One ascends so high that they say it is the highest place in the world. On reaching these heights, one finds a plain between the mountains, with a great lake, whence issues a very fine river. There is the finest pasture in the world: a lean beast will fatten in ten days. There is great abundance of all kinds of game. There is also an enormous number of wild sheep, of very great size. Their horns reach a length of quite six spans, the smallest being three or four spans. From these horns the shepherds make great bowls out of which they eat. With them too they make enclosures where they pen their cattle by night. There are also large numbers of wolves that kill and eat many of those sheep. Hence large quantities of horns and bones are found, great piles of which are made along the roads to point out the way to travellers when the ground is covered with snow. To cross this plain one rides no less than twelve days. It is called Pamier. During all those twelve days, you find no houses nor grass, so that travellers must bring their food with them. Not a bird is to be seen flying on account of the great altitude and the cold. And I tell you that, on account of this great cold, fire does not burn so clearly, nor is it of the same colour as elsewhere, and it cooks food less well.

Let us now quit this subject, and tell you of other things, proceeding towards north-east and east.

Here is told of a country called Belor

When one has journeyed twelve days, as I have said, one must journey forty more, between north-east and east, always through mountains and hill-slopes and valleys, crossing many rivers and deserts. During all those days, one finds no habitations or grassy regions, so that the traveller must take all necessaries with him. This region is called Belor. The people live in the mountains at great altitudes. They are idolaters and very wild, and live only by the chase. They dress in the skins of animals. They are exceedingly evil folk.

We will now leave this region and speak of the province of Cascar.

Here is told of the Kingdom of Cascar

In past times, Cascar was a kingdom, but nowadays it is subject to the Great Kaan. The people worship Mahomet. There are many cities and towns, the largest and noblest city being Cascar. The country is situated to the east and north-east. They live by trade and handicrafts. They have splendid gardens and vineyards, and fine farms. The district is fertile and abounds in all necessaries. There is great plenty of cotton, and also flax and hemp. From this country, many merchants go forth about the world for the purpose of trading. The people are very miserly and wretched, for they eat badly and drink badly. Among the Turks in this land there are a few Nestorian Christians, with a Church and Law of their own. The folk of the country have their own language. The province extends for five days' journey.

We will cease speaking of this region and tell you of Samarcan.

Here is told of the great city of Samarcan

Samarcan is a very great and noble city. The inhabitants are Christians and Saracens. They are subject to a nephew of the Great Kaan's; he is, however, no friend of his, and on the contrary has frequent quarrels with him. This city lies towards the north-west. It has splendid gardens, and a plain full of all the fruits one could possibly desire.

I will tell you of a great marvel that happened in this city.

You must know, then, that not many years ago Chagatai, carnal brother to the Great Kaan, turned Christian; he was the Lord of this country and of many others. When they saw that their Lord had turned Christian, the Christians of the city of Samarcan rejoiced greatly. They therefore raised a great church in the city in honour of St. John the Baptist; and such was the name of the church. Taking possession of a very fine stone that belonged to the Saracens, they used it as the pedestal of a column that stood in the middle of the church, holding up the roof. Now, it happened that Chagatai died. When the Saracens saw that he was dead, they who had been and still were exceedingly sad on account of the stone placed in the church of the Christians, decided among themselves to recover it by force. This they might easily do, being ten times more numerous than the Christians. So some of the Saracen elders went to the church of St. John, and told the Christians that were there, that they wanted the stone which had belonged to them. The Christians answered that they were ready to give them anything they might ask for, if they would but leave the stone, for, were it removed, the damage to the church would indeed be too great. The Saracens replied they wanted neither gold nor treasure, but their stone at all costs. What more shall I tell you? The lordship belonged to the Great Kaan's nephew whom I mentioned, and he commanded the Christians to restore the stone to the Saracens within two days. When they received that order, the Christians were exceedingly sad, and knew not what to do. Well, there occurred the miracle I will tell you of. You must know that on the morning of the day on which the stone was to be returned, the column that rested on it rose of itself, by the will of Our Lord Jesus Christ, to a height of no less than three spans from the stone, remaining in place just as if the stone were beneath it. So the column has remained ever since, and so it is to the present day. And this was then and is still held to be one of the great miracles that have occurred in the world.

We will now leave this subject and tell of a province called Yarcan.

Here is told of the province of Yarcan

Yarcan is a province extending to the length of five days' journey. The inhabitants follow the Law of Mahomet, but among them there are a few Nestorian Christians. They belong to the same nephew of the Great Kaan's of whom I told you before. They have great abundance of everything, and especially of cotton. The greater number of them have one foot very big and the other small: and yet they walk quite well.

They also mostly have goitres, and this is due to the nature of the water they drink.

But as there is nothing else worth mentioning in our book, let us cease speaking of this and tell you of Cotan.

Here is told of the great province of Cotan

Cotan is a province between east and north-east, and it is eight days' journey in length. They are subject to the Great Kaan. The inhabitants all worship Mahomet. There are very many cities and towns. The noblest city, and the capital of the kingdom, is called Cotan, which is also the name of the province. It has abundance of everything. Cotton grows there in considerable quantities, as well as flax, hemp, and corn. There are many vineyards, farms, and gardens. The people live by trade and handicrafts. They are no warriors.

We will now quit this province, and tell you of another called Pem.

Here is told of the province of Pem

Pem is a province five days' journey in length, between north-east and east. The people worship Mahomet, and are subject to the Great Kaan. There are many cities and towns. The noblest city, which is the capital of the kingdom, is called Pem. There are rivers, in which abound the stones called jasper and chalcedony. There is abundance of everything. Cotton grows in considerable quantities. The people live by trade and handicrafts. And I will add that they have the following custom: if a man is married and must leave his wife to go on a journey, so as to remain absent more than twenty days, the wife, as soon as he has set out, takes another husband; this she may do with impunity, as it is their custom. The husbands, too, wherever they go, can take another wife.

And you must know that all the provinces I have mentioned, from Cascar onwards, and others yet that we shall come across further on, belong to Great Turkey.

We will now quit this place, and we will tell you of a province called Charchan.

Here is told of the province of Charchan

Charchan is a province of Great Turkey, between north-east and east. It was once a fine and fertile region, but the Tartars have ravaged it considerably. The people worship Mahomet. There are many cities and towns, and the capital of the kingdom is Charchan. There are large rivers, that bring down jasper and chalcedony, which the traders take to Cathay, obtaining great profit, as they are both plentiful and of good quality. The whole province is all one stretch of sand; from Cotan to Pem it is also all sandy, and it is sandy too from Pem hither. The water is often bad and bitter, but in several places fresh and sweet water is to be found. If a hostile army happen to pass through the country, the people flee with their women and children and cattle, advancing for two or three days' journey into the sands to localities where they know that water is to be found and that they can live with their cattle. And I assure you no one can discover whither they have gone, because the wind covers up with sand the tracks they have made, so that no trace is left: it would seem as if no one, man or beast, had passed there. Even thus as I tell you do they escape from their enemies. You must also know that when they bring in their corn they store it far from their houses, in certain caves in the midst of the sands; this they do for fear of armies; from the caves they carry home what is needful month by month. If a friendly army happen to pass through the country, they only take away their cattle, for they do not want them to be taken away from them and eaten; for the soldiers do not pay for what they take.

When one leaves Charchan, one travels no less than five days across the sand, finding bad and bitter water; only here and there does one come across good and sweet water. There is nothing else worth mentioning in our book.

At the end of five days, one reaches a city called Lop, which is at the beginning of the Great Desert, where travellers collect provisions for the crossing of the desert. We will hence leave this subject, and proceed in our account.

Here is told of the city of Lop

Lop is a large city on the border of the Great Desert, which is called the Desert of Lop. It stands between the east and the north-east, and belongs to the Great Kaan. The inhabitants worship Mahomet. And you must know that those who wish to cross the Great Desert take a week's rest in this city in order to refresh themselves and their animals. At the end of the week, they take with them food for a month for man and beast, and, leaving the city, enter the desert.

You must know, too, that this desert is said to be so long that it takes a year to cross it from one end to the other, but where the width is least, it is a month's journey. It is all mountains and sand and valleys, and nothing eatable is to be found in it. After riding a day and night, however, one finds some drinking water in winter, sufficient not indeed for a large number of people, but for some 50 or 100, with their animals. And across the desert one must always ride a day and a night to find water. In three or four places the water is brackish and bitter, but elsewhere it is good. In all there are about twenty-eight places with water. There are neither beasts nor birds, for they find nothing to eat. But you must know that even such a marvel is to be found there as I shall tell you of.

Know, then, that when one travels by night across this desert, if anyone happen, through falling asleep or through any other cause, to remain behind or leave his companions, then, when he wishes to rejoin them, he hears spirits speaking to him as if they were his companions, for sometimes they even call him by name. And often a traveller is thus led astray, and never found again, so that many have died or disappeared in this way. And you must also know that these spirit-voices are heard in the daytime too; and one seems at times to hear the sound of various instruments, and especially of drums. Hence, travellers crossing the desert hang bells round their horses' necks by night, in order not to be led astray.

In this way, then, does one cross this desert, and with even as much hardship as I have told you. But now we will cease speaking of this desert, of which we have told you everything, and tell of the provinces one finds when one comes out of it.

Here is told of the great province of Tangut

After thus riding thirty days across the desert of which I have spoken, one reaches a city called Sachiu, belonging to the Great Kaan. The province is called Tangut. They are all idolaters, or, rather, there are also Christian Turks, who follow the Nestorian Law, and some Saracens too. The Idolaters have a language of their own. The city stands between north-east and east. The inhabitants do not live by trade, but by the profit they obtain from the corn they cultivate.

They have many abbeys and monasteries, all of which are full of all kinds of idols, to which they offer great sacrifices, and pay great honour and worship.

And you must know that those who have children,

breed a sheep in honour of the idols, and on New Year's Day, or on the feast of the child's idol, they who have bred the sheep, take it and their children, before the idol, which they worship devoutly, together with their children. After this they have the sheep cooked. They then take it again into the presence of the idol with great reverence, and leave it there until they have recited their offices and uttered prayers to the idol to save their children. And they say that the idols eat the substance of the meat. Having done this, they take the meat that has lain before the idol, and carry it home, or whithersoever they will, and, calling together their relatives, eat it with great reverence and festivity. The priests of the idols receive the head, feet, entrails, and skin, and also part of the flesh. After they have eaten the meat, they collect the bones, and carefully store them in a chest.

And you must know that all the idolaters in the world, when they die, are burnt. And when these idolaters are carried from their houses to the place where they are to be burnt, their relatives have wooden houses built in several places along the way, complete with porticoes, and covered with cloths of silk and gold. When the corpse arrives before these houses thus draped, the procession pauses, and the men cast abundance of wine and food in front of the dead man. This they do because they say that he will be received in the next world with as much honour. When the body reaches the place where it is to be burnt, the kindred have men, horses, camels, sheep and coins as large as bezants, cut in paper, all of which they burn together with the corpse. And they say that in the next world the dead man will have as many slaves and animals and sheep and coins as the paper ones they burn. And I also tell you that when they carry the corpse to be burnt, all the instruments in the place are played before it.

And another thing I tell you too, namely that when

one of these idolaters dies, the astrologers are sent for, and are informed concerning the dead man's nativity, that is to say when he was born, in what month, on what day, and at what hour. And the astrologer, having ascertained this, does his magic by means of his devilish arts, and after that tells them on what day the body should be burnt. I assure you that some are kept without being burnt for a week, and some a month, and some six. And during all that time the dead man's family must keep him in the house, even as I have told you, for they would never dream of having him burnt until their sorcerers tell them that they may do so. They cannot, in fact, as they say, remove the body from the house except under the planet under which the man was born, or at least under such a planet as is not contrary to it. They assert that otherwise the dead man can bring down many evils upon the house; and they give this as the reason when, as often happens, demons harm or kill someone in the house. During all the time the corpse remains unburnt, and lies in the house, they keep it as follows: they take a coffin made of boards a span broad, well joined together with pitch and mortar, and splendidly painted, and place the body in it, covering it up with such cloths, especially prepared with camphor and other spices, as prevent the corpse stinking for those in the house. Every day, as long as the dead man remains there, his relatives, namely those that live in the house, set a table for him with food and drink as if he were alive, and place it in front of the coffin containing the corpse, leaving it there for as much time as would be necessary to partake of the meal; and they say that his soul eats the food. Thus they keep the body until they take it away to be burnt. And another thing, too, that they do, that I will tell you of: often enough these astrologers tell the kindred that it is not good that they should carry the dead body through the main door, and they attribute this to some star or other influence, that is in opposition to that door. Hence the kindred have it removed through another door and at times even have a wall pulled down, and carry the corpse through the hole. And all the idolaters in the world perform these practices I have told you of.

Now we will leave this subject, and speak of other cities, situated towards the north-west, near the borders of the desert.

Here is told of the province of Camul

Camul is a province that once was a kingdom. There are many cities and towns in it, but the principal city is called Camul. The province lies between two deserts, for on one side stretches the Great Desert, and on the other side a small desert, three days' journey in extent. The people are all idolaters, and have a language of their own. They live by the fruits of the earth, for they have abundance of food and drink, which they sell to travellers passing through there. They are a merry people, for they do nothing but play instruments and sing and dance, and indulge greatly in bodily pleasures. And they delight, too, in writing, after their own fashion, and in reading.

And I assure you that if a stranger comes to one of their houses to lodge, the master is exceedingly glad. He orders his wife to do everything that the stranger may desire, and he himself leaves the house, and goes about his business. He remains away two or three days going to his country-houses, and from there sends everything that his guest may need, but against payment. The stranger meanwhile remains in the house with the wife, and does according to his will, lying in bed with her, as if she were his own wife; and they make great merriment. And all the husbands in that city and province are thus cuckolded by their wives, but I assure you that they think it no shame. And the women are beautiful, merry, and wanton.

Now, it happened in the days when Mongu Kaan, Lord of the Tartars, was king, that he was informed how the men of Camul thus prostituted their wives to strangers. So Mongu Kaan forbade them, under grievous penalties, thus to lodge strangers in their houses. When the men of Camul received this order, they were greatly vexed. For about three years they obeyed the king, but at last, seeing that their lands no longer yielded their usual fruits, and that many evils befell their households, they took counsel, and decided to do what indeed they did, even as I shall tell you. They took a most beautiful gift and sent it to Mongu, begging him to let them follow, as regards their women, the customs handed down to them by their fathers, and telling him that their fathers had said that their idols were most pleased with this favour they showed to strangers, by giving them their wives and goods, and that for this reason their crops and their labour prospered. When Mongu Kaan heard this, he said, "Since you want your shame, have it then." So he consented that they should have their will. And I assure you that they have ever since followed that custom, and still do so.

Here we will cease speaking of the province of Camul, and tell you of other provinces that lie between north and north-west.

And you must know that that province belongs to the Great Kaan.

Here is told of the province of Icoguristan

Icoguristan is a large province and belongs to the Great Kaan. It has many cities and towns, but the principal city is called Carachoco. This city has many other cities and towns dependent upon it. The inhabitants worship idols. But there are many Christians who follow the Nestorian Law. There are also some

Saracens. The Christians often intermarry with the Idolaters.

They say that the king, who first ruled them, was not of human origin, but was born of one of those swellings that the sap produces on the bark of trees, and that we call *esca*. From him descended all the other kings. These Idolaters are exceedingly learned, according to their own laws and customs, and constantly apply themselves to the liberal arts. The land produces corn and excellent wine. But in winter the cold there is greater than is known to exist in any other part of the world.

Here is told of the province of Ghinghintalas

Ghinghintalas is a province also situated on the borders of the lesser desert, between north and north-west. It extends for sixteen days' journey. It belongs to the Great Kaan. There are cities and towns in it in great numbers. There are three kinds of people—Idolaters, Mohammedans, and some Turkish Christians of the Nestorian Church. On the borders of this province, towards the north is a mountain with an excellent vein of steel and *ondanique*. In the same mountain there is a vein from which salamander is obtained. For you must know that salamander is not an animal, as people say, but is such as I shall tell you. It is a truth that you all know, that by nature no animal, no living creature, can live in the fire, as every animal is composed of all four elements. As people had no certain information concerning the salamander, they thought, and still do think, that it is an animal, but this is not the truth, which is as I will now tell you. You must know, then, that I had a comrade, Zurficar by name, who was a very wise Turk, and who lived three years in that province, by order of the Great Kaan, to extract the salamander, the steel, the *ondanique*, and so forth. For it is the Great Kaan's custom to send a lord to rule over that province for three years at a time, and to oversee the mining of the salamander. My friend explained the thing to me, and I myself witnessed it. For you must know that when you have extracted some of the substance from the vein in the mountain, if you try to break it up, it remains united, making threads like wool. Hence, when one has this vein, one has it dried, and then pounded in great brazen mortars, and finally washed. Thus there remains the threads of which I have spoken, whereas the soil is worthless and is thrown away. The threads, which look like wool, are then carefully spun, and made into napkins. The latter, however, are by no means white. But they put them into the fire, and leave them there awhile; and so the napkins become as white as snow. And whenever any of these salamander napkins show stains or spots, they are put into the fire and left there awhile, and they become as white as snow.

This is the truth concerning the salamander, even as I have told you, and all the rest that is said about it is lies and idle tales.

And I will also tell you that in Rome there is a napkin that the Great Kaan sent to the Pope as a splendid present, when he sent the two Polo brothers to him as envoys, in order that the sacred shroud of Our Lord Jesus Christ might be wrapped up in it. And on that napkin are golden letters, saying *Tu es Petrus et super hanc petram edificabo ecclesiam meam.*

Now we will cease speaking of this province, and tell you of another, which lies between north-east and east.

Here is told of the province of Suchu

On leaving this province of which I have told you, one rides ten days between north-east and east. And all this time one finds no dwellings, or almost none.

Nor is there anything worthy of being recorded in our book.

At the end of the ten days, one reaches a province called Suchu, in which there are many cities and towns. The principal city is called Suchu. There are both Christians and Idolaters. They belong to the Great Kaan. The great General Province to which this province, as well as the other two I have just told you of, belong, is called Tangut. All over its mountains, rhubarb is found in great quantities. Here merchants purchase it, and then carry it all over the world. The travellers who pass through this province dare not, however, cross those mountains with any other animals than native ones, for there grows on them a poisonous grass, such that animals that eat of it lose their hoofs; the native animals, instead, know this grass, and avoid it. The people live by the fruits of the soil, and hardly do any trading. The province is healthy everywhere, and the inhabitants are dark-skinned.

Now I will leave this place, and tell you of a city called Canpchu.

Here is told of the city of Canpchu

Canpchu is also a city of Tangut, and a very large and noble one, the capital and mistress of the entire province. The people are idolaters, and there are also some who worship Mahomet. There are Christians, too, who possess three fine large churches in the city. The Idolaters have many abbeys and monasteries after their fashion, and they have, too, an infinite number of idols. And I assure you that some of them are ten paces long; some are of wood, others of clay, others again of stone, but all are covered with gold, and are of excellent workmanship. The large idols are in a lying posture, and all round them are many other small idols, which seem to be paying them humble homage.

And as I have not yet told you everything about the idolaters, I will tell you all about them here.

Know, then, that the regulars among the idolaters live more virtuously than all the other idolaters. They avoid lechery, though they do not hold it a grievous sin. For, according to their conscience, they can lie with a woman without committing a sin if she asks them for their love, whereas they consider it a sin if the man asks for the woman's love. Yet I assure you that if they find that a man has lain with a woman against nature, they condemn him to death. They have feasts for their idols at different times, just as we have for our saints, and they also have a kind of calendar in which the feasts of the idols are marked on the appointed days. And I will add, too, that they have moons, as we have months. In certain moons there is a period of five days during which no idolater would for anything in the world kill beasts or birds, or eat the flesh of animals killed during those days. During those five days they live more virtuously than at other times. Among these idolaters there are some religious who never eat meat from one year's end to another; but the lay-folk do not abstain from it except at the periods stated.

They may take as many as thirty wives, more or less according to their wealth, and the number they can keep. The husbands give to their wives, as their portion, cattle and slaves and money, according to their means. But you must know that the first wife is held by the husband to be superior to the others. And I may add that if the husband finds that one of his wives is of no use, or displeases him, he can simply turn her out, and do as he will. They take to wife their cousins and their father's widows, with the exception of their own mother. They do not consider sinful many things that we consider grievously so, for they live like beasts.

But of this we have said enough, and so we will

leave the subject, and tell you of other lands towards the north.

And you must know that Messer Niccolò, Messer Matteo, and Messer Marco lived a whole year in the city of Canpchu for certain business of theirs, which it is not necessary to mention here.

We will then leave this place, and travel sixty days northward.

Here is told of the city of Ezina

When one leaves this city of Canpchu, one rides for twelve days before reaching a city called Ezina, which stands on the border of the desert of sand, towards the north. It belongs to the province of Tangut. The inhabitants are idolaters. They have abundance of camels and cattle. There are many excellent lanner and saker falcons. The people live by the fruits of the earth and by cattle breeding. They are no traders.

In this city one collects victuals for forty days, for you must know that, on leaving Ezina, one rides northwards for forty days across a desert, without dwellings or hostelries. Nor do any people live there, except in summer, in the valleys and on the mountains. But plenty of wild animals are to be found there, including quantities of wild asses. There is abundance of water, and plenty of fish. There are many pine-woods.

When one has ridden northwards for forty days, one reaches a certain province. You shall hear which it is.

Here is told of the city of Caracoron

Caracoron is a city of three miles in circuit, and is all built of wood and clay, and surrounded with an earthen rampart, for stone is scarce there. Near it there stands a very large fort, in which there is a most beautiful palace where the governor of the city lives.

This was the first seat of the Tartars when they left their country.

I will tell you about the Tartars, and how they made a lord for themselves, and spread over the world.

How the Tartars rebelled against Prester John

You must know, then, that the Tartars lived towards the north, in the neighbourhood of Chorcha and Bargu. In that country there were vast plains, without any dwellings, such as cities and towns, but with good pastures, large rivers, and abundance of water. They had no King of their own, but they paid tribute to a mighty monarch, whom in their tongue they called Unc Kan, which in the French language we call Prestre Johan This was the Prester John, of whose great power the whole world speaks. The Tartars paid him as tribute one beast out of every ten. Now, it happened that they multiplied exceedingly, and when Prester John saw that they were such a numerous people, he feared that they might be dangerous, and so decided to disperse them over several districts. Thus he sent them some of his barons to carry this out. And this is how it was done. Every time a lord subject to Prester John rebelled, three or four of these Tartars out of every hundred were chosen, and sent against him. In this way their power was decreased. Similarly did Prester John act in his other affairs. And when the Tartars saw what he meant to do, they were exceedingly aggrieved. They all departed together and went so far northwards through desert regions that Prester John could do them no more harm. And they rebelled against him, and paid no tribute. Thus they remained some time.

How Chinghis became the first Kaan of the Tartars

Now it happened, in the year 1187 after Christ's Incarnation, that the Tartars made a king for themselves, whose name, in their language, was Chinghis Kaan. He was a man of great worth, great wisdom, and great prowess. And you must know that when he was elected king, all the Tartars in the world, scattered over those distant regions, came to him, and acknowledged him as their Lord. And this Chinghis Kaan wielded his rule well and worthily. What more shall I tell you? There came such a multitude of Tartars that truly it was a wonder. And when Chinghis Kaan saw that he had so many subjects, he furnished them with bows and other weapons such as they use, and set out to conquer other countries. And I tell you that he conquered no less than eight provinces in a short time. This could happen quite naturally because in those days those lands and provinces either had a popular government or had each its own lord or king; hence, not being united, they could not singly resist against such a great multitude. But he did them no injury, nor did he deprive them of their goods, but took them with him to conquer other peoples. In this way did he conquer such a great number of peoples as you have heard. And when these peoples saw how worthily this lord exercised his dominion, and how good he was, they went most willingly with him.

When Chinghis Kaan had thus gathered together so great a multitude of people, enough to cover the whole earth, he thought of conquering the whole world.

Hence he sent envoys to Prester John—and this was 1200 years after the birth of Christ—to tell him that he wished to take his daughter to wife. When Prester John heard that Chinghis Kaan was demanding his daughter of him, he was wroth, and said: "How then is Chinghis Kaan not ashamed of asking for my daughter in marriage? Knows he not that he is my liegeman and my servant? Return, then, to him and tell him that I will sooner have my daughter burnt alive than give her to him to wife. And tell him in my name that it behoves me that I should put him to death for the disloyal traitor that he is against his Lord." Then he commanded the envoys to go straightway from his presence, and never to return.

When they had heard this, the envoys at once departed, and travelled until they reached their Lord. And they told him everything that Prester John had bidden them say, without any omission, and all in due order.

How Chinghis Kaan mustered his men to attack Prester John

On hearing the insolent message that Prester John sent him, the heart of Chinghis Kaan swelled so, that it nearly burst within his breast. For indeed I assure you, that he was too great a prince to suffer it. After a time he spoke, and said in a loud voice, so that all around him could hear, that he would no longer keep his dominion if the impudent message of Prester John were not paid for at a higher price than any insult had ever been paid for. And he said he must soon show Prester John whether he was his servant.

He then had all his men mustered, and made the greatest warlike preparations that had ever been seen or heard of. He sent word to Prester John to defend himself as well as he could, and that he himself would attack him with all his host.

When Prester John knew for certain that Chinghis Kaan was bearing down upon him with such a multitude, he took the matter lightly, and treated it as a trifle, for he said that they were no soldiers. All the same, he said to himself that he would do everything in his power in order to capture him, if he really did come, and put him to an evil death. Hence he mustered and fitted out all his men, throughout many a distant province, and gathered together so great an army that no one had ever heard tell of a greater.

In this way, even as you have heard, they got themselves ready on either side. But why should I make a long story of it? Know, then, in very truth that Chinghis Kaan came with all his host to a vast and fair plain that was called Tenduc, and that belonged to Prester John; and there he pitched his camp. I assure you that it was such a multitude of men, that no one could tell their number. There he received tidings that Prester John was coming, and he rejoiced greatly, for that was a fine and vast plain, fit for a mighty battle. Therefore he awaited him there, and longed for his arrival in order to come to grips with him.

But here the story leaves off telling of Chinghis Kaan and his men. We will return to Prester John and his host.

How Prester John and his host went out to meet Chinghis Kaan

The story tells, then, that when Prester John heard that Chinghis Kaan was coming against him with all his men, he himself advanced against him with the whole of his host. And they marched until they reached that great plain of Tenduc, and there pitched their camp, some twenty miles from that of Chinghis Kaan. And both sides rested in order to be fresh and strong on the day of battle.

Even as you have heard, these two mighty hosts lay in the plain of Tenduc. One day Chinghis Kaan called his astrologers to him, of whom some were Christians and other Saracens, and bade them tell him who was to win the battle, whether he or Prester John. The astrologers performed their magic arts. The Saracens were unable to tell him the truth, but the Christians revealed it openly. In his presence they took a green cane and split it in two, lengthways; one half they put on one side, and the other half on the other side, and no one held either part. One half of the cane they called Chinghis Kaan, and the other half Prester John. Then they said to Chinghis Kaan, "Sire, look carefully at the two canes, and mark well that this one is called by your name, and the other by the name of Prester John; he will be the victor whose cane shall go over the other when we have spoken our charms." Chinghis Kaan replied that he was most willing to see, and bade the astrologers show him as quickly as possible. Then the Christian astrologers took the Psalter, and read certain psalms, and performed their incantations. The cane bearing the name of Chinghis Kaan, without anyone touching it, joined the one bearing the name of Prester John, and lay above it. And this occurred in the sight of all those present. And on seeing this Chinghis Kaan rejoiced greatly.

And since he found the Christians had spoken the truth, he ever after showed great honour to Christians, and at all times held them truthful and trustworthy.

Here is told of the great battle fought between Prester John and Chinghis Kaan

After two days, both sides armed, and fought fiercely together. And it was the greatest battle that had ever been seen. There was great slaughter on either side, but at length Chinghis Kaan remained victor. Prester John was killed in battle and from that day lost his land, for Chinghis Kaan went on fighting until he had conquered the whole of it. And you must know that, after this battle, Chinghis Kaan ruled six years longer, and conquered many fortresses and provinces. But at the end of six years he attacked a stronghold called Caaju, and he received an arrow-wound in the knee, of which he died. This was a great pity, for he was valiant and wise.

Now I have told you how the Tartars first took a king for themselves, namely Chinghis Kaan. And I have also told you how at the beginning they overcame Prester John. Now I will tell you of their manners and customs.

Here is told of the Kaans who reigned after Chinghis Kaan

You must know that after Chinghis Kaan, Cui Kaan became Lord; the third was Batui Kaan; the fourth, Alton Kaan, the fifth, Mongu Kaan; the sixth, Cublai Kaan, who now reigns, and is greater and more powerful than all the others. For if all the power of all the other five were put together, it would not equal that of Cublai. Nay, still more will I say: not all the Emperors of the world and all the Kings, both Christian and Saracen, would be able to put together as much power as this great Cublai Kaan can wield. And I will clearly prove this to you in our book.

You must know that all the great kings descended from the line of Chinghis Kaan are taken to be buried to a great mountain called Altai. And wheresoever the Great Lords of the Tartars may die, were it a hundred days' journey from that mountain, they must be taken there to be buried. Another wonder I will also tell you : when the corpses of these great Kaans are taken to that mountain, be it for a distance of forty days' march, or more, or less, all the people met along the road followed by the corpse, are put to the sword by those who accompany the body, who say, "Go and serve your lord in the next world." For they truly believe that all those whom they slay, must serve their Lord in the next world. The same is also done with the horses, for, when the Lord dies, they kill all the best horses the Lord had; and they kill them in order that he may have them in the next world. And you must know that when Mongu Kaan died, more than 20,000 men, who met the corpse when it was being taken to its burial were killed.

And as we have begun speaking of the Tartars, I will tell you many more things.

During the winter, the Tartars live in the plains and the warm regions, where there is grass and good pasture for their cattle; in summer they live in cool places, on mountains and in valleys, where they find water and woods and pasture for their cattle, and also because in cold places there are no flies and other such pests to molest them and their animals. And for two or three months they go ever higher and higher up, pasturing all the while, for they would not have enough grass, considering the multitude of their cattle, if they always pastured in the same place. They have wooden houses, covered with felt, and round in shape; and they take them about with them wherever they go, on four-wheeled carts, for the wooden laths of which they are made, are so well bound and so cleverly arranged, that they are very light to carry. Every time they pitch and erect their house, the door is to the south. They have beautiful two-wheeled carts, so covered with black felt that, were it to rain for ever, nothing inside the cart would become wet. They have them drawn by oxen and camels. On these carts they carry their wives and children, and their property. And you must know that the women do the buying and selling and all that is needful for their husband and household, for the men do nothing but hunt and fight and fowl and rear falcons and goshawks. They live on meat, milk, and game, and they also eat Pharaoh's rats, which abound in summer all over those plains. They eat horse-flesh and dog-flesh, and in general all kinds of flesh. They drink mare's milk. For nothing in the world would they touch another man's wife, for they hold it too wicked and scandalous a deed. The women are good and faithful towards their husbands, and look after the households very well. Their marriages are made as follows. Each man can take as many wives as he will, even a hundred if he have the means to keep them. The man gives a dowry to the woman's mother, but the woman gives nothing to the man. But you must know that they consider the first wife as the most legitimate and best. They have more children than any other people, for they have so many wives as I have told you. They can marry their cousins, and if the father dies, his firstborn can take his father's wives to himself, with the exception of his own mother. They can also take the wife of their own brother, if the latter dies. When they take a wife, they have sumptuous weddings.

Here is told of the God of the Tartars and of their Law

You must know that their Law is as follows. They say that there exists a heavenly God, to whom they daily burn incense, and of whom they ask nought else but intelligence and health. Then they have a God they call Natigai, whom they consider an earthly God, who protects their children, their cattle and their crops. They pay him great worship and honour, and everyone keeps him in the house, for they make him of felt or cloth, and keep him in their homes. They also make the wife and children of this God; his wife they place on his left hand, and his children in front of him. And they pay them great honour. When they sit down to eat, they take some of the fat, and grease the God's mouth with it, and also the mouths of his wife and children. Then they take some broth, and sprinkle it outside the door, that the other spirits may have some too. When they have done this, they say that their God and his family have had their part. Thereupon they eat and drink.

And you must know that they drink mare's milk, but I assure you that they prepare it in such a way that it seems white wine. It is excellent to drink, and they call it *kemis*.

Their manner of dressing is as follows: the wealthy wear cloths of gold and of silk, and fine skins, such as sable and ermine and vair and fox, all in the richest fashion. And all their equipment is surpassingly beautiful and of great value.

Their arms are bows, swords, and maces, but above all they make use of the bow, as they are excellent archers. On the body they wear armour made of buffalo hide or of other boiled hides, which are very strong.

They are very good and valiant in battle, and I will tell you how they endure hardship better than all other men: many a time, if it is necessary, they can remain a whole month, whether resident in one place or on the march, without any other food than a little mare's milk and the game they may themselves catch, and all the time their horses will feed on the grass they find, so that they need not take barley or straw with them. They are most obedient to their leaders, and I assure you they will, if necessary, remain the whole night on horseback, with all their armour on, their horses cropping the grass all the while. Of all troops in the world, they are the best in enduring fatigue or hardships, the least costly, and the finest for conquering lands and kingdoms.

Their troops are ordered as I shall tell you. Know, then, that when a Tartar Lord goes out to fight, taking with him, say, 100,000 horsemen, he arranges everything as you shall hear. He places an officer over every ten, one over every 100, one over every 1000, and one over every 10,000 men, so that he has to deal only with ten persons; and he who is placed over 10,000 men, only has ten men to deal with, he who is placed over 1000 men, only has ten men to deal with, and similarly he who is placed over 100 men, only has ten men to deal with. And in this way that you have heard, each man is responsible to his superior. And when the commander of 100,000 men wishes to send a force somewhere, he orders the commander of 10,000, to give him 1000 men, and the commander of 10,000 men orders the commander of 1000 to give him his part, and the latter orders the commander of 100, who orders the commander of ten, each to give their respective parts of the 1000 men required. Thus all know at once what they are to do, and each gives his part. For they are the most obedient in the world in carrying out orders. And you must know that their word for 100,000 is *tuc* and for 10,000 is *toman*; the *tomans* may be counted by thousands, by hundreds, and by tens.

When the army is on the march for some purpose or other, whether in the plains or in mountainous country, they send 200 men two days' march ahead as scouts, and as many they place behind and on the flanks. This they do in order that the army should not be attacked by surprise. When they have to march a very long distance, they take no equipment with them, especially such as is needful for sleeping. They live, for the most part, as has been said, on mare's milk, and, between horses and mares, each man has eighteen; when one horse is tired, they take another. They carry two leather bottles where they put the milk to drink. Likewise they carry a small earthenware vessel or pot, in which they cook their meat; if they are without it, they empty the belly of some animal, fill it with water, and put inside pieces of the meat they wish to cook; after that they put it on the fire, and, when it is cooked, they eat all altogether the meat and the vessel. They carry a small tent, under which they shelter from the rain. Another thing, too, I will tell you: when necessary, they will ride as much as ten days without eating, and without lighting a fire, living on the blood of their horses, each man opening one of his horse's veins, and drinking the blood. They also have dried milk, of the thickness of paste, and they dry it as follows: they boil the milk, and then put in another dish the fat that gathers at the top, of which they make butter, for as long as it remains in the milk it would be impossible to dry it; then they place the milk in the sun, and so it dries. When they go campaigning, they take some ten pounds of this milk, and, when necessary, they take half a pound of it in the morning, and put it in a little leathern flask of the shape of a wine-skin, with as much water as they want; as they ride, the milk in the flask is churned up and melts; then they drink it.

When they join battle with their enemies, they defeat them as follows. They consider it no shame to flee, and they attack the enemy now here and now there, on all sides. They have trained their horses so well, that they turn in all directions as readily as dogs. When they are driven back and flee, they fight with the same valour and energy as when they face their enemy, for, in the very midst of the flight, they turn round with their bows, and shoot a shower of arrows, killing many of the enemy's horses and men. So, when the enemy think they have defeated and routed them, they are lost, for their horses are killed, and they too. And when the Tartars see that they have killed many men and horses, they wheel around, and all together fall upon the enemy, with such vigour and bravery, that they vanquish and overwhelm them. In this way they have won many a battle, and defeated many an army.

All these that I have told you are the manners and customs of the true Tartars, but I must say that nowadays they are greatly degenerate. For those who live in Cathay have adopted the habits and manners and customs of the Idolaters, and have for the most part abandoned their own Law. And those who live in the Levant follow the fashions of the Saracens.

Justice is dealt out as I shall tell you. If a man steal some small thing for which he need not be put to death, he is given seven blows with a stick, or seventeen, or twenty-seven, or thirty-seven, or forty-seven, and so on up to one hundred and seven, increasing always by ten according to the value of what he has stolen. Many die of this beating. And if a man steal a horse, or commits another theft for which the penalty is death, he is cut in half with a sword. But if the thief is capable of paying, and prepared to give nine times the value of the stolen goods, his life is safe. For a homicide there is no way of escape. Even if a man only threatens to strike another with a weapon, his hand is cut off. He who wounds is wounded in a like manner.

Every lord or other person who owns cattle, has them branded with his own mark, whether they be horses, mares, camels, oxen, cows, or other large animals. Then they let them graze on the plains and mountains without any keeper. If they get mixed up, each animal is returned to the man whose brand it bears. The sheep and rams are entrusted to shepherds. Their cattle are all very big, fat, and fine.

I will also tell you of another very strange custom of theirs, which I was forgetting to put down. You must know that if there are two men of whom one has lost a son of tender age, or at any rate unmarried, and the other likewise an unmarried daughter, they unite their families by marriage. They in fact give the dead girl as a wife to the dead boy, and make out the contract. Then they burn this contract, and they say that the smoke which rises into the air, goes to their children in the next world, so that they come to know of it, and consider one another as husband and wife. They arrange a great wedding feast and banquets, scattering here and there some of the meats they eat, thinking that they go to their children in the next world. Another thing they do too. They paint and draw on paper men, in the semblance of slaves, and horses, cloths, bezants, and other objects, and then they burn them.

They say that all these things that they have drawn and burnt will be possessed by their children in the next world. And when they have done all this, they consider themselves related, and they respect this relationship as if their children were alive.

Now I have clearly shown you the customs and practices of the Tartars. Another most notable subject I have not however yet spoken of: I mean of the Great Lord of all the Tartars and his wonderful Imperial Court. But I shall tell you about it in this book all in the proper place, for these are such marvellous things that they must be set down in writing. But now we must return to our story, to the great plain where we were when we began telling of the Tartars.

Here is told of the plain of Bargu, and of sundry customs of its inhabitants

When one leaves Caracoron and Altai, where the dead Kaans are buried, as I told you above, one rides northwards across a region called the plain of Bargu. It extends to a distance of no less than forty days' journey. The inhabitants are called Mecrit, and they are wild. They live by the chase. The most plentiful animals are stags; and I assure you they ride upon them. They also live on birds; for there are many lakes, pools, and marshes, and the plain is bounded to the north by the Ocean. During the greater part of summer, when those birds moult, they gather together near those waters, and when they are quite naked and cannot fly, then the people catch them at will. They also live on fish. They have the same habits and customs as the Tartars. They are subject to the Great Kaan. They have neither corn nor wine. In summer they have plenty of game, both beasts and birds, but in winter there is neither beast nor bird there on account of the great cold.

When one has journeyed forty days, one comes, then, to the Ocean Sea. Here are mountains where peregrine falcons nest. For you must know that no man or woman or bird or beast is to be found there, except a certain kind of bird called *bargherlac*, on which these falcons feed. They are the size of partridges. Their feet are like those of parrots, their tails like those of swallows. They are very swift fliers. When the Great Kaan wants nestlings of the peregrines, he sends thither to fetch them.

In the islands round about in that sea, gerfalcons breed. And I tell you in very truth that that place is so far to the north that the North Star is left somewhat behind to the south. And I must also tell you that the gerfalcons that breed in these islands I have just spoken of, are so numerous that the Great Kaan can have as many as he wants of them. Do not think that those that are brought to the Tartars from the lands of the Christians are taken to the Great Kaan; they are brought to the Levant, to Argon and other kings of the Levant.

Now we have clearly told you everything concerning the northern provinces as far as the Ocean Sea. Henceforward, we will tell you of other provinces on the way to the court of the Great Kaan. And we will first return to a province of which we have already spoken in our book, called Canpchu.

Here is told of the great kingdom of Erginul

When one leaves this Canpchu of which I have told you, one journeys for five days through a region where many spirits can be heard speaking, especially at night. At the end of these five days, one reaches, towards the east, a kingdom called Erginul. It belongs to the Great Kaan. It is part of the great province of Tangut, which includes several kingdoms. The inhabitants are partly Turkish Christians of the Nestorian Church, and partly Idolaters and worshippers of Mahomet. There are many cities, and the principal city is Erginul. From this city, travelling to the south-east, one can reach the regions of Cathay.

In this south-easterly direction, towards the regions of Cathay, one finds a city called Silinju. Silinju is also the name of the province. There are many cities and towns in it. It also is part of Tangut, and belongs to the Great Kaan. The people are Idolaters, but there are some who worship Mahomet, and there are also a few Christians. There are wild oxen in great quantities, as big as elephants, and very fine to look upon; they are all hairy, except on the back, and they are black and white. The hair is three spans long, and is as fine as silk. Messer Marco brought some of it to Venice as something remarkable, and such it was judged by all who saw it. They are so beautiful that they are a marvel to look upon. Of these oxen they have many tame: they take wild ones and make them breed, so that they have an enormous number of them. They use them as beasts of burden, and they work with them, and I assure you that they do as much work, and are as strong as two ordinary oxen.

In this land is produced the best and finest musk in the world, and it is found in the way I will tell you. You must know in very truth that there is a little animal, the size of a gazelle, but shaped as follows: it has a very thick coat, like that of a deer, feet like a gazelle, no horns, tail like a gazelle, and four slender teeth, two above and two below, some three fingers long, two of them growing upwards and two downwards. It is a fine animal. The musk is found in this way: at full moon there grows near the navel of this beast, between the skin and the flesh, an imposthume of blood; when the hunters catch the animal, they cut away the imposthume together with the skin, and take it out; then they dry it in the sun. That blood is the musk that gives such a strong perfume. The flesh of the animal is very good to eat. And you must know that there is an immense number of those beasts in this country, and the musk is as good as I have told you. Of one of these beasts Messer Marco brought the head and feet to Venice.

The people live by trade and handicrafts, and have great quantities of corn. The province stretches for a distance of twenty-five days' journey. There are pheasants there twice as big as those of our own countries, for they are the size of peacocks, or little less. They have a tail ten spans long at most, and there are many with tails nine, eight, or at least seven spans long. There are also pheasants of the shape and size of ours. There are other birds, too, of various kinds, with very beautiful and gaily coloured plumage.

The people, as we said, are idolaters; they are fat, with short noses and thick hair. They have no beards, but only a few stray hairs on their chins. The women have no hair at all except on their heads, and nowhere else have they any. They are splendidly white, have a beautiful skin, and are very well made in every limb. And you must know that they delight greatly in sensual pleasures, and take many wives, for neither their Law nor their customs forbid it; thus they can take as many as they desire or can keep. And I will also tell you that if there is a woman who is beautiful, but of humble birth, she may be taken to wife for her beauty by a great baron or nobleman, who gives the mother a sufficiently large sum of money, according to the agreement they come to.

Now we will leave this place, and tell you of another province towards the east.

Here is told of the province of Egrigaia

When one leaves Erginul and rides towards the east for eight days, one reaches a province called Egrigaia, where there are many cities and towns; it forms part of Tangut. The principal city is called Calachan. The inhabitants are idolaters, but there are also three churches of Nestorian Christians. They are subject to the Great King of the Tartars. In this city are made camlets of camel-hair, the best and finest in the world. They also make some out of white wool, namely white camlets, which are exceedingly fine and beautiful; and they make great quantities of them. From there, traders carry them to many parts of the world, and especially to Cathay.

We will now leave this province, and tell you of another province towards the east, that is called Tenduc; and we shall enter the lands of Prester John.

Here is told of the great province of Tenduc

Tenduc is a province that lies to the east, in which there are many cities and towns. It belongs to the Great Kaan, for the descendants of Prester John are the subjects of the Great Kaan. The principal city is called Tenduc. The king of this province belongs to the lineage of Prester John, and he too is Prester John. His name is George. He rules the land for the Great Kaan, not indeed all the land that Prester John held, but only a part of it. But you must know that the Great Kaans have always given daughters of their own or other kinswomen of theirs as wives to the Kings of the lineage of Prester John reigning in Tenduc. Further, Prester John is a Christian, and hence most of the people become Christians too.

In this province are found the stones from which azure is made; they are both plentiful and of good quality. There are excellent camlets of different colours, from camel's hair. The people live by breeding cattle, and by the fruits of the soil. There is also a certain amount of trade and industry.

The rulers, as I have said, are Christians, but there is also a good number of idolaters, and of those who worship Mahomet. There is a race called *Argons*, which in our language means "bastards"; they are sprung, in fact, from two races, namely that of the Tenduc idolaters and that of the worshippers of Mahomet. They are much handsomer than the other inhabitants of the country, more intelligent, and better traders.

And you must know that in that province was the principal seat of Prester John when he was Lord of the Tartars and of the other provinces and kingdoms round about. And to this day his descendants still live there. The George that has already been mentioned, belongs to the lineage of Prester John, even as I have told you, and is the sixth King ruling after him. And that is the place that in our country is known as Gog and Magog, but they call it Ung and Mungul. In each of these provinces there was a separate race; in Ung lived the Gogs, and in Mungul the Tartars.

Here is told of the city of Sindachu and of other countries

[When one leaves the province of Tenduc, one enters another province seven days' journey in breadth.] And as one rides across that province for seven days towards the east in the direction of Cathay, one finds many cities and towns, the inhabitants of which are Mohammedans or Idolaters, though there are a few Turkish Christians of the Nestorian Church. They live by trade and handicrafts, for they make cloths of gold, which they call *nascisi* and *nac*, and also silk cloth of different kinds. For, as we have many different kinds of woollen cloths, they have many different kinds of cloths of gold and of silk. They are subject to the Great Kaan. There is a city called Sindachu, where they make all sorts of things for the equipment of an army. In the mountains of this province there is a place called Idifu, where there is an excellent silver mine, whence abundance of silver is obtained. They have a great deal of game, both beasts and birds.

Now we will leave this province and these cities, and travel on for three days.

Here is told of the city of Chagannor

When one has journeyed three days, one finds a city called Chagannor, which in our language means "White Pool," where there is a great palace belonging to the Great Kaan. For you must know that the Great Kaan likes very much living in his palace in this city, because there are many lakes and rivers, in which there are quantities of swans. And also there are beautiful plains, rich in cranes, pheasants, partridges, and many other kinds of birds. On account of the excellent fowling, the Great Kaan likes staying there, as he enjoys himself; for he goes fowling with gerfalcons and hawks, and catches many birds, to his great pleasure and delight.

There are five kinds of cranes, which I will describe to you. The first kind is all black like a crow, and very big. The second kind is all white; it has most beautiful wings, with round eyes all over them, like those of a peacock, but of a brilliant gold; the head is red and black, and the neck black and white; it is much larger than all the other kinds. The third kind is like ours. The fourth kind is small, with beautiful long vermilion and black feathers near the ears. The fifth kind is all grey, with a very well-shaped black and red head, and is exceedingly large.

Near this city there is a valley in which the Great Kaan breeds a great number of quails, or what we call Great Partridges. In summer he has millet and panic grass sown on the hill-sides, as well as such other grasses as those birds like, and he orders that none of these grasses be picked, in order that the birds may have plenty to feed on; and in winter, too, he has millet-seed thrown to them, and the birds are so used to being fed, that when seeds are thrown to them and the man whistles, they immediately come, wherever they may happen to be. The Great Kaan has had many little houses built, where they shelter at night, and there are many men to look after them. When he comes to these parts, the Great Kaan has plenty of these birds—as many as he wants. In winter, when they are very fat, as he does not live there on account of the cold, he has them loaded on camels and brought to him, wherever he may be staying.

Now we will leave this place, and travel on three days between north and north-east.

Here is told of the city of Chandu and of a wonderful palace of the Great Kaan

When one leaves the city I have just told you of and travels for three days, one reaches a city called Chandu. It was built by the Great Kaan who now reigns, and whose name is Cublai Kaan. In this city Cublai Kaan had an immense palace made of marble and stone, with halls and rooms all gilt and adorned with figures of beasts and birds, and pictures of trees and flowers of different kinds. It is most wondrously beautiful and marvellously decorated. This palace is situated within the city, but on one side it is bounded by the city-wall, and from that point another wall runs out enclosing a space of no less than sixteen miles, with numerous springs and rivers and meadows. Into this park one cannot enter except from the palace. And the Great Kaan keeps all kinds of animals in it, namely stags and fallow-deer and roebucks, in order to feed his gerfalcons and hawks, which he keeps there in mew. Of gerfalcons alone there are more than two hundred. He goes himself once a week to see them in mew. And often enough the Great Kaan rides about this walled park, taking a leopard with him on his horse's croup; when the fancy takes him, he lets it go, and with it takes a stag or a fallow-deer or a roebuck and has it given to the gerfalcons in mew. This the Great Kaan does for amusement.

And you must know that in the middle of that walled park, where there is a very fine wood, the Great Kaan has had another great palace built, all of cane; it is a kind of pavilion, with fine painted and gilt columns, and at the top of each column is a large dragon, with its tail coiled round the shaft; with its head and two legs, the one stretched to the right and the other to the left, it holds up the roof. Inside, the palace is all gilt, and adorned with figures of beasts and birds of exquisite workmanship. The roof is also made of canes, but it is so well varnished, with such strong varnish, that no amount of rain can do it any damage. And I will tell you how they make a palace of canes. You must know that these canes are more than three palms in breadth, and are from ten to fifteen paces long. They are slit in two, lengthways, from knot to knot, so that one gets two tiles. And the tiles made from these canes are so thick and large that one can cover and build a whole house with them. This palace I have told you of, was all made of canes. The Great Kaan had had it built in such a way that it could be moved whenever he wanted. It was braced by over two hundred silk cords.

The Great Kaan lives there three months a year—June, July and August. He lives there at that season both because it is cool there, and because it is most pleasant. During those three months the cane palace is left standing; during the rest of the year it is taken to pieces. He had it made in such a way that it can be put together and taken down as he pleases. But on the twenty-eighth day of the August moon, the Great Kaan leaves Chandu and that palace; every year on that same day—I will tell you why. You must know that he has a stud of horses and mares, all as white as snow, without a spot of any other colour, and there is an enormous number of them—over ten thousand mares alone. No one can drink the milk of those mares unless he belongs to the imperial family, namely to the lineage of Chinghis Kaan. There is however also another race of people who may drink of that milk, called Horiat; it is an honour done them by Chinghis Kaan on account of a victory that they once helped him to win. And you must know that these white mares are held in such reverence, that when they go along the road, not even a nobleman, however great he were, would pass through the midst of them, but waits till they have gone by, or else goes on until he has passed beyond them. Further, the astrologers and idolaters have told the Great Kaan, that every year, on the twenty-eighth day of the August moon, he must scatter some of the milk on the ground and in the air, in order that the spirits may drink of it. And the idolaters say that it is necessary that the spirits should have this milk to drink, that they may protect all the things belonging to the Great Kaan, both men and women, beasts and birds, corn and everything else. And to perform this sacrifice, he is obliged to leave Chandu, and go elsewhere.

But we will not yet leave this place. First I will tell you of another marvel that I had forgotten. You must know, then, that when the Great Kaan lives in this palace of his, if it is rainy or cloudy, or the weather is otherwise bad, he has wise astrologers and sorcerers who, by the might of their wisdom and of their incantations, drive away all clouds and bad weather from the palace; the weather keeps fine above the palace, and the bad weather goes to an entirely different place. These wise men who perform this wonder are called

Tebet and Kesmur, which are the names of two races of idolaters. They know more of diabolical arts and enchantments than any other people on earth. What they perform is by the art of the Devil, but they make others believe that it is done through their great sanctity, and by the help of God. These people go about all dirty and filthy, never giving a thought to their self-respect or to those who see them; their faces are covered with mud, and they never wash or comb their hair, but ever go about in an exceedingly sordid condition. They also have another custom that I will tell you of: when someone is condemned to death and executed by the authorities, they take him, and then cook and eat him; but if a man die of a natural death, they will not eat him.

Know, too, that these *Bacsi*—namely, those I have just spoken of as being skilled in so many charms—perform a very great wonder, even as I shall tell you. When the Great Kaan sits in his principal hall, at his table, which is over eight cubits high and at no less than ten paces' distance from the cups full of wine, milk, and other beverages, placed in the middle of the hall, these wise sorcerers I have mentioned, called *Bacsi*, bring it about by means of their arts and enchantments, that these cups filled with drink, rise up by themselves above the floor, and go before the Great Kaan without anyone touching them. When he has drunk, the cups return to the place they came from. This is performed in the sight of ten thousand persons. And it is true and credible, without any lie. Indeed, those who are learned in necromancy will assure you the thing is possible.

I will tell you also that when the feasts of their idols come round, these *Bacsi* go to the Great Kaan and say to him: "Sire, the feast of such and such an idol is approaching"—and they name the idol they mean, and then add: "You know, gracious Lord, that this idol is wont to bring bad weather, and do injury to our possessions, to our cattle, and our crops, unless he receive offerings and holocausts. For this reason we pray you, gracious Lord, to have such and such a number of black-faced sheep given us, and so much incense, and so much aloes-wood, and so much of this, and so much of that, in order that we may do great honour, and perform sacrifice to our idol, that he may protect our persons and cattle and crops." These things do the *Bacsi* say to the barons around the Great Kaan and to those who have authority; and the latter repeat it to the Great Kaan. Then the *Bacsi* get all they want in order to solemnize the feast of their idol. And when they have received what they have asked for, they pay great worship to their idol, with songs and feasting. For they incense it with all the sweet perfumes of their good spices, and cook the meat, placing it before the idol, and sprinkling the broth here and there; for they say that the idols take their fill of it. Thus then do they honour their idols on their feast-days, for you must know that each idol has its feast on an appointed day, like our saints.

They have immense abbeys and monasteries, some of them indeed as large as small cities, containing over two thousand monks after their fashion, who dress more decently than the rest of the people. They have their head and beards shaven. They hold for their idols the greatest festivals ever heard of, with the greatest profusion of songs and illuminations ever seen. Moreover, among these *Bacsi*, there are some who, in accordance with their rules, may take wives. And so they do: they marry and have many children.

And I will tell you, too, that there is another kind of religious called *Sensin*. They are men of great abstinence, according to their customs, and lead even as hard a life as I will describe. You must know that all their lives they eat nothing but bran, that is, husks left after making wheat-flour. They take this bran and, putting it into hot water, leave it there awhile, until all the white flour has left the husks, which they then eat, thus tasteless. And though they eat nothing but this bran I have spoken of, they fast many a day in the year. They possess large idols, and numbers of them, and sometimes they worship fire. And I assure you that the other monks say that these who live in such great abstinence are what we should call Patarins, or heretics, because they do not worship their idols in the same way as they, for there is a considerable difference between them, that is, between the various rules. The *Sensins* would not take a wife for anything in the world. They have their heads and chins shaven. They wear black and yellow clothes made of hemp; and even if they were to make them of silk, they would have them of the colours I have mentioned. They sleep on mats, that is on wooden trellises. They lead the hardest lives one can imagine.

Their monasteries and their idols are all feminine, that is, have women's names.

Now we will leave this subject, and tell you marvellous wonders concerning the very great King of Kings of all the Tartars, namely the very noble Great Kaan, whose name is Cublai.

Here is told about the Great Kaan who now reigns, and whose name is Cublai Kaan, and here is told too how he keeps his court and governs well all his peoples, and also what his conquests were

Now I will begin telling you in this book of ours all the wondrous things and all the mighty marvels, concerning the Great Kaan who now reigns and whose name is Cublai Kaan, Kaan meaning in our language "Great Lord of Lords." And truly he has a right to such a title, for everyone must know for very truth that this Great Kaan is the most puissant of men, in subjects, lands, and treasure, that there is on earth or ever was, from the time of our first father Adam to this day. And that this is true I will show you clearly in this book, so that you shall be convinced that he is the greatest Lord that now lives or that ever has lived. And I will tell you why.

Here is told of Naian's rebellion against his nephew the Great Kaan

You must know, then, that Cublai descends in a direct Imperial line from Chinghis Kaan, for the Lord of all the Tartars must belong to that lineage. He is the sixth Great Kaan, namely he is the sixth Great Lord of all the Tartars. And he obtained the Lordship 1256 years after the birth of Christ; that was the year he began to reign. He obtained the lordship by his own valour and courage and great wisdom; for his brothers and relations opposed his claim. Still he made it good with his prowess, though you must know that the lordship truly belonged to him by right. From the day he began to reign to this present year, 1298, forty-two years have elapsed; he must not be less than 85 years old.

Before he was Lord, he took part in almost every war; he was a valiant soldier and a fine leader. But since he became Lord he has only gone campaigning once; this was in 1286, and I will tell you why.

You must know that there was a certain Naian, an uncle of Cublai Kaan, who was left, when a young man, lord and master of many lands and provinces, so that he could muster quite 400,000 horsemen. His ancestors had previously been vassals to the Great Kaan, and he also was a vassal of his. But, as I have said, he was a young man—only thirty years old—when he found himself the lord of so many lands as to be able to muster quite 400,000 horsemen. Hence he declared that he would no longer remain a vassal of the Great

Kaan, and that indeed he would deprive him of his lordship if only he might. So this Naian sent messengers to Caidu, a great and puissant Lord, and nephew to the Great Kaan, against whom he had rebelled, for he hated him heartily. Naian, then, sent him word that he should attack the Great Kaan from one side, with a view to depriving him of his lands and of his lordship, and that he himself would attack him from the other side. This Caidu replied that he was quite willing, and promised to be ready with his men at the appointed time, and to march against the Great Kaan. And you must know that he was powerful enough to muster and put into the field quite 100,000 horsemen. What more shall I tell you? These two barons, Naian and Caidu, got ready, and gathered together an immense force of horsemen and foot-soldiers in order to attack the Great Kaan.

How the Great Kaan marched against Naian

When the Great Kaan heard of this, he by no means lost heart, but, like the wise and valiant man he was, got ready with his men. He swore he would no longer wear crown or keep any lands, if he did not succeed in putting these two disloyal traitors to an evil death. He immediately had guards placed at all the passes that led to the countries of Naian and Caidu, so that they might not get to know what he meant to do, and at once ordered that all the people who lived within ten days' journey from the city of Cambaluc should come together as quickly as possible. And you must know that he made all his preparations within the space of twenty-two days, and so secretly, that no one knew anything, apart from those of his council. He mustered no less than 360,000 horse and 100,000 foot. He assembled such a small force because he only took those armies of his that were near him. His other armies, twelve in number, and immense, were so far away campaigning, in order to conquer lands in divers parts, that he could not have had them at the proper time. For, had he collected all his forces together, he would have had as many horsemen as he could have wished for, and such a mighty multitude would have come as no one could possibly believe or hear of. And these 360,000 horsemen he mustered, were merely his falconers and other men about him. For, had he summoned the armies that he constantly keeps to garrison the province of Cathay, a period of thirty or forty days would have been necessary, and the preparations would have become known; thus Caidu and Naian would have joined forces, and would have taken refuge in strong and advantageous positions. But the Great Kaan wished, instead, to act so quickly as to take Naian by surprise, and attack him when alone.

And as here it is to the point to say something of the Great Kaan's armies, I will tell you that in all the provinces of Cathay and Manji, and all over the rest of his territory, there are many disloyal and faithless peoples who would fain rebel against their Lord. Hence it is indispensable to keep an army in every province that has large cities and a numerous population. These armies are stationed in the country, at a distance of some four or five miles from the cities, which may have neither gates nor walls—nothing, in fact, that may prevent the soldiers from entering them at will. The Great Kaan changes these armies, and the captains who command them, every two years. Thus curbed, these peoples live quietly, and cannot make the least movement of revolt. Besides the money that the Great Kaan always gives them from the income of the provinces, these armies live on their cattle, which they possess in immense quantities, and on the milk they send to be sold in the cities, where they themselves buy whatever they stand in need of. These armies are scattered in different places at distances of thirty, forty, or sixty days' journey. And if only the Great Kaan had wished to assemble but half of them, they had been a marvellous and incredible multitude.

When the Great Kaan had mustered those few men I have told you of, he bade his astrologers enquire whether he would vanquish his enemies, and whether he would get the better of them. And they told him that he would have them at his mercy. So the Great Kaan set out with all his men, and marched on until, after twenty days, he reached a great plain, where Naian was with all his troops, which amounted to quite 400,000 horsemen. They arrived one day very early in the morning, and in such a way that the enemy knew nothing, for the Great Kaan had had all the roads occupied, so that no one could come or go without being taken. So the enemy knew nothing of their arrival. And when the army of the Great Kaan arrived, Naian was in his tent, lying in bed with his wife, and disporting himself with her, for he loved her dearly.

Here we come to the battle between the Great Kaan and Naian his uncle

What more shall I tell you? At dawn on the day of the battle, the Great Kaan appeared on a hill that rose over the plain where Naian was encamped. The latter and his men felt perfectly secure, for they had not the least idea in the world that anyone might be coming there to do them harm. This is why they lay in such security, without guards to their camp, nor any scouting-parties either in front or behind.

The Great Kaan was on the hill, as I have said, upon a bartizan borne by four elephants, full of crossbow-men and archers, with his flag above him, bearing the figures of the sun and the moon, and so high that it could be seen from all sides. The four elephants were all covered with very stout boiled hides, overlaid with cloths of silk and gold.

His army was drawn up in thirty divisions of 10,000 men each, all armed with bows. The Great Kaan divided his force into three groups, prolonging those on either wing very much, so that they should surround Naian's army. This was done in a moment. In front of each division there was a body of 500 foot with swords and short spears, who acted as follows: every time the horsemen seemed to be about to charge, each foot-soldier jumped on to the croup of the horse nearest to him, behind the rider, and went off together with him. When the horse stopped, they dismounted and killed the enemy's horses with their spears.

Even so, then, as you have heard, the Great Kaan had drawn up his army in divisions round Naian's camp, ready to fight with him.

When Naian and his men saw that the Great Kaan had surrounded the camp with his army, they were sore dismayed. Running to take their arms, they immediately prepared themselves, and arrayed their ranks wisely and in good order.

Both the sides were now ready, and nothing remained but to join battle. Then one might have seen and heard many an instrument played (especially certain two-stringed ones, with a very pleasant sound), and many a bugle blown, and many a loud voice singing. For you must know that the Tartars have this custom: when they are arrayed and drawn up to fight, they wait, before joining battle, for the signal to be given by their leader's *naccars* or kettle-drums; and until the *naccars* sound, the majority play on their instruments and sing. This is why on either side there was so much playing and singing.

When all were quite ready on both sides, then the Great Kaan's *naccars* began to sound, first on the right and on the left wings. And as soon as the *naccars* began sounding, all delay ceased, and they charged upon one another with bows and spears and maces and lances (but only a few of the last); but the foot-soldiers had cross-bows and many other weapon. What more shall I tell you? The struggle began, exceedingly cruel and fierce. Now one might have seen arrows flying, for all the air was full of them, as if the rain were falling. Now one might have seen horsemen and their mounts falling dead to the ground. There was such lamentation and uproar, that one could not have heard God's thunder. And you must know that Naian was a baptized Christian, and in this battle bore the Cross of Christ on his ensign.

But why should I make a long story of it? You must know that this was the most perilous battle and the fiercest that ever was seen; nor, in our own times, have so many men ever been seen on a field of battle, especially horsemen. So many were killed on either side, that truly it was a wonder. The battle raged from morning till noon, for the devotion of Naian's men was so great, on account of his generosity, that for love of him they would rather die than turn their backs in flight. But in the end the Great Kaan had the victory. When Naian and his men saw that they could hold out no longer, they began to flee, but this helped them not at all, for Naian was taken prisoner; and all his barons and subjects surrendered, with all their weapons, to the Great Kaan.

How the Great Kaan had Naian put to death

And when the Great Kaan heard that Naian was taken, he ordered him to be put to death. Then he was put to death even as I shall tell you: he was most tightly rolled up in a carpet, and so beaten about hither and thither, that he died. And he was put to death in this way because they will not allow that the blood of the imperial lineage be shed on the ground or that the sun and the air see it.

When the Great Kaan had won that battle in the

way I have told you, all the men and barons of Naian paid homage to the Great Kaan, and swore fealty to him. They were of four provinces. I will tell you which these four provinces were: the first was Choreha, the second Cauli, the third Barscol, and the fourth Sikintinjin.

How the Great Kaan defended the Cross of Christ

After the Great Kaan had done this and won the battle, the different kinds of people present, Saracens, Idolaters, and Jews, and many other peoples who do not believe in God, mocked the Cross that Naian had borne on his standard. And they said to the Christians who had been present: " See how the Cross of your God has aided Naian who was a Christian ! " The mockery and the gibes were so loud, that they reached the ear of the Great Kaan. And when the Great Kaan heard them, he angrily rebuked those who mocked the Cross in his presence. Then, calling many Christians who were there, he comforted them, saying, " If the Cross of your God has not aided Naian, there was good reason for it; for, as it is good, it can only do what is good and just. Naian was a disloyal traitor, who fought against his liege, so that what has happened to him is most just. And the Cross of your God has done very well in not helping him contrary to justice. For, in that it is a good thing, it cannot do but what is good." The Christians then answered the Great Kaan, " Most puissant Lord, indeed what you say is sooth. For the Cross would not commit evil or treachery, as Naian did, who was a disloyal traitor to his Lord. And he has justly received what he deserved."

Such were the words that passed between the Great Kaan and the Christians concerning the Cross that Naian had borne on his standard.

Here is told why the Great Kaan did not become a Christian

When the Great Kaan had defeated Naian as I have told you, he returned to his capital of Cambaluc; and there he remained in the midst of great rejoicings and festivities. And as for the other baron, who was king and whose name was Caidu, when he heard that Naian had been vanquished and put to death, he was most dejected, and no longer made war, being now terrified and greatly afraid of being treated as Naian had been.

The Great Kaan returned to Cambaluc in November, and there he remained until the month of February or March, when our Easter occurs. Then, knowing that this was one of our principal feasts, he summoned all the Christians, and desired them to bring him the Book of the four Gospels. When this was done, he had the Book incensed many times with great ceremony, and devoutly kissed it, bidding all the barons and lords present to do the same. And this he always does on all the principal feasts of the Christians, such as Christmas and Easter. He acts similarly on the principal feasts of the Saracens, Jews, and Idolaters. And on being once asked the reason of this, he answered, "These are four prophets who are adored and worshipped by all the world. The Christians say their God was Jesus Christ, the Saracens Mahomet, the Jews Moses, and the Idolaters Sagamoni Borcan, the first man of whom an idol was made. I honour and revere all four, and thereby also the one who is the most powerful in Heaven and the most true, and I pray him to aid me." But, from what he lets be seen, it is certain the Great Kaan considers the Christian faith to be the truest and best, for he says that it commands nothing but what is full of all goodness and holiness. And in no way will he suffer the Christians to bear the Cross before them, for on it was scourged and killed so great and mighty a man as Christ. Someone might ask, "As he considers the Christian faith to be the best, why does he not embrace it and turn Christian?" The reason is this, even as he stated it to Messer Niccolò and Messer Maffeo, when he sent them as envoys to the Pope; for at times they spoke to him concerning the faith of Christ. He said, "How would you have me become a Christian? You see that the Christians in these parts are so ignorant, that they achieve nothing and can achieve nothing. And you see, too, how these Idolaters do all they will, and when I sit at table, the cups standing in the midst of the room, full of wine or drinks or other things, come to me without anyone touching them, and I drink from them. They oblige bad weather to go whither they will, and perform many marvels. And, as you know, their idols speak to them, and prophesy all that they wish to know. But if I turned to the Christian faith and became a Christian, then my barons and other men who do not turn to the same faith, would say to me, 'What reason has urged you to be baptized and to follow the faith of Christ? What power or miracles have you seen in him?' And these Idolaters say that what they perform is performed thanks to their holiness and to the power of their idols. Then I should not know what to answer; so there would be great scandal among them, and these Idolaters, who work such wonders with their arts and wisdom, could easily bring about my death. But do you go to your Pontiff, and beg him in my name to send me a hundred men learned in your Law, who may in the presence of these Idolaters reprove them for their practices, and tell them that they too know how to perform such things, but will not, for they are done by the acts of the devil and of evil spirits; and let them so restrain the Idolaters, that they shall no longer have power to work these wonders in their presence. Then, when we see this, we shall denounce them and their Law; so I shall be baptized, and when I am baptized, all my barons and lords will be baptized too, and their subjects will receive baptism, and so there will be more Christians here than in your own countries."

And if, as we said in the beginning, men had been sent by the Pope, capable of preaching our faith to these peoples, the Great Kaan would have become a Christian, for it is known for certain that he was greatly desirous of doing so.

Now you have heard how the Great Kaan only went campaigning on that one occasion. For on all his other wars and business, he sent his sons and barons. But that time he would that no one should go but himself alone, for too great and evil did the presumption of that baron seem to him.

Now we will tell you of what he did to the barons who bore themselves well in the battle, and what to those who were cowardly.

How the Great Kaan rewarded the barons who bore themselves well in battle

You must know that the Great Kaan has twelve wise barons, whose task is that of enquiring and learning what the captains and soldiers do, especially in the actions and battles in which they take part, and reporting to the Great Kaan.

Well, as for those who bore themselves well, the one who was captain of 100 men he made captain of 1000, and the one who was captain of 1000 men he made captain of 10,000, and further, according to their rank, he gave them silver cups and Tablets of Authority, fine armour, beautiful jewels of silver and gold, pearls and precious stones, and horses. And you must know that he who is captain of 100 men has a silver tablet, he who is captain of 1000 men a tablet of gold or of gilt silver, he who is captain of 10,000 a gold tablet with a lion's head. And I will tell you the weight of those tablets. Those of the captains of 100 or 1000 men weigh 120 *saggi;* that with the lion's head, 220 *saggi.* And on all these tablets is inscribed an order which says: " By the might of the great God and of the great grace He has granted to our Emperor, blessed be the name of the Great Kaan. And let all those who shall not obey him be killed and destroyed." And I must further tell you that those who possess these tablets, also have certain warrants, in which all the duties of their rank are put down in writing.

We have now told you of these things, but we will tell you still more about them. Know, then, that he who has a great command, say over 100,000 men, or who is the leader of a great army, has a golden tablet of 300 *saggi* in weight, inscribed with words saying what I have told you above; below these words is the picture of a lion, and above them are drawn the sun and the moon. Further they have warrants for their great commands and powers. Moreover, those who have this splendid tablet, must, every time they go riding, carry a small umbrella over their heads as a token of their great command. And every time they sit down they must do so on a silver chair. To these, too, the Great Lord gives a tablet with a gerfalcon; this tablet he gives to the very great barons, in order that they may have full authority, even as he himself. He who has such a tablet may claim from any great prince his whole army for a body-guard. And, if one of these barons wishes to send someone, say a messenger, he may, if he will, take a king's horses for the purpose. And if I say " a king's horses," it is that you may know that he may take anyone's.

Now we will leave this subject, and resume our account of the wonderful things that concern the Great Kaan. We have already told you of his lineage and of his age. We will now tell you of his personal appearance and conduct.

Here is told of the personal appearance and conduct of the Great Kaan

The personal appearance of the great King of Kings whose name is Cublai, is as follows. He has a fine figure, neither tall nor short, but of middle height. He has the proper amount of flesh, and is exceedingly well shaped in all his limbs. His countenance is white and red, like a rose, his eyes black and beautiful, his nose shapely and well placed.

He has four wives, all of whom he considers legitimate. (The eldest of the sons he has by his four wives must by law be the Lord of the Empire when the Great Kaan dies.) They are all called Empresses, the proper name of each being added. Each of them has a court of her own. None has less than three hundred most beautiful and handsome maidens. They also have many eunuchs as pages, and many other servants, both male and female. Hence each lady has 10,000 persons in her court. And every time the Great Kaan wishes to lie with one of these four wives of his, he summons her to his chamber, and sometimes he himself goes to her chamber.

He also has many concubines, and I will tell you how he obtains them and uses them. You must know that there is a province where lives a race of Tartars called Ungrat. The city is likewise called Ungrat. The people there are most beautiful and white. When he pleases, for the most part every two years, the Great Kaan sends envoys to that Province to find him the most beautiful damsels, according to a certain scale of beauty that he gives them—four hundred or five hundred of them, or more or less, as he pleases. And the beauty of these damsels is appraised in this way. When the envoys arrive, they summon all the damsels in the province; and there are appraisers, especially deputed for this task, who look at and examine one by one the members of each of them, their hair, their face, their eyebrows, their mouth, their lips, and their limbs, and see that they are all in due proportion to the rest of their body. Then they appraise some at 16 carats, others at 17, 18, 20, or more or less, according as they are more or less beautiful. And if the Great Kaan has ordered that those to be brought to him should be of 20 or 21 carats, the required number of that value is taken to him. When they come to his presence, he has them appraised once more by other appraisers, and out of the whole number he chooses for his own chamber some 30 or 40 of those that are valued highest. Then he has one given to each of the wives of his barons, to have them sleep in the same bed with them, and see carefully whether they are virgins, and perfectly healthy under every point of view, whether they have a quiet sleep or else snore, whether their breath is good and sweet, or else evil, and whether they in any way have an unpleasant odour. When they have been thus diligently examined, those that are found to be beautiful and good and sound under every aspect, are appointed to wait on the Lord in the way I will tell you. Six of those maidens remain in the Lord's chamber for three days and three nights, and wait on him in bed, and do all that he may need. And the Great Kaan does with them as he pleases. At the end of the three days and three nights, six other damsels come; and so they go on, changing every three days and nights, until all have had their turn. Then they begin again. True it is that while some of the six remain in the Lord's chamber, the others stay in a neighbouring room. And if the Lord needs to have something brought to him from outside, as for example food or drink or anything else, the damsels within the Lord's chamber tell those in the next room what they are to get ready, and they at once get it ready. Thus the Lord is not waited on by anyone else but the damsels. And the others, who were appraised at less carats, live in the palace with the rest of the damsels belonging to the Lord, and are taught how to sew and make gloves and do other kinds of noble work. And when some nobleman is seeking for a wife, the Great Kaan gives him one of them, together with a large dowry. In this way he marries them all splendidly. But someone might object: "Are not the men of that province aggrieved that the Great Kaan should take away their daughters?" Certainly not; indeed they repute it a great grace and honour. And greatly do those who have beautiful daughters rejoice, that the Great Kaan should deign to accept them, for they say, "If my daughter was born under a good planet and with good fortune, the Lord will the better be able to work out her destiny and marry her nobly, which I myself should not be able to do." And if his daughter misbehaves, or else things go ill with her, then the father says, "This has happened to her, because her planet was evil."

Here is told of the sons of the Great Kaan

And you must know further that, by his four wives, the Great Kaan has twenty-two sons. The eldest was called Chinghis in memory of the good Chinghis Kaan, and he was destined to be Kaan and Lord of the whole empire; indeed, already during his father's lifetime he had been confirmed Lord. Now, it came to pass that he died. But he left a son called Temur, and this Temur will be the Great Kaan and Lord. And rightly so, since he is the son of the eldest son of the Great Kaan. And I assure you that this Temur is wise and valiant, and has already many times clearly proved his worth in battle.

And you must also know that, by his concubines, the Great Kaan has no less than twenty-five more sons, all good and valiant in arms. And each of them is a great baron.

And I tell you, too, that of the sons he has had by

his four wives, seven are Kings of immense provinces and kingdoms. And all of them rule their lands well, like the wise and worthy men they are. There is a good reason for it too, for I assure you that their father, the Great Kaan, is the wisest man, and most gifted in every way, the best ruler of peoples and empire, and the man of greatest worth, that ever sprang from the race of the Tartars.

Now I have told you of the Great Kaan and his sons; I will next tell you how he keeps his court and of his habits.

Here is told of the palace of the Great Kaan

Know, then, in truth that for three months in the year, namely December, January, and February, the Great Kaan lives in the capital of Cathay, called Cambaluc. In this city he has his great palace, and I will tell you how it is built.

All round the city there is a first row of walls, square in shape, each side being eight miles long. All along the wall there is a deep ditch, and in the middle of each side a gate through which pass all the people who come to this city. Then there is a space of a mile, where the troops live. Then you come to another square wall, twenty-four miles long. [This is the real city wall, and we will speak of it later. The Great Kaan's palace is within this wall, but, to reach it, two more rows of walls have to be passed.]

First of all there is a great square wall, with sides a mile long, that is to say, it is four miles all round. It is exceedingly thick, quite ten paces high, and all white and embattled. In each corner stands a most beautiful and rich palace, where the Great Kaan's warlike equipment is kept, such as bows, quivers, saddles, bridles, bow-strings, and all else that is necessary for an army. Further, in the middle of each side is another palace similar to those in the corners; hence, all round there are eight palaces in all. And all eight of them are full of the Great Lord's war-equipment. And you must know that in each palace there is only one kind of thing. Thus, in one there are bridles, saddles, stirrups and all other kinds of harness for horses; in another, bows, bow-strings, quivers, arrows, and other things belonging to archery; in another again, there are breastplates, corslets, and other such objects of boiled leather; and so on, in the others. On the southern side of this wall, there are five gates: one large gate in the middle, which is only opened when the Great Kaan goes in or out, and on either side of it two smaller gates, through which all the other people pass. Two more very large gates, also for the many, are placed, one on the one side, and one on the other, towards the corners.

Within this wall is another wall, the enclosure being rather greater in length than in breadth. Round it, also, are placed eight palaces, built like the others, in which likewise the Great Kaan's war-harness is kept. In this wall too, on the south side, are placed five gates, just like those in the wall in front of it. The remaining sides, both of this wall and of the other I mentioned before, have one single gate.

In the middle of these circuits of walls rises the Great Kaan's palace, which is built as I shall tell you. It is the largest that was ever seen.

Towards the north, it touches the last of the walls we have spoken of, but, on the south side, there is an empty space before it, where the barons and soldiers walk. It has no upper floor, but the basement is ten palms higher than the ground surrounding it, and the roof is surpassingly high. Flush with the floor of the palace, there is a marble wall, running all round, two paces wide. The palace is built in the centre of the wall, so that the whole of the wall around is like a vestibule to the palace, round which one can walk, and from which one can see outside. The outer edge of the wall holds up a fine pillared balcony, that one can look out of. On each side of the palace is a great marble staircase, which leads from the ground to the top of the marble wall, and by which one reaches the palace. The inside walls of the halls and rooms are all covered with gold and silver, and on them are painted beautiful pictures of ladies and knights and dragons and beasts and birds and divers other things. The ceiling is also made in such a way that one sees nothing else on it, but pictures and gold. The great hall is so vast and large that quite six thousand men could banquet there. There are so many rooms as to surpass all belief. The beauty and size of this palace are so great that no one on earth, who had the necessary skill, could have planned or built it better. The roof is varnished in vermilion, green, blue, yellow, and all other colours; and so well and cunningly is this done, that it glitters like crystal, and can be seen shining from a great way off all round. And you must know that the roof is so strongly and firmly built that it lasts for years without number.

Moreover, behind the palace there are great houses, and halls, and rooms where the personal effects of the Kaan are kept, namely all his treasure—gold, silver, gems, and pearls, and gold and silver dishes; and there his ladies and concubines live; and there, too, he has all things done for his personal convenience. And no one may enter that place.

Between the two walls of which I have spoken, there stretch meadows with fine trees, full of animals of different kinds, such as white stags, and the animals that make musk, and roebucks, and fallow-deer, and vair and many other kinds of beautiful animals. The space between the two walls is all full of these fine beasts, with the sole exception of the roads along which the people pass. The meadows are beautifully grassy, for all the roads are paved, and raised no less than two cubits above the ground, so that mud never collects on them, nor does the rain-water stop on them, but flows off into the fields beneath, thus nourishing the soil, and making the grass grow in abundance.

Again, towards the north, at the distance of an arrow's flight from the palace, but within the two walls, the Great Kaan has had a little hill or mound made, quite a hundred paces high, and over a mile in girth. It is covered with trees that never lose their leaves, but always remain green. And you must know that if the Great Kaan is told that in a given place there is a beautiful tree, he has it taken, wherever it be, roots and all, and with a great deal of soil, and has it carried on to the little hill by elephants. And were the tree as big as you will, he would be sure to do so. In this way there are in that place the finest trees in the world. And I will add that the Great Lord has had the whole of that hill covered with dust of lapis lazuli, which is surpassingly green. Thus all the trees are green and all the hill is green too, all that strikes the eye is green. Hence it is called the Green Hill.

On that hill, right at the top, rises a fine big palace, which is all green too. And I assure you that the hill, and the trees, and the palace are all so fair to look upon, that those who see them feel great delight and joy at the sight. And the Great Lord caused that hill to be made in order to have this fine sight, and derive comfort and pleasure from it.

In the same space between the walls, towards the north-west, is a large lake made by man, very broad and deep, and excellently planned, the making of which furnished the soil for the aforesaid hill; into it there flows a smallish river—into which the Great Kaan has caused many kinds of fishes to be put. Here the beasts go to drink. Out of the lake flows the river we have mentioned, and, passing along an aqueduct near the hill, it feeds another very large and deep lake, situated between the Great Kaan's palace and that of his son Chinghis; and the soil removed to dig this lake also served for the making of the hill. In these lakes there are many kinds of fishes, and every time the Great Lord wants some, he has them in abundance. And the river flows out at the other end of the lake, and proceeds on its course. But in the two points where the river enters and leaves the lake, there are iron and copper nets which prevent the fish from getting out. There are also swans and other water-fowl. And over the water, from one palace to the other, there is a bridge.

Here is told of the palace of the Prince who is to reign after the Great Kaan

And I will tell you, too, that near his palace, the Great Kaan has had another built, similar to his own, down to the last detail. He has had it made for that son of his who is to reign and become Lord. This is why he has had it made in the same way, just as large, and with the same circuits of wall as his own, which I have described to you above. There lives the son of Chinghis, whom I have mentioned above, and who is to reign after him: he kept and followed all the customs and manners of the Great Kaan, being destined to become Lord as soon as the Great Kaan dies. He already possesses the bull and seal of empire, but not with an authority as absolute and complete as that of the Great Kaan himself.

Now I have told you about the palaces. I will next tell you of the city of Taidu, in which these palaces are, and why and how it was built.

Here is told of the great city of Taidu

You must know that there was in that place an ancient city, both large and noble, called Cambaluc, which in our tongue signifies " the city of the Kaan." And the Great Kaan knew from his astrologers that the city would revolt, and cause the greatest trouble to the Empire. Hence he had a new one built near it, separated from the other merely by a river. All the Cathayans, namely those who were natives of the province of Cathay, he ordered to leave the old city, and go and live in the new one, which he had built and called Taidu. In the old city he only left those who he was sure would not rebel, since the new city could not hold as many people as lived in the old one, which was very large. How large Taidu was, I will now tell you.

It measures 24 miles in circuit, and it is square, with all its sides exactly equal. It is surrounded by earthen walls, ten paces broad at the base, and twenty paces high. The walls are not, however, as broad at the top as at the bottom, for they become narrower as they rise, so that at the top they are but three paces broad. They are all embattled and white. The city has twelve gates, and over each gate there is a very large and beautiful palace, so that, as there is also a palace at each corner, each side of the wall has three gates and five palaces. In these palaces there are immense halls where are kept the arms of those who guard the city.

And I assure you that the streets of the city are so straight and broad that one can see from one end to the other of them, and they are so arranged that from each gate one can see the opposite one. There are many beautiful palaces, many beautiful hostelries, and many beautiful houses. And everywhere along the main streets there are rooms and shops of every kind. All the plots of ground on which the houses are built, are square, and laid out with straight lines, and in each plot there are large and spacious palaces, with their proper courtyards and gardens. These plots are given to the heads of families, so that so-and-so of such a family has received such a plot, and so-and-so of such another family has received such another plot; and so on. And round each of these square plots, there are beautiful streets, along which one walks. In this way the whole of the inner city is arranged in squares, just like a chess-board; and it is so beautiful, and so skilfully arranged, that it is not possible to describe it.

In the middle of the city, there is an immense palace, with a large clock, that is to say, a bell, which is struck three times at night, to warn the people that from that moment no one may go out into the streets. Once that bell has struck three times, no one dares go about the city, except it be for some urgent reason, as for a woman in labour or for a sick person; and those who do thus go about, must carry a light with them.

I will also add that each of those twelve gates has to be guarded by a thousand men. But you must not think that this is due to any fear of assailants; it is in honour of the Great Lord who lives there, and in order that brigands may do no mischief within the city. Further, on account of the astrologers' words, a certain amount of suspicion is felt towards the people of Cathay.

Outside the city, beyond each gate, are large suburbs, so built that the suburb of each gate borders on those of the next two. They stretch to a distance of three or four miles, so that the inhabitants of the suburbs are more numerous than those of the city. In each suburb, to a distance of perhaps a mile from the city, there are many beautiful fondacos in which the merchants lodge, who come from different lands; to each nation a given fondaco is assigned, that is, as we should say, one to the Lombards, another to the Germans, another again to the French. There are, too, twenty-five thousand harlots, counting those of the suburbs of the new city together with those in the old city, who serve men with their bodies for money. They have a general overseer; there is an overseer, too, for each hundred and for each thousand, but they are all responsible to the general. The reason why these women have an overseer is that, every time envoys arrive at the Great Kaan's court on business of his, and stop in Taidu at his expense—and indeed they are provided for in the most honourable manner—this overseer's duty is to give every night one of these harlots to the said envoys and to every man in his train. And every night they are changed, receiving no wages, for this is the tribute they pay to the Great Kaan.

Further, guards ride all night about the city, in groups of thirty or forty, seeing whether anyone is abroad in forbidden hours, namely, after the third stroke of the bell; and if they find anyone, they take him, and straightway put him in prison. Next morning, the proper officers question him, and if they find him guilty of some misdeed, they give him a certain number of blows with a stick, according to the seriousness of the offence; and at times people die of those blows. For this is how they inflict punishments for crimes, nor will they shed blood, since the *Bacsi*, that is, their wise astrologers, have told them that it is wicked to shed human blood.

We have told you of the city of Taidu. Now, [as we have touched upon the suspicion in which the Cathayans are held], we will tell you how once the Cathayans wanted to rebel in the city.

How the Cathayans of Taidu tried to rebel

You must know that, as we shall tell you later on, the Great Kaan has entrusted to twelve men the task of attending, as seems best to them, to all territories, governments, and everything else. Among these twelve men, there was a Saracen, Acmat by name, a shrewd and capable man, who above all others enjoyed great power and influence with the Great Lord, who loved him so much that he gave him every liberty, for, as was found after his death, this Acmat laid such a spell over the Kaan with his sorceries, that the latter placed absolute faith in his words, paying them the closest attention. Thus he was able to do all that he wished. He it was who distributed all governments and offices, and punished all offenders. And every time he wished to encompass the death of someone he hated, whether justly or unjustly, he would go to the Lord, and say, "Sire, such a man is worthy of death, for he has offended your Majesty in such a way." Then the Lord would say, "Do what thou thinkest most fitting." And straightway he would have the man put to death. Hence, seeing the complete liberty he enjoyed, and that the Lord placed absolute trust in his words, no one dared cross him in anything whatsoever. There were none so great or so powerful as not to fear him. And if someone was accused before the Lord on a capital charge, and wished to defend himself, he could not bring forward his defence, there being no one to whom he might do so, for none dared go counter to Acmat. In this way he made many a man die unjustly. Besides, there was no beautiful woman but that, if he had a mind to her, he had her, taking her as wife if unmarried, or otherwise obtaining her consent in some other way. When he heard that so-and-so had a fair daughter, he had his pimps, who would go to the girl's father, and say, "What wilt thou do? Thou hast this daughter: give her in marriage to the *Bailo*—for they gave Acmat a title like our *Bailo* or *Vicar*—and we shall see to it that he gives you such and such a government or office for three years." And so that father would give him his daughter. Then Acmat would say, to the Lord, "Such and such a government is vacant, or will be on such a day. This man is fit to have it." And the Lord would answer, "Do as thou thinkest most fitting." So Acmat would at once invest the man with the government. Thus, partly through ambition of having governments and offices, partly because he was feared, this Acmat either got all the most beautiful women as wives, or else otherwise had his will of them. He also had sons—some twenty-five of them—who occupied the highest offices. And some of them, in their father's name and under his protection, committed adultery like him, and performed many heinous and wicked deeds. This Acmat had gathered together a great treasure, for who ever wished for some government or office, sent him a large present.

This man, then, continued wielding his power for twenty-two years, but at last the men of the land, namely the Cathayans, seeing his infinite crimes and infamous misdeeds, that surpassed all bounds, both at their wives' expense and at their own, and being no longer able to bear with him in any way, decided to kill him, and to rebel against the government of the city. Amongst them there was a Cathayan named Chencu, who was leader of a thousand men, and whose mother, daughter, and wife had all been debauched by Acmat. In his indignation, he spoke to another Cathayan, Vancu by name, the leader of ten thousand men, concerning Acmat's destruction, saying that they should encompass it when the Great Kaan, after staying as usual three months at Cambaluc, left the city to go to Chandu, where he also spent three months. At the same time his son Chinghis also used to leave, in order to go to his usual resorts, and Acmat remained behind to keep and guard the city, sending word to the Great Kaan at Chandu concerning any emergency that might arise, and receiving orders from him as to how to deal with it. Having decided upon this, Vancu and Chencu determined to make their intentions known to the more important Cathayans in the land, and, by common consent, informed their friends in many other cities of their plan. This was that, on a certain day appointed for the purpose, as soon as they saw the fire-signals, they should slay all men with beards, and signal by means of beacons to the other cities to do likewise. And the reason why they said that all bearded men were to be slain, was that the Cathayans are by nature beardless, whereas Tartars, Saracens, and Christians wear beards. And you must know that all the Cathayans detested the Great Kaan's dominion, because he placed Tartars and, still oftener, Saracen governors over them; and they could not bear this, as it made them seem slaves. For the Great Kaan had no legal right over the province of Cathay, which he had taken by force, and so he did not place any faith in the people, but entrusted the government of the land to Tartars, Saracens, and Christians who belonged to his train, and were faithful to him; he entrusted it, that is, to persons who did not belong to Cathay.

Now the aforesaid Vancu and Chencu, on the appointed day, entered into the palace by night. And Vancu sat upon a throne, and had many lights lit before him. He then sent a messenger of his to the *Bailo* Acmat, who lived in the old city, to tell him, in the name of the Great Kaan's son Chinghis, supposed to have just arrived during the night, that he should straightway come to the palace. When Acmat heard this, he marvelled exceedingly, and went at once, for he had great fear of Chinghis. On passing through the city-gate, he met a Tartar called Cogatai, who commanded the twelve thousand men that constantly guarded the city; and Cogatai asked him, "Whither are you going so late?" "To Chinghis, who has just arrived," said Acmat. "How is it possible that he should have come so secretly that I should know nothing about it?" said Cogatai. And so he followed Acmat with some of his men. Now you must know that the Cathayans had said to themselves, "As long as we succeed in killing Acmat, we need not have fear of anything else." The moment Acmat entered the palace, and saw so many lights burning, he knelt before Vancu, thinking him to be Chinghis; and Chencu, who stood there ready with a sword, cut off his head. On seeing this, Cogatai, who had stopped at the entrance of the palace, cried " Treason! " and straightway shot an arrow against Vancu as he sat on the throne, and killed him. Then, calling his men, he took Chencu, and sent a proclamation round the city to the effect that whosoever was found out of doors should straightway be put to death. When the Cathayans saw that the Tartars had discovered the plot, and that they themselves were left without leaders, the one being killed and the other captured, they withdrew into their houses, and were no longer able to make signals to the other cities to rebel as had been decided.

So Cogatai at once sent messengers to the Great Kaan, to tell him all in due order what had happened. And the Great Kaan commanded that he should diligently examine the Cathayans and punish them for their misdeeds in proportion to their guilt. When morning came, Cogatai duly examined all the Cathayans, and many he destroyed and killed, having found that they were the ringleaders in the conspiracy. The same was done in the other cities, too, when it became known that they also had taken part in the plot.

When later the Great Kaan returned to Cambaluc, he wished to know the reason why all these events had come about, and so he discovered that this accursed Acmat, both he and his sons, had committed as many and as heinous misdeeds as we have before recounted. And it was found, too, that he and seven of his sons—for not all of them were wicked—had taken an infinite number of women as wives, without counting those whom they had taken by force. Then the Great Kaan had the whole of the treasure brought to the new city, that Acmat had collected in the old city, and he added it to his own; and it was found to be incalculable. Then he ordered Acmat's body to be taken out of its tomb, and cast on the road, that the dogs might tear it to pieces. And Acmat's sons who had followed in their father's footsteps, he had flayed alive.

Then he pondered over the accursed sect of the Saracens, to whom every sin is permissible, and who may kill anyone who does not follow their Law, and he bethought him how the accursed Acmat and his sons did not think that they were committing any sin; and so he greatly despised that sect and held it in abomination. Summoning the Saracens, he forbade them to do many things that their Law commanded. He ordered them, in fact, that they should take wives for themselves according to the Law of the Tartars, and that they should not slaughter cattle in the way they did, in order to eat the flesh, but that they should rip up their belly.

And at the time these things came about, Messer Marco was in the country.

Now we will cease speaking of this, and return to the subject we left off. We have told you of the city. We will now tell you how he, namely the Great Kaan, holds his court, and other things, too, we will tell you concerning him.

How the Great Kaan has a guard of twelve thousand horsemen

You must know that the Great Kaan, to keep his state, has a guard of twelve thousand horsemen. They are called *Kesitan*, a word that in our language signifies " Faithful Knights of the Lord." But he does not keep them because he is afraid of anyone, but as a sign of his majesty.

These twelve thousand men have four captains, one to each group of three thousand. For three days and three nights, three thousand of them remain on guard in the palace, eating and drinking there. After the lapse of three days and three nights, they go away, and another group of three thousand come, and remain on guard for three days and three nights, and so on, until all four groups have had their turn. Then they begin again. And so it goes on all the year round. The nine thousand who are not on duty, also remain in the palace in the day-time, except such of them as have to go on the Kaan's business, or on their own, as long as it is permissible, and only with their captain's leave. And if something were to happen to one of them, if, for example, his father, or a brother, or other relative were on the point of death, or if some other evil were impending, so as to prevent his returning quickly, he must ask for the Great Kaan's leave. During the night, the nine thousand go home.

How the Great Kaan keeps table at high feasts

When the Great Kaan holds his court and receives at his table, the manner of it is as follows.

The Great Lord's table is much higher than the others. He sits on the north side, so as to look towards the south. Near him, on his left, sits his first wife; on his right, but rather lower, so that their heads are on a level with the Great Lord's feet, sit his sons, his grandsons, and all his kinsfolk who belong to the Imperial line. Slightly higher than the others, sits the heir-presumptive. Then come the other barons, sitting at other tables, lower still. It is the same with the ladies, for all those of the Great Kaan's sons and grandsons and relatives, sit on the left, also lower; then come all the ladies of the barons and knights, they, too, seated lower still. And everyone knows the place that belongs to him, for the Great Kaan has fixed it. But you must not suppose that all the company sits at tables; the greater number of the knights and barons eat in the hall upon carpets, and have no tables. The tables are so placed that the Great Lord can see everyone. They are an immense multitude. Outside the hall, more than forty thousand people eat. For many people flock in, with splendid gifts, namely such people as come from foreign parts, bringing strange things with them, and such, too, as have held a command in the past and wish to have another. All these people come on the days when the Great Kaan holds his court, and keeps open table.

In the middle of the hall where the Great Kaan holds the banquet, stands a beautiful contrivance, very large and richly decorated, made like a square coffer, three paces wide along each side, and cunningly wrought with beautiful gilt sculptures of animals. In the middle, it is hollow, and in it stands a great vessel of pure gold, holding as much as a large cask: it is full of wine. All round this vessel, namely at each corner, there are smaller ones, of the size of a firkin; in these there are excellent drinks; in one there is mare's milk, in another camel's milk, and so on. On the coffer stand the Great Kaan's cups, in which he is offered drink. The wine, or precious beverage, as the case may be, is drawn into large gold vessels, big enough to contain sufficient wine for eight or ten men. Of these vessels, one is placed on the table for every two guests. Each of the two guests has a golden cup with a handle, and with it he draws his drink from the large golden vessel. And so with the ladies, every two of whom have one of the large vessels and two cups, like the men.

And you must know that those vessels and cups are of great value. I assure you that the Great Kaan has so much gold and silver plate, that no one who has not seen it, can believe it.

You must also know that there are certain barons whose duty it is to assign their proper places to the strangers who arrive without knowing the customs of the great court. These barons constantly go hither and thither about the hall, seeing whether those sitting at the tables lack anything, and if there be anyone who wants wine or milk or meat or anything else, they at once have it brought by the servants.

At all the doors of this hall, and indeed of any other place where the Lord may be, stand two tall men, as big as giants, one on either side, with staves in their hands, for no one may touch the threshold of the door, but must step over it. And if by chance anyone does touch it, these guards strip him, and, to get his clothes back, he must pay a forfeit. If they do not strip him, they give him the appointed number of strokes. If, however, there are strangers who do not know the order, there are barons appointed to inform them of it and to introduce them. This is done because it is thought to bring ill luck if anyone touches the threshold. When people leave the hall, however, as some are the worse for drink, so that they could not look to where they are stepping, the order is not enforced.

You must also know that many great barons are also appointed to take charge of the Great Kaan's food and drink; and their mouths and noses are muffled up with beautiful silk and gold cloths, in order that no breath or odour of their bodies may come near the Great Kaan's food and drink.

When the Great Kaan is about to drink, all the numberless instruments of every kind that are in the hall begin to play. A page offers him the cup, and then straightway steps back three paces, and kneels. At the very moment the Great Kaan takes the cup, all the barons and other people present, fall on their knees, and make signs of great obeisance. Then the Great Kaan drinks. And every time he drinks they do as you have heard.

Of the food I will not speak, for anyone can understand that it is in great abundance.

I will add that no baron or knight may take part in the banquet, unless he takes his first wife with him; and she eats with the other ladies.

When they have eaten, and the tables are removed, there enters the hall, into the presence of the Great Lord and of all those people, a crowd of jugglers and tumblers and other such persons, who know how to do all kinds of wonderful things. And they give great pleasure to the Great Lord, and all the people are delighted, and laugh and enjoy themselves. After this, the guests leave, and everyone returns to his hostelry or home.

Here is told of the high feast that the Great Kaan holds on his birthday

You must know that all the Tartars celebrate their birthdays. The Great Kaan was born on the twenty-eighth day of the September moon, and so on that day they celebrate the greatest feast held in those parts, with the exception of their New Year's Day, as I shall tell you later.

On his birthday, the Great Kaan dresses in wondrous robes of beaten gold, and twelve thousand barons and knights also dress in the same colour and after the same fashion. But though their robes are of the same colour and fashion, yet they are not so costly; but all the same they are of silk and gold. And all of them have great golden belts. This raiment is given them by the Great Kaan. And I assure you that some of these robes are adorned with precious stones and pearls to the value of 10,000 gold bezants. Robes of this value are not rare. And you must know that thirteen times a year does the Great Kaan give rich robes to these twelve thousand barons and knights; and all these robes are similar to his own, and of great value. It is truly a wonderful thing, as you may see, and such as no other Lord in the world, but he, could possibly do or keep up.

You must further know that on his birthday all the Tartars in the world, all provinces and all lands subject to him, give him great presents, varying according to the rank of the giver, and to the established custom. Great gifts are brought him by many others, too, namely those who wish to ask for some office. (Their requests are seen to by twelve barons appointed by the Great Lord to distribute offices according to the applicants.) And on that day all idolaters, and all Christians, and all Saracens, and all other kinds of people, utter solemn prayers to their idols and gods, with much singing and burning of incense, and great illuminations, to preserve their Lord for them and grant him long life and joy and health.

Such, then, even as I have told you, are the rejoicing and feasting on his birthday. Now we will cease speaking of this feast, which we have fully described, and tell you of another great festivity that he celebrates at the beginning of the year, and that is called the White Feast.

Here is told of the splendid feast held by the Great Kaan on their New Year's Day

You must know that their New Year's Day comes in February. The Great Kaan and all his subjects celebrate it as I shall tell you.

It is the custom that the Great Kaan and all his subjects, both men and women, old and young, should on that day dress in white robes, if they have but the means to do so. This they do because white clothes seem to them an excellent thing and of good omen. So they dress in white on New Year's Day, that they may be lucky and happy all the year. And on that day, all peoples, and provinces, and lands, and kingdoms, subject to the Great Kaan, send him great gifts of gold, and silver, and pearls, and precious stones, and many splendid white cloths. This they do in order that their Lord may during the whole year, have treasure in abundance, and be happy and joyful. And I tell you, too, that the barons and knights, and all the people, exchange presents of white things, and they embrace and greet one another with joy and mirth. And they say to one another, as we also do: "May all that you do this year be lucky and fortunate." And this they do in order to enjoy prosperity and good fortune all the year.

And you must also know that on that day more than a hundred thousand splendid white horses are given to the Great Kaan; and if they are not absolutely white all over, they are at least almost completely white. Of white horses there is great abundance in those parts. When they make gifts to the Great Kaan, it is their custom that the giver should, if he can, follow this observance, namely give nine times nine units of the thing given. Thus, if the present is one of horses, nine times nine horses are given, namely eighty-one; if it is gold, then nine times nine pieces of gold; if it is cloth, nine times nine pieces of cloth; and so on for all things.

On that day, too, his elephants are taken out, which amount to no less than 5000, and are all covered with fine cloths, bearing figures of birds and beasts. Each of them bears on its back two surpassingly beautiful and richly-wrought coffers, full of the Lord's plate, and of other precious things necessary for the White Court. Then there follows an immense number of camels, also covered with rich cloths, and loaded with the things necessary for this feast. And all file past the Great Lord; it is the finest sight that ever was seen.

I must add, too, that, on the morning of that feast, before the tables are set out, all the kings and all the dukes, marquesses, counts, barons, knights, astrologers, leeches, and falconers, together with many more officers and rulers of peoples, lands, and armies, all gather together in the presence of the Great Kaan. And those who find no room, stand outside the hall where the Lord may see them. And this is how they are disposed. First there are the Kaan's sons, his grandsons, and his kinsfolk of the Imperial lineage. Then there are the kings; then the dukes; then all the other ranks, one after the other, in the proper order. When all are seated, each in his appointed place, then a high prelate rises, and says in a loud voice: "Bow and adore!" As soon as he has uttered these words, straightway all bow down and touch the ground with their foreheads, and they raise up a prayer to the Kaan, and adore him as if he were a god. Then the prelate says: "God save and preserve our Lord for long, in joy and happiness." And all answer: "May God do so." And again the prelate says: "May God increase and multiply the empire of our Lord, and make it ever greater, and may He keep all his subjects in tranquil peace and goodwill; and may everything prosper in all his lands." And all answer: "May God do so." In this way do they adore him four times. Then the prelate goes to a beautifully decorated altar, on which lies a red tablet bearing the name of the Great Kaan; and there is also a magnificent censer. The prelate then incenses the tablet and the altar with great reverence. And all the others do the same, and then return to their places.

When all have done so, then they give the gifts I have told you of, that are so immensely precious and so splendid. When all the gifts have been given, and the Great Kaan has seen everything, then the tables are laid out. When the tables are laid out, then all the people sit down in the order I told you of before: the Great Lord, that is, sits at his high table, and with him, on his left, his first wife, and no one else. Then all the others sit, in the order that I have already described, all the ladies being on the side of the Empress, even as I said. And he keeps table in the way I have told you before. And when they have finished eating, the jugglers come and amuse the court, as I also have told you. And at the end all return to their hostelries and homes.

Now I have told you of the White Feast held on New Year's Day. I will next return to a most noble custom of the Kaan's, of which I have already said something, namely the duty on the part of certain barons to wear certain robes when they are bidden to come to the feasts.

Here is told of the twelve thousand barons who are bidden to the feasts; and how they are provided with robes by the Great Kaan

You must know that, by order of the Great Kaan, there are thirteen feasts (which the Tartars celebrate with great solemnity according to the thirteen moons of the year), in which the twelve thousand barons we mentioned, called *Kesitan*, namely the "Guards faithful to the Lord," are obliged to take part. To each of them he has given thirteen suits of clothes, all of different colours, to be worn only on the aforesaid feasts. They are most splendidly adorned with pearls and precious stones, and other wonderful things, and are of immense value. Further, to each of the twelve thousand barons, he has also given a most beautiful and valuable gold belt. And he has given to each boots of *camu*, very cunningly worked with silver thread, which are most beautiful and valuable. And they are all so nobly and splendidly attired, that, when they are dressed, they all look like kings. And for each of the thirteen feasts, one particular dress is to be worn. These dresses are always ready, but they are not made anew every year, for they last some ten years, more or less. The Great Kaan has thirteen dresses similar to those of his barons—I mean, similar in colour, for otherwise they are more splendid and more valuable, and more richly adorned. And every time he dresses like his barons.

Now I have told you of the thirteen dresses that the Lord gives to his twelve thousand barons—156,000 in all, so magnificent and valuable as to represent such a treasure as can scarcely be counted, to say nothing of the belts and boots, which are also worth a large sum. And all this the Great Lord does in order to give greater splendour and dignity to his feasts.

And now I will tell you of another thing that seems to us a marvel and that I was forgetting, though it is worthy of mention in our book. You must know that a large lion is brought before the Great Lord. And as soon as the lion sees the Great Kaan, it crouches down before him, making signs of great obeisance; and you would think it knew him for its lord and master. It remains before him unchained. And truly it is a marvellous sight.

Now we will leave this subject, and tell you of the great hunting that the Great Lord causes to be done, as you shall hear.

How the Great Kaan has ordered that his people shall supply him with game

You must know that during the three months that the Great Kaan passes in the city of Taidu (namely, December, January, and February), he has ordered that, up to a distance of some sixty days' journey all round, everyone should hunt and fowl. According to this order, every Lord of men and lands must send him all the large animals, such as wild boars, stags, fallow-deer, roebucks, bears, and so forth—or, rather, I should say, the greater number of them. And this is how they catch them: every Lord in the province takes with him all the hunters in the country, and goes with them to the places where the animals are to be found; there they surround them, and kill them by means of dogs, or, more often, with arrows. In this way do all the people I have mentioned hunt. They then gut the animals that are to be sent to the Great Kaan, and place them on carts, and so despatch them. This is done by those who live within a distance of thirty days' journey, and the number of animals they send is enormous. Those who live further away, up to sixty days' journey, do not send the meat on account of the distance, but send the hides, instead, all ready and tanned, as the Kaan uses them for making the equipment necessary for his armies and wars.

Now I have told you about the chase; we will next tell you of the wild animals that the Great Kaan keeps.

Here is told of the lions, leopards, and lynxes that the Great Kaan has trained for the chase; and here is also told of the eagles

You must know that the Great Kaan has many leopards, all excellent for the chase and for catching game. He also has a large number of lynxes trained to hunt, and very good for the chase. He has many very big lions, too, much bigger than those of Babylon; they have very fine coats, and are of a beautiful colour, being striped lengthways in black, red, and white. They are trained to take wild boars, wild oxen, bears, wild asses, stags, fallow-deer, and other beasts. And I assure you it is a splendid sight to see those lions catch their quarries. When lions are taken to the chase, each lion is put in a cage on a cart, and a little dog with him. The reason they are placed in cages is that otherwise they would be too fierce and anxious to fall on the game, and it would be impossible to hold them. They have, moreover, to be led to the windward of the game, for if the latter scented them, they would flee, and not wait for them to approach.

He also has a multitude of eagles, trained to catch wolves, foxes, deer and roes; and they take many of them. Those trained to catch wolves are remarkably big and powerful. For you may be sure there is not a wolf, however big, that can escape them.

You are now informed of these things. I will next

tell you how the Great Kaan keeps an enormous number of excellent hounds.

Here is told of the two brothers who look after the hounds

You must know that among the barons at court there are two who are own brothers, one called Baian, and the other Mingan. Their title is that of *Cuiuci*, a word that means "those who look after the mastiffs." Each of these brothers has ten thousand men at his orders, and each group of ten thousand is dressed in one colour, the two colours being vermilion and yellow. Every time they go out hunting with the Great Lord, they wear this livery I have told you of. Out of the ten thousand, two thousand have, each of them, charge of one, two, or more mastiffs; so the number of mastiffs is immense. When the Great Kaan goes out hunting, one of these two brothers goes on one side of him, with his ten thousand men and quite five thousand hounds, and the other brother goes on the other side, with his ten thousand and their hounds. They all go abreast, and at a short distance of one another, so as to occupy the space of more than a day's march, and then they gradually converge. No wild animal they come across can escape. It is truly marvellous to see this hunt, and the behaviour of those hounds and hunters. For I assure you that when the Great Kaan rides out with his barons hunting over these plains, you will see these hounds, some here, some there, hunting down bears or stags or other animals; it is really a glorious sight.

It is part of the duty of these brothers to furnish the Great Kaan's court every day, from the beginning of the month of October to the end of March, with a thousand head of beasts and birds, except quails. Fish, too, they have to provide, as best as they may, counting as one " head " as much fish as three persons could eat at a meal.

I have now told you of those who look after the hounds. We will next tell you what the Great Kaan does during the other three months.

Here is told how the Great Kaan goes hunting in order to take beasts and birds

After passing the three months of December, January, and February in the city I have mentioned, the Great Kaan leaves in the month of March, and goes south, keeping at a short distance from the Ocean Sea, which is only two days' journey away. He takes with him no less than ten thousand falconers, and quite five hundred gerfalcons, besides a multitude of peregrine and saker falcons. He also takes numbers of goshawks for catching water-fowl. You must not, however, suppose that he keeps all these falconers near him in one place, he distributes them here and there, in groups of a hundred or two hundred or more. These groups go out fowling, and the greater part of the birds caught, they take to the Great Kaan. And when the Great Lord goes fowling with his gerfalcons and other birds, he takes with him no less then ten thousand men, disposed in twos, who are called *Toscaor*, a word that in our language signifies " men who watch." And that indeed they do, for they are posted here and there, in couples, so as to cover between them a large tract of land; and each of them has a whistle and a hood, to call in the birds, if necessary, and hold them. So when the Great Kaan gives orders to let his birds fly, there is no need for those who do so to go after them, since there are these men I have mentioned, scattered about the country, who keep their eye on them so well that the birds can go nowhere without the men going there too. And if the birds need help, the men straightway give it.

All the Great Kaan's birds, as well as those of the barons, have a little silver tablet attached to their legs, bearing the name of the owner and of the keeper. In this way the birds are recognised as soon as they are taken, and returned to their owners. And if one does not know whose the bird is, it is brought to a baron called *Bularguchi*, a word signifying "the keeper of things without an owner." For you must know that if a horse or a sword or a bird or anything else is found, without its owner being known, it must at once be brought to that baron, and he has it taken and put away. If he who finds it does not straightway give it up, he is held to be a thief. And those who have lost something go to that baron; if he has the object, he at once has it handed over. He is always stationed at the highest point of the camp with his banner, so that those who have lost or found anything, may see at once where he is. In this way all that is lost cannot but be found again and returned.

And when the Great Kaan goes on this expedition I have told you of, in the neighbourhood of the Ocean Sea, there is no lack of fine sights in the way of the hunting of birds and beasts. There is no amusement in the world equal to it. And the Great Kaan always goes on four elephants, in a beautiful wooden chamber, all lined inside with cloths of beaten gold, and covered outside with lions' skins. He always remains inside it when fowling, as he is troubled with the gout. The Great Lord always keeps in it twelve of his best gerfalcons. There are also many barons and ladies to amuse him and keep him company. And when he goes journeying in that chamber placed on the elephants, you must know that if the barons who ride round him, cry out: "Sire, cranes are passing!" then he has the chamber uncovered above, and, on seeing the cranes, he has the gerfalcons he wants, brought to him, and casts them. The gerfalcons fight at length with the cranes, and generally take them. The Great Lord watches the sight, remaining in his bed, and finds great pleasure and amusement in it. And all the barons and knights ride round their Lord. And truly there never was, nor do I believe there is now, any man on earth able to have so much pleasure and delight as the Kaan, and to procure it with such ease.

So the Great Lord travels on until he reaches a place called Cachar Modun. Here he finds his tents pitched, and those of his sons, barons, and concubines; more than ten thousand tents in all, and every one richly adorned and beautiful. And I will tell you how the Great Kaan's tents are made.

They are more than one, as I shall tell you. The tent in which he holds his court is so large that it can contain a thousand knights; its door opens to the south, and in it, as in a pavilion, stand the barons and other people. Then there is another tent, connected with this one, facing west, in which the Lord lives; it is a kind of pavilion reserved for his use. When he wishes to speak to anyone, he summons him within. Behind the large hall, is a spacious and fine chamber where the Great Lord sleeps. There are also other chambers and tents, but they do not communicate with the large one. The large halls and the chamber are built as I shall tell you. Each of the two halls has three pillars of spice-wood, very cunningly carved and gilt. On the outside, they are all covered with lions' skins, which are most beautiful, for they are all striped in black and red and white; and they are so well arranged that the rain and the wind can do no injury within. Inside they are all lined with ermine and sable, which are the most beautiful, fine, and costly furs in existence. For you must know that a sable fur sufficient for a man's mantle is worth 2000 gold bezants, if good, and 1000 if of the ordinary kind. The Tartars call it the queen of furs. The animals are of the size of a weasel. Now, those two halls of the Great Kaan are lined with these skins, worked and decorated in a marvellous way.

And the chamber in which the Kaan sleeps, and which is connected with the two large halls, is also covered outside with lions' skins, and lined inside with sable and ermine. It is most cunningly constructed and arranged. And the ropes that brace the halls and the chamber are all made of silk. Those three tents are so valuable and costly, that no petty king could pay for them.

Around these tents stand all the other tents, excellently constructed and arranged. The Lord's concubines also have splendid tents. And the gerfalcons and hawks and other birds and beasts have many immense tents. What more shall I tell you? Know in very truth that there are so many people in that camp that verily it is a marvel. One would think the Kaan was in his finest city. For people flock from all sides. And, further, he brings all his servants with him, and with him are also his leeches, and astrologers, and falconers, and other officers in great number. And everything is as orderly as in his capital.

And you must know that he remains there till spring, that is to say, till about the season of our Easter. And during all that time he never ceases fowling in the lakes and rivers, catching cranes, swans, and other birds in abundance. His people, too, scattered on all sides around him, send him plenty of venison and game. And, all the time, he lives there in the midst of the greatest pleasure and entertainment; nor would anyone believe it, who had not seen it, for his splendour and delight are much greater than I have told you.

Another thing I will add, too; no merchant or artisan or peasant dare keep any falcon, or other bird for fowling, or any dog fit for the chase throughout the whole of the Great Kaan's dominions. And no baron or knight or any nobleman whatsoever dare hunt or fowl near the place where the Great Kaan lives, in some parts to a distance of five days' journey, and elsewhere to a distance of ten or even fifteen days' journey, unless he be entered in the rolls of the Captain of the Falconers, or have a special privilege. But beyond the limit of twenty days' journey, in all the other provinces and lands, barons, knights, and noblemen can hunt, and keep birds and hounds as they please. Know, too, that throughout all the lands where the Great Kaan holds sway, no king, no baron, no one, in a word, dare take or chase hares, fallow-deer, roebucks, stags, or any other animal of this kind, between the months of March and October; and this is in order that they may breed. And who should transgress this order, would be made bitterly to rue it, for so the Great Kaan has decreed. But I assure you that his commands are so respected, that often enough hares and deer and the other animals I have mentioned come right up to people, and no one touches them or does them any harm.

Even as you have heard, then, does the Great Lord remain in that place till, more or less, the time of our Easter. Then he goes away with all his people, and returns straight to the city of Cambaluc, along the same road by which he came, ever hunting and fowling, to his great entertainment and delight.

And when he reaches his capital city of Cambaluc, he stays in his principal palace three days, and no longer. He holds a great Court and gives splendid banquets, and has great pleasure and solace with his ladies. Truly it is a wondrous sight to see the great magnificence displayed by the Great Kaan during those three days.

[You have now heard how the Great Lord goes hunting and how he holds his Courts and has great entertainments on his return from Cachar Modun. I will now tell you how immense multitudes foregather in Cambaluc, and many things of great value are brought thither.]

Here is told of the great city of Cambaluc, of the many people that foregather in it, and of the precious things that are brought thither

You must know that, counting those inside and those outside the city (namely in the suburbs which, as you know, are twelve, and very large, stretching beyond each of the twelve city-gates), the houses and inhabitants of Cambaluc amount to such an immense number, that it is not possible to count them. There are many more inhabitants in the suburbs than in the city, for in them dwell and lodge all the merchants and other such people who come for their business; and they come in great numbers, both because the Lord lives in the city, and because Cambaluc is such a good market that many merchants and others go there for their business. And I assure you that the suburbs have as fine houses and palaces as the city, if you except, of course, that of the Great Lord. And within the city no dead man is buried: if an idolater dies, they carry him to the place where the body is to be burnt, which is beyond the suburbs; the same is done with the dead of other religions; they too are buried beyond the suburbs. Nothing sinister is allowed in the city. Another thing I will also tell you—no sinful woman may dwell within the city—I mean no women of the town who give themselves to men for money: they live in the suburbs. And there is an enormous number of them, such as no one can believe, for I assure you there are twenty thousand of them, who prostitute themselves for money. And yet they all find employment, on account of the great number of merchants and strangers that come and go every day. And as the number of harlots is such as I have told you, you may see from that whether or not there be an immense population in Cambaluc.

You must also know in very truth that there is no city in the world to which such rare and costly wares are brought. And first of all I will tell you what they are. All the rare things that come from India are brought to Cambaluc—precious stones, and pearls, and all kinds of other rarities. And also all the beautiful and costly products of Cathay and of the other provinces are brought thither. This is on account of the fact that the Lord lives there, as well as all those ladies and barons, and the immense multitude of people, and the soldiery, and all the other persons who come for the courts held there by the Great Lord. For this reason I have told you, rarer and costlier and more abundant wares are brought to Cambaluc than to any other city in the world, and more things are bought and sold there than elsewhere. For example, I tell you that a thousand cart-loads of silk enter Cambaluc daily. For they make much gold and silk cloth; indeed almost all the cloth they make is of silk, for they have great quantities of it, but no flax, and but little cotton and hemp. Moreover, round about Cambaluc, there are more than two thousand cities, at various distances, from which people come to sell goods, and procure for themselves whatever they may need. No wonder, then, that Cambaluc is as great a mart as I have said.

Now that I have told you all this clearly and in detail, I will next tell you about the mint and the money made in this same city of Cambaluc. We will show you clearly that the Great Kaan can do and spend much more than I have said or can say in this book. And I will show you why.

How the Great Kaan makes people use paper for money

You must know that in this city of Cambaluc is the Great Lord's mint, and it is so arranged that one may well say that the Great Kaan is a perfect alchemist! And I will straightway prove it to you.

Know, then, that he has money made as follows.

He has the bark taken of a certain kind of tree, that is to say of the mulberry-tree, the leaves of which are eaten by silkworms; then he has the thin layer of skin that lies between the bark and the trunk, removed; and he has this shredded and pounded into a kind of paste, together with glue; this he then has rolled out into sheets, something like paper, which are completely black. When the sheets are ready, he has them cut up into pieces of different sizes, but all of a rectangular shape, of greater length than breadth. The smallest piece is worth half a small tornesel; then there is one worth a whole tornesel (a small one, of course); then there is one worth half a silver *grosso*; then one worth a whole silver *grosso* (equivalent to a Venetian silver *grosso*); then there are some worth two, five, and ten *grossi*, and others worth one, two, three, or more bezants, up to ten. And all these sheets bear the Great Lord's seal. For you must know that all that money is issued with as much authority and solemnity as if it were of pure gold or silver. To each piece, certain officers, duly deputed for this task, write their names, and set their seals. When the money is all ready, the chief of these officers, especially deputed by the Kaan, smears the seal entrusted to his keeping with vermilion, and presses it on the paper, so that the impress of the seal smeared with vermilion remains upon it. Then that particular piece of money becomes authentic. And if anyone were to forge it, he would suffer capital punishment. The Great Kaan has this money made in such quantities, that he could pay with it for all the coin in the world.

When this paper-money has been prepared in the way I have told you, he has all payments made with it, and he has the money spent in all the provinces and kingdoms and lands that he rules over. And no one dares refuse it on pain of death. Yet I assure you that all his subjects, of all countries and peoples, readily accept that paper in payment, for wherever they go,

CHINESE BANK NOTE OF THE REIGN OF HUNG-WU (1368-1398)

they can pay for anything with it—wares of all kinds, pearls, precious stones, gold and silver. They buy what they want, and then pay with that paper. The paper given for ten bezants, does not reach the weight of one.

Further, many times a year merchants arrive in Cambaluc in groups, bringing pearls, precious stones, gold, silver, and other things, such as gold and silver cloths, and they offer all these things to the Great Kaan. The latter sends for twelve wise men, who see to these things and have much experience, and he bids them examine what the merchants bring, and have it paid what they consider the proper price. Then these twelve wise men look at the things and, appraising them according to their consciences, straightway have the value paid, to the advantage of the merchants, in the paper-money I have told you of. The merchants accept it very willingly, having to use it for all the purchases they make throughout all the lands of the Great Lord. And you may well believe that the things the merchants thus bring in the course of a year amount to quite 400,000 bezants in value. The Great Lord has everything paid for in that paper.

And I will also tell you that several times a year a proclamation is issued in the cities, to the effect that whoever possesses precious stones, pearls, gold or silver, is to bring them to the Great Lord's mint. And all do so, and they bring an enormous quantity of them. And they are all paid in paper. Thus the Great Lord has all the gold and silver, and all the pearls and precious stones of all his lands.

Another thing I will also add, that is worth telling you. When, through long use, those pieces of paper get torn or spoilt, they are taken to the mint, where new ones are given in exchange, three being, however, left out of every hundred. Yet another thing is worth telling in this book: if a man wishes to buy gold or silver for the purpose of making plate or girdles or anything else, he goes to the Great Lord's mints, taking that paper with him, and gives it in payment for the gold and silver he buys from the chief officer of the mint. All the armies, too, are paid in that kind of money.

Now I have told you how and why the Great Lord has, and cannot but have, the greatest treasure of any man on earth. But I will say still more: all the princes in the world do not together possess the wealth that the Great Kaan alone has.

I have told you in detail how the Great Kaan has money made out of paper. I will next tell you of the great officers of State, who are sent from Cambaluc on the Great Kaan's business.

Here is told of the two councils of barons set over all the Great Kaan's affairs

As has already been said before, the Great Kaan appoints twelve great and powerful barons, to decide upon everything that concerns the armies, namely as regards changing their stations, replacing or transferring their commanders, furnishing reinforcements according to the greater or lesser importance of a war, and so on. Moreover they have to distinguish between the brave and valiant fighters, and the cowardly and worthless ones, by promoting the former and degrading the cowardly and timid ones. So, if a leader of a thousand has borne himself in a cowardly fashion in some action, these barons, considering him unworthy of his command, degrade him, lowering him to the rank of a commander of a hundred. But if he has borne himself nobly and valiantly, they declare him worthy of a higher command, and make him leader of ten thousand. All these things, however, are done with the knowledge of the Great Lord. Thus, when they wish to lower or degrade someone, they say to the Kaan, " So-and-so is unworthy of such a command." He then answers, "Let him be degraded, and reduced to a lower rank." And so it is done. But if they wish to promote someone, because he deserves it, then they say, "Such and such a leader of a thousand is worthy of being a leader of ten thousand," and then the Kaan confirms this, and gives the man the Tablet of Authority belonging to his command, as we said before. After that, he gives him great gifts, in order to encourage the others to be valiant.

The office of these barons, then, is called *Thai*, which is saying as much as "Supreme Court"; there is, in fact, no higher authority above them, other than that of the Great Lord himself.

Besides these barons, the Great Lord has also appointed twelve more very great barons, to whom he has entrusted all the affairs of thirty-four provinces. I will tell you how they set to work, and also about their establishments.

I will begin by saying that these twelve barons live in the city of Cambaluc in a very beautiful and vast palace with many halls, and comprising many different buildings. For every province there is a judge and a body of clerks; they all live in the palace, each in a house of his own. The judges and clerks transact all the necessary business concerning the province to which they are assigned. They act according to the will and orders of the twelve barons aforesaid.

Moreover you must know that the authority of the twelve is even as great as I shall tell you. They nominate the governors of all the thirty-four provinces. When they have invested someone they consider fit and worthy, with such an office, they inform the Great Kaan; the latter confirms the appointment, and has the gold or silver tablet pertaining to the post given to the person. Further, these barons have to see to the collecting of tributes and dues, and the use and employment thereof, as well as to all the rest of the

Great Kaan's affairs concerning the above-mentioned provinces, with the exception of his armies.

These twelve are called *Shieng*, which also means "Supreme Court," for they have no higher authority above them, other than that of the Great Kaan himself. The palace in which they live is also called *Shieng*. In the whole court of the Great Kaan there is no authority higher than theirs, for truly they have the power of doing much good to whomsoever they will.

Neither of these courts, namely the *Thai* and the *Shieng*, has anyone above it, except the Great Kaan, yet the *Thai*, or court to which the care of the armies is committed is reputed nobler and greater than any other.

I shall not at present tell you the names of all those provinces, for I shall deal with them in detail in the course of this book. We will hence leave this subject, and tell you how the Great Lord sends his envoys, and how they find horses ready for their journeys.

How from the city of Cambaluc many roads lead out into sundry provinces

You must know that from this city of Cambaluc many roads lead out into sundry provinces; I mean one road leads to one province, and another road to another province. Each road bears the name of the province to which it leads. [And the Great Kaan has arranged that when his envoys ride along those roads, they should find everything they need ready for them.] For the way the Great Kaan's messenger-service works, is truly admirable; it is indeed arranged in a most excellent manner.

You must, in fact, know that along those roads the envoy of the Great Kaan who leaves Cambaluc and rides twenty-five miles, reaches at the end of that stage what in their language is called a *yanb*, that is, in our language, a horse-post station. There the envoy finds a very large and fine palace, where the Great Kaan's envoys lodge, with splendid beds, furnished with rich silk sheets, and with everything else that an important envoy may need. And if a king should go there, he would be splendidly lodged. Here the envoys also find no less than four hundred horses, always kept there by the Great Kaan's orders, in readiness for any envoys of his that he may send somewhere.

These post-stations I have mentioned are placed every twenty-five or thirty miles, along all the principal roads that lead to the provinces which I have mentioned before. In each of these the envoys find three or four hundred horses ready at their disposal. They also find as beautiful palaces as I have told you of, where they lodge with as much magnificence as I have said above. And this is so in all the provinces and kingdoms of the Great Lord.

And even when the envoys have to traverse roadless and mountainous regions, without houses or hostels, the Great Kaan has had post-stations built there, with the palace and all the other things, such as horses and harness, that the other stations have. Only the distances are larger, for they are placed at thirty-five, and even more than forty miles, from one another. The Great Kaan also sends people to live there and till the soil, performing the necessary services for the posts. Thus large villages are formed.

In this way, even as you have heard, the Great Kaan's envoys can go everywhere, and have hostels and horses ready for every day's journey. And truly this is the most splendid proof of magnificence and greatness that ever was given at any time by Emperor or King, or by any other mortal whatsoever. For you must know that more than 200,000 horses are kept in those stations merely for the envoys, while the palaces are more than 10,000, all richly furnished as I have told you. It is so wonderful a thing, and indicates such wealth, that it can hardly be described.

Someone might wonder how there are people enough to perform all these duties, and how they live. The answer is that all the Idolaters, and the Saracens likewise, each take six, eight, or ten wives, according to the number they can keep, and beget an infinite number of children. Thus you come across many of them who have more than thirty sons, all armed, following them. This is on account of the many wives. We, instead, have only one wife, and if she is barren, a man will end his days with her without begetting a single son; so we have not so many people as they. As for food, they have enough, since, for the most part, they make use of rice, panic, and millet, especially the Tartars, the Cathayans, and those of the province of Manji; and in their countries these plants yield a hundred measures for every one of seed sown. These people have no bread, but merely cook those three kinds of grain with milk, or else meat, and so eat them. In those parts wheat does not yield so much, but they eat what they have of it in the form of pan-cakes or other kind of pastry. In their countries no arable land is left barren. Their cattle increase and multiply immensely, and so, when they go campaigning, there is none of them but takes six, eight, or more horses for his personal use. Hence one may easily understand how it is that in those parts there is such a multitude of people, and how they can live in such plenty.

Another thing, too, I will tell you, that I had forgotten, but which is connected with the subject I dealt with above. You must know that every three miles, between the stations, there is a village, of some forty houses, where live foot-runners who also carry messages for the Great Lord. I will tell you how. They wear a broad belt, hung all around with bells, that they may be heard from afar when they are on the road. They always go at full speed, and only run three miles. At the end of the three miles, there is another messenger standing ready, waiting for the one who is coming, having heard him a long way off. When this messenger arrives, the other takes from him whatever he is carrying, receives a slip of paper from the clerk, and sets off at a run; he then goes three miles, when the same thing happens as at the previous station. And I assure you that in this way, by means of these runners, the Great Lord has news in a day and a night from places at a distance of ten days' journey. For you must know that these runners cover in a day and a night the distance of ten days' journey; thus, in two days and two nights, they carry news from a distance of twenty days' journey, and similarly in ten days and ten nights, they carry news from a distance of a hundred days' journey. And I assure you that many a time these men carry to the Kaan in one single day fruit from a distance of ten days. Thus, for example, often enough, during the proper season, fruits are picked one day in the city of Cambaluc and next day, towards evening, are brought to the Great Kaan in the city of Chandu, at a distance of ten days' journey. At each of these three-mile-stations, a clerk is appointed to register the day and hour one messenger arrives and the day and hour the other leaves. And this is done at all the stations. And there are certain men who are appointed to go and inspect these stations every month, and to see whether there be runners who have not been diligent, and punish them.

The Great Lord exacts no tribute from these runners or from those who live in the stations, and indeed pays them out of his own purse.

As for the horses of which I have spoken as being kept in such numbers in the stations in order to carry the envoys, I will tell you how the Great Lord has arranged matters. He asks himself, "What city is near such and such a station?" "Such and such a city." Then by his orders the Governors of the city enquire, by means of experienced men, how many horses that city can keep up for the envoys; and if the figure be, say, a hundred, the city receives orders to place a hundred horses at the nearest station. Then he has enquiries made as to the number of horses all the other neighbouring towns and villages can maintain, and each is given orders to keep at the stations as many horses as it can afford. The cities come to mutual agreements, since sometimes, before arriving at the next station, there is yet another city that gives its share. These cities keep the horses with the tributes they owe to the Great Kaan. Thus, for example, if a man is assessed with a tax that might keep a horse and a half, he is bidden to contribute to that extent to the cost of the nearest station. But you must know that the cities do not constantly keep four hundred horses at each station, but only two hundred a month actually working, while the other two hundred are fattening; at the end of a month, the fattened horses are placed at the station, and the others are sent to fatten; and so it goes on. And if it happen that in some place there be a lake or river that the runners or horse-messengers have to cross, the neighbouring cities constantly keep three or four boats ready for the purpose. And if it be necessary to traverse a desert several days' journey in breadth, where there are no dwellings, the city nearest to the desert is obliged to give the Lord's envoy horses, victuals, and escort as far as the other side; but these cities are helped by the Lord for such expenses. Thus, then, all the stations are provided for, so that they cost the Great Lord nothing for horses, as he furnishes with animals of his own only those placed in uninhabited regions.

I will also tell you that when it is necessary that the horse-messengers should go in great haste in order to inform the Kaan at once of the rebellion of some land or baron, or to bring him tidings that may be urgently needed by him, the horse-messengers can cover 200 and even 250 miles a day. And I will show you how.

When the messenger wishes to go at such speed, and cover in a day as many miles as I have said, he bears the tablet with the gerfalcon, to show that he must go as quickly as possible. If there are two messengers, they leave the place where they happen to be on two good horses, that are strong and swift. They swathe their bellies, and bind their heads, and then set off at full speed as fast as they can ride. When they approach the next station, they sound a kind of horn, that can be heard a long way off, as a signal that horses should be got ready. So they go on until they reach the end of the first stage of twenty-five miles; then they find ready two new horses, fresh and swift. They straightway spring to the saddle, without resting at all, and, once they are mounted, immediately set off again at full speed; nor do they stop until they arrive at the next station. Here they find more horses ready; they jump on to them as swiftly as before, and set off again. Thus they go on until evening comes. Even in this way do these messengers cover as much as 250 miles in order to bring news to the Great Lord. And, when necessary, they even cover three hundred. And if the case is very urgent, they also ride by night; if there is no moon, the men of one station run in front of them with lights as far as the next station. Still, by night these messengers do not go so fast as by day, on account of those who run before them with lights, and who cannot go so quickly. These messengers are very much prized.

Let us now leave this subject of the messengers, for we have told you everything about it clearly enough. We will next tell you of the bounty that the Great Lord shows twice every year towards his subjects.

How the Great Kaan has help given to his subjects in case of diseases of crops or cattle

Know, then, further, in very truth, that the Great Lord sends messengers throughout all his dominions—lands, kingdoms, and provinces—to see whether his subjects' crops have suffered from the weather, or from locusts or other plagues. And if they find that in some place the people have suffered damages, and lack corn, he not only exempts them from that year's tribute, but also himself has them furnished with corn, in order that they may have enough to eat and sow. And this is truly a great bounty on the part of the Great Lord.

This he has done in summer. In winter he has the same done for the cattle. Thus, if his messengers find that a man has lost his cattle on account of a murrain, he has some of his own given to the man, taking them from those he receives as tithes from the provinces; so he has him helped, and also exempts him for that year from all tribute.

But we will also tell you of another act of bounty on the part of the Great Kaan. If lightning strikes a flock of sheep or a herd of any other kind of animals, belonging to one or more persons, however large the flock or herd may be, the Great Kaan does not take the tithe for three years. Similarly, if lightning chance to strike a ship loaded with merchandise, he will take no duty on the cargo or any share of it, for he considers it ill luck if lightning strike someone's property. For the Great Kaan says to himself, "God hated this man, and hence has struck him with lightning." So he will not have it that such goods, struck by the wrath of God, should enter his Treasury.

Even as you have heard, does the Great Lord help and aid his subjects. Now that I have told you of this, I will tell you of something else.

How the Great Kaan has trees planted along the highroads

Now you must know the Great Kaan has bidden that on the highroads along which his messengers, as well as merchants and other people, travel, trees should be planted on both sides, at a distance of two paces from one another. And truly they are so high and big, that they can be seen from afar. The Great Kaan has had this done so that people should be able to see the roads and not miss their way, for you will find these trees even along desert roads; and then they are of great comfort to traders and wayfarers.

Along the roads, then, in every province and kingdom, the Great Kaan has trees planted so long as the soil makes it possible. In sandy and desert tracts, and on rocky mountains, where it would be impossible, he has stone cairns and pillars set up to show the way. And he has certain barons to whom he has committed the task of seeing to it that those roads are constantly kept in good condition. Further, as regards what we have said about the trees, the Great Kaan has them planted all the more willingly as his soothsayers and astrologers have told him that he who plants trees lives long.

We have told you of the trees along the roads. We will now tell you of something else.

Here is told of the wine that the Cathayans drink

You must know that in the province of Cathay most of the people drink such wine as I will tell you of. They make a drink of rice, adding many good spices, and prepare it so excellently, that it is better to drink than any other kind of wine. It is very clear and fine; it makes a man drunk sooner than any other wine, as it is very hot.

Now we will leave this subject, and tell you how stones are burnt like wood.

Here is told of a kind of stone that burns like wood

You must know that all over the province of Cathay there is a kind of black stone, which is dug out of the mountains like any other kind of stone, and burns like wood. These stones make no flame, except a little at the beginning when they are lit, like charcoal, and by merely remaining red-hot they give out great heat. They keep alight better than wood. If you put them into the fire at night and kindle them well, I assure you that they remain alight all night, so that you will still find the fire burning in the morning. And you must know that these stones are burnt all over the province of Cathay. True it is that there is no lack of firewood, namely, logs, but there is such a multitude of people, and so many stoves, that is to say baths, are constantly being heated, that the wood would not suffice; for there is no one but, if he can, goes at least thrice a week, and every day in winter, to the stoves to have a bath; every nobleman and rich man, further, has a bath in his own house to wash in. Thus the supply of wood would never be enough for so many fires. Hence they make great use of those stones not only because they are cheaper, but also because in this way they can save much wood.

Now we have told you of this subject, and we will next tell you of another thing, namely how the Great Lord sees to it that corn be not dear.

How the Great Kaan has immense stocks of corn gathered and stored, in order to be able to come to the aid of his subjects

You must know in very truth that when the Great Lord sees that corn is abundant and cheap, he has immense stocks of it gathered and stored in large buildings set apart for the purpose, in every province, and he has it looked after so well that it will not rot for three or four years. Of course, he lays in stocks of every kind of corn, such as wheat, barley, millet, rice, panic, and so on. And he has immense quantities of them stored. So, when certain kinds of corn lack, and there is dearth, then the Great Lord has recourse to these stocks, which, as I have said, are immense. Thus, for example, if wheat is being sold at one bezant for each measure, he has it sold at four measures for a bezant. And he distributes such an amount of it, that all can get some. Thus everyone has plenty of corn.

In this way the Great Lord provides for his people, against the dearth of corn. And this he does throughout all the lands over which he reigns.

Now we have told you this, and will next tell you of another matter, namely of the Great Lord's charity.

How the Great Kaan gives many alms to the poor

Now that I have told you how the Great Lord ensures abundance of corn for his people, I will next tell you how he gives many alms to the poor of the city of Cambaluc. You must know that he has a list drawn up of honourable and worthy families of Cambaluc who have fallen through some misfortune into indigence, and who, being unable to work, lack food. To these families, that may be of six, eight, ten, or more, or less persons, the Great Lord has wheat and other kinds of corn given, so that they may have sustenance for the whole year. And the number of these families is very considerable. When the proper time comes round, these families apply to the officials entrusted with all the Great Kaan's expenses, who live in a palace set apart for this purpose. They then show a paper stating how much they have received for their sustenance in the previous year, and so are provided for, to that extent, for the coming year. The Great Kaan also provides them with clothes, as he receives tithes on all wool, silk, hemp, and other materials of which clothes are made; these materials he has woven and made into cloth, in a building set aside for the purpose, where they are stored; and as all craftsmen are obliged to give him a day's work every week, the Great Kaan has clothes made out of the pieces of cloth, distributing to the aforesaid poor families such as are suitable for winter or summer, as the case may be. He also provides his army with clothes, and in every city has woollen cloth woven, paying for it with the city's tithes. And you must know that, according to their ancient customs, before they knew the Law of the Idolaters, the Tartars never gave alms; indeed, if a poor man went up to them, they drove him away rudely, saying, " Go with the curse of God, for if He loved you as He loves me, He would have done some good to you." But since the wise men of the Idolaters, and especially the *Bacsi* we mentioned before, told the Great Kaan that it was virtuous to provide for the poor, and that his idols would be greatly pleased thereby, he provided for the poor in the way we have said. And I assure you that if anyone goes to the Kaan's court to ask for bread, he is not denied it, alms being given to all those who go there; not a day passes but the proper officials dispense more than thirty thousand dishes of rice, or panic, or millet. This is done all the year round. Truly this is great bounty on the part of the Lord, who is merciful towards the poor among his subjects. And his subjects are so grateful to him for this, that they adore him like a god.

Now I have told you about this. We shall hence speak of other things, and also of the many astrologers in the city of Cambaluc.

Here is told of the astrologers of Cambaluc

What with Christians, Saracens, and Cathayans, there are in the city of Cambaluc some five thousand astrologers and soothsayers, whom every year the Great Kaan has provided with food and clothing, like the poor we have spoken of, and who constantly practice their arts in the city.

They have an astrolabe of their own on which are written the planetary signs, the hours, and the points of the whole year. Every year these Christian, Saracen, and Cathayan astrologers, each sect by itself, examine in this astrolabe the course and nature of the whole year, that is, the course of each moon; for they can see and discover what general conditions each moon will produce in the course of the year, according to the natural course and disposition of the planets and constellations, and according to their different properties: they see, namely, that such a moon will be marked by thunderstorms and tempests, another by earthquakes, another again by lightning and violent rains, and yet another by disease and pestilence, by wars and infinite discord, and so on for each moon. And they say that such things should happen according to the natural course and order of events, but that the power of God can make things more or less. Further they make many little booklets, in which they enter all that is to happen in that year, according to each moon; these booklets are called *tacuini*, and are sold at the price of one *grosso* to those who wish to buy them, in order to know what is going to happen that year. Those of them who are found to have come nearest to the truth are considered the most perfect masters of their art, and receive the greatest honour.

Moreover, if anyone has to undertake some important work, or to set out for some distant country for reasons of trade or for any other business, in a word, if anyone has to do something, and wishes to know beforehand how it will turn out, he applies to one of these astrologers, and says to him, "Look into your books, and see how the heavens are at present, for I should like to go on such and such business." Further, he tells him the year, day, hour, and point of his nativity. For, from the day a child is born, it is taught what to say concerning its nativity. This is the method they follow. You must know that the Tartars count their years by twelves, each year of the twelve having a special sign of its own. The first has the sign of the lion; the second, of the ox; the third, of the dragon; the fourth, of the dog; and so on, up to the twelfth. Thus, if a man is asked when he was born, he answers, "in the course of the year of the Lion, on such a day or on such a night, and at such an hour and such a point of such a moon"; that is to say, he will state the precise circumstances of his nativity, and the sign of the year, all which things fathers of children diligently enter in a book. When the tale of twelve years is told, and the twelfth sign is reached, they begin again with the first, and so go on, always in the same order. Thus, when someone asks an astrologer or soothsayer what will be the issue of his undertakings, and informs him of the day, hour and point of the moon of his nativity, as well as the sign of its year, the soothsayer, on inspecting the constellation and finding the planet under which the man was born, can tell him all in due order what will happen to him on his journey, or what will be the luck, good or bad, that his projects will have, in the course of all his affairs. So, for example, if he be a trader, the planet just then in the ascendant may be unfavourable to his trading, and he will have to wait for a more propitious planet; or perhaps the constellation directly opposite the city-gate through which he has to pass, may be contrary to his particular one, so that he must leave by another gate, or else wait for another constellation. Similarly, the soothsayer will be able to tell him that in such a place and at such a time he will meet with robbers; that at such another place and time he will come across rain and storm; elsewhere his horse will break its leg; elsewhere, again, he will lose part of his wares, or make gains. And so he will foretell him, as regards his return, all particulars, both good and bad, according as the stars are for or against him.

[We have told you of the astrologers of Cambaluc. We will now tell you certain things about the religion of the Cathayans, of their beliefs concerning the soul, and of certain customs of theirs.]

Here is told of the Law of the Cathayans, and of certain customs of theirs

You must know that Messer Marco found the people of Cathay superior to all others in excellence of customs and depth of learning, for they are ever intent upon their studies and scientific pursuits. Only one custom did he find among them that is to be abhorred, and that he entirely refrained from. They speak well and clearly, they greet you courteously, with a smiling and pleasant face, and they eat at table with gentlemanly elegance. And so it is with other things. They have great respect for their parents. And if a son causes them displeasure, or fails to help them at need, there is a public office to which is committed the sole task of severely punishing ungrateful sons, when they are proved to have behaved ungratefully towards their parents.

They are all idolaters, and take no thought for their consciences or of their souls, but merely of bodily pleasures and satisfactions.

They believe that as soon as a man dies, he is born again into another body, and that, according as his conduct in life has been virtuous or wicked, he passes from good to better, or from bad to worse. Thus, if he was a plain man and bore himself well while alive, he will be born again after his death from the womb of a noble woman; if, then, during his life as a nobleman, he behaves well he will be born again from the womb of a countess; then having again died, he will be born again of a princess; and so on, step by step, until he becomes a god. Similarly, if the son of a nobleman has borne himself ill, he will be born again as a peasant, and then as a dog, ever descending lower and lower.

And this is how they worship their gods. Each man keeps at home, hanging on one of the walls of his room, a statue representing the Supreme God of the Heavens, or else merely the god's name written on one of the walls. And they worship him as follows: They burn incense daily, raise their hands and gnash their teeth three times, praying the god to grant them good understanding and a long, happy, and joyful life. Stretched on the floor, they have another statue called *Natigai*, who is god of the things of the earth, to whom they only pray for earthly things, for such, namely, as are born on the earth. Near this god are his wife and children. They worship him in the same way, offering incense, gnashing their teeth, and raising their hands; they pray to him for fair weather, for the fruits of the earth, for children, and for other such things.

For malefactors who have been taken and put in prison for some crime or other, a time comes, every three years, as fixed by the Great Kaan, when they are all set free. They then go their ways, but a mark is branded on the jaw so that they may be recognised.

Further, the Great Kaan who now reigns, forbade all gambling and swindling, which once were more customary among these people than in any other place in the world. And in order to wean them from these habits, he used to say to them, " I have conquered you by the force of my arms, and all that you possess is mine; if you gamble, it is my property you are staking." Not, however, that he took anything away from them.

I will not omit adding how the subjects and barons

of the Great Kaan conduct themselves when they go into his presence. First of all, within a range of half a mile from the place where the Great Kaan happens to be, all the people are meek, peaceful, and quiet, out of reverence for his majesty, so that not a sound or noise is heard, or the voice of anyone shouting or speaking loudly. And all barons and noblemen carry with them a beautiful little vase, into which to spit while they are in the presence-chamber, for no one would dare to spit on the floor; and when they have spitten, they cover it up and put it away. They also have certain beautiful white leather buskins that they carry with them; when, on arriving at the court, they have to enter the presence-chamber because the Lord summons them, they put on those white buskins, and hand those they take off to the servants. This they do in order not to soil the carpets of silk and gold or of other materials, that are so beautiful and cunningly wrought.

Now I have told you all about this. We will hence tell you of other things : we will depart from the city of Cambaluc and go into the interior of Cathay, and speak of the great and splendid things it contains.

Here the book begins to tell of the great province of Cathay, and first of all of the river Pulisanghin

You must know, then, that the Great Lord sent Messer Marco, the author of this book, as an envoy into the parts lying to the west. He left Cambaluc, and travelled westwards for no less than four months' journey. We will hence tell you all that he saw, both on his outward journey and on his return.

After leaving the city of Cambaluc and travelling ten miles, one reaches a large river called Pulisanghin, which flows into the Ocean Sea, and on which many merchants sail with great quantities of wares. Over this river there is a most beautiful stone bridge, truly the finest in the world, and without equal. And I will tell you why.

You must know that it is no less than 300 paces long and eight paces broad, so that as many as ten horsemen can cross riding abreast. It has twenty-four arches, and twenty-three pillars on which the arches stand. It is all of grey marble, most excellently worked and put together. Along each side there is a parapet of marble slabs and columns, made as I shall tell you. The way that leads up to the bridge is rather broader at the bottom than at the top, but once you reach the top, the bridge is of one width all the way, as if it had been drawn with a line. At the beginning of the bridge, there stands a very large and tall marble column, resting upon a marble tortoise, with a big marble lion at the foot; another very beautiful lion, big and well-made, lies on the top of the column. At the distance of a pace and a half from this column, there is another, precisely the same as the first, with two lions. Between the two columns, to prevent people from falling into the water, is a grey marble parapet all adorned with different sculptures, and set into the columns. Thus it is, all along the bridge, from one end to the other. The descent from and the ascent to the bridge are similar. So that it is a truly splendid sight.

Now that we have told you of this beautiful bridge, we will tell you of other things.

Here is told of the great city of Jonju

After crossing that bridge, one travels thirty miles towards the west, always finding fine hostelries and vineyards and gardens, and most fertile fields and excellent springs. Then one at last comes to a city called Jonju, which is both large and beautiful. It contains many monasteries of the idolaters. The people live by trade and handicrafts. Beautiful gold and silver cloths, and very fine sendals are made there. There are also many hostelries for travellers.

One mile out of this city, one finds two roads, one leading to the west, and the other to the south-east. The westerly road is that of Cathay, the other leads towards the great province of Manji.

And you must know that travelling across the province of Cathay, towards the west, one finds, at ten days' journey from Jonju, the city of Taiuanfu. And all the time one comes across many fine cities and towns, with much trade and industry, beautiful fields, and splendid vineyards. The wine is taken to those parts of Cathay where it is not produced. There are also many mulberry-trees, from the leaves of which the inhabitants obtain much silk. The population is everywhere very friendly on account of the many cities, which are close to one another, while the cities themselves are so thickly populated, that along the road there is always a crowd of travellers. And this is due to the large amount of merchandise that is constantly being carried between the cities, and to the fairs that are held in each of them.

There is nothing else worth mentioning. I will only add that after travelling for five of the ten days I have mentioned, there is a finer and larger city than the others, called Acbaluc, where end, in this direction, the hunting preserves of the Great Kaan, within which no one dares go hunting except the Great Kaan himself and his servants, and those who are entered upon the rolls of the Captain of the Falconers. But beyond this limit anyone may hunt, provided he be a nobleman. The Great Kaan, however, hardly ever went hunting in those parts, and for this reason the wild animals increased and multiplied to such an extent, especially the hares, as to damage the crops of the whole province. When the Great Kaan was informed of this, he went there with all his court, and the number of animals caught was incalculable.

We will now leave this subject and tell you of a kingdom called Taiuanfu.

Here is told of the kingdom of Taiuanfu

After riding ten days from Jonju, one reaches a kingdom called Taiuanfu. The capital thereof is the city we have just mentioned, also called Taiuanfu, a very large and beautiful city, in which there is much trade and industry. Here are made great quantities of the war-gear needed by the Great Lord's armies. There are many fine vineyards, which produce wine in great abundance. And this district is the only part of the province of Cathay that produces wine, but from there it is taken all over the province. There is also a great deal of silk, for they have immense numbers of mulberry-trees and silk-worms.

On leaving Taiuanfu, one rides towards the west for seven days through a most beautiful region, where there are many cities and towns, all carrying on much trade and industry. Many a trader goes out from there into divers lands, getting great gain thereby.

At the end of the seven days, one reaches a city called Pianfu, which is both large and important, and where there are many merchants. The people live by trade and handicrafts. Great quantities of silk are produced there.

We will now leave this subject, and tell you of a very large city called Cachanfu. But first of all we will tell you of a noble castle called Caichu.

Here is told of a certain castle in the province of Taiuanfu

On leaving Pianfu, and riding two days westwards, one reaches a fine castle called Caichu, which was built in time past by a king who was known as the Golden King. In this castle there is a most beautiful palace with an immense hall, where, in splendid paintings, are the portraits of all the kings that ruled that province in the past; it is indeed a splendid sight. The hall is all gilt, and adorned with fine paintings. And all this was done by the various kings who ruled over that province.

This Golden King was a great and powerful prince, and while he lived in that castle, he kept only most beautiful damsels for his personal service, and he had a multitude of them at his court. When he went to take an airing in the grounds of the castle, he rode in a cart drawn by these damsels, who could easily do this because the cart was small and light. They also did everything that the king might need or wish for. And he proved himself a worthy prince, ruling nobly and according to justice.

I will now tell you a pretty story concerning what befel between him and Prester John, just as the people of those parts are wont to tell it.

How Prester John captured the Golden King

You must know, then, that, according to what they relate, this Golden King was at war with Prester John, and held so strong a position that Prester John could not attack him or in any way hurt him. And on this account Prester John was most dejected. So seven of his squires said to him that they would bring him the Golden King alive. Prester John answered that he would willingly let them try, and that he would be most thankful to them if they but succeeded. Taking leave, then, of Prester John, the seven squires all set out together, with a goodly band of yeomen, and went straight to the Golden King, telling him they had come from distant lands to enter his service. The king bade them be welcome, adding that he would give them honour and satisfaction.

Thus, even as you have heard, Prester John's seven squires entered the service of the Golden King. At the end of about two years' stay, they had become very dear to the King on account of their excellent service.

What more shall I tell you? The King trusted them as if all seven were his sons. But now you shall hear what those seven false squires did; and indeed it came about, because no one can guard against treachery and disloyalty. Know, then, that one day the Golden King went out for amusement with only a few followers, amongst whom were the seven false squires. When they had passed a river a mile away from the castle I have mentioned, the seven squires, seeing that the King had no followers who could defend him against them, thought that the opportunity offered to do what they had come for. They therefore put their hands to their swords, and told the King that either he went with them, or they would slay him. On seeing this, the King was greatly astonished, and asked them: "What is this, my good sons? What is it that you are saying? Whither am I to go?" And they answered: "You shall come with us to our Lord, Prester John."

When the King heard these words, he was so aggrieved, that he almost died of anguish. And he exclaimed: "Have pity, my sons! Have I not shown you sufficient honour beneath my roof? And will you place me in the hands of my enemy? Truly, if you do this, you will be committing a wicked and disloyal deed." But they answered that so it must be.

Thus, then, they led him to Prester John. And when Prester John saw him, he rejoiced greatly and said to him: "Not well, but *ill*-come be thou." And the other answered nothing, for he knew not what to say. Then Prester John ordered him to be led out, and put to mind the cattle. And thus it was that the Golden King was put to mind the cattle. This did Prester John do out of his spite towards him, to show him how he despised him, and to prove to him his nothingness, as compared with himself.

So he remained two years minding the cattle, closely guarded all the while, so that he might not escape.

Then Prester John had him summoned to his presence, had rich garments given to him, and received him honourably. Then he said to him: " Sir King, art thou now satisfied that thou wast no man to make war upon me?" " Truly, my good Lord," answered the king; " Well do I know, and always did know, that I was in no way a man to stand against you." " Since thou sayest so," replied Prester John, " I have no more to ask; henceforward I will grant thee service and honour."

Then Prester John had horses and arms given to the Golden King, and, giving him also a fair retinue, let him go. So the Golden King went his way, and returned to his kingdom; and from that time he was the friend and servant of Prester John.

We will now leave this subject, and tell you of something else.

Here is told of the great river Caramoran

On leaving this castle and riding some twenty miles westward, one reaches a river called Caramoran, so wide that there is no bridge that can span it; for truly it is very broad and deep and swift. It flows into the Ocean Sea. Along the river there are many cities and towns, with many merchants and thriving trade. In the region it crosses, there is a great deal of ginger, and abundance of silk. The number of birds there is prodigious, for you can have three pheasants for a Venetian *grosso*, or, rather, for an *aspre*, which is worth but little more. In the neighbourhood of the river there also grow great quantities of large canes, a foot or a foot and a half thick, that the inhabitants use for many of their needs.

After crossing the river, and riding two days towards the west, you reach a noble city called Cachanfu. The inhabitants are all idolaters, for as you know, the people of the province of Cathay are all such with a sprinkling of Christians and Saracens. It is a city thriving with trade and handicrafts. They have great abundance of silk, of ginger, galingale, spikenard, and many other kinds of spices, which are not brought into our countries. Much gold and silk cloth of all kinds is made there.

There is nothing else worth mentioning, and so we will leave this place and proceed, telling you of a noble city, called Kenjanfu, which is the capital of a kingdom.

Here is told of the great city of Kenjanfu

When one leaves the city of Cachanfu I have spoken of, one rides eight days westward, all the time passing many cities and towns, all of them thriving with trade and handicrafts, and many a fair garden and field. Further, the whole region is full of mulberry-trees, namely the trees on the leaves of which silk-worms feed. All the people are idolaters, apart from a few Turks, who are Nestorian Christians, and a handful of Saracens. There is plenty of game, both beasts and birds.

After travelling for those eight days, as I have said, one reaches this great and noble city of Kenjanfu, which is truly large and beautiful, and the capital of the kingdom of Kenjanfu, that once was a noble, wealthy, and powerful kingdom, ruled by many excellent and worthy kings; now, however, its lord and sovereign is a son of the Great Kaan's, called Mangalai, for his father presented him with this kingdom, and crowned him king thereof. The city is thriving with trade and handicrafts. They have great quantities of silk. Gold and silk cloths of all kinds are made there. They also make equipment of all sorts for the armies. They have all the necessaries of life in great abundance and very cheap. The city lies to the west, and the people are idolaters, but there are also some Turkish Nestorians and a few Saracens.

Outside the city stands the palace of king Mangalai,

which is a fine palace, as I shall tell you. It rises in a broad plain, full of rivers, lakes, marshes, and springs. In front of the palace is a very thick and high wall, some five miles in circuit, and very well built and embattled. Inside the wall there are great quantities of wild beasts and birds. In the middle stands the palace, which is so large and fair, that no one could imagine a fairer. There are many splendid halls and many fine chambers, all painted and adorned with beaten gold, and with the finest azure, and numberless marbles. This Mangalai rules his kingdom excellently, with justice and equity, and is greatly beloved by his subjects. The soldiers are quartered around the palace, and the abundant game furnishes them with plentiful sport.

We will now leave this kingdom, of which we will say no more. And we will tell you of a very mountainous province, called Cuncun.

Here is told of the frontiers between Cathay and Manji, and first of the province of Cuncun

On leaving this palace of Mangalai, one travels three days westward across a very fair plain, all the time passing many a city and town, the inhabitants of which live by trade and handicrafts, and have abundance of silk. At the end of three days' journey, one reaches high mountains and great valleys belonging to the province of Cuncun. And both on the mountains and in the valleys there are cities and towns. The people are idolaters, with a sprinkling of Turkish Nestorians and Saracens, and live by the fruits of the fields and of the forests and by the chase. For you must know, that they have many forests, with plenty of wild animals—lions, bears, lynxes, fallow-deer, roes, stags, and many more—so that they take them in large numbers, and get considerable gain therefrom.

Thus one rides twenty days through mountains and

valleys, and forests, ever coming across cities and towns and good hostelries, where travellers can lodge comfortably.

We will now leave this region, and tell you of another province, even as you shall hear.

Here is told of the province of Acbaluc Manji

At the end of the twenty days' journeying through the mountains of Cuncun, I have mentioned above, one reaches a province called Acbaluc Manji, which is all level. It has many cities and towns. It lies to the west. The people are idolaters. They live by trade and handicrafts. And you must know that ginger grows in this province in such quantities that it is carried all over the great province of Cathay, and the inhabitants derive great profit and gain from it. They have wheat, rice, and other kinds of grain in large quantities, and cheap; and indeed it is a land abounding in every good thing. The capital is called Acbaluc Manji, words signifying "the White City on the frontier of Manji."

The plain is two days' journey in extent, and they are most pleasant days on account of the wealth of the place, as I have told you, and of the many cities and towns. At the end of the two days, one comes to great mountains and valleys, and many large forests. So one goes on for no less than twenty days travelling westward, and passing many cities and towns. The people are idolaters. They live by the fruits of the soil, by the chase, and by cattle-breeding. There are lions, bears, lynxes, roes, fallow-deer, and stags; there are also quantities of the little animals that make musk.

We will now leave this region, and tell you of others, all in due order and clearly, even as you shall hear.

Here is told of the great province of Sindufu

When one has travelled twenty days westward through the mountains, as I have said, one reaches a plain where is a province, which also borders on Manji, and which is called Sindufu. Sindufu is also the name of the capital, which was once a great and noble city, and had powerful and wealthy kings. It has a circuit of no less than twenty miles, but now it is divided as I shall tell you. You must know that when the king of this province died, he left three sons; hence he divided the city into three parts, and gave one to each son. Each of these parts has its own wall, but all three are contained within those of the whole city. And you must know that the three sons of that king all became kings too, and each had vast dominions and a large treasure, for their father had been very powerful and rich. But the Great Kaan conquered this kingdom, and dispossessed the three brothers, keeping their lands for himself.

Now you must know that several large rivers, flowing down from the mountains far away, cross this city. These rivers surround it on all sides, and flow through it in various directions. Some of these are half a mile broad, others 200 paces, others again 150, some more, some less, and they are very deep. A great quantity of fish is caught in them. As these rivers flow out of the city, they all join and form a very large river, called Kiansui, which flows into the Ocean Sea, at a distance of some 80 or 100 days' journey. Along this river stand many cities and towns. There is great shipping on it, I mean an immense multitude of ships, such a number as no one who has not seen them, could ever credit. The amount and quantity of great merchandize that traders carry up and down this river is also so vast, that no one, who has not seen it, could possibly believe it. So big is the river, that you would rather think it a sea than a river.

I will tell you, too, of the great bridges inside the city, that span the various rivers that flow through it. Over these rivers there are many fine, big bridges, built of stone, and eight paces wide, varying in length according to the width of the river. All along either side, they have fine marble columns, that hold up the roof of the bridge. For all these bridges have very beautiful wooden roofs, painted in red with fair pictures, and covered with tiles. From one end to the other of each bridge, there are, on either side, little booths in which many trades and industries are plied. These little booths, however, are made of wood, and they are brought there in the morning and removed in the evening. There are also, on the bridges, the Great Kaan's Customs, that is to say, the officials who receive his dues, namely the tolls on the wares that are sold upon the bridges. And I assure you these tolls on the bridges are worth quite a thousand golden bezants a day.

The people are all idolaters.

On leaving this city, one rides five days across plains and valleys, passing many towns and villages. The people live by the fruits of the soil. There are many wild animals—lions, bears, and many more. They also live by handicrafts, for fine sendal and other cloths are made there. They, too, belong to the province of Sindufu.

At the end of these five days' journey, one reaches a much devastated province, called Tebet. We will tell you of it in the next chapter.

Here is told of the province of Tebet

At the end of the aforesaid five days' journey, one enters, then, a much devastated province, for it was laid waste in war by Mongu Kaan. There are many cities and towns and villages there, all ruined and destroyed.

One proceeds for twenty days through uninhabited places, where congregate large numbers of wild animals, such as lions, bears, lynxes, and many more, so that it is a dangerous journey. The following means of defence has been invented. There grow in those parts certain remarkably big and thick canes; for I assure you they are quite three palms in girth and fifteen paces long. The distance between the joints is quite three palms. Now, the merchants and other travellers who cross those regions by night, take some of these canes and burn them, for, as they burn, they make such reports and explosions as to terrify the lions and bears and other wild animals, and make then run away as fast as they can; nor for anything in the world would they go near the fire. Such fires, then, do the people make in order to protect their own animals from the wild beasts which are so numerous in that part of the country. For they have multiplied exceedingly on account of those regions being uninhabited. And no one could traverse them, but for those canes which make such reports as they burn, that they frighten the animals away. And I will also tell you—for indeed it is worth telling—how far away these reports can be heard, what terror they instil, and what the results are.

Know, then, that they take these canes when they are green, and throw them on to a good log-fire. When they have lain some time on the fire, the canes begin to warp, and burst in the middle, and as they burst they make such a report as can be heard at night ten miles away. And I assure you that if one is not accustomed to hearing them, one is struck dumb, so terrible is it to hear. And those who are not used to it, have to take some cotton, and fill their ears with it, and then swathe their heads and faces, covering them with all the clothes they have. And so, I assure you, when horses hear it, without ever having done so before, they are so terrified, that they break their halters and all the ropes with which they are bound, and gallop off. This has happened to many a traveller. But when one has horses that one knows have never heard it, one covers up their heads, especially their eyes and ears, and ties their four legs with iron hobbles, so that, when they hear the canes bursting, they cannot run away, even if they would. In this way, then, even as I have told you, do the travellers escape during the night, both they and their animals, from the lions and lynxes and other evil beasts that abound in that region.

And during all those twenty days' journey, one finds no hostelries, nor any supplies, except perhaps every three or four days; hence it is necessary to take with one food for both men and beasts.

At the end of these twenty wearisome days, during which one comes ever across so many fierce and cruel wild beasts, that are so dangerous and terrible, one reaches a region where there are many small towns and villages among the mountains. And their customs as regards marriage are as follows.

You must know that no one would for anything in the world take a virgin to wife, for they say that a woman who has not had commerce with many men is worthless; for they believe that a woman who has not been known by a man is hated by the gods, so that the men abhor and avoid her, since, were she dear to their idols, men would seek her out and desire her. This, then, is what they do. You must know that when strangers from foreign lands pass through this region, and set up their tents in order to rest, the old women from the towns and villages bring their daughters to the tents, arriving in groups of twenty to forty at a time, and offer the girls to the men, that they may have their will of them, and lie with them. So the men take them and disport themselves with these girls, keeping them as long as they like—but always in that place, for they may not take them away anywhere else. Later, when the men have had their will of them, and wish to leave, then each must give the girl with whom he has lain some jewel or other token, so that, when the time comes for her to marry, she may prove that she has had a lover. And every girl must procure over twenty such tokens for herself in this way, and these, as soon as she gets them, she hangs round her neck, to show that she has had many lovers, and that many men have lain with her. And the one who has the greatest number of tokens, and can show that she has had most lovers, and has lain with the greatest number of men, is esteemed more than the others; they marry her more readily, and say that she is more beloved of the gods than the others. And if it were to happen that one of them were to remain with child by some traveller, the child is kept by him who marries the girl, together with the other children, and with the same rights as they. But once they have married these women, they look after them closely, for they consider it a villainous deed to touch another man's wife, and they all carefully avoid it.

Now I have told you of the marriage customs, which were well worth relating. That is a fine country for young men from sixteen to twenty-four to go to!

The people are idolaters, and truly an evil lot. For they hold it no sin to rob and injure travellers, and they are the greatest brigands and robbers in the world. They live by the chase—both of beasts and of birds—by the fruits of the soil, and by breeding cattle. And you must also know that in that country there are many animals that make musk, and that in their language are called *gudderi*. There are so many of them that the perfume can be smelt all over the country, on account of the musk that these animals shed at every moon. For, as has been said before, there forms, near the navel of these creatures, an imposthume, like an excrescence, full of blood; and that blood is musk. But at every moon, this imposthume, being too full, sheds some of that blood; hence, as there are many of these animals in those parts, so that the musk is sprinkled in many places, the whole province smells of it. And those evil people have many excellent dogs which catch great numbers of these *gudderi*, so that they have large quantities of musk. They have no coinage, not even the Great Kaan's paper-money, but use salt as money. They dress very poorly, for their clothes are made of the skins of animals, of canvas, and of buckram. They have a language of their own, and they are called Tebet.

This province of Tebet is immensely large, and I will briefly tell you more about it, as you shall hear.

Here more is told of the province of Tebet

Tebet is an immensely large province, with a language of its own. They are idolaters, and border on Manji and on several other provinces. There are many great brigands. It is so vast a province that it contains eight kingdoms, and an infinite number of cities and towns. There are, in several parts, rivers, lakes, and mountains where gold-dust is found in considerable quantities. Cinnamon grows there in great abundance. Amber and coral find a market in this province, and at a very high price, for they hang them as a token of great joy around the necks of their women and idols. I will add, too, that in this province are made many camlets, and other kinds of cloth, both of silk and of gold. And there are many kinds of spices that never were seen in our countries. They have cleverer sorcerers and astrologers, after their fashion, than all the other provinces around them. For, by means of their diabolical arts, they perform the most terrible sorceries and the greatest wonders to see and listen to. Thus they produce storms and lightning at will, and, also at will they make them cease. They perform infinite marvels, but it is not well to tell them in our book, for too great would be people's amazement.

They are a barbarous people. They have very large mastiffs, as big as donkeys, very good for catching wild animals, and especially the wild oxen they call *beyamini*, which are very large and ferocious, as well as abundant. They also have various other kinds of dogs for the chase, and many excellent lanner and saker-falcons, that are very good fliers, and catch birds very well.

Now we will leave this province of Tebet, of which we have briefly told you everything, and we will speak of another province called Gaindu. But, as regards Tebet, you understand that it belongs to the Great Kaan; and all the other kingdoms and provinces and regions described in this book also belong to the Great Kaan, except those we mentioned at the beginning of the book, which belong instead to the son of Argon, as I told you. Apart from them, then, all the others described in this book belong to the Great Kaan; and even if you do not find it written, you must understand that it is as I have said.

But we will now leave this subject, and tell you of the province of Gaindu.

Here is told of the province of Gaindu

Gaindu is a province lying towards the west. (But if I say *west*, you must not think that these countries are to the west of *us*; it is that we have started from regions in the east and north-east, and travelled towards the west; hence we describe them as lying *to the west*.) Once Gaindu had a king of its own, but ever since it has been subject to the Great Kaan, the latter sends his own governors there. The people are idolaters, and subject to the Great Lord. There are very many cities and towns; the capital is also called Gaindu, and stands near the borders of the province. There is a great salt lake, in which many pearls are found; they are perfect as to colour, but, instead of being round, they are, so to speak, gnarled, as if four, five, six, or more pearls were united in one. The Great Kaan does not allow anyone to fish for them, for, if he let every one gather as many as are to be found, so many would be gathered, that they would become worthless, and lose their value. Of course, when the Great Kaan wants any, he has them fished for himself alone; but no one else may do so, without being put to death. And I will add that there is a mountain there, where one might find enormous quantities of a kind of stone called turquoise, that is very fine. But the Great Lord does not allow it to be extracted except by his own orders.

And you must know that in this province they have the custom I will tell you of, as regards their women.

No man holds it a villainy if a foreigner or any one else debauches his wife or daughter or sister or any other woman he may have in the house. Indeed he welcomes it if any one lies with them, for the belief is that thereby their gods and their idols will be more favourable to them, and grant them the things of this world in great plenty. This is why they give their women to foreigners with such generosity as I shall tell you. For you must know that when a man of this region sees a stranger coming to his house to lodge there, or for some other reason, he straightway leaves the house, and bids his women satisfy every desire of the stranger. He then goes on his business, to his fields or vineyards, and does not return as long as the stranger remains in his house. And I assure you that many a time the stranger will stay there even three days, lying with the wretch's wife. And to show that he is still in the house, the stranger makes use of this sign: he has his hat or some other object hung outside: and this means that he is still within. And as long as the wretched husband sees this signal outside his house, he does not return. And this they do all over the province. The Great Kaan, indeed, forbade this custom, but they have not left off following it, for they all observe it willingly, and no one accuses the other.

In the towns and villages situated on the mountains near the roads, there are many men with beautiful wives, who bestow them on passing merchants that they may have their pleasure of them. And the merchants give these women some bit of fine linen, say half an ell of it, or some other gewgaw of little worth. And when he has had his pleasure, the merchant mounts his horse again and rides off. Then the husband and wife cry after him in derision: "You, there, where are you going? Let us see what you are taking away of ours! Show us, you pariah, what you have gained! See instead what you have left us, what you have forgotten!" (And so saying they show him the bit of linen they have earned from him.) "This we have of yours, you wretch, and you carry nothing away with you!" And so they laugh at him. Such is their custom.

And I will tell you the kind of money they have. You must know that they have gold in rods, and its value is according to its weight in *saggi*. But they have no coined money. Their small change is as I shall tell you. They have certain briny water with which they make salt. They boil this water in pans; after it has boiled an hour, it hardens into a kind of paste. This they then put into a mould. The pieces are as big as a two-penny loaf, and can weigh about half a pound; they are flat below and round above. When they are ready, they are placed near the fire on very hot stones, and so they dry and become hard. Upon this kind of money the Great Lord's seal is printed. It can only be made by the officials of the Great Kaan. Eighty of these salt-loaves are worth one *saggio* of fine gold. Such is the small change they use.

But the merchants go with this money among the people who live in the wild and unfrequented parts of the mountains, and there they get a *saggio* of gold for sixty, fifty, and even forty of these salt coins, according as the place is more or less wild, and distant from the cities and from civilised people. This is because the inhabitants cannot always, for lack of buyers, sell their gold when they want; and the same applies to their musk and other things. Hence they sell their gold cheap, all the more as they find it in the rivers and lakes, as I have said. These merchants also travel over the mountains and regions of the aforesaid province of Tebet, where this salt-money is also used. And they get great gains and profit, for these people use the salt-money both to buy themselves necessaries and to season their food. In the cities, however, they only use broken pieces for their food, and use the whole pieces as money.

They have immense numbers of the animals that make musk, and the hunters catch them, and take the musk of which they have great quantities. They have plenty of excellent fish that they get in the lake I have mentioned, where the pearls are to be found. There are also many lions, lynxes, bears, fallow-deer, and roes, and abundance of birds of all kinds. They have no wine made of grapes, but prepare it with wheat and rice, together with many different spices; it is an excellent drink. In this province there are plenty of cloves. They grow on a small tree, with leaves like a laurel, but somewhat longer and narrower; it bears little white flowers, like our clove. They also have quantities of ginger, and of cinnamon, too, as well as many spices that, as they never come to our countries, are not worth mentioning.

Now we will cease speaking of this part of the province containing the capital, for we have told you all that is necessary about it, and we will speak of the rest of the province.

When one leaves this city of Gaindu, one rides quite ten days, passing through many cities and towns. The nature of the people is the same, and they have the same customs as those I have described. They have plenty of game, both beasts and birds.

At the end of those ten days' journey, one reaches a large river called Brius, where the province of Gaindu ends. In this river great quantities of gold-dust are found. There is plenty of cinnamon. The river flows into the Ocean Sea.

Now we will cease speaking of this river, as there is nothing more worth mentioning, and we will tell you of another province called Carajan, even as you shall hear.

Here is told of the great province of Carajan

After crossing this river, one enters the province of Carajan, which is so large that it comprises no less than seven kingdoms. [And I will tell you of the first of them, which is called Yachi.]

It lies towards the west. They are idolaters, and subject to the Great Kaan, but their king is the latter's grandson, Esentemur, who is a great king, both wealthy and powerful. As he is also wise and valiant, he governs his dominions excellently well.

After leaving the river I have told you of, one rides five days to the west, passing through many cities and towns, in regions where very good horses are bred. The people live by cattle-breeding and by the profit they get from the soil. They have a language of their own, which is surpassingly difficult to understand.

At the end of the five days, one finds the most important city, called Yachi, which is the capital of the kingdom, and very large and noble. There are many merchants and craftsmen in it. There are different kinds of people: some of them worship Mahomet, others are idolaters, and a few more are Nestorian Christians. They have abundance of wheat and rice, but they do not eat wheaten bread, because it is unhealthy in that province; they eat rice instead. With rice and spices they prepare a very fine, clear drink, that makes one drunk like wine. Their money is as I shall tell you.

They use white porcelain, namely the shells one finds in the sea, such as are hung around a dog's neck. Eighty of them are worth a silver *saggio*, that is to say two Venetian *grossi*; and you must know that eight *saggi* of fine silver are equivalent to one *saggio* of fine gold. They have briny wells from which they get salt, enough to provide the whole district with it. And I assure you the King draws no little profit from that salt. And I will also tell you that they care little if a man lies with another man's wife, provided it be by the woman's will.

We have now told you of this kingdom, and will next tell you of the kingdom of Carajan; but first I will tell you something else I had forgotten.

You must know that they have a lake, quite a hundred miles in circuit, in which there is an immense quantity of the best fish in the world, large in size and of many different kinds. Moreover, I will add that they eat raw the flesh of chickens, sheep, oxen and buffaloes. The poor people go to the slaughter-house and get raw liver, just as it is taken from the animal; they then cut it up small, put it into a garlic sauce, and so eat it. Thus they do with other meats also. And the noblemen, too, eat raw meat; but, after having it minced very small, they put it into a garlic sauce mixed with excellent spices, and then eat it with as much pleasure as that with which we eat cooked meat.

And now we will tell you of the kingdom of Carajan I have just mentioned.

Here is still told of the province of Carajan

On leaving the city of Yachi, and travelling ten days westward, one reaches the kingdom of Carajan, the capital of which is also called Carajan. They are idolaters, and subject to the Great Kaan. And the king is Cogachin, who is a son of the latter. Gold-dust is found in the rivers of this province. In the lakes and on the mountains, gold is also found in larger pieces. Indeed they have so much gold that I assure you they give one *saggio* of it for six of silver. In this province, also, they use as money the porcelain shells I mentioned before. These are not, however, found in the country, but come from India.

In this province there are great snakes or serpents of such immeasurable size as to strike you dumb; and they are truly hideous, both to look upon and to hear of. I will tell you how big and long they are. Know, then, that in very truth there are some ten paces long, as big as a large cask, for they have a girth of some ten palms. These are the biggest. In front, near the head, they have two short legs, without feet, but furnished with three claws, one large and two small, like those of falcons and lions. They have a very big head, and eyes larger than a big loaf; their mouth is so big, that they can swallow a man whole; their teeth are enormous. They are so immeasurably large and fierce, that there is no man or beast that does not fear them; all are terrified by them. There are also smaller ones, five to eight paces in length.

And this is how they are captured. You must know that in the daytime, on account of the great heat, they remain underground; at night they come out to feed, and they take all the animals they can catch. They go to drink in the rivers, lakes, and springs. They are so long, heavy and big, that, when at night they go out across the sand to feed or drink, they make great furrows in it, so that you would think a full cask of wine had been dragged along. In the places where they see that these snakes pass, the hunters who go to catch them, place a certain trap. When they see that, in order to drink, the snake usually follows a given course leading to some steep bank, they plant on the slope of the latter a big and strong wooden stake so deep into the ground as to be barely visible; on the top of the stake is fitted a steel blade, as sharp as a razor or as a lancepoint; this sticks out about a palm above the stake, and is slightly inclined in the direction from which the snake usually comes. Of such stakes and blades the hunters plant a large number. When the proper time comes round, the snake or serpent goes down towards the river to drink, and since on reaching the place where these blades are, it tumbles rapidly on, on account of the steep slope, it strikes so hard against these blades, that it is ripped up from the breast to the navel, so that it dies on the spot. The hunter knows that the beast is dead from the cries of the birds, and so goes up to the place; for otherwise he would not dare to approach. Thus, then, do the hunters catch these serpents.

When they have caught one, they take out the gall from its belly and sell it very dear. For you must know that it is much used as physic. Thus, if a man is bitten by a mad dog, he is given a little of it to drink—a small pennyweight—and he recovers immediately. Again, if a woman has difficulties in travail, and suffers and cries greatly, they give her a little of this gall, and as soon as she has drunk it, she is straightway delivered. The third use is when a man has a tumour; they put a little of this gall on it, and in the space of a few days the man is well again. For such reasons, then, the gall of these animals is very much prized in that province. Moreover, the flesh of these serpents is sold at a high price, as it is excellent to eat, and the people like it very much.

I will add that these snakes also go to the dens where lions, bears, and other wild beasts bear their young, and devour them all, parents and cubs, if they can but get at them.

Further I will tell you that in this province large numbers of horses are bred, which are taken to India to be sold. And you must know that they cut off two or three joints from the horses' tails, to prevent their hitting their riders with them, and flapping their tails as they run, for they think it most unseemly, that a horse should flap its tail as it runs. And you must also know that the people of this province ride with long stirrups, like Frenchmen. (I say *long*, because the Tartars and almost all the other peoples use short stirrups, on account of their being archers, since, when they shoot an arrow, they are wont to raise themselves on their horses.)

They wear armour of buffalo-hide, and have lances, shields, and arbalasts; and they poison all their arrows.

All of them, both the men and the women, are always provided with poison, especially such of them as intend mischief. This is in case one of them should be taken after committing some crime, and have to submit to torture. For, rather than endure the sufferings of the bastinado, they put the poison into their mouths and swallow it, in order to die as quickly as possible. But as the authorities are prepared for this, they always keep dog's dung ready, so that, should a prisoner take poison for the reason we have stated, they immediately make him swallow the dung in order to make him vomit the poison. Such is the remedy found by the authorities, and it has very often been put into practice.

I will also tell you of another thing that these people used to do before the Great Kaan conquered them. If it happened that a handsome and noble man, or any other person who had a fine shadow, came to lodge in the house of a man of this province, they killed him at night with poison or with some other means. But you must not suppose they did so in order to steal his money, but because they thought that his fine shadow and his good graces, as well as his wisdom and his soul, remained in the house. And so they killed many a man for this reason, before the Great Kaan conquered them. But ever since the Great Kaan conquered them —which was some thirty-five years ago—they no longer indulge in this evil practice, out of fear of the Great Lord, who does not allow it.

We have now told you of this province. We will now tell you of another country, even as you shall hear.

Here is told of the great province of Zardandan

When one leaves Carajan, one travels five days westward, reaching a province called Zardandan. They are idolaters, and subject to the Great Kaan. The principal city of this province is called Vochan. All the people have gold teeth; that is to say, each tooth is covered with gold. They make a gold case, fitted to their teeth, and cover both the upper and lower ones. This the men do, but not the women. Moreover the men have all round their arms and legs certain bands or strips of black dots, made as follows. They take five needles tied together, with which they prick their flesh until the blood flows; then they put a black dye on, which cannot come off. And they consider it noble and elegant to have these bands of black dots. Further, the men are all gentlemen, after their fashion, and do nothing but go campaigning or hunting or fowling. The women do everything, as also the men captured in war, whom they keep as slaves. These men and the women do everything that is necessary.

When a woman has been delivered of a child, the latter is washed and swathed, and then the woman's husband gets into bed, keeping the child with him. Thus he lies in bed some twenty days—or longer, according to the local custom—without getting up, except for some necessity. All his friends and relatives come to see him, and keep him company, making great festivity. This they do because they say that the woman has had a hard time of it carrying the child in her womb, and so, they say, for a certain time, twenty days or more, she is to have no more of it. Thus, as soon as a woman has borne a child, she gets up, and sees to all the household affairs, and serves her husband who remains in bed.

They eat all kinds of meat both raw and cooked. And they also eat rice cooked with meat and other things, according to their fashion. They drink wine, which they make with rice and good spices; and it is excellent. For money they have gold, but they also use porcelain shells. And I assure you that they give one *saggio* of gold for five of silver; this is because there is no silver mine at less than five months' journey. For this reason merchants come with much silver, and change it with these people, giving five *saggi* of it for one of gold. From this the merchants make great profits and gains.

These people have neither idols nor churches, but worship the founder of the family; for they say: "From him are we descended." They have no alphabet, nor any kind of writing. Nor is this any wonder, for they are born in impassable regions, in great forests and vast mountains, through which one cannot go in summer for anything in the world, for at that season the air is so bad and impure, that no foreigner would be able to survive. But when they have any business with one another, they take a round or square piece of stick, and split it in two; and one takes one half and the other takes the other half. But before they split it, they make two or three notches in it, or as many as they wish. So, when one of them comes to pay another, he gives him the money or whatever it is, and gets back the piece of stick the other had.

And you must know that in all these provinces I have mentioned, namely, Carajan, Vochan, and Yachi, there are no leeches. When one of their noblemen falls ill, they call their magicians, namely the devil-charmers and those who keep the idols. When these magicians are come, the sick man tells them what he feels. Then the magicians begin to play their instruments, and sing and dance round, until one of them falls flat to the ground or on the floor, foaming at the mouth, and looking dead. When the other magicians (for several of them come) see that one of their comrades has fallen as I have told you, then they begin to speak to him, asking what disease the sick man has. And he replies: "Such and such a spirit has stricken him, because he has displeased him in some way." And so he mentions the name of the spirit. Then the magicians say: "We beg thee to forgive him, and to take whatever thou wilt in exchange for his recovery." When these magicians have said many things and uttered many prayers, the spirit inside the body of the fallen man, replies. And if the sick man is to die, the spirit answers saying: "This sick man has so grievously offended such and such a spirit and is so wicked, that he will not forgive him for anything in the world." This is the answer that those who are to die receive. But if the sick man is to recover, the spirit inside the body of the magician answers, saying: "He has sinned much, yet he shall be forgiven. But if the sick man wishes to recover, let him take two or three sheep, and prepare ten or more costly and excellent beverages." Then the reply specifies that the sheep must be black-faced or of some other kind, and adds that all this is to be offered to such and such an idol and such and such a spirit, and that so many magicians and women—of those who serve the spirits and idols—are to be present at the offering, and that great praises and festivity are to be made in honour of the spirit and idol. When the magicians have received this answer, the sick man's friends straightway perform what the magicians tell them. They take the sheep of the kind prescribed, and they prepare such beverages, as the spirit has asked for, in the quantity and of the excellence commanded. They slaughter the sheep, and sprinkle their blood where they are told, in due honour and sacrifice to the spirit. Then they cook the sheep in the sick man's house, and there the prescribed number of magicians and women foregather. When they have all come, and the sheep and drinks are ready, they begin to make music, and dance, and sing certain lauds to the spirits; they sprinkle some of the broth and some of the drinks, and, moreover, go incensing here and there with incense and aloes-wood. And they make a great illumination. When they have done this for some time, then one of them falls to the ground, and the others ask him whether the sick man has been forgiven, and is to recover. He answers and says that the sick man is not yet forgiven, but that they are to do such and such another thing, and then he will be forgiven. And it is done at once. Then the spirit answers that as the sacrifices and everything else have been performed, the sick man is forgiven and will soon recover. When they have received this answer, and have sprinkled the broth and the beverages, and made great illuminations, and burnt much incense, they say that the spirit is at last on their side. Then the magicians and the women—namely those in the service of the spirits—eat the sheep, and drink the beverages, with great mirth and festivity. Then they all go home again. After all this has been done, the sick man recovers at once, for these responses almost always come true. But if by chance the sick man were not to recover, then they say that the sacrifice has been impaired, namely that those who prepared the food tasted it before the idol had been given its share. These ceremonies are not performed for any ordinary man, but only once or twice a month for some rich nobleman. And the custom is still observed all over the provinces of Cathay and Manji, and by almost all the idolaters, for they have no great numbers of leeches.

Now we have told you of the way of living and of the customs of these people, and how these magicians can charm spirits. We will now cease speaking of this people and this province, and tell you of others, as you shall hear.

How the Great Kaan conquered the kingdom of Mien and Bangala

But you must know that I had forgotten to tell you of a glorious battle which took place in the kingdom of Vochan, and which is worthy of being mentioned in this book. We will hence describe it to you in detail, explaining why and how it came about.

You must know that in the year 1272 after Christ's Incarnation, the Great Kaan sent a large army into the kingdoms of Vochan and Carajan in order to protect them from other peoples that might ravage them. For as yet the Great Kaan had not sent any of his sons there, as he was to do later, when he made Esentemur king, who was the son of a deceased son of his. Now, there was a king of Mien and Bangala, who was very powerful in lands, treasure, and people, and not subject to the Great Kaan, though before long the latter was to defeat him, and deprive him of the two kingdoms I have mentioned. Well, it happened that this king of Mien and Bangala, on hearing that the Great Kaan's army was at Vochan, said to himself that it was necessary that he should fall upon it with such a force as might suffice to destroy it, so that the Great Kaan should never again think of sending another army into that province. So this king made great preparations, and I will tell you what they were. You must know then, in very truth that he got together two thousand very large elephants, and on each of them he had a very strong wooden tower placed, very cunningly made, and suitable for fighting; and in each tower there were at least twelve soldiers, but in some there were sixteen, and even more. He further mustered quite 40,000 men, including horsemen and a small number of foot-soldiers. He made, that is, all his preparations as became the great and puissant monarch that he was. For truly his army was capable of carrying out a great enterprise. What more shall I tell you? When he had completed all these preparations I have mentioned, he did not delay any longer, but straightway set out with all his men, in order to attack the Great Kaan's army at Vochan. And so they marched on without encountering any adventure worth mentioning, until they were at three days' journey from the Tartar army. Here the King pitched his camp in order to rest his men.

Here is told of the battle between the Great Kaan's army and the King of Mien

When the leader of the Tartar army knew for certain that this king was coming against him with so great a force, he could not but be uneasy, for he had only 12,000 horsemen. Still he was certainly a most valiant man and a good leader. His name was Nescraddin. So he disposed and exhorted his men very well, and made every effort, to the best of his ability, in order to defend the country and his people. But why should I make a long story of it? You must know that the Tartars, 12,000 horsemen in all, came to the plain of Vochan, and there halted, waiting for the enemy to come to attack them. And by doing so they showed that they possessed much wisdom and were well led. For you must know that by the side of the plain, was an immense forest, thick with trees.

Thus, then, as you have heard, did the Tartars await the enemy in the plain. But we shall cease speaking of them a moment, for we shall be telling of them again presently; let us instead speak of their enemy.

Now you must know that the king of Mien and his men, after a brief rest, raised their camp, and set out again; and so they marched on until they came to the plain of Vochan, where the Tartars were all ready for them. When they reached that plain, at about a mile's distance from the enemy, the king arrayed his elephants, with their castles containing the fighting men, all well armed. He then marshalled his horsemen and foot soldiers skilfully and prudently, like the wise king he was. When he had thus ordered and prepared everything, he set out against the enemy with his entire force.

When the Tartars saw them advancing, they did not betray any signs of dismay, but on the contrary showed themselves most valiant and hardy. For, in fact, you must know that they all advanced together, properly and wisely arrayed, against the enemy. When they were near, and nothing remained but to begin the fight, the horses of the Tartars, on seeing the elephants, were so overcome by terror, that it was impossible for their riders to make them go on towards the foe; in spite of all efforts, they kept on turning back. And the king and his men, together with the elephants, kept on advancing.

Here is still told of the same battle

On seeing this, the Tartars were sore dismayed, and knew not what to do, for they clearly understood that, should they be unable to make their horses advance, all would be lost. However they succeeded in overcoming the difficulty very skilfully; and I will tell you what they did. You must know, then, that when the Tartars saw their horses were so terrified, they all dismounted and, leading the horses inside the wood, tied them to the trees. Then they took their bows, and, drawing them, shot their arrows against the elephants. They shot so many that it was truly a wonder. And the elephants were cruelly wounded. The king's men, too, also let fly showers of arrows upon the Tartars, and pressed hard upon them, but the Tartars were much better soldiers than their enemies, and defended themselves with great prowess. What more shall I tell you? Know that when the greater part of the elephants had thus been struck by arrows as I have said, they turned in flight towards the king's own men, and with such fury that the whole world seemed to be collapsing. They only stopped when they reached the forest, into which they forced their way, breaking the towers, and smashing and crushing everything. For they went hither and thither in the wood, with the fury born of fear. When the Tartars saw that the elephants had turned tail in this way, they delayed not a moment, but straightway mounted their horses, and fell upon the king and his men. They began the fight with arrows, and it was a most cruel and terrible one, for the king and his men defended themselves valiantly. So, when they had shot all their arrows, they took up their swords and maces, and fell furiously upon one another. The fiercest blows were exchanged. Now could one see men giving and receiving mighty blows with swords and maces. Now could one see horsemen and horses hewn down. Now could one see hands and arms and bodies and heads cut off. For you must know that many a man fell to the ground, dead or mortally wounded. The noise and uproar were so great that one would not have heard God's thunder. Terrible and fierce were the melley and the struggle on all sides. But you must know that without doubt the Tartars had the best of it. Truly in an ill hour had the battle begun for the King and his men, so many of them were slain on that day. And when the struggle had lasted till after midday, the King and his men were reduced to such a sorry plight, and so many of them lay slain, that they could no longer hold out. For they saw clearly enough that if they tried to do so, they would all be killed. Hence they would remain no longer, but fled as fast as they could. When the Tartars saw that the enemy had turned tail, they hewed them down, and gave them chase, slaying them so mercilessly that truly it was a pitiful sight to see. When they had pursued them for some time, they ceased doing so, and entered the woods, in order to capture some of the elephants. And you must know that they cut down great trees to lay them in front of the elephants, and bar their passage; yet even this was not enough to enable them to catch them. But the king's own men who had been taken prisoners, succeeded in capturing them; for the elephant is more intelligent than any other animal. And so they captured over two hundred elephants. After that battle, the Great Kaan began to keep elephants in large numbers.

Thus, then, went the battle, and the Tartars had the victory. And this was because the host of the king of Mien and Bangala was not armed like that of the Tartars, and also because the elephants in the first rank were not protected with armour in such a way as might enable them to withstand the enemy's first arrow-shower and fall upon them and disarray their ranks. But, what is still more important, the king should never have attacked the Tartars in that position, with the forest behind him, but should have awaited them in the open country, where they would have been unable to withstand the attack of the first armed elephants, and then, with his two wings of horsemen and foot soldiers, he would have surrounded and destroyed them.

How one goes down a great descent

On leaving this province of which I have spoken, one begins to go down a great descent. And you must know that one rides no less than two and a half days constantly down hill. During these two and a half days, there is nothing worth mentioning, except that there is a large place where a great market is held, for all the people of the district go thither on certain fixed days, three times a week. They exchange gold for silver, giving one *saggio* of gold for five of silver. Here foregather merchants from very distant countries, and exchange their silver for these people's gold; and I assure you that they get great profit and gain thereby. And as for the people of the country who bring the gold, no one can go to their homes where they live, in order to do them any harm, so strong and impassable is the region they inhabit. Indeed no man knows where they live, for no one ever goes there but themselves.

After these two and a half days' descent, one reaches a province towards the south, on the borders of India, called Mien. One travels fifteen days through difficult country and great forests, where there are elephants and unicorns in great numbers and many other kinds of wild beasts. There are neither men nor dwellings. For this reason we will say no more of these forests, but tell you a story, as you shall now hear.

Here is told of the city of Mien

Now, you must know, that when one has travelled for those fifteen days over difficult ground, one finds a city called Mien, which is very large and noble, and is the capital of the kingdom. The people are idolaters, and have a language of their own. They belong to the Great Kaan. And in this city there is a very noble thing that I will tell you of.

You must know that once there was in this city a rich and powerful king. When he was about to die, he bade that on his tomb, namely on his monument, two towers should be built, one of gold and one of silver, made as I shall tell you. They were built of fine stone, and one of them was covered with gold, quite a finger in thickness; and the whole tower was covered with it, so that it seemed made entirely of gold. It was quite ten paces high, and of a breadth duly proportionate to its height. The upper part was round, and hung all about with gilt bells, which tinkled every time the wind blew among them. The other tower was of silver, and in every way similar to the first, being made in the same way, of the same size and shape. Moreover the tomb itself was covered partly with gold and partly with silver. This the king had had done for his glory, and for his soul's good. And I assure you that they were the finest towers in the world to look upon, and of immense value. When they were touched by the sun, they shone and could be seen glittering from a great distance.

Now thus, even as I shall tell you, was this province conquered by the Great Kaan. You must know that at the Great Kaan's court there was a large number of jugglers and tumblers, and the Great Kaan said to them that he wished to send them to conquer the province of Mien, and that he would give them leaders and help. This he designed doing, in order to show the king of Mien how much he despised him, and to punish him for having taken up arms against him. The jugglers replied that they would willingly do so. Hence they set out with the leaders and the help that the Great Kaan gave them. What more shall I tell you? Know that these jugglers, together with the men who accompanied them, conquered this province of Mien. When they had conquered it, and had come to the noble city of Mien, they saw those two splendid and rich towers, and greatly marvelled at them. So they sent word to the Great Kaan, to tell him what those towers were like, and how beautiful and precious they were, adding that, if he wished, they would break them up, and send him the gold and silver. But the Great Kaan knew that that king had had them built for his soul's good, and in order that he might be remembered after his death, and so he answered that he would not have them broken up, but wished them to remain even as the king, who had built them, had bidden. Nor was this any wonder, for I assure you that no Tartar touches anything belonging to the dead, or upon which the judgement of God has fallen—be it by lightning or pestilence—nor will he receive any tribute on such things.

They have many elephants and wild oxen, both large and fine; they have also great numbers of stags, fallow-deer, roes, and all kinds of other animals.

Now I have told you of this province of Mien. We will therefore leave it, and tell you of a province that is called Bangala, as you shall hear.

Here is told of the great province of Bangala

Bangala is a province lying towards the south, which, in the year 1290 after Christ's Nativity, when I, Marco, was at the Great Kaan's court, had not yet been conquered, but the Kaan's armies and men were already there to conquer it. You must know that this province has a king and a language of its own. They are most wretched Idolaters. They are on the borders of India. There are many eunuchs, and from this province all the nobles and gentlemen of the neighbouring provinces are provided with them. They have oxen as tall as elephants, though not so bulky. The people live on meat, milk, and rice. They have much cotton. They carry on a thriving trade, for they have spikenard, galingale, pepper, ginger, sugar, and many other kinds of precious spices. Indian merchants come to this province, and buy the eunuchs I have mentioned, and also many slaves, and then they take them to divers other countries to sell them again. Eunuchs and slaves are very numerous, because all who are taken prisoners by those people, are straightway castrated, and then sold.

There is nothing else worth mentioning in this country. We will leave it, and tell you of another province, lying towards the east, and called Caugigu.

Here is told of the great province of Caugigu

Caugigu is a province lying towards the east. It has a king. The people are idolaters, and have a language of their own. They have submitted to the Great Kaan, and pay him a yearly tribute. And you must know that their king is so given to sensual pleasures, that he has no less than 300 wives; for, when there is a beautiful woman in the district, he at once marries her. There is plenty of gold in this province. They have great abundance of many kinds of precious spices, but, as the country lies far from the sea, their wares have no great value, and are given at low prices. They have a great number of elephants, as well as wild asses, and many other animals of various sorts. There is plenty of game. They live on meat, milk, and rice. They have no grape-wine, but they make an excellent wine with rice and spices. All the people, in general, both the men and the women, have their skins painted in the way I will tell you. All over their bodies they have pictures drawn of lions, dragons, birds, and other things, made in such a way with needles that they are indelible. This is how they do it: first of all a man has the outlines of as many and such figures as he wishes, drawn in black all over his body—on his face, neck, belly, hands, legs, and, in short, everywhere. When this is done, his hands and feet are tied, and two or more people hold him down. Then the artist takes five needles tied together in such wise, that four are placed as it were at the corners of a square, while the fifth is in the middle; with these same needles he pricks the patient's body all over, following the outlines of the drawings. As soon as these pricks are made, a black liquid is straightway poured over them, so that the figures outlined become visible by means of the pricks. But they suffer such agony during the process, as might be thought to suffice them for purgatory! Yet they do it because it is a sign of great nobility;

and the more they have of these pictures, the greater and handsomer they consider themselves. And many of them die as a result of being painted in this way, for they lose a great deal of blood.

We will now cease speaking of this province, and tell you of another, called Aniu, that lies towards the east.

Here is told of the province of Aniu

Aniu is a province lying towards the east, and belonging to the Great Kaan. They are idolaters. They live by breeding cattle and by the fruits of the earth. They have a language of their own. The women wear round their arms and legs gold and silver bracelets of very great value. The men, too, wear them, but finer and more precious than those of the women. They have many excellent horses, which they sell in great numbers to the Indians, who carry on a thriving trade in them. There are also large quantities of buffaloes, oxen, and cows, as the country is exceedingly fertile, and rich in pasture. They have great abundance of all necessaries.

And you must know that from Aniu to Caugigu, which is beyond it, there is fifteen days' journey, and from Caugigu to Bangala, which is beyond it again, thirty days.

We will now leave this province, and pass on to another, called Toloman, which is quite eight days' journey to the east.

Here is told of the province of Toloman

Toloman is a province situated to the east. The people are idolaters, and have a language of their own; they belong to the Great Kaan. They are very handsome people, not quite white, but brown. They are very good soldiers. They have plenty of cities, but there is an especially large number of towns, situated on very high and impregnable mountains. When they die, they have their bodies burned; the bones that are left and cannot be burned, they take and put into little caskets, which they carry up great high mountains, and place in large caverns, hanging them in such wise that no one, man or beast, may touch them.

Much gold is found there. The money they use as small change consists of the porcelain shells I have told you of. All those other provinces, too, namely Bangala, Caugigu and Aniu, spend gold and porcelain shells. There are not many merchants, but the few that there are, are exceedingly rich, and carry on a thriving trade. They live on meat, milk, and rice. They have no grape-wine, but make an excellent wine with rice and spices.

We will now cease speaking of this province, as there is nothing else worth mentioning, and we will tell you of another called Chuju, lying to the east.

Here is told of the province of Chuju

Chuju is a province lying to the east. When one leaves Toloman, one travels twelve days along a river, on whose banks are many cities and towns; but there is nothing worth mentioning. After these twelve days' journey on the river, one reaches the city of Chuju, which is very large and noble. They are idolaters and subject to the Great Kaan. They live by trade and handicrafts. And you must know that they make splendid cloths of tree-bark, in which they dress in summer. They are soldiers. They have no other currency that the Great Kaan's paper, of which I have spoken. For I must add that we are now back again in the countries where the Great Kaan's paper is spent.

There are so many lions, that no one may sleep out of doors at night, for the lions would instantly devour him. And I will also add that when people travel on this river and stop somewhere for the night, if they do not keep at a good distance from the banks, the lions will spring on to the boat, and snatch a man, and go away and devour him. But I must also say that the people know how to defend themselves; and this is how they do it. Though the lions are very big and dangerous, I will tell you one thing that will surprise you: there are dogs in that country that have the pluck to attack them. There must, however, be two of them. With two dogs one man can kill a big lion; and I will tell you how. If a man, riding along with bow and arrows, and with two very big dogs, meets with a large lion, the dogs, that are plucky and strong, rush at the lion very boldly, the moment they see him. One attacks him from behind, and the other barks in front of him. The lion turns now towards the one, and now towards the other, but the two dogs do not let themselves be caught. And so the lion, seeing that he cannot catch them, ends by going away. But as soon as the dogs see that the lion is going away, they run after him, and bite him in the thighs or in the tail. The lion turns fiercely, but cannot catch hold of them, for the dogs know well how to defend themselves. What more shall I tell you? The lion is very much frightened by the great noise made by the dogs, and sets off to find a tree against which he may stand at bay, and face the dogs. And as the lion goes on, they keep on biting him behind. And the lion turns now to the right, and now to the left. Meanwhile the man takes his bow, and shoots one, two, or more arrows, as many as are necessary to kill the lion. In this way they kill many of them. For a lion can put up no defence against a man on horseback with two good dogs.

They have much silk and wares of all kinds in great abundance, which are carried, along the river I mentioned, to divers lands.

And you must know that one travels along that river for twelve more days, ever passing very many cities and towns. The people are idolaters and belong to the Great Kaan. Their currency is the Great Lord's paper money. They live by trade and handicrafts. And they are good soldiers.

At the end of the twelve days, one reaches Sindufu, which has been spoken of before in this book. On leaving Sindufu, one rides for no less than seventy days across provinces and lands where we have already been, and of which we have written previously in this book. At the end of the seventy days, one finds Jonju, where we have already been. Leaving Jonju, one travels on for four days, coming across many cities and towns. The people are busily engaged in trade and handicrafts. They are idolaters, and have the currency of the Great Kaan, their Lord, namely paper. At the end of the four days, one finds the city of Cachanfu, which lies to the south, and belongs to the province of Cathay.

We will now tell you what this city of Cachanfu is like, even as you shall hear.

Here is told of the city of Cachanfu

Cachanfu is a large and noble city of Cathay, situated towards the south. They are idolaters, and burn their dead. There are also some Christians, who have a Church in the city. They are subject to the Great Kaan, and have paper money. They live by trade and handicrafts, for they have abundance of silk. They make large quantities of gold and silk cloth, and sendals. This city has many other cities and towns dependent upon it. It is crossed by a large river, on which great quantities of merchandise are carried to Cambaluc, for, by many channels and canals, they make the river flow as far as that city.

We will now leave this place, and travel southward three days. And we will tell you of another city called Changlu.

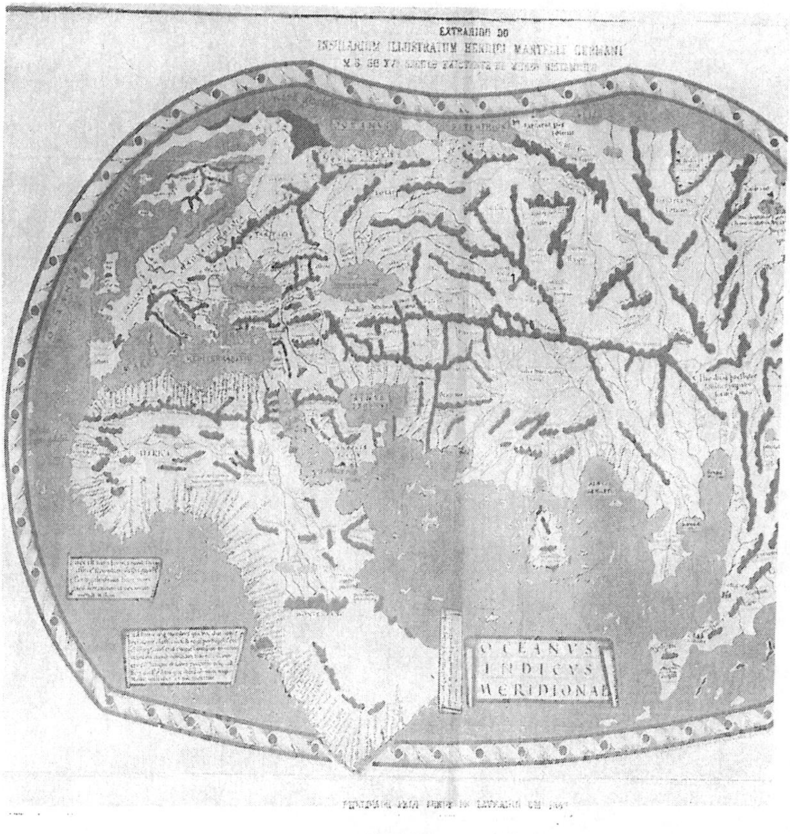

MAP OF HENRICUS MARTELLUS

Here is told of the city of Changlu

Changlu is also a very large city lying towards the south. It belongs to the Great Kaan, and is part of the province of Cathay. Their currency is paper. They are idolaters, and burn their dead. And you must know that in this city, and in its surrounding district, salt is made in immense quantities; and I will tell you how. Know, then, that they take a certain soil, that is very salt; they make great piles of this soil, and throw a great deal of water on it; by means of channels, they then gather the water which has passed through that soil and absorbed the salt in it; they then put it into large broad iron pans, no more than four fingers high, and boil it for a long time. Thus the salt is formed, which is beautiful, and very white and fine-grained. And I will add that this salt is carried into many lands all around; thereby the people make great gains, and the Great Lord derives a considerable revenue and profit.

In this region there grow very large peaches, weighing quite two small pounds each.

As there is nothing else worth mentioning, we will now leave this city, and tell you of another called Changli, situated to the south. We will now tell you about it.

Here is told of the city of Changli

Changli is a city of Cathay, lying towards the south. It belongs to the Great Kaan. They are idolaters and have paper currency. It is at a distance of five days from Changlu, and, during those five days, one passes through many cities and towns, all belonging to the Great Kaan, and thriving with trade, and hence very profitable sources of income to him. And you must know that through the middle of the city of Changli there flows a large and broad river, along which immense quantities of merchandise are carried up and down—silk, spices, and other precious wares.

We will now leave Changli, of which we will say no more. And we will tell you of another city, called Tandinfu, at six days' journey from the other, towards the south.

Here is told of the city of Tandinfu

On leaving Changli, one travels six days towards the south, ever passing numerous towns and cities of great wealth and splendour. They are idolaters, and burn their dead. They are subject to the Great Kaan, and have paper currency. They live by trade and handicrafts. They have great abundance of all the necessaries of life. But there is nothing special worth mentioning, and so we will speak of Tandinfu.

Tandinfu is a very large city. In past times it was a great kingdom, but the Great Kaan conquered it by force of arms. But I assure you that it is the noblest city in the entire region. There are very important merchants in it, engaged in considerable trade. They have so great an abundance of silk, that it is truly a wonder. They have many a beautiful and pleasant garden, full of all kinds of good fruit. And you must know in truth that this city of Tandinfu has dependent upon it eleven imperial cities, namely, cities that are noble and of great wealth. They are centres of great and profitable trade, as they have silk in immense quantities.

You must know too, that in the year 1272 after Christ's Incarnation, the Great Kaan sent to this city and province one of his barons, Litan Sangon by name, to provide for their peace and safety, for which purpose he gave the said Litan 80,000 horsemen. But when Litan had sojourned some time in this province with his men, he, like the traitor he was, decided upon the great treachery that I will now tell you of. He plotted with the elders of all the cities of the province, and decided with them that they would rebel against the Great Kaan. And this they did, having on their side the support of the entire province. They rebelled against the Great Kaan, and obeyed him in nothing. When the Great Kaan was informed of this, he sent two of his barons, called Aguil and Mongatai, and together with them no less than 100,000 horsemen. But why should I make a long story of it? Know in very truth that these two barons and their men fought against Litan who had rebelled, and against all the men that he could muster, who amounted to about 100,000 horsemen besides an immense number of foot-soldiers. But fate willed it that Litan should lose the battle, and be killed, together with many others. After Litan's defeat and death, the Great Kaan had enquiries set afoot as to who had been responsible for this treason; and all those who were found guilty were put to a cruel death. All the others were forgiven, and no harm was done to them. And ever since they have been loyal subjects.

But now we will leave this subject, as we have told you all about it in due order, and we will tell you of other countries. [But before I do so, as we are once more in Cathay, I wish to inform you of certain other customs of the Cathayans, and first of all I wish to show you how virtuous are their maidens, and speak of the life they lead.]

Here is told of certain customs of the Cathayans

You must know that the maidens of Cathay are without peer as regards virtue, and the keeping of the ornament of modesty. They do not indulge in noisy and unseemly merry-making; they do not dance ; they importune no one ; they are not ever at the window, looking at the faces of the passers-by, or offering their own for inspection. They lend no experienced ear to improper discourses, and haunt no feasts or places of amusement. If it happen they go abroad on some fitting errand, as for example to the temples of their idols, or on a visit to some relative or kinsman, they go in the company of their mothers, without looking shamelessly into peoples' faces, and wearing certain pretty hats of theirs, which prevent them from looking upwards. Thus, when they go walking, they always keep their eyes turned towards their feet. In the presence of the elders, they are most modest, never uttering an idle word, nay, never saying a single word unless they be questioned. They keep to their rooms, attending to their work, and rarely do they enter the presence of their father or brothers, or of any of the elders of the house. Nor do they give ear to gallants.

And the same is to be said of the boys and youths, who never presume to speak in the presence of their elders unless they be questioned. What more shall I say? So great is the sense of modesty among them, that is to say among relatives and kinsmen, that two of them would never dream of going together to the baths.

Further, if a man wishes to give his daughter in marriage, or she is asked of him by another, he vouches to the future husband that she is a virgin. Indeed, the father and the future husband bind themselves with bonds and contracts, for, should the contrary turn out to be the case, the marriage would not be valid. When these bonds and contracts have been solemnly stipulated and signed by them, then the maiden, for the purpose of testing her virginity, is led to the baths, where she is awaited by her own mother and by the mother of her future husband, as well as by their kinswomen, and certain matrons, representing both parties, who, being especially deputed for this purpose, have first of all to test the maiden's virginity by means of a dove's egg. And if the women who represent the future husband are not satisfied with this test, seeing that it is quite possible to contract the privy parts of a woman by means of drugs, one of the said matrons ably introduces into the maiden a finger wrapped in a thin white cloth, and slightly scratches the virginal vein in such wise, that the cloth is slightly soiled with the virginal blood. For that blood has such a property and virtue, that it cannot by any washing be removed from a cloth that is soiled with it. And if it does perchance disappear, it is a sign that the girl has already been polluted, and that the blood is not that of a pure maiden. After this test, if the girl is proved a virgin, the marriage is valid; otherwise it is not; in which case the father, on the strength of the bond signed, has to pay a fine.

And you must know that in order to preserve their virginity, girls walk so daintily that one foot is never more than a finger's length in front of the other, for often enough a virgin's privy parts become distended if she moves in too unseemly a way.

All this must be understood as applying to the natives of the province of Cathay, since the Tartars are not so particular, for their wives and daughters go riding with them, so that it may be supposed that the virginity of the latter may suffer somewhat thereby. The inhabitants of the province of Manji follow the same custom as those of Cathay.

[And, concerning the ways of the Cathayans, I will tell you certain other things that are right worthy of being recorded in our book, as you shall hear.]

Here is told of other customs of the Cathayans

You must know that the Idolaters have eighty-four idols, each of which has a name of its own. And the Idolaters say that a particular virtue has been assigned to each idol by the heavenly God; thus one is concerned with the finding of lost objects, another with granting fertility and good weather to the fields, another again with protecting cattle, and so on for every contingency, both good and bad. And every idol is called by its own name, and they know the particular office and virtue of each.

As for the idols who are concerned with the finding of lost objects, they consider such two small wooden statues, that have the appearance of boys of some twelve years of age, which they deck out with beautiful ornaments: near them in their temple there constantly lives an old woman, who is a kind of verger. If, then, someone loses an object because he has been robbed of it, or does not remember where he has put it, or for any reason cannot find it, he goes or sends to the aforesaid old woman, in order that she may question the idol about it. She first of all bids him incense the idols, and he incenses them. After the incense has been offered, the old woman enquires of the idol concerning the object lost, and they answer her according to the circumstances. Then the old woman says to the man who has lost the object: "Look in such a place, and you shall find it." If instead someone has taken it, she says: "So-and-so has it; tell him to give it you; and if he denies it, come back to me, and I will see to it that he returns it to you; for otherwise I shall bring it about that he shall cut his hand or his foot, or fall and break his arm or his leg, or else that some other evil come upon him, so that he will be obliged to give it back to you." And experience shows in truth that it is so. In fact, if anyone has stolen something from another, and continues to deny it, and to disregard the order to make restitution, then, if it be a woman, when she is doing something in the kitchen with a knife or attending to some other duty, she will cut her hand or fall into the fire, or else some other evil will come upon her; or if it is a man, similarly, when he is hewing wood, he will cut his foot, or break his arm or his leg or some other limb. And as the people know by experience that this happens to them because of their denying, they straightway make restitution of what they have stolen. If, however, the idols do not at once reply, the old woman says, "The spirits are not here; go away, and come back at such an hour, for meantime the spirits will come, and I shall question them." So the man returns at the appointed hour, and in the meantime the spirits have given their response to the old woman. This response they give whispering in a low and husky voice, like a hiss. Then the old woman thanks them in this wise: she raises her hands in their presence, gnashing her teeth thrice, as if to say: "Oh, what a worthy and holy and virtuous thing!"—And if the man has lost horses, she tells him, "Go to such a place, and there you shall find them," or else, "Robbers have found them in such a place, and are leading them away with them towards such another place; run, and you shall find them." And everything is found to be precisely as she says. In this way nothing is lost, but one may succeed in finding it again. And, when they have recovered what they have lost, they offer to the idols, as a sign of respect and devotion, something like an ell of some fine cloth, as for example, of gold or silk.

And I, Marco, found in this way a ring that I had lost; not, however, that I made them any offering or paid reverence to them.

[So we have told you of these customs, that were right worthy of being mentioned; but now we will return to our subject], and we will tell you of a country lying towards the south, and called Sinjumatu.

Here is told of the noble city of Sinjumatu

On leaving Tandinfu, one rides three days southward, ever passing through cities and towns, all noble and wealthy, and thriving with trade and handicrafts. There is a great deal of game of all kinds, both beasts and birds. They have an abundance of everything.

And after travelling for these three days, one reaches the noble city of Sinjumatu, which is very large and rich, and also has thriving trade and crafts. They are idolaters, and belong to the Great Kaan. Their currency is paper. You must know, moreover, that they have a river from which they get great profit; I will tell you how. You must know that it is a great river, flowing down from the south to this city of Sinjumatu; and the people of the city have made two rivers of this one large river, for they have made one half flow to the east, and the other to the west; thus the one goes to Manji and the other traverses Cathay. Further, this city possesses such immense shipping, I mean such a number of ships, that no one who has not seen them can believe it. Do not, however, imagine that the boats are big in themselves, though they are such as are suitable for a large river. And you must know that these boats carry so great a quantity of merchandise to Manji and across Cathay, that it is truly a wonder; and when they come back, they do so fully laden. It is indeed a marvel to see the quantities of goods carried up and down the river.

Now we will leave Sinjumatu, and tell you of another land lying towards the south. It is a great province called Linjin.

Here is told of the great city of Linjin

On leaving the city of Sinjumatu, one journeys southward for eight days, always coming across many cities and towns, all very noble, large, and wealthy, with thriving trade and handicrafts. They are idolaters, and burn their dead. They are subject to the Great Kaan. Their currency is paper.

At the end of the eight days, one finds a city called Linjin, like the province; it is the capital of the kingdom. It is a most noble and wealthy city. The people are good soldiers. Still, they engage considerably in trade and handicrafts. They have quantities of game, both beasts and birds. They have abundance of food-stuffs. All over the province they have an immense amount of jujube fruits, which are twice as big as dates, and the people of the province eat bread made of these jujubes.

This city also is on the river I mentioned above. They have bigger ships than those I spoke of, and much precious merchandise is carried in them.

We will now cease speaking of this city and province, and proceed to tell you of other new things. We will deal with a city called Pinju, which is very large and noble.

Here is told of the city of Pinju

On leaving the city of Linjin, one journeys three days southward, ever coming across many goodly cities and towns. They belong to Cathay. They are idolaters, and burn their dead. They are subject to the Great Kaan. They are like those of whom I have spoken previously. Their currency is paper. There is also the best game in the world, both beasts and birds. They have great abundance of all the necessaries of life.

At the end of three days, one reaches a city called Pinju, which is very large and noble, and thriving with trade and handicrafts. They have immense quantities of silk. This city is on the confines of the great province of Manji. In this city merchants load their carts with wares of sundry kinds, and carry them to many cities and towns in Manji. It is a city that brings in large profit to the Great Kaan.

There is nothing else worth mentioning, and so we will leave this city, and tell you of another, called Chinju, also lying to the south.

Here is told of the city of Chinju

On leaving the city of Pinju, one travels two days southward, passing through very fine regions, rich in all good things, with plenty of game of all kinds, both beasts and birds.

At the end of two days, one reaches the city of Chinju, which is very large and wealthy, prosperous with trade and handicrafts. The people are idolaters, and burn their dead with fire. Their currency is paper, and they are subject to the Great Kaan. There are splendid plains and beautiful fields. They have abundance of wheat and of every other kind of grain.

There is, however, nothing else worth mentioning; hence we will leave this place, and tell you of other lands further on.

On leaving the city of Chinju, one journeys quite three days towards the south, crossing fair regions, and fine towns and villages, and beautiful cultivated lands and fields, with plenty of game, both birds and beasts, and abundance of wheat and of all other kinds of grain. They are idolaters, and subject to the Great Kaan. Their currency is paper.

At the end of the three days, one reaches the great river Caramoran, which flows out of the land of Prester John, and is very big and broad. For you must know that it is a mile wide. It is very deep, so that large boats can navigate it. It has abundance of large fish. On the river there are quite 15,000 boats, all belonging to the Great Kaan, for the purpose of carrying his armies to the islands in the sea, for the sea is only one day's journey away from this place. These boats need twenty sailors each, and carry about fifteen horses with their riders, as well as their weapons and provisions. But not only in this place is the number of boats past all belief, but in many other places too, wherever, in fact, a city stands on the banks of the river.

On either bank, facing one another, there are two cities; one is called Coiganju, and the other Caiju. One is large and the other is small.

And now, passing this river, we enter the great province of Manji. I will tell you how this province of Manji was conquered by the Great Kaan.

You must not, however, think that we have dealt,

point by point, with the whole of the province of Cathay, but barely with a twentieth part of it. I have kept to the road that I, Marco, used to follow when crossing this province, describing the cities I passed on my way, and omitting all mention of those to the right and left, and in the interior, for it would have made too long a tale to speak of them all.

How the Great Kaan conquered the great province of Manji

You must know that the Lord and King of the province of Manji was Facfur, who was a very great and powerful king as regards treasure, subjects and territory, so that there were few greater than he in the world; and indeed there was none wealthier and more powerful, except the Great Kaan himself. But you must know that he was not a good soldier; he found all his pleasure in women, and in doing good to the poor. In his province there were no horses, nor were the people used to battles and weapons and armies; and this was because the province of Manji is surpassingly strong by nature. For all the cities are surrounded by broad and deep sheets of water, so that there is not one of them that is not environed by an expanse of water at least an arrow-shot in breadth, and very deep. Thus all cities are entered by bridges. And I may add that, had the people been good soldiers, they would never have lost the province. But they were neither valiant, not accustomed to carry arms, and so they lost it.

Well, in the year 1268 after Christ's Incarnation, the Great Kaan now reigning, namely Cublai, sent thither a baron of his, called Baian Chincsan, which means Baian of the Hundred Eyes. And you must know that the King of Manji knew from his astrologers that he could not lose his kingdom except to a man with a hundred eyes. So this Baian came to Manji with the immense army of horse and foot that the Great Kaan gave him. Further he had a large number of boats to carry both horsemen and foot-soldiers, should the need arise. When he had come with all his men to the threshold of Manji, namely to the city of Coiganju that we have now reached, and of which we will tell you later, he invited the inhabitants to submit to the Great Kaan. And they answered that they would not. On seeing this, he advanced, and reached another city; and this city also refused to surrender. And so he advanced still further. This he did because he knew that the Great Kaan was sending another great army after him. What more shall I tell you? He went to five cities, without being able to take any, for none of them was disposed to surrender. But when he came to the sixth, Baian took it by force, and had all that were in it put to death. Then he took another, then a third, so that it came about that in this wise he took twelve, one after the other. But why should I make a long story of it? You must know in very truth that when Baian had taken as many cities as I have told you, he went on straight to the capital of the kingdom, which was called Kinsai, where the King and Queen were. And when he saw Baian with his army, the King was overcome by fear. Together with many men, he abandoned the city on no less than a thousand ships, and took refuge in the islands of the Ocean Sea. The Queen remained in the city with many men, and made every effort to defend it as well as she might. Now it happened that one day the Queen asked what was the name of the leader of the enemy's army, and so she was told that it was Baian of the Hundred Eyes. When she heard the name, she remembered that the astrologers had said that a man with a hundred eyes was to deprive them of the kingdom. Hence she surrendered to Baian. And as soon as she had surrendered, all the other cities and the whole kingdom surrendered, for none put up any defence. And indeed that was a great conquest, as in the whole world there was not a kingdom worth the half of this one, for the King had such wealth that it was truly a marvel.

And I will tell you something of his bounty. You must know that every year he had no less than 20,000 little children looked after, and I will tell you how. In that country children are exposed as soon as they are born; this is done by the poor women who cannot bring them up. The King had all these little ones taken charge of, and the constellation and planet recorded under which each had been born. Then he had them nourished in many different places by wet nurses, that he kept in great numbers. When a rich man had no children, he went to the King, and had as many as he wished given to him, choosing those he liked best. Further, if, when one of those children had grown, the father or the mother wished it back, the King had it handed over to them, if they could prove in writing that it was theirs. Again, when the boys and girls reached an age at which they could be married, he gave one of the girls as wife to one of the boys, presenting them with enough to live upon comfortably. In this way, every year he brought up quite 20,000 of both sexes.

Another thing this King used to do. When he went riding along the roads, and happened to see two fine houses with a small one in between, he used to ask why this house was so small, and not as big as the others; when he was told that it belonged to a poor man without the means to improve it, he used to bid that the small house should be made the same in size and beauty as the other two on either side of it.

Further, I will add that this King always had in attendance over a thousand youths and maidens, all dressed at his expense in fine rich clothes.

He governed his kingdom so well, that no one ever committed a crime there; during the night, the shops were left open, and nothing was ever found missing.

One could travel at night, just as in the daytime. One cannot describe the magnificence of that kingdom.

I have told you of the King; I will now tell you of the Queen. She was taken to the Great Kaan. And when the Great Lord saw her, he treated her honourably and had her splendidly waited upon, like the great Lady she was. As for the King her husband, he never left the islands of the Ocean Sea; and he died there.

So we will cease speaking of him and his wife, and of this subject, and will resume telling you of Manji. We will relate, all in due order, of their manners and customs, and of other things about them, even as you shall clearly hear. And we will begin at the beginning, namely with the city of Coiganju.

Here is told of the city of Coiganju

Coiganju is a very large, noble, and wealthy city, lying to the south-east, at the entrance to the province of Manji. The people are idolaters, and burn their dead. They are subject to the Great Kaan. There is an immense number of ships, for you know that, as I have already told you, it stands on the great river called Caramoran. I will further tell you that in this city there arrives an immense amount of merchandise, as it is the capital of the region. Many cities in fact have their wares carried thither, for from there they are distributed along the river to many other cities. Further, in the city salt is made; more than forty other cities are provided with it from here. The Great Kaan hence draws a very large income from this city, on account of the salt, and the dues on the great trading that is carried on there.

Now we have told you of this city; we will therefore leave it, and tell you of another city, called Paukin.

Here is told of the city of Paukin

On leaving Coiganju, one travels one day towards the south-east, along a causeway which is at the entrance of Manji. This causeway is made of very fine stones, and there is water along it on either side, for on the one side there are vast marshes and, on the other side, first there are marshes, and then deep water, on which boats sail. One cannot enter the province except along this causeway, unless one goes by boat.

At the end of the day's journey, one reaches a city called Paukin, which is very large and beautiful. They are idolaters, and burn their dead. There are also some Turkish Nestorian Christians, who have a church there. They are subject to the Great Kaan. Their currency is paper. They live by trade and handicrafts. They have silk in great abundance. Cloths of gold and silk of many kinds are made there. They have in great plenty the necessaries of life.

There is, however, nothing else worth mentioning, and so we will leave this city, and tell you of another, called Cauiu.

Here is told of the city of Cauiu

On leaving the city of Paukin, one travels one day to the south-east. Then one reaches a city called Cauiu, which is very large and noble. They are also idolaters, have paper currency, and are subject to the Great Kaan. They live by trade and handicrafts. They have great abundance of the necessaries of life. They have fish in immense quantities. Game, too, they have, both beasts and birds, in great plenty, for I assure you that one can get three good pheasants for one Venetian silver *grosso*.

We will now leave this city, and tell you of another, called Tinju.

Here is told of the city of Tinju

Now, you must know that on leaving the city of Cauiu, one travels for one day, ever coming across great numbers of villages, fields, and farms, after which one reaches a city called Tinju, which is not very large, but rich in every earthly blessing. The people are Idolaters, have paper currency, and are subject to the Great Kaan. They live by trade and handicrafts, for they derive great gains and profits from many different wares. It lies towards the south-east. They have many boats, and plenty of game, both beasts and birds.

You must also know that, on the left side, towards the east, at three days' distance from here, is the Ocean Sea. And everywhere between here and the Ocean Sea, salt is made in very great quantities. And there is a city called Chinju which is very large, wealthy, and noble, and so much salt is made in this city that it is sufficient for the whole province. And I assure you that the Great Kaan draws an immense revenue therefrom; indeed it is so big that one could hardly believe it without having been there. They are idolaters, have paper currency, and are subject to the Great Kaan.

We will now leave this place, and return to Tinju; and we will leave Tinju also, for we have already told you of it, and will tell you of another city called Yanju.

Here is told of the city of Yanju

On leaving the city of Tinju, one travels for one day to the south-east, through a very fine country, where there are many towns and villages. Then one reaches a great and noble city called Yanju. And you must know that it is so large and powerful that it has twenty-seven other cities dependent upon it, all of them large, wealthy, and thriving with trade. In this city resides one of the Great Kaan's twelve barons, for it has been chosen as one of their twelve seats. They are idolaters.

They have paper currency, and are subject to the Great Kaan. And Messer Marco in person, he of whom this book speaks, held the government of this city for three years by order of the Great Kaan. They live by trade and handicrafts, for great quantities of equipment for horsemen and men-at-arms are made here. For you must know that in this city, and all around in its district, are stationed many troops.

There is nothing else worth mentioning. And so we will leave this place, and tell you of two great provinces that form part of that of Manji. They lie towards the west, and as there are many things to be related about them, we will tell you of all their customs and manners. And first of all we will deal with one that is called Nankin.

Here is told of the province of Nankin

Nankin is a province lying to the west, and is part of Manji; it is a most noble and wealthy province. They are idolaters. They have paper currency, and are subject to the Great Kaan. They live by trade and handicrafts. They have abundance of silk. They make gold and silver cloths of all kinds. There is great plenty of all kinds of grain, and of all the necessaries of life, for it is truly a most fertile province. They have abundance of game, both beasts and birds. They burn their dead. There are many lions. There are many wealthy merchants, from whom the Great Kaan receives much tribute and revenue.

We will now leave this place, as there is nothing else worth mentioning, and we will next tell you of the noble city of Sanianfu, which is well worthy of being spoken of in this book of ours, so great is its importance.

Here is told of the city of Sanianfu

Sanianfu is a large and noble city, which has no less than twelve other large and noble cities dependent upon it. There is much trade and industry there. They are idolaters, have paper currency, and burn their dead. They are subject to the Great Kaan. They have abundance of silk, and make gold and silk cloths of many different kinds. They have plenty of game, both beasts and birds. Sanianfu possesses all the noble things that a noble city should possess.

And you must know that this city held out three years after all the rest of Manji had submitted. All this time a large army of the Great Kaan's remained encamped before it, but it could approach it only from one side, namely from the north, for on all the other sides there was a vast and deep lake. The Great Kaan's army could hence besiege it only from the north, and from all the other sides the inhabitants received food enough across the water. And I assure you that they would never have taken it but for a circumstance I will tell you of.

Know, then, that when the Great Kaan's army had besieged this city three years without being able to take it, they were greatly dejected. Then Messer Niccolò, Messer Matteo, and Messer Marco said: "We will find you a way to make the city surrender straightway." And those of the army replied that it would please them greatly. These words were exchanged in the presence of the Great Kaan, for the envoys of the army had come to tell the Great Lord how it was that the city could not be taken by siege, since there was no way of preventing supplies from arriving from certain parts. And the Great Kaan said: "It is necessary that a way be found to take the city." Then it was that the two brothers and Messer Marco their son and nephew said: "Sire, we have among our followers certain men who can build mangonels, capable of throwing such large stones, that the citizens will not be able to endure them, but will surrender as soon as the mangonel has shot into the city." The Great Lord replied to Messer Niccolò and to his brother and his son, that it would please him greatly, and told them to have this mangonel built as quickly as possible.

So Messer Niccolò, his brother, and his son, who had among their followers an Alan and a Nestorian Christian, who were excellent masters of this craft, bade them build two or three mangonels, capable of throwing stones of 300 pounds in weight; and the two of them built three such mangonels; and they were fine and big, and capable of throwing stones of 300 pounds in weight to a great distance. Of these stones they had over sixty, all round and of the same size. When the mangonels were ready, the Great Lord and the barons of his court saw them with pleasure, and had them tried in their presence, making them throw several stones of the size we mentioned; and they were much astonished, and praised the work greatly. Then the Great Lord had the mangonels taken to his army, that was besieging the city of Sanianfu without being able to capture it. When they arrived, they were set up, and the Tartars thought them the greatest wonder in the world. What more shall I tell you? When the mangonels had been set up and made ready, a stone was cast into the city. And it fell among the houses, breaking and smashing everything, and making an immense din and uproar. When the citizens saw this evil thing, that they had never seen before, they were aghast, and so terrified, that they were at their wits' ends. They took counsel together, but they could find no way of escape from these mangonels. They said that they would all be killed, if they did not surrender. So they decided to surrender at all costs. Hence they sent word to the commander of the army that they wished to surrender on the same conditions as the other cities of the province, and remain under the lordship of the Great Kaan. And the commander of the army replied that he was willing. And so he received the citizens, and they surrendered. And this came about thanks to the efforts of Messer Niccolò, Messer Matteo, and Messer Marco. And it was no small achievement. For you must know that this city, with its province, is one of the best that the Great Kaan possesses, and he obtains much revenue and profit from it.

Now we have told you of this city, and how it surrendered on account of the mangonels that Messer Niccolò, Messer Matteo, and Messer Marco had built. We will now leave this subject, and tell you of a city called Sinju.

Here is told of the city of Sinju

You must know that on leaving the city of Yanju, one reaches, after travelling fifteen miles, a city called Sinju, which is not very large, but possesses many boats, and carries on considerable trade. They are idolaters, and subject to the Great Kaan. Their currency is paper. It stands on the banks of the greatest river in the world, called Kian, which varies in breadth between six and ten miles; its length is 120 days' journey. Into it flows an infinite number of other rivers, all of them navigable, coming down from many different countries, and duly increasing it in size. On account of the river, this city has a very large number of boats, which carry many things, including the most varied merchandise. Hence it is a city that yields much revenue and tribute to the Great Kaan.

And I assure you that this river is so long, and crosses so many regions, and has so many cities on its banks, that I may assert that there are more boats on it laden with more precious and costly wares, than sail on all the rivers and seas of the Christians put together. For I can state that I have seen quite 10,000 boats at one time in this city; and all of them sailed on that river. And I have heard tell from the official that gathers the Great Kaan's revenues, that 200,000 boats sail on that river annually, counting only those that go up. If then this city, which is not very large, has so many boats, you may imagine how many there are in the other cities. And you must know that this river traverses more than sixteen provinces, and over 200 large cities stand on its banks, all with a greater number of ships than this one, not to mention the cities and towns standing on its tributaries, which also have plentiful shipping. And all these ships carry wares to this city of Sinju or from it to other cities. And the principal commodity traded along the river is salt. The merchants load the boats with it in this city, and then they carry it to all the regions along the banks of the river; they also go into the interior, leaving the river, and sailing up its tributaries, thus furnishing all the surrounding districts with salt. Hence from all places on the sea-coast where salt is made, it is carried to the same city of Sinju; here it is loaded on boats, and carried to the aforesaid places. They also carry iron. When they come down again, the boats carry to this city wood, coals, hemp, and many other wares of different kinds which are furnished to the regions along the coast. Still, the shipping is not sufficient to carry all this merchandise, so that much is carried on rafts. Great, therefore, is the revenue that the Great Kaan receives from this city, or rather from its harbour.

In many places in this river rise mounds and rocky hillocks, on which monasteries of the Idolaters, and other edifices, are built. One constantly passes villages and inhabited places.

The boats are covered, and have a single mast, but they can carry a great deal of cargo, for I assure you they can bear a freight of four to twelve thousand *cantars*, reckoning as we do in our country.

Now that we have explained everything properly to

you, we will leave this place, and proceed to tell you of another city called Caiju. But first of all I wish to tell you another thing I had forgotten, for it is worthy of mention in our book. You must know that not all the boats have hempen ropes; only the masts and sails are provided with them. The lines with which the boats are towed up-stream, are made of cane. The canes used for the purpose are those long and thick ones I have mentioned before, that reach a length of fifteen paces. They split them, and then tie them together, making in this way ropes quite 300 paces long, and stronger than if they were made of hemp. Moreover, every boat has eight to twelve horses to tow it up the river.

We will now leave this subject, and return to Caiju.

Here is told of the city of Caiju

Caiju is a small city. It stands to the south-east. They are idolaters, are subject to the Great Kaan, and have paper currency. It stands on the river. In this city vast quantities of corn and rice are collected, and from there they are carried by water to the great city of Cambaluc, where the Great Kaan's court is. But if I say " by water," I do not mean by sea, but by rivers and lakes. On the corn from this city lives a great part of the Great Kaan's court. He it is who had the water-ways constructed from this city to Cambaluc. He made great ditches, both wide and deep, from one river to another, and from one lake to another, and then he made the water flow in them, so that they look like large rivers. And quite big boats sail on them. In this way does one travel from Manji to the city of Cambaluc. One can also go by land, for all along the water-ways there is also a causeway made with the soil removed to make the ditches. Thus, as you have heard, one may go either by water or by land.

In the middle of the river, opposite this city, is a

rocky island, on which is a monastery of the Idolaters, with two hundred brethren. In this great monastery there is an immense number of idols. And you must know that the monastery has many other idolatrous monasteries dependent upon it, being like an archbishop's see with us.

We will now leave this place, and cross the river, and tell you of a city called Chinghianfu.

Here is told of the city of Chinghianfu

Chinghianfu is a city of Manji. The people are idolaters, are subject to the Great Kaan, and have paper currency. They live by trade and handicrafts. They have abundance of silk. They make gold and silver cloths of divers kinds. There are great and wealthy merchants. There is plenty of game, both beasts and birds. They have corn and victuals in great quantities.

There have been two churches of Nestorian Christians here since the year 1278 after Christ's Incarnation. I will tell you how it came about. You must know that there had never been any Christian monastery there, not anyone who believed in the God of the Christians till the year 1278, when Marsarkis, a Nestorian Christian, became governor in the Great Kaan's name for three years. This Marsarkis it was who had two churches built. From that time there have been Christian churches, whereas before there were neither churches nor Christians.

We will now leave this subject, and tell you of another great city called Canju.

Here is told of the city of Canju

On leaving the city of Chinghianfu, one travels three days to the south-east, ever passing many cities and towns, all thriving with trade and handicrafts. They are all idolaters, are subject to the Great Kaan, and have paper currency.

After three days, one reaches the city of Canju, which is very large and noble. The people are idolaters, and are subject to the Great Kaan. Their currency is paper. They live by trade and handicrafts. There is abundance of silk. They make gold and silk cloths of divers kinds. There is plenty of game, both beasts and birds. They have great quantities of the necessaries of life, for it is a very fertile land.

And I will tell you of an evil action committed by the people of this city, and how they paid for it dearly. You must know that when the province of Manji was conquered by the Great Kaan's troops under Baian, it happened that this Baian sent a party of his men, who were Alans and Christians, to take this city. It had two circuits of walls. Having got beyond the first circuit, the Alans found an immense quantity of good wine, and drank so much of it that they all became drunk, and slept like logs. When the citizens, who were within the second circuit, saw that their conquerors were in such a state that they seemed all dead, they lost no time: that same night they killed every one of them, so that not one remained alive. When Baian, the leader of the great army, heard that the people of this city had killed his men thus treacherously, he sent thither a large host. The city was stormed, and I assure you that, once they had taken it, they put everyone to the sword. Even, thus, as you have heard, were so many people killed in this city.

We will now leave this place, and proceed, telling you of a city called Suju.

Here is told of the city of Suju

Suju is a large and very noble city. They are idolaters, are subject to the Great Kaan, and have paper currency. They have immense quantities of silk. They live by trade and handicrafts. They make a great deal of silk cloth for clothes. There are great and wealthy merchants. It is so large a city that it has a circuit of sixty miles. The population is so immense that it is beyond all counting. I assure you that, if they were soldiers, the men of Manji would conquer all the rest of the world. But they are no soldiers; instead they are wise merchants, and clever in all handicrafts; and among them there are great natural philosophers, and great leeches who are learned in the secrets of nature. There are many magicians and diviners.

You must know moreover that in this city there are quite 6000 stone bridges, under which, one, and even two, galleys abreast might pass. Further I will tell you that in the mountains around tnis city, rhubarb and ginger grow in great quantities, so that for a Venetian *grosso* you could have quite sixty pounds of fresh ginger, which is exceedingly good.

Know, too, that this city has sixteen other cities dependent upon it, all large and thriving with trade and handicrafts.

Further, you must know that " Suju," the name of this city, means, in our language, " Earth "; and there is another city near it called " Heaven." They received these names because they were such noble cities. Of the city called " Heaven " we will tell you later.

We will now leave Suju, and proceed to a city called Vuju. Know, then, that this Vuju is at a day's distance from Suju. It is a very great and wealthy city, thriving with trade and handicrafts. But as there is nothing new worth mentioning in it, we will leave it, to tell you of another city called Vughin.

This Vughin is also a very large and noble city. They are idolaters, are subject to the Great Kaan, and have paper currency. There is great abundance of silk, and of many other kinds of costly merchandise. They are clever traders and craftsmen.

We will now leave this city, and tell you of the city

of Changan, which is very large and wealthy. They are idolaters; are subject to the Great Kaan, and have paper currency. They live by trade and handicrafts. They make sendal of many kinds in great quantities. They have plenty of game, both beasts and birds.

There is nothing else worth recording; hence we will leave this place and proceed to tell you of other cities. And our subject will be the noble city of Kinsai, which is the capital of the kingdom of Manji.

Here is told of the city of Kinsai

On leaving the city of Changan, one journeys three days through a beautiful district, where one finds many noble and wealthy cities and towns, engaged in trade and handicrafts. They are idolaters, and subject to the Great Kaan. Their currency is paper. They have abundance of all the things that are necessary for a man's bodily welfare.

After these three days, one reaches the most noble city of Kinsai, which is as much as to say, in our language, the "City of Heaven."

Seeing that we have now come to this city, we will tell you of its great splendour; and it is truly worth while, for verily it is the noblest and richest city in the world. To tell you of its splendour we will follow the lines of the written description sent by the Queen of this kingdom to Baian, the conqueror of the province, that he might acquaint the Great Kaan with it, in order that the latter, learning of the magnificence of the city, might not have it destroyed or devastated. We will explain everything in due order, as it stood in that writing. And all that was in it was true, as I, Marco Polo, was later able to see with my own eyes.

First of all, the writing stated that the city of Kinsai was about one hundred miles in circuit, and this is because [apart from the immense number of people] the streets and canals are very broad; and then there are the open places, where the markets are held, and which, on account of the multitudes which assemble there, must be exceedingly vast and spacious.

The city is situated as follows: on one side, it has a beautifully clear fresh-water lake; on the other side, there is a very large river, which flows into every part of the city along a multitude of canals, large and small, that carry away all the refuse; it then flows out into the lake, and thence into the Ocean. For this reason the air is good.

All over the city, one can go about either along the streets or on these canals. Both are so wide, that carts and boats respectively can go along them comfortably, carrying necessaries to the inhabitants. The city has 12,000 bridges, most of which are of stone, and a few of wood; but those that cross the principal canals and the main street are arched up so high, and are so cunningly built, that a large boat can pass beneath them without lowering its mast; yet, carts and horses cross them, so well have the streets been kept level, in spite of the height of the bridges. Smaller boats can pass under any of the other bridges. Nor need it astonish you that the bridges are so many, for, as I have said, the city stands, so to speak, on water, so numerous are the streams that surround and cross it. Hence many bridges are necessary so that people may go to all parts of the city.

At one of the corners of the city there is a ditch, that bounds it on that side, some forty miles long and very broad, filled with water from the river. It was made by the ancient kings of the province in order to drain off the water of the river every time it rose above its banks. It also serves as a defence, for the soil that was extracted in making it was piled up on the inner side and looks like a little hill surrounding the city.

Besides an infinite number of others in the different quarters of the town, there are ten principal squares, with sides half a mile long. In front of them is the main street, forty paces broad, running straight from one end of the city to the other; it is crossed by many level and comfortable bridges. One finds one of these squares every four miles, and they are, as we have said, two miles in circuit. Behind the squares, and parallel to the street, there is a very wide canal, on the near bank of which are built large stone warehouses where all the traders that come from India and elsewhere store their wares and goods in order to have them ready to hand near the squares. Three times a week, there is a gathering in each of these squares of forty to fifty thousand people, who come to the market, bringing with them everything one may desire in the way of food-stuffs, for there is ever an immense abundance of every kind of victuals such as, of beasts, fallow-deer, roebucks, stags, hares, and rabbits, and of birds, partridges, pheasants, francolins, quails, chickens, capons, and more ducks and geese than one could ever tell, for so many are bred in that lake, that for a Venetian silver *grosso* one has a couple of geese or two couple of ducks. Then there are the shambles, where bigger animals are slaughtered, such as calves, oxen, kids, and lambs, the flesh of which is eaten by the rich and the great. But the people of lower birth do not abstain from unclean flesh. In those market-squares there are ever vegetables and fruit of all kinds, especially certain very big pears, weighing ten pounds each, white as paste inside, and very sweet-smelling; at the proper season, there are very exquisite peaches, both white and yellow. The country produces neither wine nor grapes, but excellent dried grapes and wine are brought there from outside; but the natives do not appreciate the wine much, being used to their own, made of rice and spices. Further, every day an immense quantity of fish is brought from the Ocean Sea, to a distance of twenty-five miles up-stream. There is also plenty of fish from the lake, for there are many fishermen there, who do nothing else but fish; the kinds vary according to the season, but it is always fat and tasty on account of the refuse from the city. When one sees that enormous quantity of fish, one would never think that it could all be sold. Yet in a few hours it is all gone, so great is the number of people used to living luxuriously, eating both fish and meat at the same meal.

All the aforesaid ten squares are surrounded by tall houses. Below these, are shops, where all sorts of crafts are carried on, and all kinds of wares sold, such as spices, jewels and pearls. In some shops nothing else is sold but wine of rice and spices, which they always make fresh, and which is cheap.

Many streets lead into these squares. In some of them there are numerous cold baths, staffed by attendants of both sexes, who bathe the men and women who go there, for they are used from childhood to wash themselves with cold water at all seasons. They say that this is a very healthy practice. In those baths they also keep some rooms with hot water for foreigners, who would not be able to stand the cold water, not being used to it. They are in the habit of bathing every day, and would not eat unless they had previously washed.

In other streets, live harlots, of whom there are so many that I dare not say the number. Nor do they only live in the neighbourhood of the squares, where for the most part are the places especially assigned to them, but also all over the city. They live in great splendour, with many perfumes and numerous servants, in finely decorated houses. These women are very clever and expert in their allurements and endearments, and ever have appropriate words ready for every kind of person. So, when foreigners have once tasted of them, they remain, so to speak, beside themselves, and are so taken by their sweetness and charm, that they can never forget them. Thus it is that, when they return home, they say they have been in Kinsai, namely in the City of Heaven, and long to be able to return there.

In yet other streets live all the leeches and all the astrologers, the latter of whom also teach reading and writing. Similarly with all the other numerous arts: each has streets assigned to it near those squares.

Moreover, in each square there are two large palaces, one at either end, where are officers specially deputed by the Great Lord to settle at once any differences that may arise among the traders or the people living in the neighbourhood. It is also the duty of these officers to make sure every day that the proper guards (of which we will speak in due course), have been kept on the bridges; and if they have not, they punish at their discretion.

Along the main street of which we have spoken as running from one end of the city to the other, there stand on either side houses and very large palaces, with their gardens, and next to them houses of craftsmen who work in their shops. At all hours one meets people going about on their business. When one sees such a crowd, one would not think it possible to find food enough to feed them. But every market-day all the squares we spoke of are full of people and merchants, who bring food on carts and boats. And everything is sold. To take an example, from which you may see the quantities of victuals, meat, spices and everything else that is bought and sold there, I, Marco, heard from one of those who attend to the Great Kaan's customs, that every day forty-three loads of pepper were consumed in the city of Kinsai, each load amounting to 223 pounds.

In the Queen's statement it was also remarked that this city possessed twelve guilds, one for each of the principal crafts, namely the twelve most thriving ones, for the minor ones are infinite in number. And it was also stated that each guild had twelve thousand workshops, that is, twelve thousand houses, with not less than ten men in each shop, while in others there were fifteen, twenty, thirty or forty men—not all of them, of course, master-craftsmen, but under the orders of one. And this great number of them is necessary, for this city supplies many other cities of the province. The merchants are so many and wealthy, that no one could tell the whole truth, so extraordinary it is. And I will add that the great men and their wives, as well as the heads of the shops I have mentioned, do nothing with their own hands: they live with as much delicacy and cleanliness as if they were kings. And their women, too, are most delicate and angel-like.

And you must know that when the aforesaid King of Manji was reigning, there was a law that everyone was to follow his father's craft. Even if a man possessed 100,000 bezants, he could not practise any other craft than his father's, nor could he leave it. But you must not suppose that they were obliged to work with their own hands, but only to keep men, as we said before, who practised the craft. But the Great Kaan does not hold them to this. If any craftsman has become so rich as to be able to leave his craft, and is desirous of doing so, he is in no way obliged to continue practising it. And the reason the Great Kaan gives for this, is as follows. If a man practises a craft because he is poor, and cannot otherwise procure his livelihood, and then, in course of time, prospers to the extent of being able to lead an honoured existence without working, why should he be compelled to practise a craft against his will? It were as absurd and unjust as to cross those to whom the gods show favour.

On the south side, as I have said, there is a lake, quite thirty miles in circuit. All around stand many fine palaces and houses, belonging to noblemen and other great men, and they could not be more beautifully planned and built, or more sumptuous. There is also a great number of abbeys and monasteries of the Idolaters.

I will further tell you that in the middle of the lake there are two islands, on each of which stands a most wonderful and sumptuous palace, with more rooms and pavilions than one can imagine; and these palaces are so admirably and so splendidly decorated, that you would think they belonged to an Emperor. When one wishes to hold a wedding-feast or any other kind of banquet, one goes to those palaces. There they hold their weddings and feasts, for there they find all the things that are necessary for a banquet, such as crockery, dishes, plates, table-linen, and so forth, all which things were made by the people of Kinsai themselves, and are kept there by the community in those palaces for that precise purpose. And sometimes there may be a hundred people, some for a banquet, others for a wedding-feast, and yet all find accommodation in different rooms and pavilions, and all is so well arranged, that no one is in anyone else's way.

Besides this, there are on that lake great numbers of barges or boats, both large and small, for pleasure-parties. Ten, fifteen, twenty, and even more people can get into them, for they are from fifteen to twenty paces long, with a broad, flat bottom, so that they can float without heeling to either side. If a man wishes to amuse himself with women or friends, he takes one of these boats, which are always kept furnished with fine tables and chairs, and all else that is necessary for a feast. They carry on board excellent wines and delicious sweet-meats. Each boat has a deck and boards, on which stand men with poles; these they stick into the bottom of the lake (which is no more than two paces deep), and so push the boat whithersoever they are bidden. The inner side of the deck is painted in various colours with figures, and so is the rest of the boat. All round there are windows, made to open and shut, in order that those who sit banqueting along the sides of the boat may look in all directions, and feast their eyes upon the varied beauties of the places through which they are being taken. And, in very truth, sailing thus about the lake gives you greater pleasure and solace than any other you may have on this earth, for the lake stretches along one side of the city, all the size and beauty of which can be seen from the boats—with all its palaces, and temples, and monasteries, and with its gardens planted with immensely tall trees, all along the shore.

Thus one constantly finds these boats on the lake, full of people bent on pleasure, for the inhabitants of this city, once they have finished their daily work, be it a craft or be it trade, have no other thought than that of spending the rest of the day amusing themselves in such wise with their women-folk, or else with public women; they are then only intent upon their bodily pleasure and amusement, feasting in company. Besides going in those boats, they also drive about the city in carriages. Of these carriages I will say something further on, as they form one of the favourite amusements of the inhabitants of Kinsai within the city, just like the boats on the lake.

In the city there are many beautiful houses, very well built, and gorgeously decorated. They take such delight in decorations, paintings, and buildings, that the expense they go to for these purposes is truly remarkable.

Here and there throughout the city there are great stone towers, whither the people carry all their chattels when a fire breaks out in the city. And you must know that outbreaks of fire are very frequent there, for there are many wooden houses.

The citizens are idolaters, are subject to the Great Kaan, and have paper currency. They eat all kinds of flesh, including that of dogs and of other unclean animals, such as no Christian in our parts would eat for anything in the world. Both the men and the women are white and handsome. The majority always dress in silk; this is due to the great quantities of silk they have, for, besides what is produced in the territory of Kinsai, traders constantly bring more from other provinces. The real natives of the city are peaceful, for they were educated to be so by their Kings, who were of that disposition. They are incapable of handling arms, nor do they keep any in their houses. You never witness or hear of any quarrel or violent difference of opinion among them. They carry on their crafts and trade with great honesty and truthfulness. They love one another, so that, with all the good-will that exists among both the men and the women, who are neighbours, you would think that a whole quarter of the town formed a single family. Great indeed is their mutual intimacy, without trace of jealousy or suspicion towards their women, for whom they show the greatest respect; in fact, a man who should hold loose speech with a married woman would be considered a great scoundrel. They are likewise very friendly towards the strangers who visit them for purposes of trade, and willingly receive them in their houses, entertaining them with the greatest kindness, and giving them help and advice on their business. On the other hand, they detest seeing soldiers, even those of the Great Kaan's garrison, as they see in them the cause of their losing their native Kings and Lords.

You must further know that on each of the 12,000 bridges there is always a guard of ten men; they are posted under a porch, five by day, and five by night. Thus in all there are always 60,000 guards on duty. The purpose of this is to protect the city against evil doers, and to prevent any bold adventurer from raising a revolt in the city. At each of the stations of these guards, there is a great wooden tabernacle with a large basin, and a clock to show the hours both of the day and of the night. And always, at the beginning of the night, when one hour has passed, one of the guards strikes once on the tabernacle and the basin, and so the district around hears that it is one hour of the clock. At the second hour, two blows are struck, and so they do every hour, increasing the number of blows every time. The guards never sleep, but always remain vigilant. On the following morning, at daybreak, they begin again striking one hour, as on the previous evening, and so they go on, hour by hour. Some of them go about the quarter, to see if anyone keeps lights or fires on beyond the legal hour. If they find someone who does so, they mark his door, and next morning call him up before the officers; and if he has no adequate excuse, he is condemned. If they find someone walking abroad during the night in forbidden hours, they arrest him, and next morning bring him up before the officers. Similarly, in the day time, if they see some poor man who is incapable of working because he is crippled, they make him go and live in the hospitals, of which there is a great number in the city, having been founded by the ancient Kings, and richly endowed by them; but if the man is healthy, they oblige him to follow some craft. As soon as they see an outbreak of fire in a house, they proclaim the fact by striking in the tabernacle, and straightway the guards of the other bridges come to put it out, and to save the property of the merchants and others, by taking it to the towers we mentioned, or else by carrying it on boats to the islands in the lake; for at night no citizen would dare to leave his house or go where the fire is, except those whose property is endangered, and they are helped by the guards, who are never fewer than one or two thousand.

Another thing I will tell you. In several places within the city there are mounds of earth, at a mile's distance from one another, with, on the top of them, a timber tower where hangs a wooden tablet. A man holds this with one hand, and with the other hand strikes it with a mallet, and the sound can be heard a long way off. These tablets are struck thus every time a fire breaks out, or if any disorder comes about in the city. As soon as that happens, the tablets are immediately struck.

The Great Kaan has the city very well garrisoned, keeping a large number of men there, both horse and foot, and both inside the city and in the neighbourhood; and he sends there the greatest and most faithful of his barons. The reason of this is that Kinsai is the capital and principal city of the province of Manji, and the wealth within it is immense, so that the Great Kaan draws from it such an enormous revenue, that one would hardly believe it. The Great Kaan also has the city so well garrisoned and by so many troops, lest it should rebel.

You must also know that in this city the streets are paved with stones and baked bricks; similarly all the streets and roads of the province of Manji are paved, so that one can traverse the whole province either on horseback or on foot without getting soiled with mud. As, however, the Great Kaan's messengers could not ride quickly on paved roads, a strip is left unpaved for them down one side of each road. Further, the main street of Kinsai, that we mentioned above, is likewise paved with stones and bricks for ten paces on each side, but in the middle it is all covered with a fine minute gravel, with channels that discharge the rain-water into the neighbouring canals, so that the street is always dry.

Up and down this street there constantly pass certain long covered carriages, furnished with silk cloths and cushions, and seating half a dozen people. Every day they are taken by men or women, for pleasure drives. One constantly sees great numbers of these carriages, going down the centre of the main street; the people in them go to the gardens, where they are received by the gardeners in certain cool shady shelters prepared for the purpose; here they remain, enjoying themselves all day with their women-folk, and in the evening they drive home again in those same carriages.

Further, in that city there are no less than 3000 baths or "stoves." The people take great pleasure in them, and go thither several times a month, for they keep their bodies very clean. And I assure you that they are the finest, best, and largest baths in the world, so large indeed, that a hundred men or women can bathe in them at the same time.

I will also tell you that twenty-five miles away from this city, between east and north-east, there is the Ocean Sea. On the shore is a city called Ganfu, with an excellent harbour, to which come very large ships, with immense quantities of costly merchandise from India and elsewhere. The city of Kinsai is connected with the harbour by a river, up which ships can come as far as the city, and further still, for the river flows through other regions too.

I will add that the Great Kaan divided the province of Manji into nine parts; that it is to say, he made nine vast kingdoms of it, giving each a King. All nine are great Kings, but you must understand that they are officers of the Great Kaan's. The accounts of each kingdom are rendered yearly to the Great Kaan's agents, every source of revenue being accounted for. Like all other officers, they are changed every three years. In this city of Kinsai resides one of the nine Kings, and he has more than 140 large and wealthy cities dependent upon him.

Another thing I will tell you, which will fill you with amazement. You must know that the cities of Manji are no less than 1200, and they are all garrisoned on behalf of the Great Kaan, as you shall hear. Know, then, that those that have the smallest number, have a garrison of 1000; the others are garrisoned, some by 10,000, some by 20,000, and some by 30,000 men. The total number of troops is such as can hardly be counted. But you are not to suppose that all these are Tartars; they are Cathayans. Nor are all the troops that garrison a city mounted; on the contrary, a large number is composed of foot-soldiers. The Tartars themselves, being horsemen, do not live in cities situated in marshy places, but only in those built on hard, dry soil, where they can practise horsemanship. To the cities lying in marshy regions, the Great Kaan sends Cathayans, or the people of Manji—or rather, such of them as are soldiers. Every year, in fact, the Great Kaan has chosen from among his subjects those that appear fit to carry arms, and has them enlisted in what are called his "armies." The men that are thus taken from the province of Manji are not put to garrison their own cities, but are sent to other cities, at twenty days' journey. Here they remain for four or five years; after that, they return home, and others are sent in their place. The same applies to the Cathayans.

The greater part of the revenues of these cities that enter the Kaan's treasury, is used for the upkeep of these garrisons. And if it happens that a city rebels—for often enough the population, taken by some sudden fit of fury or savagery, slays its governors—the number of troops that neighbouring cities send immediately, is so immense that the rebellious city is destroyed. For it were a lengthy business to bring an army up from some other province of Cathay—a matter of two months.

The city of Kinsai constantly has a garrison of 30,000 men.

In a word, I assure you in very truth that, for its wealth and for the revenues and profit that the Great Kaan draws from it, the province of Manji is so fabulous as to be beyond all telling, and all belief, too, unless one has seen it. The splendour of this province can hardly be described. I will therefore stop, for I have now but little else to tell you. Yet, there are still a few things I wish to say, and then we will leave the place.

Know, then, that all the inhabitants of Manji have

the customs I will describe to you. As soon as a child is born, the father or the mother has note taken of the day, point, and hour of its birth, and of the constellation and planet under which it was born. Thus everyone knows his own nativity. When a man intends to go on a journey abroad, he goes to the astrologers, and tells them his nativity. They then tell him whether it is well or not that he should set out. And many a time they are induced to give up their journey. Similarly, if a marriage is to take place, the astrologers first examine whether the planets under which the bride and bridegroom were born, are in accord or not with one another; if they are, the wedding takes place; if they are not, it falls through. [Thus it is in all other important matters.] For you must know that their astrologers are exceedingly learned in their art and in diabolical incantations, and the people have great faith in them, for what they say so often comes true. Of these astrologers and magicians, there is a great number in every public square.

Further, when a dead body is carried to be burnt—unless it be that of a man of very humble birth—all his relations, male and female, dress in hemp as a sign of mourning, and follow the body. They take musicians with them, and, as they go, chant prayers to their idols. On reaching the spot where the body is to be burnt, they stop. It is their custom to have great numbers of figures of horses, male and female slaves, camels, silk cloths, and coins cut out in paper. These they throw into the flames, and burn them together with the dead man. And they say that the latter will in the next world have all the slaves and animals in flesh and blood, and the money in gold. And they say, too, that all the honour that is paid to the man as he burns, will also be paid him in the next world, and in the same measure, by their gods and idols.

On account of this belief, as long as they are sure of having these honours when they are dead, they have no fear of death, being convinced of receiving the same honours in the next life. Further, the people of Manji are excitable above all others and very often will kill themselves out of sorrow or excitability. If, for example, it happen that one man slaps another's face, or pulls his hair, or again offends or hurts him in some other way, and that the offender is too exalted and powerful for the other to take his revenge, the latter will, out of his great chagrin, go and hang himself at the offender's door, in order to bring greater contumely and contempt upon him. Thus, once the offender has been discovered, on the evidence furnished by his neighbours, he is condemned to make reparation; that is to say, when the dead man is burned, he must hold a fine feast in his honour, according to their customs, with musicians, servants and so on, as we said before. The chief reason why the unfortunate wretch hangs himself is precisely this—namely, that the rich and powerful man should render him honour at his funeral, in order that he himself may be similarly honoured in the next life.

In this city stands the palace of the king who was Lord of Manji, and of whose flight I have told you. It is the finest and most splendid in the world, and I will tell you something about it.

You must know that King Facfur's predecessors had had a large tract of country—some ten miles in circuit—surrounded by very high battlemented walls. This territory was divided into three parts. Into the central part [namely, into the palace proper], one entered by a very lofty gate. Once inside, one saw on either side twenty very broad and large pavilions, on the ground level, and all of the same size and shape; the [gilt] ceilings were held up by painted columns, all worked in gold and in the finest blues. At the end, one saw the principal pavilion, larger than the others, and likewise painted, with gilt columns and gold-decorated ceiling; on the walls all around, were painted with great skill the stories of previous Kings; there were also the figures of many beasts and birds, of knights and ladies, and of many other wonderful things. It was a marvellous sight to look upon. On all the walls and ceilings, one saw nothing but paintings and gold. Here, every year, on certain days sacred to his idols, King Facfur used to hold his court, receiving at his table the principal lords, the most important master-craftsmen and the wealthiest artificers of the city of Kinsai. Ten thousand people at a time could comfortably sit down to a banquet in the pavilions. This court lasted ten or twelve days; and it was a marvellous sight, passing all belief, to see the magnificence of the guests, all dressed in silk and gold, with so many precious stones on their persons. For each one made every effort to go there making the greatest possible show of wealth and splendour.

Behind this large pavilion of which we have spoken as standing opposite the main entrance, was a wall with a door in it, cutting off this part that we have seen from the rest of the palace. Passing through this door, one entered another great edifice, something like a cloister, with a portico all round, supported on pillars. Here were several chambers for the King and Queen, also decorated in various ways; and so were all the walls. From this cloister one went into a passage, six paces wide, and roofed over; it was so long that it went down to the lake. On either side of this passage were ten courts, built like long cloisters, with porticoes all round. In each cloister, or court, were fifty chambers with their gardens. In these chambers lived a thousand maidens that the King kept in his service. At times the King would go with the Queen, and with some of the maidens, to disport himself on the lake, in boats all covered with silk, or to visit the temples of the idols.

The other two parts of the great enclosure were taken up by woods, by gardens filled with all the good fruits one can imagine, and by many lakes, with all kinds of fish. There were many fountains, too, and all sorts of animals, such as roe-deer, fallow-deer, stags, hares, and rabbits. Here the King went to take his pleasure with his damsels, some in carriages, and some on horseback. And no man was allowed to enter there. He would make the damsels run after the game with dogs; and once they were tired, they would go into the woods standing round the lakes, and, leaving their clothes there, would come out again naked, and go into the water, swimming about, some one way, and some another. And the King would watch them with great delight, and then go home again. Sometimes the King would have his meal taken out into the woods, which were dense with tall trees, and he would then be waited upon by the damsels. Thus, ever dallying with women, he grew up without knowing what arms were; and the result was that, on account of his cowardice and worthlessness, the Great Kaan deprived him, as you have heard, of all his state, to his great shame and ignominy.

All these things were told me, when I was at Kinsai, by a very wealthy merchant of that city, who was then very old and had in past times been intimate with King Facfur. This man knew all about the King's life, and had seen the palace when it was in perfect condition. And it was he who took me to see it. As the new King appointed by the Great Kaan over this part of Manji lives there, the first part of the palace, namely, the pavilions, is just as it used to be, but the chambers of the damsels have fallen into ruin, and one can only see some remains of them. Likewise the wall that surrounded the woods and gardens, is fallen down, and there are now neither trees nor animals.

And you must know, too, that in this city there are 160 *toman* fires, that is, 160 *toman* houses; a *toman* is the equivalent of ten thousand. In other words, there are 1,600,000 houses, among which there are very many large palaces. There is only one church of Nestorian Christians.

And as I have told you of the city, I will add yet another thing that is quite worth mentioning. You must know that all the burgesses of this city—and this applies to all the other cities as well—have the following custom. Everyone has written up over the door of his house his own name, that of his wife, those of his children, of his sons' wives, of his slaves, and of all those who belong to his household; and there is also mention of the number of horses he keeps. If it happen that one of those whose names are written up, dies, the name is cancelled; if, instead, a child is born, its name is added to those of the others. In this way the governor of every city knows how many and what people he has dependent upon him. This is done throughout the whole of the province of Manji, and also in Cathay. There is another excellent custom, too, that I will tell you of: you must know that all those who keep hostelries and lodge travellers, write down the name of the persons they have lodged, and the day and month that they have been there. Thus the Great Kaan may at any moment know who comes and goes about his lands. And it is indeed a custom that shows great wisdom.

Further, I will tell you that in the province of Manji almost all the poor sell their sons and daughters; they sell them to the rich and noble, in order that the sum they receive may help them to live, and that the children themselves may be more comfortably off.

[One more thing, before we leave this city.] I will not pass over a miracle that came to pass when Baian was besieging it. When King Facfur took flight, many of the citizens of Kinsai also embarked, and fled along a broad and deep river, that flows down one of the sides of the city. As they were thus fleeing, all of a sudden the water disappeared, leaving the river-bed quite dry. When Baian heard of this, he hastened to the spot, and obliged all the fugitives to return to the city. And, high and dry across the river-bed, was found a fish that was truly marvellous to look upon: it was quite 100 paces long, but its breadth was out of all proportion to its length. It was all hairy. Many had the daring to eat of it, but not a few of them died. And I myself, Messer Marco Polo, have with my own eyes seen the head of that fish in a temple of idols.

I have told you part of what might be told of Kinsai. I will now tell you of the immense revenue that the Great Kaan draws from this city and its territory, which forms only one of the nine parts of Manji.

Here is told of the great revenue that the Great Kaan draws from Kinsai

I now wish to speak of the immense revenue that the Great Kaan draws from this city of Kinsai, that I have been telling you about, and from the lands dependent upon it, which form only a ninth part of the province of Manji. And in the first place, I will speak of the salt, which is the product that yields most.

You are to know that the salt of this city normally yields 80 *tomans* of gold; as a *toman* is the equivalent of 70,000 *saggi* of gold, the 80 *tomans* amount to 5,600,000 *saggi* of gold. (The value of a *saggio* is greater than that of a gold florin or a gold ducat.) It is truly something fabulous, an enormous sum. The salt-revenue is so large in this city because it is situated in a region near the sea, close to lagoons or marshes, where, in summer time, the water congeals, and salt is gathered in enormous quantities. No less than five kingdoms are supplied with the salt they need from this city of Kinsai.

Having told you of the revenue drawn from the salt, I will now tell you of that drawn from other goods and wares.

You must know that the production of sugar is immense in this province, as in the other eight provinces of Manji—twice greater, indeed, than in the whole of the rest of the world. And this also implies an enormous revenue.

But instead of telling you of each commodity separately, I will speak of all the spices together.

Know, then, that all spices yield three and a third per cent. The thirtieth part, that is, three and a third per cent., is also paid on all goods brought by traders to this city by land, and on all those that the traders carry from here to other cities, either by sea or by land. On the goods that are brought hither by sea, ten per cent. is paid. Of all that is produced in the district, whether animals or fruits of the soil, a tenth part belongs by right to the Great Kaan.

Great, too, is the revenue accruing from the rice-wine, from coal, and from all the twelve guilds I mentioned above as possessing 12,000 shops each. The revenue drawn from these guilds is immense, because everything pays duty. Considerable revenue is also obtained from silk, of which they have such abundance. But why should I make a long story of it? Know that ten per cent. is paid on silk, and this amounts to an incalculable sum.

To conclude, I, Marco Polo, who have often heard the calculations made of the revenue dues accruing from all these goods, assure you that normally, and exclusive of the salt-revenue, they amount every year to 210 *tomans* of gold, equivalent to 14,700,000 *saggi* of gold. Truly this is the greatest sum that has ever been heard of in the way of revenue. And this is only one of the nine parts of the province, even though it be the largest and wealthiest. You may imagine from this, what is the revenue the Great Kaan draws from the whole of Manji.

All this revenue, however, is used by the Great Kaan for the upkeep of the armies that garrison the various cities and districts, and for the purpose of alleviating poverty in the cities themselves.

We will now leave the city of Kinsai, seeing that we have told you a great deal about it. And so we will proceed, and tell you of a city called Tanpinju.

Here is told of the great city of Tanpinju

On leaving the city of Kinsai, one rides one day to the south-east, ever coming across houses and farms and very delightful gardens, and passing through a region abounding in all the necessaries of life. At the end of this day's journey, one reaches the city I have just mentioned, namely Tanpinju, which is very fine and large, and belongs to the government of Kinsai. They are subject to the Great Kaan, and have paper currency. They are idolaters, and burn their dead in the way I have described above. They live by trade and handicrafts. They have great abundance of all the necessaries of life. There is nothing worthy of special mention, and so we will leave this place, and tell you of Vuju.

On leaving the city of Tanpinju, one journeys three days to the south-east, ever coming across cities and towns, all of them fine and large, lying in a region full of all good things, both plentiful and cheap. The people are idolaters. They are subject to the Great Kaan, and have paper currency. They, too, belong to the government of Kinsai. There is nothing especially worth mentioning. At the end of three days' journey, one reaches a city called Vuju. This Vuju is a large city. They are idolaters, and subject to the Great Kaan. They have paper currency, and live by trade and handicrafts. They also belong to the government of Kinsai. There is nothing that we wish to mention in our book, and so we will proceed, and tell you of the city of Ghiuju.

Know, then, that, on leaving the city of Vuju, one

journeys two days to the south-east, ever passing through so many cities and towns, that you would think you were crossing one single city. They have abundance of everything. They have certain big canes, the biggest and longest in the whole country, for you must know that some are four palms in girth, and quite often paces long. There is nothing else worth mentioning. At the end of the two days' journey, one reaches a city called Ghiuju, which is very large and beautiful. They are subject to the Great Kaan, are idolaters, and belong to the government of Kinsai. They have a great deal of silk. They live by trade and handicrafts. They have abundance of all the necessaries of life. There is nothing else worth mentioning, and so we will leave this place, and proceed.

On leaving the city of Ghiuju, one journeys four days to the south-east, ever coming across many cities, towns, and villages. They have great abundance of all the necessaries of life. Here, too, they are all idolaters. They are subject to the Great Kaan, and have paper currency. They also belong to the government of Kinsai. They live by trade and handicrafts. There is plenty of game, both beasts and birds. There are very many lions, both big and fierce. In the whole of Manji they have no sheep, but numbers of buffaloes, oxen, cows, goats and swine. There is nothing else worth mentioning, and so we will leave this region, and proceed, telling you of other things.

At the end of those four days' journey, after leaving the city of Ghiuju, one reaches the city of Chanshan, which is very large and beautiful. It is situated on the top of a mountain, and surrounded by the two channels of a river, which is divided by the mountain into two parts, flowing in opposite directions, one to the south-east and the other to the north-west. This city also belongs to the government of Kinsai, and is subject to the Great Kaan. They are idolaters. They live by trade and handicrafts. There is nothing else worth mentioning, and so we will leave this place, and proceed.

Know, then, that on leaving Chanshan, one rides three days through a most beautiful region, with many cities, towns, and villages, where there are many merchants and craftsmen. They are idolaters and subject to the Great Kaan. And they, too, are under the government of Kinsai. They have abundance of the necessaries of life. They have plenty of game, both beasts and birds. There is nothing else worth mentioning, and so we will proceed.

And you must know that at the end of the three days, one reaches the city of Cuju, which is very large and beautiful. They are subject to the Great Kaan, and are idolaters. And this is the last city under the government of Kinsai. From this point onwards Kinsai has no authority. There begins another kingdom, namely another of the nine parts of Manji, and it is called Fuju.

Here is told of the kingdom of Fuju

On leaving the city of Cuju, the last of the kingdoms of Manji, one enters the kingdom of Fuju. Of this we will now begin speaking.

One journeys six days to the south-east, over mountains and valleys, and through regions thickly studded with cities, towns, and villages. They are idolaters, and subject to the Great Kaan. They belong to the government of Fuju, of which we have now begun speaking. They live by trade and handicrafts. They have great abundance of all the necessaries of life. There is plenty of game, both beasts and birds. There are many big and fierce lions. They have immense quantities of ginger and galingale, so that for a Venetian *grosso* you would get something like eighty pounds of fresh ginger. They also have a kind of fruit that looks like saffron, but is not; it serves the same purpose, however, as saffron.

There are other things worth mentioning. Thus, you are to know that the people eat all sorts of unclean things; they will even willingly eat the flesh of a man, if it be one who has not died of disease. They will eat the whole of a man who has died a violent death, and they say that it is excellent food. Those who go campaigning, that is, the soldiers, do as follows. They have their hair cropped all round, and have a blue mark, like the blade of a sword, painted in the middle of their faces. They all go on foot; except their commander. They carry a lance and a sword, and are the cruellest men in the world; they ever go about killing people, and drinking their blood, and then eating them. They are always on the look-out for an opportunity of killing someone, to drink his blood, and then eat him.

We will now quit the subject, and tell you of something else. You must know that, after journeying three days only of the six I mentioned above, one comes to the city of Kenlinfu, which is very large and noble; it is subject to the Great Kaan, and belongs to the government of Fuju. It is bordered by a large river, spanned by three splendid bridges, among the finest and most beautiful in the world; they rest, at one end, on the city-walls; they are quite a mile long, and nine paces broad; they are all built of stone, with fair marble columns. They are so wonderfully beautiful, that the building of one alone must have cost a treasure. The people live by trade and handicrafts. They have silk in abundance. There are large quantities of ginger and galingale. They make a great deal of cotton cloth with twisted threads, enough to supply the entire province of Manji. They have beautiful women. There is yet another curious thing that is worth mentioning: I assure you they have featherless hens, with a skin like that of a cat; they are all black. They also lay eggs like our hens, and they are very good to eat. There are so many lions, that it is dangerous to travel through the region, except in large companies. There is nothing else worth mentioning, and so we will depart from this place, and proceed.

During the remaining three days of the six I mentioned above, one passes many a city and town, with many traders, and plenty of merchandise, and also with many craftsmen. They have abundance of silk. They are idolaters, and subject to the Great Kaan. There are quantities of game, both beasts and birds. There are big, fierce lions, which do much mischief to travellers. At the end of the three days, and proceeding another fifteen miles, one comes to the city of Unken, where they have an enormous quantity of sugar. From this city the Great Kaan gets all the sugar that is used at his court—enough to represent a considerable sum in value. You must also know that in these parts, before the Great Kaan subjected them to his lordship, the people did not know how to prepare and refine sugar so well as is done at Babylon. They did not let it congeal and solidify in moulds, but merely boiled and skimmed it, so that it hardened into a kind of paste, and was black in colour. But after the country had been conquered by the Great Kaan, there came into these regions some men of Babylon, who had been at the court of the Great Kaan and who taught them how to refine it with the ashes of certain trees.

There is nothing else worth mentioning, and so we will proceed.

On leaving this city of Unken, one rides for fifteen miles, and then one reaches the noble city of Fuju, which is the capital of the kingdom. We will therefore tell you what we know of it.

Here is told of the city of Fuju

Know, then, that the city of Fuju is the capital of the kingdom called Choncha, which is one of the nine parts of the province of Manji. A great deal of trade is carried on in this city, and there are many merchants and craftsmen. They are idolaters, and are subject to the Great Kaan. A vast number of troops is quartered in this city, for several of the Great Kaan's armies are stationed in it. This is because often enough the cities and towns of the region rebel, since, as we have said elsewhere, they have no fear of death, believing, as they do, that they will lead an honoured existence in the next world; another reason is that these people live in strong positions in the mountains. Whenever a city rebels, the soldiers stationed at Fuju go there at once, and take the city, and destroy it. This is why several of the Great Kaan's armies are quartered in this city.

You must also know that, along one side of the city, there flows a large river, quite a mile broad. It is spanned by a beautiful bridge, built on large rafts. These rafts are held in place by strong anchors, and have stout thick planks nailed over them. In this city are built many boats that sail on the river.

In this region there are many lions, which they catch in a special trap. In suitable places they dig two very deep ditches, one beside the other, leaving between them a strip of earth, perhaps an ell broad. Along two sides, they then erect a high hedge, leaving the other two sides, parallel to the strip of earth, open. At night, the man who has made the ditches, chains a little dog on the strip of ground between them, and then goes away, leaving it alone. The dog, being thus chained up and abandoned by its master, keeps on barking. It must be a white dog. The lion, however far it may be, hears the dog's bark, and rushes fiercely towards the animal. On seeing it looming in the dark, it wishes to spring upon it, and so falls into the ditch. In the morning, the owner of the ditches comes, and kills the lion. They eat the flesh, which is excellent, and sell the skin, which is very costly. And if, instead, the man wants to take the lion alive, he has the proper means for pulling it alive out of the ditch.

In that region there are also certain animals called *papioni*, which look rather like foxes. They nibble and damage the canes that produce sugar. When traders cross the region with their caravans, and stop somewhere to rest and sleep, these animals approach stealthily by night, stealing everything they can steal, and carrying it away, thus causing considerable loss to the traders. The latter, however, succeed in catching them as follows. They take large gourds, and cut them in the upper portions, so as to make a hole big enough for one of these animals to force its head through. To prevent the hole opening further under the pressure of the animal's head, they make little holes all round, through which they pass a cord. After this, they smear the bottom of the gourds with fat and then place many of these gourds all round the caravan, at a certain distance from it. Thus, when one of these animals approaches to carry something off, it smells the fat in the gourds, and, running up to one, tries to put its head in, but without success. Being, however, greedy of the food inside, it pushes violently, until it succeeds in forcing its head in. But then it cannot pull it out again, and, as the gourd is light, it lifts it up with its head, and carries it off with it. Then it cannot see where it is going, and the merchants can catch it at will. The flesh of these animals is very good to eat, and the skins sell very dear.

Further, in this region enormous geese are bred, weighing quite 24 pounds each. They have a large gizzard on their neck, and, above the bill, near the nostrils, a kind of swelling like that of swans; only it is much bigger.

In this province, sugar is produced in such quantities as to be beyond all belief. There is much trade in pearls and precious stones. This is due to the fact that many ships come there from India, with crowds of merchants, who traffic in the Indian islands. For you must know that at six days' journey from this city is the port of Zaitun, on the Ocean Sea, whither many ships come from India with a great deal of merchandise; they then sail from this port up the river I mentioned before, as far as this city of Fuju; from there the merchandise is carried into different parts, either by the same river or by land. In this way much precious merchandise comes from India.

They have great abundance of all the necessaries of life. There are beautiful and pleasant gardens, with much excellent fruit. Indeed, it is a fine and admirable city under every aspect.

[Besides idolaters, there are also some in this city who follow the Law of Christ.] In order that you may know how this has come about, I will tell you something that is quite worth recording.

When Messer Matteo, who was Messer Marco's uncle, and Messer Marco himself were in this city, there was in their company a certain wise Saracen, who said to them: "In such and such a place there is a race of people of whom no one knows what Law they follow; they are not Idolaters, for they have no idols; they do not worship fire; they do not profess the Law of Mahomet; nor do they seem to be Christians. If it so please you, let us go and speak with them; mayhap you will discover something as to what they are." And so they went, and began speaking with them, questioning them concerning their customs and their creed. But these people almost seemed to fear lest they were being questioned with the purpose of depriving them of their religion. Then Messer Matteo and Messer Marco, guessing the cause of their fear, encouraged them to speak, saying: "Have no fear, for we are not come here to do you any harm, but rather for your good, indeed for the bettering of your condition." They feared, in fact, that Messer Matteo and Messer Marco had been deputed by the Great Kaan to make this enquiry, and that evil might come to them thereby. But Messer

Matteo and Messer Marco kept on visiting that place every day, becoming familiar with them, and taking interest in their affairs. And so at last discovered that they followed the Law of Christ. For they had books, and Messer Matteo and Messer Marco, reading in them, began to interpret what was written there, and to translate it, word by word, out of the original tongue. And so they found that they were the words of the Psalter. Then they asked them whence it was that they had received that Law and rule of life. And they answered, saying: "From our fathers." In a certain temple of theirs, in fact, they had three painted figures, representing three apostles—three of the seventy who went about the world preaching—and said that in ancient times their fathers had been instructed by them in the law of Christ, that the Faith had been kept alive among them for 700 years, but that they had long been without teaching, so that they did not know the most essential things. "One precept alone has been handed down to us from our fathers, namely that, according to our books, we celebrate and pay reverence to those three as to apostles." Then said Messer Matteo and Messer Marco: "Ye are Christians, and so are we. We counsel you to send to the Great Kaan, and tell him of your condition, that he may recognise you, and that ye may freely profess your Law and rule." For, on account of the Idolaters, they did not dare to profess and follow their Law openly. So they sent two of their number to the Great Kaan. And Messer Matteo and Messer Marco further instructed the messengers that they should first present themselves to a certain man who was the head of the Christians at the court of the Great Kaan, in order that he should explain their condition to the Great Lord himself. And thus the messengers did. What more shall I tell you? He who was the head of the Christians went into the presence of the Great Kaan, and told him that these people were Christians, and were to be recognised as such in his dominions. But when he who was the head of the idolaters heard this, he raised an objection, saying that this was not to be, and asserting that these people were, and had always been, Idolaters, and that everyone had always considered them such. Hence there was a great discussion over this in the presence of the Great Kaan. But at last the latter, becoming wroth, dismissed everyone from his presence, and, summoning the messengers, asked them whether they wished to be Christians or Idolaters. And they answered him, that, if it pleased him and was not unbecoming to his majesty, they would fain be Christians, as their fathers had been. Then the Great Kaan had the necessary writs issued to them, stating that they were to be called Christians, and that all the rules of the Christians, and all the rites demanded by that Law, were to be valid for them. And it was found that, scattered here and there throughout the province of Manji, there were over 700,000 families who followed this Law.

There is nothing else worth mentioning, and so we will say no more, but will proceed, and tell of other things.

Here is told of the city of Zaitun

You must know that, on leaving Fuju, one crosses the river, and journeys six days to the south-east, ever coming across many fine and wealthy cities, towns, and villages, where there is great abundance of everything. There are mountains and valleys and plains. There are immense forests, with a great many trees that produce camphor. There is plenty of game, both beasts and birds. They live by trade and handicrafts. They are idolaters. They are subject to the Great Kaan, and belong to the government of Fuju; that is, they depend upon its ruler.

At the end of the five days, one reaches a very large and noble city, called Zaitun.

Here is the harbour whither all the ships of India come, with much costly merchandise, quantities of precious stones of great value, and many fine large pearls. It is also the port whither go the merchants of Manji, which is the region stretching all around. In a word, in this port there is such traffic of merchandise, precious stones, and pearls, that it is truly a wondrous sight. From the harbour of this city all this is distributed over the whole of the province of Manji. And I assure you that for one shipload of pepper that goes to Alexandria or elsewhere to be taken to Christian lands, there come a hundred to this port of Zaitun. For you must know that it is one of the two greatest harbours in the world for the amount of its trade.

And I assure you that the Great Kaan receives enormous revenues from this city and port, for you must know that all the ships that come from India pay ten per cent., namely a tenth part of the value of all the goods, precious stones, and pearls they carry. Further, for freight the ships take 30 per cent. for light goods, 44 per cent. for pepper, and 40 per cent. for aloes-wood, sandal-wood, and other bulky goods. Thus, between the dues and the freight, traders have to give half of what they carry. Yet, on the remaining half, they make such great profits, that they look forward to returning with more merchandise. It is therefore easy to believe that the Great Kaan draws an immense revenue from this city.

The river that enters the harbour of Zaitun is very large and broad, and flows very rapidly. On account of its velocity, it hollows out many channels for itself, that is to say, it divides in many places into many different branches. It is itself a branch of the river that flows past the city of Kinsai. At the point where it leaves the main channel, stands the city of Tiunju. There are five beautiful bridges that span the river, the largest being quite three miles in length. These bridges are built as I shall tell you. The piers are composed of great stones placed one on the top of the other, and shaped as follows: they are thick in the middle, and taper towards the ends, which are pointed, both towards the sea, on account of the strong flow when the tide climbs up the river, and towards the river itself, on account of the velocity of its current.

They are Idolaters, and subject to the Great Kaan. It is a most pleasant land, abounding in all the necessaries of life. To this city there come from Upper India all those who wish to have their bodies painted with needles, in the way we described before, for there are in it many great masters of this craft.

I will further tell you that in this province, in a city called Tiunju, they make porcelain dishes, of all sizes, the finest that can be imagined. They are made nowhere else, but only in this city. Thence they are distributed throughout the world. There are quantities of them, and they are cheap, so cheap, indeed, that for a Venetian *grosso*, you can get three of them, and such fine ones, that you could not imagine finer. These dishes are made of such a kind of earth as I shall tell you. You must know that the inhabitants of this city collect a certain mud or putrid earth, making great heaps of it, and leaving them for thirty or forty years, exposed to the wind, the rain, and the sun. All those years they do not touch it, and during this time, this earth becomes refined, so that the dishes made with it are blue, shine wonderfully, and are exceedingly beautiful. They cover them with such colours as they wish, and then bake them in ovens. And you must know that when a man makes heaps of this earth, he does so for his children, for, on account of the long time that it must lie idle to become refined, he cannot hope to derive any personal profit from it, or make use of it himself; his son, who comes after him, will obtain profit therefrom.

I will add that the inhabitants of this city have a

speech of their own. But you must know that throughout the whole of the province of Manji, there is but one language, and one manner of writing. Still, there is a certain difference in speech between the various districts, as, amongst us, between Lombards, Provençals, and Frenchmen. The difference, however, is not such, in the province of Manji, as to prevent the people of one city from understanding the speech of those of other districts.

I have now told you of this kingdom of Fuju, one of the nine parts of Manji. From it the Great Kaan obtains greater profit and revenue, than from any of the others, with the exception of that of Kinsai. And this is solely due to the great revenue from the port of Zaitun.

Of the nine kingdoms of Manji, we have told you only of three, namely Yanju, Kinsai, and Fuju. Of these you have been well informed. Of the other six we should also be able to tell you much, but it were too vast a subject to deal with. Moreover, of those three kingdoms, we have given you a detailed account because Messer Marco himself traversed them. For they were on his way. Of the other six, he heard and learned many things, but, as he did not traverse them, his description could not be as full as for the others. Hence we will be silent concerning them.

We have, then, told you enough concerning Manji, and Cathay, and many other provinces, of their peoples, beasts, birds, gold, silver, precious stones, pearls, and merchandise, and of the habits and customs of the inhabitants, and of many more things, as you have heard. Our book, however, does not yet contain all that we wish to record in it, since we still have to tell you all about the Indians—many things, namely that are quite worth recounting to those who do not know them; for there are quantities of marvellous things in India that do not exist in any other part of the world, and it is most right and fitting and profitable to put them into our book. And the master shall put them all down in detail, even as Messer Marco Polo has related and told them.

And in very truth I tell you that Messer Marco lived so long in India, and learned so much of their life, and customs, and trade, that not for a long time has there been anyone better informed than he. Truly some of the things we shall tell are so wonderful, that those who hear them will be not a little amazed. But nevertheless we will record them all, one by one, even as Messer Marco himself related them, stating them to be the truth. And we will begin straightway, as you shall in due time hear in this book.

Here the book begins to tell of India, and of all the wonders that are there, and of the different peoples; and first of all it tells of the ships, which sail thither.

Now that we have told you, as you have heard, of so many provinces on the continent, we will quit this subject, and enter India, to tell of all the wonders that are there. And first of all we will begin with the ships upon which the merchants go to India and return.

You must know that they are built as I shall tell you. They are made of a wood that is called fir, and of pine. They have a deck. On this deck, there are, in most of them, sixty cabins, in each of which a merchant can live comfortably. They have one rudder and four masts. Often they add two more masts, which can be set up and taken down again as the occasion demands. Some of the ships, namely the bigger ones, also have, inside them, thirteen tanks or compartments, made of strong boards firmly joined together; thus, if the ship should chance, by any accident, to spring a leak, either as the result of striking against a rock, or because a hungry dolphin gives it a blow, and staves in some part of it (which happens often enough, for when the ship is sailing by night, and churning up the water along its sides, if it chance to pass near a dolphin, the animal, seeing the foaming water, thinks it is something to eat, and, darting quickly forward, strikes the ship, often staving in a part), then the water flowing through the leak falls into the bilge, which is always kept empty. Thereupon, the sailors ascertain where the leak is, and empty out the flooded compartment, transferring everything into the neighbouring ones; the water, in fact, cannot pass from one compartment into another, so well and strongly built are the partitions separating them. After this has been done, they stop the leak, and replace the cargo previously displaced.

As for the fastenings, I shall begin by saying that these ships are double, namely, there are two layers of planks all round. They are caulked both within and without, and made fast with iron nails. They are not pitched, because they do not possess pitch. They paint them instead in another way, as I shall tell you, for they have a certain stuff which they consider better than pitch. They take lime and finely chopped hemp, pounding them together with a certain tree-oil. By pounding these three things together, I assure you one gets something as sticky as bird-lime. With this they paint their ships. And it is quite as good as pitch.

You must know that some of these ships need 300 sailors, some 200, and some 150, and more or less according to their size. Moreover, they carry a much larger cargo than our ships: they are so big that they can carry 5000, and some of them even 6000, baskets of pepper. Once they had even bigger ships than now, but the violence of the sea had so damaged the landing-places in the islands, that in many localities there was no longer water enough for such large ships. Hence they made smaller ones.

And you must know, too, that they also use oars, each of which is pulled by four rowers.

Moreover, the large ships are accompanied by two

or three smaller ones, manned by 60, 80, or even 100 sailors, and laden with much merchandise, as they are capable of carrying even 1000 baskets of pepper. They have at least two of them, and one is bigger than the other. These smaller ships can also be propelled with oars, and are very often used to tow the large ships by means of ropes or lines. They are tied to one of the large ships with ropes, and go on ahead, pulling the ship after them, whether it be going with oars, or else sailing with the wind on the beam; not, however, when the wind is astern, for then the sails of the large ship would take the wind out of those of the others, and the latter would be run down.

Further, the large ships generally have some ten dinghies to render them various services, such as laying out the anchors, fishing, and so forth. These dinghies are carried slung to the sides of the large ships. The smaller boats we mentioned above also carry some of these dinghies.

I will add that when a large ship has sailed a year, and is to be overhauled, namely repaired, they do as follows: over the two layers of planks they nail a third layer all round the ship. Thus it has triple sides. Then they caulk and paint it over again. That is how they repair it. When they next repair the ship, they nail on a fourth layer of planks. Thus they go on, until there are six layers. After that, the ship is discarded, and no longer used for sailing on the sea.

Another thing I will also tell you—namely how, when a ship is to set out, they make an experiment, in order to discover whether its voyage shall be prosperous or not. The men in the ship take a wicker hurdle, with cords tied to the four corners and to the middle of each side, namely, eight cords in all, the loose ends of which are all tied together to a long rope. Then they look for a drunkard or a madman, and tie him to this hurdle—and indeed no one in his senses and sober would run such a risk. This they do when a stiff gale is blowing. They hold the hurdle up against the wind, which catches it, and carries it up into the air, while the men hold on by the long rope. If the hurdle, as it soars in the wind, begins to dip, they pull the rope a bit, and the hurdle rights itself; then they pay out some of the rope, and the hurdle rises again. If it dips once more, they pull in the rope as much as is necessary for the hurdle to right itself again, and then pay the rope out once more. In this way the hurdle might soar up to such a height as to disappear, were the rope but long enough. And the experiment consists in this: if the hurdle soars straight up, they say that the ship for which the experiment is being made will have an easy and prosperous voyage, and all the merchants flock to it in order to load their wares, and sail upon it. If, instead, the hurdle fails to rise, no merchant will set foot on the ship for which the experiment is made: they say that it will not reach its destination, and all sorts of evils will befall it. And the ship does not leave the harbour that year.

Now I have told you of the ships on which the merchants go to India and return. We will hence leave this subject of the ships, and tell you of India. But first of all I wish to say something of the many islands that lie in the Ocean Sea, which we have now reached. These islands are situated to the east. We will begin with an island called Chipangu.

Here is told of the island of Chipangu

Chipangu is an island towards the east, in the high seas, 1500 miles from the continent. It is a very large island. The people are white, courteous, and handsome. They are idolaters. They are independent, and know no lordship but their own.

You must know that they have immense quantities of gold, because it is found on the spot in great abundance. Moreover, no one ever brings the gold away from the country, for no one goes thither from the continent, not even merchants. This is why they have as much gold as I have said.

I will tell you, too, of a great wonder concerning one of the palaces of the Lord of this island. You must know that he has a very large palace, all covered with fine gold. Just as we roof our houses and churches with lead, so this palace is all roofed over with fine gold: so the value of it is such that one can barely calculate it. Further, the floors of the chambers, of which there is a great number, are also of fine gold, over two fingers in thickness. And all the other parts of the palace, namely the halls, and the windows, are similarly adorned with gold. I assure you that this palace is of such immeasurable wealth that if anyone told the value of it, it would be past all belief.

They have pearls in abundance, of a rose colour, very beautiful, and round, and large. They are worth as much as the white ones, more indeed. In this island some of the dead are buried, and some are burnt; and those that are buried have one of these pearls put into their mouths. This is a custom of theirs. Besides pearls, they also have abundance of many kinds of precious stones. It is a rich island, so rich that no one can tell its wealth.

And you must know that, hearing of this vast wealth, the Great Kaan, namely Cublai now reigning, decided to conquer the island. So he sent thither two of his barons, with a great number of ships, and a multitude of horsemen and foot-soldiers. One of these barons was called Abacan, and the other Vonsanichin. They were very able and valiant. What more shall I tell you? They set sail from Zaitun and Kinsai, and put out to sea. They sailed on, until they reached this island; then they landed, and occupied many plains and villages, but had not yet succeeded in taking any city or town, when there befell them the disaster I will now tell you of. For you must know that there was much envy between those two barons, and neither of them would in any way help the other.

Now, it happened one day that the north wind blew with such violence, that the invaders said that, if they did not depart, all their ships would be wrecked. So they all embarked, and left the island, putting out to sea. But they had hardly sailed four miles, when the violence of the wind increased, and the number of their ships was so great, that many fell foul of one another, and were wrecked. Only such ships as were not in close formation but were sailing separately escaped being wrecked. There was another island nearby—not a very large one. Those who succeeded in landing there, saved themselves; and there was a considerable number of them, not less than 30,000. Those who did not succeed in landing, were all drowned. And many of the ships were destroyed by being driven by the wind against the shore of the island.

When the violence of the wind and the fury of the tempest had abated, the two barons, with the ships that had kept out to sea and avoided shipwreck (and there was a large number of them), returned to this island, and took on board with them all those of any rank, namely commanders of 100, 1000, and 10,000; they could not find room for all the rest too, as they were so many. Then they left the place, and set sail towards their own country.

Those who were left on the island—a large number, as we have said—considered themselves as good as dead, and great was their despair, for they knew not how they could leave the place, and reach a safe harbour. And they saw the ships that had weathered the storm sailing homewards without giving them a thought. For thus indeed they did: they sailed on and on until they reached their country.

But let us leave those who fled, and return to those on the island who held themselves for dead men.

How the Great Kaan's host that survived the storm took the city of their enemies

You must know, then, that when the 30,000 survivors found themselves abandoned on the island, they held themselves for worse than dead, for they saw no way by which they might escape. They were filled with sorrow and despair, and knew not what to do. In such a state of mind did they live on the island.

When the Lord and the people of the large island saw that the enemy's host had been thus scattered and put to flight, and heard of those who had taken refuge on the island, they rejoiced greatly. So, as soon as the sea was calm and quiet, they embarked on numerous ships that they kept in different places, sailed straight to the small island, and landed without delay, intending to capture those that were there. When the 30,000 saw that all their enemies had disembarked, and that no one was left on the ships to guard them, then, like the cunning men they were, they did as you shall hear. While the enemy was advancing to capture them, they went round the island, which rose up high in the centre, so that whichever way round they went, they would come to the enemy's ships. And so it was. On reaching the ships, they straightway boarded them. And it was easy, since there was no one to oppose them.

What more shall I tell you? Once they were on board, they left this island, and turned their prows towards the large one. Here they disembarked, and, bearing with them the standards and ensigns of the Lord of the island, they marched to its capital. On seeing their own standards, the citizens never doubted but that these were their own troops. So they let them enter the city. Thus, as only the old men had been left in the city, the Great Kaan's men took it, and expelled all the inhabitants, except some beautiful women, that they kept for their own purposes. In this way the Great Kaan's men took the city.

When the Lord and the people of the island saw that they had lost their city, and that events had turned out this way, they almost died of grief. They returned with other ships to their island, and besieged the city, so that no one could go in or come out without their knowing. What more shall I tell you? The Great Kaan's men held that city seven months, and made every effort, day and night, to let the Great Kaan know of their plight. But it was all in vain. When they realized that it was impossible, they came to terms with the besiegers, and surrendered, on condition that their lives should be spared, but that they themselves should remain in the island for the rest of their days. This happened in the year 1269 after Christ's Incarnation.

Thus, then, as you have heard, did things go. The Great Kaan ordered one of the barons who had commanded the army, to lose his head. The other baron was sent to a certain savage island called Zorza, where the Great Kaan has many people guilty of grievous offences put to death in the following manner. When he sends someone to be put to death on that island, the skin of a newly-flayed buffalo is carefully wrapped and sewed round the man's hands. As it dries, this skin so tightens round the hands, that it cannot be removed. The man is then abandoned on the island in this condition, to die a miserable death. He cannot, in fact, help himself; he has no food, and if he wishes to eat grass, he must throw himself face downward on the ground. Thus, then, did the Great Kaan have that baron put to death. This he did to the two barons because he had heard that they had borne themselves ill.

I will also tell you of another wonderful thing, that I had forgotten. In one of the towns of the island, a group of men fell into the hands of the two barons; as they had refused to surrender, the barons commanded that they should all be put to death, and their heads cut off. And so it was done, and all had their heads cut off, except only eight of them: and it was impossible to cut off the heads of these: this was by virtue of a certain stone they possessed. Each of them, in fact, had a stone inside his arm, between the flesh and the skin, in such wise that it could not be seen outside. And this stone was charmed, and had this virtue: a man could not die by steel as long as he had it. When the barons were told why these men could not be killed with a sword, they bade them be beaten to death. And they died at once. The two barons had the stones removed from their arms, and treasured them greatly.

Thus, then, did these things happen, namely the defeat of the Great Kaan's troops. We will now quit this, and return to our subject, in order that our book may proceed.

Here is told of the different kinds of Idolaters

You must know that the Idolaters of these islands are of the same kind as those of Manji and Cathay. Further, the Idolaters of these islands, like the others, have idols with the heads of animals—of oxen, pigs, dogs, sheep, and many more. Some idols have a head with four faces; others have three heads, one in the proper place, and one on each side, over the shoulders. Some have four hands, some ten, some a thousand. These last are the best idols they have, those to which they pay the greatest reverence. When Christians ask them why they make their idols in all these different ways, they answer: "Such they were when our fathers handed them down to us. Such we will leave them to our sons and to those that come after them."

The life of these Idolaters is a tissue of such absurdities and devilries, that it is not well to dwell upon it in this book of ours, for it were too wicked a thing for Christians to listen to. We will hence cease speaking of these Idolaters, and tell you of other things.

This much, however, I will tell you, for I wish you to know it, namely, that when one of the Idolaters of these islands captures someone who is not of his friends, then, if the man cannot ransom himself with money, he invites all his friends and relatives, saying: "I wish you to come and dine with me at my house." Then he has the prisoner slaughtered, and eats him in company with his relatives—cooked, of course. And they consider human flesh the best meat that can be had.

But now we will leave this, and return to our subject. You must know that the sea in which these islands lie, is called the Sea of Chin, which means the sea opposite Manji, for in the language of the islanders, Chin means Manji. This sea stretches to the east. According to the good sailors and pilots that navigate it, and who know the truth, there are 7448 islands in it, the majority of which are inhabited. I will add that in all these islands there is no tree but has a powerful and pleasant perfume, and is valuable; no less valuable, for example, than aloes-wood, and even more. There are also many precious spices of different kinds. Further, in those islands grows abundance of a kind of pepper that is as white as snow, as well as black pepper. The amount of gold and other precious things in those islands is truly prodigious. But I must add that they are so far away, that it is a serious business going there. When the ships of Zaitun and Kinsai sail thither, they obtain great profit and gain, but they toil a whole year on their voyage, for they go in winter and return in summer, as only two kinds of wind blow there—one which carries them out, and one that brings them home again: one blows in summer, and one in winter. And you must know that this region is a great way off from India. Moreover, I will add that this sea, though I have said that it is called the Sea of Chin, yet is nothing but the Ocean Sea. They call it the Sea of Chin, just as we speak of the Sea of England, or the Sea of Rochelle; in the same way do they speak in these parts of the Sea of Chin, the Sea of India, and so on. But in every case they are all parts of the Ocean Sea.

But we will say no more of this region and of these islands, as they are much too far out of the way, and also because we have never been there. I will, however, also add that the Great Kaan has nothing to do with them, nor do they pay him any tribute, or bring him any revenue. We will therefore return to Zaitun, and there take up the thread of our book once more.

Here is told of the country of Chanba

On leaving the port of Zaitun, one sails quite 1500 miles to the west-south-west, crossing a great gulf called Keinan. To one travelling towards the north, this gulf stretches to the distance of two months' sailing. To the south-east it borders only on one province, namely Manji, but on the other side it borders on Aniu, Toloman, and many other provinces, that we mentioned before together with these. There is an infinite number of islands scattered over the gulf, most of which are inhabited. On these islands a great deal of gold-dust is found, which is collected in the sea, where the rivers flow into it. There are also great quantities of copper, and other things. The islanders trade among themselves in the wares that are found in one island and not in another. They also trade with the continent, and sell their gold, copper, and other goods, buying for themselves whatever they need. In the majority of these islands, there is great abundance of corn. This gulf is so vast, and so many people live in it, that you would almost think it a world by itself. But we must return to our original subject.

Know, then, that when one has left the port of Zaitun, and sailed 1500 miles west-south-west, crossing the lower part of the gulf of which we have spoken, one reaches a country called Chanba, which is very wealthy and large. They have a King and a language of their own, and are Idolaters. Every year they send a tribute of elephants and aloes-wood to the Great Kaan; it is the only tribute they pay. I will tell you why this King pays such a tribute to the Great Kaan.

You must know that in the year 1278 after Christ's Incarnation, the Great Kaan sent against this King of Chanba one of his barons, Sogatu by name, with a great host of horse and foot. And the latter began waging a fierce war against the kingdom. The King, who was exceedingly old, and had by no means as large an army as the Great Kaan's, being unable to defend himself in the open, held out in his cities and towns, which were so very strong, that he needed fear no one. But all the open plains and villages were ravaged and destroyed. When he saw that the baron was thus laying waste and ruining his kingdom, he was greatly grieved. So he straightway summoned some messengers, and sent them to the Great Kaan to take him the message that you shall hear. After overcoming great difficulties, the messengers reached the Great Kaan's presence, and said to him: "Sire, the King of Chanba greets you as his liege-lord. He tells you that he is of great age, and that he has long held his kingdom in peace. He now sends you word that he is willing to be your vassal. Every year he will pay you a fitting tribute of elephants and aloes-wood. Humbly he prays and begs you to call away from his land your baron and your army, who are laying waste his kingdom." Thereupon the messengers remained silent, and added not another word. When the Great Kaan had heard the message that the old King sent him, he felt pity for him. He straightway bade his baron and his army leave that kingdom, and go and conquer lands elsewhere; and they carried out the orders of their Lord: leaving at once and going to another country. And so every year this King sends as tribute to the Great Kaan an immense quantity of aloes-wood and twenty elephants, the handsomest and the largest to be found in the land.

In this way, as you have heard, did this King become a vassal of the Great Kaan, and this is the reason why he pays him the tribute of elephants and aloes-wood, as I have told you. Now we will leave this subject and tell you certain particulars about this King and his land.

Know, then, that in this kingdom no beautiful girl may get married unless the King has seen her first. If he likes her, he takes her to wife; if he does not, he gives her some money, according to her condition, in order that she may find another husband. And I will add, that, in the year 1285, I, Marco Polo, was in that kingdom, and this King at that time had 326 children, male and female, and, among them, more than 150 were men fit to bear arms.

There are very many elephants in this kingdom. They also have great abundance of aloes-wood. They have many forests of the wood called ebony, which is exceedingly black, and of which chess-men and ink-holders are made.

There is nothing else worth recording in our book; let us therefore quit this place and proceed; and we will tell you of a great island called Java.

Here is told of the great island of Java

You must know that, on leaving the kingdom of Chanba, one sails 1500 miles south-south-east, and reaches a very large island called Java. According to experienced sailors who know the matter well, it is the largest island in the world, having a compass of quite 3000 miles. It belongs to a great King. They are idolaters, and pay tribute to no one. This island is immensely rich. They have pepper, nutmegs, spikenard, galingale, cubebs, cloves, in a word all the precious spices one can think of. Great numbers of ships go thither, with many traders who buy sundry wares, from which they obtain much profit and gain. In this island there is such wealth, that no man in the world could calculate or describe it. And I will add that the Great Kaan was never able to take it on account of the great distance, and the dangers of the voyage thither. The merchants of Zaitun and Manji have in the past obtained great profit from the trade with this island, and still do so. The greater part of the spices sold in the world, comes from this island.

Now I have told you of this island, and will say no more about it, but will proceed.

Here is told of the islands of Sondur and Condur

On leaving this island of Java, one sails between south and south-west for 700 miles, after which one finds two islands, one larger and one smaller. The one is called Sondur, and the other Condur. They are two uninhabited islands, and therefore we will pass on.

One leaves these islands, and proceeds for some 500 miles to the south-east. One then reaches a continental province, called Locac, which is very large and rich. There is a great King in it. They are idolaters, and have a language of their own. They pay tribute to no one, for their land is so situated that no one can enter it to do any mischief. If it were possible to do so, the Great Kaan would soon make it submit to him. In this country there grow immense quantities of brazil-wood and ebony. They have great abundance of gold, so great, indeed, that no one could believe it without seeing it. They have elephants, and game, both beasts and birds, in great plenty. From this region come all the porcelain shells that are used as money in different countries, as I have told you.

There is nothing else worth mentioning, except that it is a wild region, whither few travellers go. The King himself does not wish anyone to go there, so that no one may know the wealth it possesses, and what its conditions are.

We will therefore leave this place, and proceed telling you of other things.

Here is told of the island of Pentan, and of other islands

You must know that when one leaves Locac, one sails 500 miles to the south, and reaches an island called Pentan, which is a very wild place. All its forests are of odoriferous trees of great value. Not far off, there are two other islands.

Let us leave this place, and proceed between these two islands for some 60 miles. The water is only about four paces deep, and big ships, when they pass through, must haul up their rudders, because they draw nearly four paces of water. After those 60 miles, one sails on to the south-east for some 30 miles; then one reaches an island that forms a kingdom; both it and its capital are called Malaiur. They have a king and a language of their own. The city is very large and noble. There is a great deal of trade in spices and other wares. For there is great abundance in that island of such products.

There is nothing else worth mentioning. And so we will leave this place, and proceed. We will tell you of Java the Lesser, as you shall hear.

Here is told of the island of Java the Lesser

After leaving the island of Pentan, and sailing some 100 miles to the south-east, one finds the island of Java the Lesser. But you must understand that it is not so small but that it has a compass of 2000 miles. We will tell you all about this island in detail.

You must also know that in this island there are eight kingdoms and eight crowned Kings. All the islanders are idolaters, and have a language of their own; indeed, each of the eight kingdoms has a language of its own. In this island there are immense riches—abundance of precious spices, aloes-wood, brazil-wood, ebony, and many other kinds of spices, that, on account of the great distance, and the dangers of the voyage, never reach our countries, and are only sent to the provinces of Manji and Cathay.

Now I intend to tell you of the nature of these peoples, one by one.

But first of all I wish to tell you one thing that will certainly amaze you; you must know that this island is so far to the south that the North Star is never to be seen there, neither little nor much. And now let us return to the subject of the peoples. And we will begin by speaking of the kingdom of Ferlec.

Here is told of the kingdom of Ferlec

You must know that in the kingdom of Ferlec the people were all idolaters, but, on account of the Saracen traders who frequent the kingdom with their ships, they have been converted to the Law of Mahomet—only, however, the inhabitants of the city. The inhabitants of the mountains are like beasts, for I assure you that they eat human flesh, and all other kinds of flesh, both clean and unclean. They worship the most varied things; the first thing they see on getting up in the morning, is to them an object of worship.

I have told you of the kingdom of Ferlec. I will now tell you of the kingdom of Basman.

Here is told of the kingdom of Basman

On leaving this kingdom of Ferlec, one enters the kingdom of Basman. This is an independent kingdom, with a language of its own; but they are people who have no Law, unless it be that of brute beasts. They call themselves lieges of the Grean Kaan, but pay him no tribute, as they are so far away that the Great Kaan's armies could never go there. Yet all the people of the island call themselves his subjects, and at times, by means of travellers passing through, send him something beautiful or curious as a gift, and especially a certain kind of black goshawk of theirs.

They have wild elephants, and great numbers of unicorns, hardly smaller than elephants in size. Their hair is like that of a buffalo, and their feet like those of an elephant. In the middle of the forehead they have a very large black horn. You must know that they do not wound with their horn, but only with their tongue and their knees. For on the tongue they have very long, sharp spines, so that when they become furious against someone, they throw him down, and crush him under their knees, wounding him with their tongue. Their head is like that of a wild boar, and is always carried bent to the ground. They delight in living in mire and in mud. It is a hideous beast to look at, and in no way like what we think and say in our countries, namely a beast that lets itself be taken in the lap of a virgin. Indeed, I assure you that it is quite the opposite of what we say it is.

They have great numbers of monkeys, of many different and strange kinds. They also have goshawks as black as crows; they are very big, and excellent for fowling.

I also wish you to know that the pygmies that some travellers assert they bring from India, are a great lie and cheat, for I may tell you that these creatures, whom they call men, are manufactured in this island; and I will tell you how. You must know that in this island there is a kind of very small monkey, with a face like a man's. They take these monkeys, and, by means of a certain ointment, remove all their hairs except round their genitals; then they stick into their chins certain long hairs to look like a beard. Then they dry them. As the skin dries, the holes into which the hairs have been stuck, close, so that the hairs look as if they had grown there naturally. Further, as their feet, hands, and certain other members are not quite the same as those of a man, they pull and shape them with their hands, and so make them similar to those of a man. Then they put these beasts out to dry, and shape them, daubing them with camphor and other things, until they look as if they had been men. But it is a great cheat, since they are manufactured even as I have told you. For such tiny men as these would seem to be, have never been seen in India or in any other more savage country.

But we will say no more of this kingdom, for there is nothing else worth mentioning. We will therefore cease speaking of it, and tell you of another kingdom, called Samatra.

Here is told of the kingdom of Samatra

You must know, then, that, when one leaves the kingdom of Basman, one enters into the kingdom of Samatra, which is situated in this same island. Here Marco Polo in person resided five months, because the weather prevented him from continuing his voyage. Here, too, the Northern Star does not appear. Nor do the north-west stars appear, neither much nor little. They are savage Idolaters, and have a rich and powerful King. They declare themselves lieges of the Great Kaan.

I will tell you in what way Marco and his men lived here five months. Know, then, that, during these five months, Messer Marco Polo, who had landed with quite 2000 followers, had great trenches dug between his camp and the interior of the island. This was out of fear of these bestial people, who devour men. The trenches abutted at either end on the harbour. On them he had five timber towers built, like battlemented scaffolds. Thus he remained five months with his men, protected by these fortifications. This was possible because of the great amount of timber in the place. By and by the islanders started coming to sell

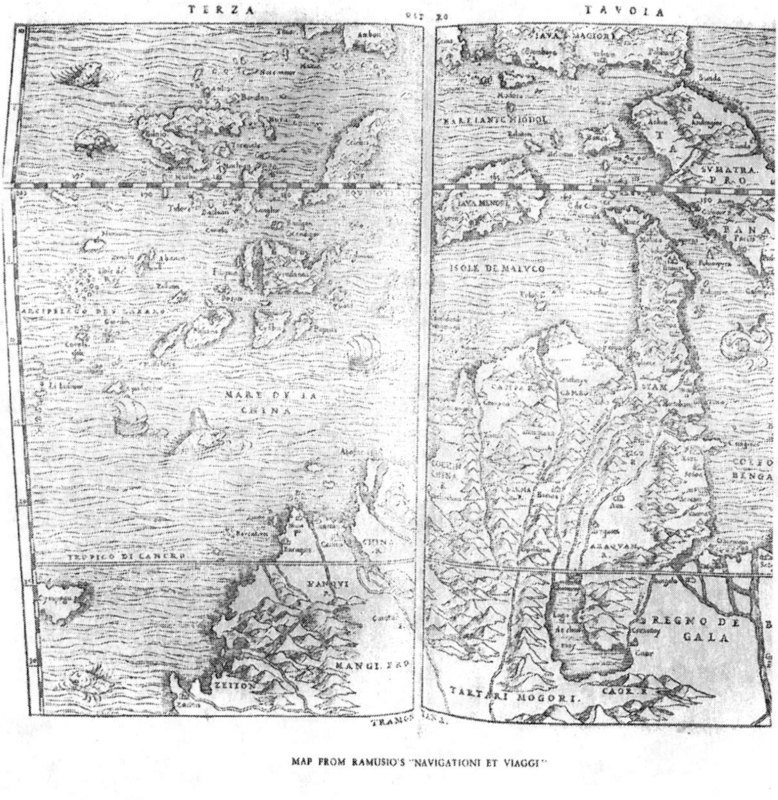

MAP FROM RAMUSIO'S "NAVIGATIONI ET VIAGGI"

victuals and other things, for mutual confidence was beginning to spring up between them.

In this region there is the finest fish in the world. They have no wheat, and live on rice. They have no wine, except such as I shall tell you of. You must know that they have a certain kind of tree, from which they cut a branch, hanging a large pot to the stump that is left; I assure you that in the course of a day and a night the pot is full. And this wine is excellent to drink; indeed its virtue is such that it cures dropsy, phthisis, and spleen. These trees are somewhat like small date-palms, and have very few branches; if one of these branches is cut at the proper season, you get a fine supply of excellent wine, as I have said. I will add that when the stump gives no more wine, they water the trees, making the necessary amount of water flow along little conduits from neighbouring streams. After an hour of this, the liquid begins to flow again, not, indeed, as red as before, but lighter in colour. Thus they have both red wine and white.

They have great quantities of Indian nuts, as big as a man's head, and delicious to eat. When they are fresh, these nuts have, inside the kernel, a certain liquid that in taste and sweetness is better than any wine or any other drink that ever was drunk.

They eat any kind of flesh, both clean and unclean.

Now we have told you of this kingdom. We will cease speaking of it, and tell you of Dagroian.

Here is told of the kingdom of Dagroian

Dagroian is an independent kingdom, and has a language of its own. It is situated on this same island, and has its own King. The people are very wild, and declare themselves lieges of the Great Kaan. They are Idolaters. First of all, I will tell you of a most evil custom of theirs, as you shall hear.

You must know that when one of them, be it a man or a woman, falls ill, the relatives send for the magicians, asking them to see whether the sick person is to recover. By means of their diabolical arts and incantations, and with the help of their idols, these magicians know whether the sick person is to recover or to die. But though we have spoken of "diabolical arts," you are not to suppose that they publicly avow this; on the contrary, they assert that they have this knowledge by virtue of their gods, and by means of their own arts. If the magicians say that the sick man is destined to die, the latter's relatives send for certain men whose office is that of putting to death the sick who are considered doomed to die. These men come and, taking the sick person, put something over his mouth, so that he dies of suffocation. Once he is dead, they cook him. Then all the dead man's kinsfolk come and eat him all up. And I assure you that they even eat all the marrow inside the bones; this they do because they do not wish that any part of his substance should remain. They say, in fact, that if any substance were to remain in the bones, it would produce worms, which would die through lack of food; and from the death of these worms great harm would accrue to the dead man's soul, for it would be a sin on its part, seeing that so many souls born of its substance would perish. This is why they eat everything up. After they have done eating, they take the man's bones, and place them in a pretty little casket, which they hang up in some large cave in the mountains, where no beast or any other evil thing may reach them.

I will add that, if only they can, they will capture any man who is not a fellow-countryman, and, if he cannot ransom himself, they slaughter him, and straightway eat him up. Now, this is a most hateful habit and an evil custom.

Now I have told you of this kingdom. We will therefore leave it, and tell you of Lanbri.

Here is told of the kingdom of Lanbri

Lanbri is a kingdom that has a King of its own, and declares itself subject to the Great Kaan. They are Idolaters. There is great abundance of brazil-wood. They also have camphor, and other kinds of precious spices. As for the brazil-wood, you must know that they sow it. When it has grown to the size of a small shoot, they root it up, and plant it again elsewhere. There they leave it for three years, and then transplant it once more with all its roots. I will add that we brought some of that seed back to Venice, and sowed it, but nothing came up. This was due to the coldness of the place.

Another thing I will tell you, that is most remarkable. You must know that in this kingdom there are men—indeed, they are the majority—with tails a palm long. These men do not live in cities, but in the open, among the mountains. The tail is not hairy, and is as big as a dog's.

There are quantities of unicorns, and abundance of game, both beasts and birds.

We have now told you of Lanbri. We will leave it, and tell you of Fansur.

Here is told of the kingdom of Fansur

Fansur is an independent kingdom. They have a King of their own, are Idolaters, and declare themselves lieges of the Great Kaan. They also belong to the island of which we have been speaking. In this kingdom grows the best camphor in the world, called Fansur Camphor; it is more costly than any other, for I assure you, it is sold for its weight in gold. They have no wheat or other kind of corn, but live on rice and milk. They have wine, that they get from trees, such as I have described before.

I will tell you another thing which is truly a wonder. You must know that in this province they have tree-flour, and I will tell you what it is like. They have a kind of very big, tall tree, that is full of flour inside. The wood of these trees amounts perhaps to three finger-breadths of bark, and all the rest is pith, namely flour. And they are such big trees, that it takes two men to enbrace one of them. This flour is put into tubs full of water, and stirred with a stick. The chaff and rubbish come up to the surface, and the flour sinks to the bottom. After this, the water is drained away, and the clean flour is left on the bottom of the tub. Then it is dressed, and various kinds of eatables are made, such as cakes, and so forth, of the kind that we prepare with wheat-flour. They are very good. Messer Marco and his companions know it well by experience, as they repeatedly ate this bread; moreover, Messer Marco brought with him some of the flour, and also some bread made with it. This bread tastes rather like barley-bread.

The wood of these trees is as hard as iron, and sinks like iron, if thrown into water. This wood will split straight down from the top to the bottom, like a cane. When the flour has been removed from the trees, the wood is left, some three fingers thick, as has been said. With this wood, the people make darts—short ones, not long ones, for if they were long, no one could wield them, or even hold them, the wood being so heavy. They sharpen the tip of these darts, and then scorch the point a little in fire. Thus prepared, these darts are superior to iron ones for piercing any armour.

Now we have told you about the kingdoms in this part of the island. Of the remaining kingdoms, in the other parts of the island, we will say nothing, never having been there. We will therefore quit this subject, and tell you of a very small island called Necuveran.

Here is told of the island of Necuveran

On leaving Java and the kingdom of Lanbri, and journeying some 150 miles to the north, one reaches two islands, one of which is called Necuveran.

On this island the people have no King, and live like beasts. I assure you that they go about entirely naked, both the men and the women, with not the least stitch to cover them. They are Idolaters.

[And I will tell you of a certain custom of theirs.] They have beautiful silk napkins or handkerchiefs, of all colours, three ells long. They buy them off passing merchants, and keep them in their houses, on poles, as a sign of their wealth and nobility, just as we keep pearls and precious stones and gold and silver dishes. They never use them, but only keep them for show. And he who has the greatest number of them, and the finest ones, is considered the noblest and the best.

And I will add that all their woods are of noble and valuable kinds of trees; you find white and red sandal-wood, Indian nuts, which they call Pharaoh's nuts, apples of Paradise, cloves, brazil-wood, and many other good trees besides.

There is nothing else worth mentioning, and so we will leave this place, and tell you of another island, called Angaman.

Here is told of the island of Angaman

On leaving the two islands of which we have just spoken, one sails westwards for 100 miles, reaching a very large and wealthy island called Angaman. They have no King. They are Idolaters, and live like wild beasts. And I will tell you of a race of men, which is quite worth mentioning in our book. You must know in very truth that all the men in this island have heads like dogs, and teeth and eyes also like dogs. I assure you that, as regards their heads, they all look like big mastiffs. They have abundance of spices. They are a very cruel people. They eat men, all those they can catch, as long as they are not of their race. They have great abundance of every variety of spiceries. They feed on rice, milk, and all kinds of flesh. They also have Pharaoh's nuts, apples of Paradise, and many other fruits, different from ours.

This island lies in so swift-flowing and deep a sea, that ships can neither anchor there nor proceed on their way, for the sea makes them drift into a bay they can never get out of again. And this is the reason: this sea, in its violence, eats its way into the land, uprooting trees, and washing them out into the bay. The number of trees constantly being washed out into the gulf, without ever leaving it again, is truly prodigious. Thus ships entering the gulf get so entangled among those trees, that they cannot move, and so they remain there for ever.

We have now told you of this island, and of its strange inhabitants. We will therefore leave it, and tell you of other things. We will speak of an island called Seilan.

Here is told of the island called Seilan

On leaving the island of Angaman, one sails, for about 1000 miles, west-south-west, reaching the island of Seilan, which, as regards size, is without doubt the largest in the world. And this is why: it has a compass of 2400 miles. Once, indeed, it was larger still, with a compass of 3600 miles, as you can see in the charts of the mariners of those seas. But the north wind blows there with such violence, that it has made the sea submerge a considerable part of the island; and this is the reason why it is no longer so big as it once was. You must also know that, on the side struck by the north wind, the island is very low and flat, so that when one reaches it on a ship from the high seas, one does not see the land until one is upon it.

We will now tell you all about this island. They have a King called Sendeman. They are idolaters. They pay tribute to no one. They go all naked, except that they cover their middles. They have no kind of grain, except rice; they also have sesame, with which they make oil. They live on flesh, milk, and rice. In this island, they also have the tree-wine of which I have told you before. They have immense quantities of brazil-wood—the best in the world.

We will now leave this subject, and tell you of the most precious thing in the world. You must know that in this island alone, and in no other part of the world, are born the noble and precious rubies. Sapphires, topazes, amethysts, garnets, and many other precious gems are also born there. Now, I will tell you that the King of this province possesses the most beautiful ruby in the world—the finest that ever was or will be seen. I will tell you what it is like. Know, then, that it is about a palm long, and quite as thick as a man's arm. It is the most resplendent thing on earth to look at. It has not the smallest flaw. It is as red as fire. It is of such immense value, that it could hardly be purchased for money. And I assure you that the Great Kaan sent envoys to this King, to tell him that he wished to buy the ruby, and that, if he would but give it, he himself would pay the price of a city. But the King said that he would not give it for anything in the world, because it had belonged to his ancestors. For this reason the Great Kaan was in no wise able to obtain it.

The islanders are no warriors, but wretched and cowardly people. If it chance that they need soldiers, they employ those of other countries, and especially Saracens.

There is nothing else worth mentioning, and so we will leave this place, and proceed, telling you of Maabar.

Here is told of the great province of Maabar

On leaving the island of Seilan, one sails some sixty miles to the west, reaching the great province of Maabar, known as Greater India. Indeed, it is the best of the Indies. It is on the mainland. You must know that in this province there are five Kings, who are own brothers; we will tell you of them, one by one. Know, too, that it is truly the noblest and richest province in the whole world. I will show you why.

Know that at this end of the province reigns one of these brothers, Sender Bandi Devar by name, who is the most important and the greatest. In his kingdom are found very large pearls, both good and beautiful. And you must know that the greater part of the pearls and precious stones that are found, come from Maabar and from the island of Seilan. I will tell you how pearls are found and gathered.

There is a bay in that sea, between the island and the mainland. Over the whole of this bay, the water is not more than ten, or at most twelve paces deep; and some parts of it are only two paces deep. In this bay, pearls are found. I will tell you how. Several traders enter into partnership, and form a single company; they then take a large boat, made for the purpose, in which each of them has a room set apart and specially prepared for him; in it there is a tub full of water, and other necessary implements. There are many of these ships, for there are many fishermen engaged in this industry, and many companies. Besides the large boat, each company also takes a certain number of small ones, which tow the large boat, and carry its anchors. The traders further hire a considerable number of men, that is to say they give them a certain sum, so that they shall remain in their service from the beginning of April to the middle of May, or as long as the fishing lasts.

[As I have spoken of the traders' expenses], I will

add that they have the following dues to pay. First of all, they give the tenth part to the King. Another part they give to the man who charms the big fish, so that they shall do no harm to those who go under water to look for the pearls: to him they give one part in twenty. These fish-charmers are Brahmins; they only charm the fish in the day time, for at night they break the spells, so that the fish can do as they please. I will add that these Brahmins also charm any other kind of beast or bird, or indeed any living creature.

When the boats, big and small, are ready, as well as all the men, the traders go to the bay I have mentioned, between the beginning of April and the middle of May, to a place called Bettalar, which is on the mainland. From here, they sail out some sixty miles into the sea, always in a southerly direction. Then they cast anchor, and the hired men enter the little boats of which we have spoken. It is they who fish for the pearls; and this is how.

On reaching the place we have mentioned, the men inside the little boats, who are in the pay of the traders, leave the boats, and dive into the water. They go down to a depth of four, five, and even twelve paces. They remain below the surface as long as they can. When they can hold out no longer, they come up again; they rest a little, and then dive down again. This they do the whole day through. When they are at the bottom of the sea, they find there certain shell-fish, commonly called sea-oysters. In these oysters are found the pearls, large and small, and of all kinds. These shells are opened, and put into those tubs full of water that are in the big boats; the pearls are found inside the flesh of the shell-fish. Through soaking in the tub, this flesh becomes soft and rotten, till it looks like white of eggs; it then floats on the top, and the pearls remain quite clean on the bottom.

In this way pearls are fished in such enormous quantities as to be past all counting. And you must know that the pearls found in this sea, or at least many of them, are carried all over the world, as most of them are round and shiny. I assure you that there are immense quantities of dues, and that the King of this country draws a vast revenue from them.

Now we have told you how pearls are found. I will add that as soon as the middle of May comes round, no more of those shell-fish are to be found, I mean of those containing pearls. True it is, however, that some 300 miles away from the place I have spoken of, one can find them; that is from September to the middle of October.

I will also tell you that in the whole of this province of Maabar there is no need for tailors or workmen to cut and sew clothes, for they all go naked, at all seasons. For I assure you that all the seasons there are temperate; thus they never suffer either heat or cold. So they always go about naked, merely covering their middles with a piece of cloth. The King goes about like the others, except that he wears certain other things I will tell you of.

Know, then, that their King goes about all naked, except that he covers his middle with a fine cloth, and wears all round his neck a necklace studded with precious stones—rubies, sapphires, emeralds, and so forth—so that it is of immense value. He also wears round his neck a fine silk thread, which hangs down in front of him to the length of a pace; on this thread are strung most beautiful large pearls and most precious rubies, 104 in all. I will tell you why they are 104. You must know that he wears these 104 gems because every day, morning and evening, he has to recite a prayer to his idols 104 times. Thus their faith and their custom bid them; thus the other Kings his ancestors did, and this duty they have handed down to him. This, then, is why he wears the 104 gems round his neck. The prayer consists of these words, "Pauca, Pauca, Pacauca"; and they say nothing else.

I will further add, that the King also wears round his arms, in three different places, certain gold bracelets, all studded with most precious stones and very large and valuable pearls. Moreover he wears, too, similar bracelets, studded with very precious stones and pearls, in three different places round his legs. Furthermore, he wears splendid pearls and other gems on his toes. It is truly a wonder to see. What more shall I tell you? Know in very truth that this King carries on his person so many stones and pearls, that the value thereof is greater than that of a goodly city. There is no one who can tell or count the great sum that the jewels worn by that King are worth. Nor is it any wonder that he has as many such jewels as I have said, for these precious pearls and stones are found in his kingdom.

Another thing I will also tell you. No one may take out of his kingdom any big or valuable stone or any pearl over half a *saggio* in weight. And you must know that several times a year he issues a proclamation throughout his kingdom, to the effect that all who possess fine pearls and valuable stones are to bring them to his court, and he will have them paid twice their value. It is a custom of his kingdom to give twice the value of all fine pearls and valuable stones. So traders and other people, when they have such fine stones, willingly bring them to court, as they are well paid. This, then, is the reason why this King is so wealthy, and possesses so many precious pearls.

I have now told you about this. I will next tell you of other wonderful things.

You must know in very truth that this King has a thousand women—five hundred wives and as many concubines. For I assure you that the moment he sees a beautiful woman or damsel, he wants her for himself. And he committed the action I will now relate to you. You must know that a brother of his had a very beautiful wife: straightway he took her, and kept her for himself. The brother, like the wise man he was, bore with the affront, and did not quarrel. This, however, is the reason why often enough he has been on the point of making war upon him. But every time this threatened, their mother showed them her breasts, saying: "If war breaks out between you, I will cut off my breasts that suckled you." And in this way the quarrel has remained dormant.

Another thing, too, I will tell you about this King, that is truly to be marvelled at. You must know that he has a large number of trusty lieges, and this is what they are like: they are the King's lieges, both in this life and in that to come, if you will but believe them. I will tell you more of this wonder. These trusty lieges wait upon their lord at court; they go riding with him; they have a very high position in his court. Wherever the King goes, these barons accompany him, and they enjoy great authority throughout the kingdom. Moreover, when the King is dead, and his body is burning on the pyre, then these barons, who were his lieges during his life-time, as I have said, throw themselves into the flames, and burn together with the King, in order to keep him company in the next world.

Further I will tell you that in this kingdom there is the following custom. When the King dies, leaving a great treasure, his surviving son would not touch it for anything in the world. For, he says: "I have all my father's kingdom, and all his subjects; so I can very well procure a treasure for myself, even as he did." So the Kings of this kingdom leave the treasure intact, and hand it on from one to the other; and each of them hoards on his own account. For this reason the treasure of this kingdom is truly immense.

I will add that in this kingdom no horses are born. So all the money, or the greater part of it, brought in by the yearly revenues, is spent by the King in buying horses; and I will tell you in what way. You must know that the merchants of Cormos, Kisi, Dufar, Eshier, and

Aden—all of them provinces abounding in all kinds of horses—buy the best horses, load them on ships, and take them to this King, and to his four brothers, who are also Kings. They sell them at no less than 500 *saggi* of gold each, which are worth more than 100 silver marks. And I assure you that this King buys quite 2000 a year; and his brothers buy as many. And at the end of the year, none of them has more than 100. They all die off, for there are no farriers, and the people do not know how to look after them; so the horses die for want of care. And I assure you that the merchants who bring the horses there to sell, neither take farriers with them, nor let any go there, for they want the horses of these Kings to die off in this way.

I will also tell you that in this kingdom there is also another custom I will mention. When a man has committed a crime, so that he is condemned to die, and the King has bidden him be put to death, then the man who is thus condemned declares that he wishes to kill himself in honour, and for the love of, such and such an idol. The King then gives his consent. Then all the relatives and friends of the man who is to kill himself, take him, and place him on a chair, giving him twelve daggers; then they carry him about the town, keeping on repeating: "This valiant man is going to kill himself for the love of such and such an idol." Even so, as I have told you, do they carry him about the town. When they reach the place of execution, he who is to die takes two of the twelve daggers, and cries out loud: "I kill myself for the love of such and such an idol." As he says these words, he straightway, with one single blow, sticks the two daggers into his thighs. Then he takes the remaining daggers, two at a time, and sticks two into his arms, two into his belly, two into his breast, and so on, until he has stuck them all into his body. And at every stroke, he calls out: "I kill myself for the love of such and such an idol." When all the daggers are stuck into him, he takes a two-handled knife, like those with which hoops are made; this he places behind his head, against the nape of his neck, and then, pulling it violently forwards, he cuts his neck. For that knife is exceedingly sharp. Once he is killed, his relatives burn his body in the midst of great rejoicings.

I will tell you that in this kingdom there is yet another custom. When a man is dead, and his body is being burnt, his wife throws herself on to the pyre, and lets herself be burnt together with her husband. The women who do this receive great praise from all. And I assure you that they are many.

I will tell you, too, that the people of this kingdom worship idols. Most of them worship an ox, because they say that the ox is an excellent animal. They would not dare eat of an ox for anything in the world, nor would they kill one. True it is that there is another race of men among them called *Gavi*, who have no scruple about eating beef. But even then they dare not slaughter an ox. Only, when an ox dies a natural death or gets killed by accident, these people do eat of it. And I will add that all their houses are smeared with ox-dung.

I will tell you that they have yet such another custom as I shall describe to you. You must know that the king, the barons, and the other people, all sit on the ground. When they were asked why they did not sit more honourably, they answered that sitting thus on the ground is more than honourable, because we were made of earth, and to the earth we shall return. Hence we can never render too much honour to the earth; nor ought anyone to despise it.

I will further add that the *gavi* I mentioned, namely all that race of people who will eat of the flesh of an ox accidentally killed, descend from those who killed St. Thomas the Apostle in the days of old. Another thing I will add, too: no member of this race of the *gavi* can enter the place where the body of St.

Thomas lies. You must know that not ten, twenty, or more men could hold one of these *gavi* where the holy body lies; nay, not ten, twenty, or more men could put one of these *gavi* into the place where the body of St. Thomas lies. The place will not receive them; and this is by virtue of the holy body.

In this kingdom no kind of grain grows, except rice alone. And I will tell you a still stranger thing, that it is well to relate. You must know that if a fine stallion covers a fine mare, all that is born is a miserable little horse with crooked legs, which is worthless, and cannot be ridden.

I will tell you, too, that these people go to war with lance and shield, but otherwise stark naked. And they are neither valiant nor good soldiers, but miserable cowards. They kill no animals, nor any living creature. When they want to eat the flesh of a sheep or of any other beast or bird, they have the animal slaughtered by Saracens, or by other people who do not follow their faith and their customs.

I will tell you, too, that they have the following custom. All of them, men and women, bathe their bodies in water twice a day, morning and evening; nor would they eat or drink until they have bathed. And those who do not bathe twice a day, are looked upon much as we look upon Paterins.

And you must know that when they eat, they only use the right hand, nor do they touch any food with the left. They do and touch all clean and beautiful things with their right hand; the office of the left hand is exclusively that of performing the ugly and unclean actions that are necessary, such as cleaning one's nostrils and anus. Moreover, they only drink out of cups, each out of his own; nor would anyone drink out of another's cup. And when they drink, they do not touch the cup with their lips, but hold it up high, so as to pour the liquid into their mouths. For nothing in the world would they touch the cup with their lips, nor would they give a stranger to drink out of their own cups. If a stranger has no drinking vessel of his own with him, and wishes to slake his thirst, they pour the wine or other liquid into his hands, and he drinks out of them; thus his hands are his cup.

I will tell you also that in this kingdom justice is even too strictly executed upon murderers, thieves, and other criminals. And as for debts, the following are the laws and institutions that are observed: if a debtor, who has been repeatedly solicited by his creditor to pay his debt, goes on putting the payment off from day to day, ever making promises, then, if the creditor can come upon him in such a way that he succeeds in drawing a circle round him, the debtor may not come out of the circle until he has satisfied his creditor, or at least given him a sufficient and reliable security that the debt will be fully discharged that same day. Otherwise, if the debtor were to be bold enough to try to come out of the circle without having paid, or given the security to pay that same day, he becomes a transgressor against law and justice, and is punished by the lord with the established penalty, namely death.

And Messer Marco witnessed an example of this in the person of the King himself. The King was debtor for certain wares to a foreign merchant, and had repeatedly put off the merchant's requests, because it was not convenient for him to pay. So, as the delay was harmful to his business, one day that the King was riding about the town, the merchant was ready and quick enough to surround the King and his horse with a circle. When the King saw this, he reined in his horse, and went no further; nor did he leave the place until the merchant had been completely paid. When the people around saw this, they marvelled greatly, saying: " See how the King obeys the Law." And to them the King replied: " Shall I, who have made the law, break it because it goes against me? Nay, I must observe it better than others."

I will also tell you that the greater number of them abstain from drinking wine; a man who drinks wine is not accepted as witness or as surety; nor is a seafaring man accepted as such. They say that a seafaring man is a desperado, and so his testimony is not accepted, but is valueless.

And you must know that no form of lechery is a sin for them.

There is such a heat there, that it is truly a marvel. That is why they go about naked. It never rains except in June, July, and August. And were it not for the rain that falls during those three months, which refreshes the air, the heat would be such that no one could survive it. But on account of this rain the heat is less than it might be.

I will tell you, too, that among them there are many men learned in an art called physiognomy, namely the art of knowing men and women, and their qualities, whether they be good or bad. They discern the qualities of a person the moment they set eyes on him.

They know precisely what it means when one meets a beast or a bird. More than anyone else, they pay attention to omens, and are expert in telling which are good and which are bad. Thus, if a man is on his way to some place, and, as he goes, hears someone snoring or sneezing, he immediately sits down where he is, and goes not a step farther. If the person who has sneezed, sneezes a second time, then the traveller gets up, and continues on his way. If he does not hear the second sneeze, he gives up his journey, and returns home.

Again, in every day in the week they say there is an unlucky hour, that they call *choiach*; thus, for example, they say that on Monday it is the hour of half-tierce; on Tuesday the hour of tierce; on Wednesday the hour of none; and so on for each day, the whole year through.

And all these things are written and defined in their books. They also know the unlucky hours from the length of shadows in feet, that is to say, by measuring the human shadow; thus, it will be a *choiach* hour when a man's shadow, against the sun, is, say, seven feet long; it will no longer be *choiach* when that measure is surpassed, either by increasing or by decreasing—for, as the sun rises higher, a shadow shortens, and, as it sinks, a shadow lengthens. Another day, the *choiach* hour will be when the shadow is twelve feet long; and when that measure is surpassed, the *choiach* will be over, too. And all these things they have set down in writing. And you must know that at those hours they abstain from trading and from any other business. Thus, it may happen that when two men are bargaining together, someone steps out into the light, and measures the length of the shadow; if it shows the period of *choiach* for that day, according to what is set down for the day, he at once says to the two: "It is choiach! Do nothing!" And they stop. Then he measures the shadow again, and, finding the hour to be over, says: "The choiach is over. Do what you please." And they are constantly alluding to this. They say, in fact, that if anyone makes a bargain in those hours he will get no profit by it—indeed, that he will have ill luck.

Again, in their houses, they have certain animals called tarantulas, which look like lizards, and climb up walls. Their bite is poisonous, and they do great harm to a man if they bite him. They make a sound as if they said "cis." That is their cry. From these tarantulas omens are drawn as follows: if two men happen to be bargaining in a house where there are some of these animals, and, as they converse, the sound of a tarantula is heard above them in the same room, they examine from what side of the buyer and the seller, the sound has come, that is, whether from the right or the left, from in front or from behind, or from above, or whatever the direction may be. And they know whether the omen is good or bad; if it is good, they conclude their bargain; if it is bad, they abandon it. They know when it is good for the seller and bad for the buyer, or bad for the seller and good for the buyer, or good for both, or bad for both. And they regulate their actions thereby. All these things they have learnt by experience.

I will also tell you that in this kingdom, as soon as a child, male or female, is born, the father or the mother has a written note taken of its nativity, namely the day, the month, the moon, and the hour of its birth. This they do because in all their affairs they regulate their actions according to the advice of an astrologer or soothsayer. These soothsayers of theirs are most expert in incantations, magic, and geomancy; and some of them also have a knowledge of astronomy.

Moreover, if a man has male children, as soon as they reach the age of thirteen, he sends them away from home, and no longer provides for their board. They say that they are then old enough to procure their own food, and to trade and earn as their fathers have done. So they give each son some 20 *grossi*, or coins of that value, in order that they may make purchases therewith, and get profit. This the fathers do in order that their sons may become experienced and quick-witted in all things, and get used to trading. And these children do as follows. All day, they do nought but run hither and thither, buying something and then selling it again. During the period of the pearl-fisheries, they buy five or six pearls from the fishermen, or as many as they can get. They then bring them to the merchants who remain at home for fear of the sun, and say: "Will you have them? I assure you they cost me so much. Let me profit as much as you think fit." And the merchants give the children somewhat over the proper price. Then they set to running about again, or else they ask the merchants: "Do you wish me to go and buy you something?" And so they become excellent and most clever traders. Thus they are able to bring all the food that is necessary for them to the houses of their mothers, who cook and dress it for them. But they get nothing to eat at their father's expense.

You must also know that in this kingdom, as over the whole of India, all beasts and birds are different from ours, with the exception of one bird alone, the quail. Their quails are, without doubt, just the same as ours; but all the others are strangely different from ours. For I assure you that their bats—namely those birds that fly by night and have neither feathers nor plumage—are as big as goshawks. Their goshawks, too, are as black as crows, and much bigger than ours; they are swift fliers, and excellent for fowling. Another thing I will tell you, that is quite worth relating: you must know that they feed their horses on meat cooked with rice, and on many other cooked foods.

I will also tell you that in their monasteries they have numbers of idols, both male and female, to whom many damsels are consecrated in the following manner. Their fathers and mothers consecrate them to whatever idols they please. Once they have been consecrated, every time the monks of the monastery containing the idol bid these consecrated damsels come to entertain the idol, they straightway go. They dance, and sing, and make great rejoicing. There are crowds of these damsels, for they have large gilds. Again, several times a month, or rather week, these damsels bring food to the idol to whom they have been consecrated; and I will tell you how they bring this food, and what they mean when they say that the idol has fed. You must know that a certain number of these damsels prepare abundant food, such as meat and other good things, and go to the monastery into the presence of the idol; then they place a table before the idol, charged with all the food they have brought, leaving it there some time. Meanwhile, all these damsels dance, and sing, and make great rejoicing. When they have kept up this merry-making for as long as it would take a baron to have his meal, they say that the spirit of the idol has eaten the substance of the food. This they then take, and eat it themselves with great gaiety and rejoicing. Then each of them returns home. Thus do these damsels do until the day they get married. And throughout the kingdom there are many such maidens who do the things I have said.

And why do they thus entertain the idols? It is because often the priests that serve the idols, say: "The god is angry with the goddess; he will have no commerce with her, nor will they speak to one another; and as they are angry and vexed with one another, unless they be reconciled and make peace, all our affairs will fare ill, and go from bad to worse, for the blessing and grace of the deities are not upon them." Then the aforesaid damsels go to the monastery, in the way we have said; and they are all naked, except that their middles are covered; and they sing in the presence of the god and the goddess. For the god stands by himself on an altar beneath a canopy; and the goddess also stands by herself on an altar beneath another canopy. And the people say that the god often takes his pleasure with the goddess, and has commerce with her, but that when they are angry, this is not so. Then those damsels come to the monastery to make peace between them. When the damsels are come, they set themselves to singing, and rejoicing, and dancing, and tumbling, and performing all kinds of tricks, in order to entertain the god and goddess, and reconcile them. And in the midst of their games, they say: "Lord, why art thou angry with the goddess, and neglectful of her? Is she not pleasing? Truly she is. May it please thee to be reconciled to her and take thy pleasure with her, for verily she is most pleasing." Then she who has thus spoken will raise one leg above her neck, and turn upon the other, in order to amuse the god and goddess. And when they have done enough of their merry-making, they go home again. The next morning the priest of the idols will announce as a great blessing, that he has seen the god having commerce with the goddess, and that peace has been made between them. Then all rejoice and give thanks.

Moreover, these maidens, as long as they are maidens, have such firm flesh, that no one can in any way grasp or pinch them in any part of their bodies. And, for the price of a small coin, they will let a man try and pinch them as hard as he likes. When they are married, their flesh remains firm, but not quite so much. On account of this firmness, their breasts do not hang down, but always remain stiff and erect.

They even have certain very light beds made of cane, so constructed that, when one is inside and wishes to sleep, one can pull them up to the ceiling by means of ropes, and fix them there. This they do in order to escape from the tarantulas we mentioned, which bite much, and also to avoid fleas and other vermin. They do it, too, for the sake of ventilation, and to avoid the heat. Not all, however, do this, but only the nobles and the elders of the house. The others sleep in the streets.

And now I will tell you of a noble law made by this King. It is this: when a man sets out on a journey by night (for they prefer to travel by night rather than by day, because it is less hot), and has a bag of pearls or other valuables, then, if he wants to sleep, he puts his bag under his head, and sleeps by the side of the road. Nor does anyone ever lose anything by theft or for any other reason. And if a man does lose anything, his loss is at once made good; but only if he was sleeping along the road; otherwise he gets nothing; indeed, suspicion is cast upon him. The authorities say, in fact: "Why were you sleeping away from the road, unless perchance you were planning some mischief against someone?" And so, instead of his loss being made good, he is punished.

We have now told you all about the customs and peculiarities of this kingdom. We will therefore leave it, and proceed to speak of another kingdom called Mutfili.

Here is told of the kingdom of Mutfili

Mutfili is a kingdom one reaches after leaving Maabar and travelling some five hundred miles to the north. It belongs to a Queen, a woman of great wisdom. [When we were there], her husband had been dead forty years. Him she had loved tenderly, bearing him the strongest affection, and so, when he died, she solemnly declared that she would take no other husband, now that he whom she had loved more than herself, was dead. And so it was, that she never married again. But I assure you that during all those forty years she has ruled her kingdom most justly and equably, nor could her husband have done so better than she. And truly she is more beloved by her subjects than any Queen or King has ever been.

They are Idolaters, and pay tribute to no one. They live on rice, flesh, milk, fish, and fruit.

And you must know that in this kingdom there are many mountains in which diamonds are found, even as you shall hear. Know, then, that when it rains in winter, the water runs down the mountains, flowing impetuously in great torrents through deep caverns. When the rain has stopped, and the water has ceased flowing, they go searching in the torrent beds, and find many diamonds. In summer too, when not a drop of water is to be seen, they find numbers of them on those mountains. But the heat is such as can hardly be borne. Moreover, on the mountains there is a multitude of serpents, both long and thick, so that those who go there do so in great fear. None the less, people go there as best they may, and find splendid diamonds—and big ones, too. And I will add that these serpents are venomous and wicked, so that people dare not go into the caverns where the evil serpents live.

I will tell you, too, that they find diamonds in yet another way. You must know that there are certain great, deep gullies, with such precipitous sides, that no one can go to the bottom of them. But this is what the people do: they take many pieces of raw and bleeding flesh, and throw them into the gullies. The places into which the flesh is thrown, are full of diamonds, which get stuck to the flesh. Now you must know that on these mountains there are many white eagles, that feed on the serpents. When they see the pieces of flesh at the bottom of the gullies, they swoop down upon them, and carry them away. Then the men, who have all the time been carefully watching whither the eagles fly, as soon as they see them settled down and tearing the flesh, hasten thither as fast as possible. The eagles fly away, and, in their fear at seeing the men suddenly coming upon them, do not carry the flesh away with them; on reaching the spot where the flesh lies, the men take it, and find plenty of diamonds stuck to it.

And they have also the following way of getting diamonds: when the eagles eat up the flesh of which I have spoken, they also eat up diamonds. So, at night, when they return to their nests, they drop the diamonds they have eaten, together with their dung. Then the people go and gather these droppings, and find quite a number of diamonds.

In these three ways you have heard, and in many more ways, too, are diamonds found. And you must know that diamonds are not found in any part of the world except in this kingdom alone. But here they are both plentiful and good. But do not suppose that the good diamonds are brought to our Christian countries; they are all taken to the Great Kaan, and to the Kings and barons of these various lands and kingdoms. It is they who possess great treasures, and purchase all the most valuable stones.

Now I have told you of the diamonds, and so we will pass to other subjects.

You must know that in this kingdom the best, and most beautiful, and finest buckrams in the world are made—and the most costly, too. For I assure you that they are like tissues of Rheims linen. Indeed, they are so beautiful, the greatest Kings and Queens might wear them as something truly regal.

They have quantities of cattle, and the biggest sheep in the world. They have great abundance and plenty of all the necessaries of life.

There is nothing else worth mentioning, and so we will leave this kingdom, and tell you of the place where the body of St. Thomas the Apostle lies.

Here is told of the place where the body of St. Thomas the Apostle lies

The body of St. Thomas the Apostle lies in a little town in the province of Maabar. The town has but a small population, and no trader goes there, because there are no wares to export, and also because the place is rather off the beaten track. Yet many, both Christians and Saracens, go thither on pilgrimage. For you must know that the Saracens of those parts hold the Saint in great reverence, and say that he was a Saracen; they believe, too, that he was a great prophet, and call him *avariun*, which means " saint."

The Christians who look after the church have many of the trees that produce wine, and of those that bear Pharaoh's nuts. Of these nuts, one is enough for a man, both as food and as drink. First of all, there is an outside husk, made up as it were of strings, which are put to many uses, and serve for many purposes. Beneath this first husk, there is an eatable substance, enough for a man's meal; it is very tasty, sweet as sugar, white as milk, and hollow like the outside husk. The inside of this is filled with water, enough of it to fill a flask; this water is clear and fresh, and of exquisite taste; when you have eaten the flesh of the nut, you have the water to drink. And so with a single nut a man can both eat and drink his fill. For each of these trees the Christian used to pay one of the four brothers of King Sender Bandi Devar a tribute of one *grosso* a month.

And you must know that in this place there is the wonder I will tell you of. The Christians who go thither on pilgrimages gather some of the soil from the place where the Saint was killed, and this soil they take away with them to their countries. Now, if anyone falls ill of a tertian, or a quartan ague, or of any other fever of the kind, they give him a potion made with this soil; and as soon as the sick man has drunk it, he is well again. And this is true of all the sick who thus drink this soil. Messer Marco himself brought some of this soil to Venice, and cured many people with it. And you must know that it is a red soil.

I will tell you, too, of a fine miracle which occurred in the year 1288 after Christ's Incarnation. You must know that the King whom we have just mentioned, having an enormous quantity of rice, filled with it both the Church of St. Thomas and all the houses round it. And this he could do because he was an Idolater. The Christians who are in charge of the church and of the Saint's body, were sore distressed when they saw that this idolatrous King was thus having the church and houses filled with rice, and that the pilgrims would have no place where to lodge. So they earnestly begged him to desist. But he, being a cruel and haughty man, would not hearken to their prayer, but filled all the buildings up according to his will, neglecting the desires of the Christians in charge of the church. Now, when the King had had all the buildings filled up with rice, whereat the brethren were sore distressed, there occurred the great miracle that I will tell you of. You must know that the night after the King had had the buildings filled, St. Thomas the Apostle appeared to him with a fork in his hand. He set it at the King's throat, and said: "Come, my man! Have my houses straightway cleared. For if thou dost not have them straightway cleared, thou shalt die an evil death." And as he said these words, he pressed hard with the fork against the King's throat, so that the King thought he felt great pain, and it almost seemed to him that he was dying. Having done this, St. Thomas departed. And the King got up very early in the morning, had all the houses cleared, and told all that St. Thomas had done to him. And it was held to be a great miracle. The Christians were overjoyed and delighted at it, and rendered thanks, and paid great reverence to St. Thomas; and greatly did they bless his name. And ever since then, the King has no longer taken the tribute for the trees, nor any other tribute from the Christians who are in charge of the church and the place, as he previously did.

Many other miracles happen there daily, such that he who should hear of them would be filled with wonder, and especially the healing of Christians who are crippled or deformed.

So we have told you of this. We will now tell you how St. Thomas was killed, according to what the people of the place say. You must know that St. Thomas was outside his hermitage in the woods, raising his prayers to the Lord his God. All around were many peacocks, for you must know that there are more peacocks here than in any other part of the world. As St. Thomas was thus saying his prayers, a certain Idolater, belonging to the race and lineage of the *Gavi*, shot an arrow from his bow, in order to kill one of the peacocks that were gathered round the Saint. Nor did he notice the latter. Just as he thought he had hit the peacock, instead he hit St. Thomas the Apostle in the middle of his right side. When he was thus hit, the Saint continued sweetly praying to his Maker, but I tell you that of that wound he died. And you must know that, before coming to the place where he died, he had converted many people in Nubia. And how and in what way this came about, we will tell you all properly and in detail, but in due time and in the proper place.

We have now told you of St. Thomas, and will therefore proceed, telling you of other things. You must know that in this country children are born black, but not so black as they become as a result of the following habit. I assure you that from the day a child is born, they anoint it once every week with oil of sesame. This makes them still blacker than they are when they are born. For truly in those parts he who is blackest is thought most of, and held superior to those who are not so black. Another thing I will add, too. I assure you in very truth that these people have all their gods and idols portrayed and painted black, and their devils white as snow. For they say that God and all the saints are black—namely, *their* God and *their* saints—and that the devils are white. For this reason, then, do they have them portrayed and painted as I have told you. I will also add that they make black statues of their idols.

And you must know that when the people of this country go campaigning, as they have great faith in the ox, and hold it for a holy thing, they take some hairs of the wild-oxen I have mentioned before. And, if they are horsemen, they attach them to their horses' manes; if they are foot-soldiers, they hang them on to their shields. And some have them tied to their hair. This they do because they believe that by virtue of these ox hairs, they will the better escape perils, and avoid troubles. And this is done by all those who go campaigning. And you must know that for this reason the hairs of wild oxen are very costly. No one who is without some feels safe.

Now we have told you of this subject; we will hence leave this place, and tell you of a province where the Brahmins live, even as you shall hear.

Here is told of the province of Lar, whence the Brahmins come

Lar is a province lying to the west, when one comes from the place where the body of St. Thomas is preserved. From this province come all the Brahmins in the world; it was their birthplace.

I assure you that these Brahmins are among the best and most trustworthy merchants in the world; for nothing on earth would they tell a lie, and all that they say is true. Indeed, you must know that if a foreign trader comes to that province in order to do business, and is ignorant of the customs of the country, he seeks out one of these Brahmin merchants entrusting him with his money and his wares, and begging him, as he does not know the local customs, to look after his business and his merchandise, that he may not be cheated. Then the Brahmin merchant takes in trust the foreign trader's business, and deals with it so honestly, both in buying and in selling, and looks after the stranger's interests with such anxious care, that he could not do better were he acting for himself. Nor does he ask for anything in return for what he does, leaving it to the stranger to give him something out of his generosity.

They eat no meat, and drink no wine. They lead a very chaste life, in accordance with their customs. They lie with no woman except their wives. They would never take from another anything that belongs to him. They would kill no living creature, nor would they ever commit any action whereby they could think they had sinned. And I will add that all Brahmins can be distinguished by a sign that they wear. For all the Brahmins in the world wear a cotton thread over one shoulder, which they tie beneath the other arm, so that it crosses both the breast and the back. By this sign they can be distinguished, wherever they go.

I will add that they have a King who is rich and powerful as regards treasure. He eagerly buys up pearls and all other kinds of precious stones; and he has established it as a rule to give double the purchase price to all the merchants of his kingdom for all the pearls they bring him from Soli, which is one of the kingdoms of Maabar, and the wealthiest and finest province of India, the one in which the best pearls are found. And the Brahmins go to that kingdom in Maabar, and buy up all the fine pearls they can find, and take them to their King. They tell him, with their customary truthfulness, what the purchase price was, and the King straightway has twice the sum paid out to them. He has never abandoned this custom. And for this reason they have brought him great quantities of very fine large pearls.

These Brahmins are Idolaters, and more than any other people in the world pay attention to omens and to meetings with beasts and birds. I will tell you something of what they do.

I will mention, for example, this custom, that they have amongst others. For every day in the week they have a special omen, such as I shall tell you. If it happen that they are bargaining for certain goods, the prospective buyer gets up, looks at the shadow cast by the sun, and asks: "What day is this?" "Such and such a day." Then he has his own shadow measured. If the length of the shadow is such as it should be on that day, he closes the bargain ; if his shadow, instead, is not of the proper length for that day, he will no way clinch the bargain, but waits until his shadow be of the length prescribed by their law. Thus the proper length of the shadow is fixed for every day in the week. And until their shadow is of the length that it should be, they will clinch no bargain nor carry on any business. As soon as their shadow reaches the proper length for the day, then they clinch all their bargains, and attend to their business.

I will tell you of a still stranger thing. When they are bargaining for some goods, either in a house or elsewhere, if they happen to see a tarantula coming—and there are plenty of them there—then, if the buyer sees it coming from a direction which seems to him to be of good omen, he straightway concludes his purchase; if, instead, the direction from which the tarantula comes, seems to him of evil omen, he abandons the bargain, and does not purchase.

I will add, too, that if, on going out of doors, they hear someone sneeze, then if it does not seem to them to be a good omen, they stop, and go no farther. And, moreover, I will tell you that if, when they are going on their way, these Brahmins see a swallow flying towards them, either in front or to the right or left, then, if it seems to them, according to their beliefs, that the swallow has come from a good direction, they proceed; if it seems to them, instead, that it has not come from a good direction, they go no farther, but turn back.

These Brahmins are also the most long-lived people in the world. And this is due to the small quantity of food they eat, and to the great abstinence they practise. Their teeth are very good, on account of a certain herb that they chew while eating, which makes them digest very well, and is very healthy for the human body. And you must know that these Brahmins do not have blood taken from their veins, nor have themselves cupped in any other part of their body.

They have among them certain regulars known as *Chughi*, who live still longer than the others, for they live from 150 to 200 years. They are very hale and hearty, so that they can go about wheresoever they will, and perform all the necessary services for their monasteries and their idols; and they do so quite as well as if they were younger. This is due to their great abstinence, in that they eat little, and only healthy food. For they are used to eating, above all, rice and milk. I will add, too, that these *Chughi*, who live so long, as I have said, also use another kind of food, that I will tell you of. And it will seem most strange to you. I tell you, then, that they take quicksilver and sulphur, and mix them together, making a drink with them; then they swallow it. And they say that it prolongs life. And in fact, thanks to it, they live much longer; and you must know that they take it twice a month. I will add that these people make use of this drink from their childhood up, in order to live longer. And, without exception, all those who live as long as I have said, make use of this drink of sulphur and quicksilver.

Further, in this kingdom of Lar there is a sect of religious, also called *Chughi*, of whose great abstinence and hard, strict life I will tell you. You must know that they go stark naked, wearing absolutely nothing, and not covering either their privy parts or any limb. They worship the ox; and most of them wear a little ox, made of copper or of gilt brass, in the middle of the forehead; of course, you understand that they have it tied on. Moreover, I will tell you that they burn ox-dung, and grind it to powder. If, as they go on their way, anyone reverently greets them, they smear his brows with this powder, as if they were performing the holiest of actions. They also smear themselves with it, in various parts of their bodies, with great devotion, with quite as much, indeed as that with which Christians bless themselves with holy water. They do not eat either out of bowls or off plates, but, as they eat, they lay their food on leaves of the apple of Paradise, and on other big leaves. Not, however, on green leaves, but on dry ones, for they say that the green leaves have a soul, and so it were a sin. I assure you that, of all people of the world, they are those who are most careful not to commit any action which they believe to be sinful; they would sooner die than commit what they consider a sin. And when others ask them why they go about naked, and why they feel no shame in showing their privy parts, they answer: "We go about naked, because we will have nothing belonging to this world, for we came into this world without clothes, and naked. And the reason why we are not ashamed of showing our privy parts, is this: we commit no carnal sin with them, and so we feel no more ashamed of showing them, than you may feel when you show your hands or your face or any other part of your body with which you commit no carnal sin. But, as you have used your privy parts for sin and lechery, so you keep them hidden, and feel ashamed of them. As for us, who commit no such sin with them, we feel no more shame at showing them, than at showing our backs." This, then, is the reason they give to those who ask them why they are not ashamed of showing their privy parts.

I will add, too, that for nothing in the world would they kill a living creature or any animal—be it a fly or a flea or a louse, or any kind of vermin—for, they say, they have souls. They may not kill them, they say, for they would be committing a sin.

I will add, moreover, that they would eat nothing green, be it grass or a root, until it is dry, for they say that green things have souls.

Further, when these people's bowels move, they go to the sea-shore, and there relieve themselves in the sand, near the water. Then they very carefully wash themselves with the water. Once they have done so, they take a little stick or rod, and therewith break up their excrements, and scatter them in the sand, until nothing is to be seen of them. If asked why they do this, they reply: "Because from this worms would spring. And as all food is dried up by the sun, the worms sprung therefrom would die through lack of food. Now, since this substance issues from our body —for without food we could not live—the death of so many souls born of our substance would be imputed to us as a most grievous sin. Thus we destroy this substance, that worms may not spring from it, only to die shortly after through lack of food, making us thereby commit a sin and a transgression."

I will add, furthermore, that they sleep all naked on the ground, without anything at all either over or beneath them. It is truly a great wonder that they do not die, but live so long as I have said.

They also practise the greatest abstinence as regards food; they fast the whole year through, and drink water, and nothing else.

Another thing I will also tell you about them. When the brethren who live in their monasteries for the service of the idols, have to be changed in their office or rank; if, for example, someone dies and another is to be put in his place, they are put to the test I will tell you of. The damsels offered to the idols are summoned, and made to caress the man who is to be promoted. They caress him here and there, all over his body, they embrace him, and excite him in every way. Then, if the man thus caressed by the damsels remains unperturbed in every way, even as he was before they began caressing him, then he is considered good, and is kept in the monastery; but if the man whom the damsels caress does not remain insensible, but reacts carnally, he is not kept, but driven at once away, for they say they will have no lecherous man among them.

They are cruel and perfidious Idolaters, even as I tell you.

The reason why they burn the dead is this: they say that if they did not burn them, worms would spring from them, and once the worms had eaten the body from which they sprang, they would have no more to eat; and so they would inevitably die. And they say that the death of these worms would be imputed as a great sin to the soul of the dead man. And this is the reason they give for burning their dead. They say that worms have a soul.

Now we have told you of the customs of these idolaters. We will hence quit this subject, and tell you a fine story we forgot, when speaking of the island of Seilan; you shall now hear it, and it will fill you with wonder.

Here is told once more of the island of Seilan

Seilan is a large island, as I have already told you in this book. Now, in this island there is a very high mountain, so precipitous and rocky that no one could scale it, were it not for what I shall tell you: on this mountain are hung many iron chains, so arranged that people can climb by means of them right up to the summit of the mountain. Now, they say that on this summit is the sepulchre of Adam, our first parent. Or rather, the Saracens say that this sepulchre is Adam's, but the Idolaters say it is Sagamoni Borcan's.

This Sogamoni was the first man in whose name an idol was made. For he was the best of men, according to their lights, that ever lived among them; he was the first that they considered a saint, and the first man in whose name they made an idol.

He was the son of a great King, both rich and puissant. But this royal youth was so piously minded that he would give thought to no earthly thing, nor did he wish to become a King. And so his father, when he saw that his son did not wish to become King, nor would give thought to any earthly thing, was sore afflicted thereat. So he made him great offers: he said he would crown him King of the land, and let him rule it according to his will; he would resign the crown to him, and renounce all authority, in such wise that his son alone should be Lord. And his son answered that he would take nought. And when the father saw that his son would for nothing in the world accept the sovereignty, his affliction was so great, that he almost died of grief. Nor was this any wonder, for he had no other son but this, nor anyone to whom to leave his kingdom.

Then the King did as follows. He decided so to act, that his son should willingly turn to earthly things, and accept the crown and the kingdom. Thus he brought it about that his son found himself in a most beautiful palace, with thirty thousand of the fairest and most pleasing damsels to wait upon him. No man dared set foot therein, but only the maidens; they alone put him to bed, and waited upon him at table, and ever kept him company. They danced and sang before him, and gave him all the solace they could, even as the King had bidden them. Yet, I tell you that all those damsels availed not to make a single thought of wantonness arise in the breast of the King's son; nay, he became more firmly chaste than ever before. And he led the most pious life, according to their lights.

And I assure you that this youth had been so delicately brought up, that he had never gone outside his palace, nor had ever seen a dead man, or anyone who was not sound and whole in all his limbs, for his father had never allowed any old or infirm person to enter into his presence. Now, it so happened that one day, as the youth was riding along the road, he saw a dead body. He was sore dismayed, as one who had never seen such a sight before. He straightway asked those who were about him, what that was, and they answered and said it was a dead man. "How," said the King's son, "do then all men die?"—"Yea, truly," answered they. Thereupon the young man said no more, but rode on, wrapped in thought. He had not ridden much further, before he met a very old man, who could no longer walk, and who had not a tooth left in his mouth, having lost them all because of his great age. When the King's son saw this old man, he asked what he might be, and why he could not walk. And those who were with him answered that the man could not walk because of his great age, and because of his great age had lost all his teeth. So, when the King's son had heard what they said concerning the dead man, and concerning the old man, he returned to his palace, and decided that he would no longer live in this wicked world, but go and seek Him who dies not, and who had made him. So he abandoned his palace and his father. He went to certain lofty and impassable mountains, and there he lived the rest of his days, leading a most holy and chaste life, and observing great abstinence. Verily, had he been a Christian, he would have become a great saint in the company of Our Lord Jesus Christ.

And when this royal youth died, the body was taken to the King his father. And when the King saw him lying dead, him whom he loved more than himself, ask not whether he was overcome by dismay and sorrow. His grief was boundless. Then the King had a statue built in his likeness, all of gold and precious stones, and had it honoured by all his subjects, and worshipped like a god.

And they say that he died eighty-four times. For they assert that when he died the first time, he became an ox; that he then died again, and became a horse. And so they say that he died eighty-four times, every time becoming an animal, either a dog or some other creature; but when he died the eighty-fourth time, they say he became a god.

To the Idolaters he is the best and greatest god they have; and you must know that he was the first idol they ever possessed, and from him all the other idols are descended.

And all this came to pass in the island of Seilan, in India.

Now you are informed how the first idol was made. And I tell you in sooth that the Idolaters come hither on pilgrimage from very distant lands, even as Christian pilgrims seek St. James. The Idolaters assert that in the tomb on that mountain lies the son of the King of whom we have told, and that the teeth and the hair and the bowl that are kept there, also belonged to this king's son, whose name was Sogamoni Borcan, which means Sogamoni the Saint. But the Saracens, who also go thither on pilgrimage in great numbers, say that it is the tomb of Adam, our first father, and that the teeth and hair and bowl are also Adam's.

Now you have heard how, according to the Idolaters, it is the son of the King, he who was their first idol and their first God, and how, according to the Saracens, it is Adam our first father. But God alone knows who he is, and what he was. For we do not believe that Adam lies in this place, as our Holy Writ says that he lies in another part of the world.

Now, it befell that the Great Kaan heard from certain Saracens that on that mountain was the tomb of Adam, and that his teeth and hair, and the bowl out of which he ate, were also there; and he decided that it were well if he possessed the teeth, and the hair, and the bowl. So he sent thither a great embassy. And this was 1284 years after Christ's Incarnation. What more shall I tell you? You must know in sooth that the Great Kaan's envoys set out with a great following, and journeyed both by land and by sea, until they reached the island of Seilan. They went to the King, and their efforts succeeded in obtaining for them two of the molar teeth, which were mighty and big; they also obtained some of the hair, and the bowl. And the bowl was of most beautiful green porphyry. And when the Great Kaan's envoys had obtained these things, they set out on their way, and returned to their Lord. When they were near the great city of Cambaluc, where the Great Kaan was then staying, they sent him word of their return, and informed him that they were bringing him what he had asked for. So the Great Kaan bade all his people, both the ecclesiastics and the others, go to meet those relics, which they were made to believe were Adam's. But why should I make a long story of it? You must know in sooth that all the inhabitants of Cambaluc went out to meet these relics, and the ecclesiastics received them, and brought them to the Great Kaan, who accepted them with great joy and feasting, and with great reverence. And I will tell you that they found in their writings that the bowl had this virtue: that if one put in it food for one man, enough was found in it to feed five men. The Great Kaan said that he had had this tested, and he asserted that it was true.

Even as you have heard, then, did the Great Kaan get the relics; and truly the money it cost him to obtain them amounted to an immense sum.

Now we have told you all this story, in due order, and in accordance with truth. We may now quit this, and proceed in our account, telling you of other things. And first of all we will tell you of the city of Cail.

Here is told of the noble city of Cail

Cail is a noble and great city. It belongs to Ashar, the eldest of the five brothers who are Kings. And you must know that at this city touch all the ships that come from the west—from Cormos, Kisi, Aden, and all Arabia—laden with horses and other wares. Traders touch at this port, because it is excellently situated, and a good market for trading. For from many different lands there come numerous merchants to buy horses and other things. The King is very wealthy in treasure; he wears many beautiful gems on his person. He is splendidly adorned. He governs his kingdom most justly, especially as regards foreign merchants, namely those that come from other lands. He protects and governs them with great equity. I will add that, if merchants go thither so willingly, it is because of this good King, who protects them so well. True it is that they also obtain great gain and profit there.

Moreover, I will tell you that this King has no less than 300 wives, and more: for it is considered a great honour there to have the largest number of wives. I will add that, when any discord arises between these five Kings, who, being born of the same parents, are carnal brothers, and war is like to break out between them, their mother, who is still alive, throws herself between them and will not let them fight. But many a time it comes about that her sons will not cease, for all her prayers, but will at all costs come to blows, and then she takes a knife, and says: "If you do not cease from this quarrel and make peace with one another, I will instantly kill myself. And first of all I will cut off from my breast the paps with which I suckled you." And when the sons see the great lamentations that their mother makes, and hear her tender supplications, then, also because they understand that it is best for them, they agree together, and make peace. And this has happened many times. But I assure you that, when their mother dies, it cannot be but a great war will break out among them, and they will destroy one another.

You must also know that the people of this city, as indeed all the people of India, have the following custom: they almost constantly keep in their mouths a certain leaf called *tambur*, which they keep chewing, spitting out the juice that it forms; this they do both out of habit and for the pleasure they derive therefrom.

Especially the nobles have this habit. The great men and the King have their leaves prepared with camphor and other spices, mixed with quicklime. So they are ever chewing this stuff; and this keeps them very healthy.

If anyone wishes to offend another, and show him his contempt by offering him an insult, he takes out of his mouth the leaf he is chewing when he chances to meet the other man, and throws it into his face, saying: "You are not worth that," namely what he has thrown into his face. The other, considering himself grossly insulted and offended thereby, straightway goes to complain to the King, stating how such and such a man has insulted him; and he asks the King's leave to avenge himself; that is to say, if the offender has intended to insult both him and his family, he asks leave to pit his own person against that of the offender, and his own family against the offender's, so as to show whether they are men of worth or no; but if he alone has been insulted, then he asks leave to pit his own person against the other's. Then the King grants leave to both parties. If the combat is to take place between the respective families, then both the principals get ready for the fight, together with their families; and the only cuirass they wear and don for their protection is the skin that their mothers first gave them. When they are on the field, they come to grips, and strike one another, wounding and killing, for their swords pierce easily, as there is nothing to keep them out. The King and a multitude of people are present at the event, and when the King sees that many lie killed on either side, and that one of the sides seems to have the advantage, and overcome the other, he places between his teeth one corner of the mantle he wears about his person, and holds the other end with his hands. Straightway the combatants cease fighting, and no further blow is struck. If, instead, the fight is between two single combatants, it takes place as follows: the two come on to the field both naked, as they are constantly wont to be, each of them holding a knife; and truly they know very well how to fight with their knives, for they are expert in covering themselves, and striking their adversary with them. And this is what they do. As you have heard, they are black. One of the two draws a white circle on the skin of the other, in any place he likes, saying to him: "Know that within this circle, and not elsewhere, I will strike you; defend yourself as best you may." The other does the same to him. [Then they start fighting with their knives.] It is well for him who is the abler, and woe to him who is less able. For whenever the other strikes him, he will feel it well enough.

Now we have told you somewhat of this city, and of the customs of its inhabitants. We will hence quit it, and tell you of the kingdom of Coilum.

Here is told of the kingdom of Coilum

Coilum is a kingdom one finds to the south-west, after leaving Maabar and travelling 500 miles. They are idolaters. There are also some Christians and Jews. They have a language of their own. Their King pays tribute to no one. Now I will tell you what one finds in this kingdom, and what it produces.

You must know that the Coilumin brazil grows there, which is of very good quality, as well as an excellent kind of ginger, also called Coilumin from the name of the country. There is abundance of pepper, too; it grows in great quantities all over the countryside, and in the woods; it is gathered in the months of May, June, and July. You are to understand that the trees that produce pepper are planted and watered—they are not wild. They also have plenty of excellent indigo. And you must know that it is made from a herb: they take the herb, removing the roots, and put it into great tubs; then they put water in, and leave the herb until it becomes rotten; after that, they put this water in the sun, which is very hot, and makes it boil and condense. Thus you get the indigo as you know it, broken up into little pieces. I will add that in this country the heat is so great, and the sun is so hot, that one can hardly bear it. For I assure you, that if you were on a river, and put an egg into the water, it would be ready cooked before you sailed on much further.

I will add, too, that merchants come to this kingdom with their ships from Manji, Arabia, and the Levant, and carry on a great trade, for they bring goods from their own countries, and go back with their ships laden with merchandise from this kingdom.

There are many strange animals, differing from those in any other part of the world. Thus, I assure you they have certain black lions, with not a spot or mark of any other colour on them. There are various kinds of parrots: some are as white as snow, with vermilion beaks and legs; others are vermilion and blue, and they are the prettiest things in the world to look at; others again are green; there are some very small ones, too, that are also exceedingly pretty. Their peacocks are much bigger and more beautiful than ours, and also different. Their hens are also different from ours. What more shall I tell you? All their things are different from ours—more beautiful, and better. They have no product that is similar to any of ours, nor any beast nor bird. And this is due to the great heat they have. They have no kind of grain except rice alone. They make a wine, or rather drink, from dates, which is very good, and makes you drunk more readily than grape-wine. They have all the necessaries of life in abundance and cheap, except that they have no grain, apart from rice.

They have many excellent astrologers. They have leeches skilled in keeping a man's body healthy.

They are all black, and go about stark naked, both

the men and the women, except that they cover their middles with splendid cloths. No act of lechery or carnal sin is held sinful by them.

As for their marriage customs, they are as I shall tell you: they marry their cousins german. If their father dies, they may marry his wife; similarly they may marry their brother's widow. These customs are shared by all the peoples of India.

Now we have told you something about this kingdom. As there is nothing else worth mentioning, we will quit it, and tell you of Comari, as you shall hear.

Here is told of the country of Comari

Comari is also a country of India, where one can see something of the North Star, which we had no longer seen since we left the island of Java. If one sails some thirty miles from here out into the open sea, one can see it, about a cubit above the water. This is not a very civilized place; indeed it is rather wild. There are strange animals of different kinds, especially monkeys: indeed some of them are so strange that you would think they were men. There are such curious apes, that it is truly a wonder. There is abundance of lions, leopards, and ounces.

There is nothing else worth mentioning; we will therefore leave this place, and go on to tell you of the kingdom of Eli, as you shall hear.

Here is told of the kingdom of Eli

Eli is a kingdom lying some 300 miles to the west of Comari. They have a King of their own, are idolaters, pay tribute to no one, and have a language of their own.

Of their customs, and of the products of the country, we will now tell you in detail. And you will be able to understand much better, because we are now approaching more civilized countries.

In this province and kingdom, there is no harbour: there is only a large river that has an excellent estuary. Pepper grows there in great abundance, and ginger too. They also have quantities of other kinds of spices. The King is very rich in treasures, but not powerful as regards soldiers. His kingdom, however, has such strong frontiers, that no one could invade it with an army in order to do it any harm. Thus the King fears no one.

Another thing I will tell you. If a ship happens to enter that estuary, and casts anchor there, without being bound for the country, they seize it, and take all its cargo, saying: "You were going to other lands, but God has sent you to us, and hence we take all your goods." So they seize all that is in the ship, and consider it their own; nor do they think they sin thereby. The same happens all over this province of India, for, if a ship is obliged by foul weather to go to a place for which it was not bound, and different from that towards which it has set out on leaving its harbour, then, whatever be the country or place at which it calls contrary to its intentions, it is taken, and all that is on board, all its cargo, is plundered. For they say: "You intended to go elsewhere, but our good fortune, our good luck, has sent you hither, so that we might have your property."

And you must know that the ships of Manji and of other countries come to this kingdom in summer; they load up in three or four, or at most eight days, and then set sail as quickly as they can, for there are no harbours, and it is most dangerous to remain. For there are beaches and sands, but not a single harbour. True it is that the ships of Manji are less afraid than others to cast anchor on beaches, for they carry such large wooden anchors as can hold in any great storm.

They have lions and other wild beasts. There is abundance of game, both beasts and birds.

Now we have told you of the kingdom of Eli; we will next tell you of the kingdom of Melibar, even as you shall hear.

Here is told of the kingdom of Melibar

Melibar is a very large kingdom lying to the west. They have a King of their own, and a language of their own. They are Idolaters, and pay tribute to no one. From this kingdom, the North Star is more visible; it appears some two cubits above the water-line.

You must know that from this Melibar—and from another province bordering on it, called Gozurat—more than a hundred ships go out every year on piratical cruises: they seize other ships, and rob the merchants. For they are wicked sea-robbers. And I will add that they take their women and little children with them; all the summer they stay out cruising, and do great harm to traders. And you must know that the greater number of the ships of these evil pirates sail hither and thither, to hunt out or lie in wait for the ships of the merchants. They also have another wicked practice: they make a cordon across the sea, that is, they spread out, at a distance of some five miles from one another; some twenty will set out, thus drawn up, so that they cover a hundred miles of sea. As soon as they see some merchant ship, they signal to one another with fires, and so no ship can cross that tract of sea without falling into their hands. But as the merchants are well aware of the habits of these wicked pirates, and know that they cannot but come across them, they go thither so well armed and prepared, that they are not afraid when they fall in with them. For they defend themselves strenuously, and inflict great losses on them. But it is of course inevitable, that the corsairs should capture a ship at times. And when these pirates do capture some merchant ship, they seize it with all its cargo. To the men, however, they do no harm, saying to them: "Go and get you other wealth; maybe you will bring more to us!"

In this kingdom there is great abundance of pepper, and of ginger, too. There is also plenty of cinnamon. Other spices there are, too, in great quantities, including turbith and Indian nuts.

Moreover, they have quantities of buckram, the gauziest and finest in the world. They have abundance of many precious wares.

I will also tell you what the merchants of other countries bring hither when they come to this country with their ships in order to purchase its products. You must know that they bring copper in their ships—in fact, they ballast their ships with this copper—and cloths of gold and silk, sendals, gold, silver, cloves, spikenard, and other such spices, that do not exist in this kingdom. All these things are exchanged for the products of the country. And you must know that ships come here from many parts, as for example from the great province of Manji. And the merchants likewise distribute what they purchase here over many countries. The wares taken to Aden are then carried on to Alexandria.

Now we have told you of the kingdom of Melibar; we will therefore leave it, and tell you of the kingdom of Gozurat, as you shall hear. But you must note that we are not giving you the names of all the cities in these kingdoms, for that would make too long a tale. You must know that in every kingdom there are many cities and towns.

Here is told of the kingdom of Gozurat

Gozurat is also a large kingdom. They are Idolaters, and have a King and a language of their own. They pay tribute to no one. The kingdom lies to the west.

From this kingdom the North Star is still more visible; it appears quite six cubits above the water-line.

In this kingdom, too, there are the worst pirates in the world. And I will tell you that they commit the atrocity you shall hear of. You must know that when these wicked pirates capture merchants, they make them drink tamarind mixed with sea-water; thus the merchants are violently purged, and void all that is inside them. Then the pirates have it all collected and examined, in case there should be any pearls or precious stones inside it. For they say that the merchants, on finding themselves captured, swallow the pearls and precious stones, to prevent the pirates finding them. This is why these wicked pirates have this cunning practice that I have told you, of giving merchants this stuff to drink.

They have quantities of pepper. They also have plenty of ginger; and abundance of indigo, too. They have plenty of cotton also, for they possess very big trees that produce it: they reach six paces in height, when they are 20 years old. But it should be noted that when the trees are as old as this, they no longer produce cotton that is good for spinning; it is used for quilting and stuffing. This is the rule as regards these trees: up to the age of 12 years, they produce good spinning cotton, from 12 to 20 they no longer produce as good cotton as when they are young.

In this kingdom immense quantities of hides are tanned; that is, they prepare skins of sheep, buffaloes, wild oxen, unicorns, and many other animals. And I assure you that they prepare such quantities, that many ships are laden with them every year. They are taken to Arabia and to many other parts. Many kingdoms and provinces are supplied with them from this country. I will add that in this kingdom they make very beautiful mats in red and blue leather, chased with figures of beasts and birds, and most delicately sewn with gold and silver threads. They are so beautiful, that it is a wonder to see them. And you are to understand that these mats I am telling you of are used by the Saracens to sleep on; and indeed one sleeps excellently well on them. Here they also make such beautiful cushions, all sewn with gold thread, that they are worth quite six silver marks apiece. And of the mats I mentioned before, some are worth quite ten silver marks. What more shall I tell you? You must know in very truth that in this kingdom are made the best and finest leather goods in the world, and the most costly.

Now we have told you all about this kingdom in due order. We will hence quit it, and go on to tell you of other kingdoms, and, to begin with, of one that is called Tana.

Here is told of the kingdom of Tana.

Tana is a great kingdom lying towards the north-west. It is a vast and excellent kingdom. They have a King of their own, and they pay tribute to no one. They are Idolaters, and have a language of their own. Pepper and other spices do not grow so abundantly here as in the other countries of which we have been telling you. There is plenty of frankincense; it is not however white, but brown. There is much trade, and great numbers of ships and merchants flock thither, for they get there excellent and beautiful hides, dressed in different ways. They also get plenty of good buckrams, and cotton, too. The merchants who go there on their ships, bring many wares, namely gold, silver, copper, and many other kinds of merchandise needed in the kingdom; and they take away with them those products of the country out of which they think they will get profit and gain.

Another thing I will add, which is not good. I tell you, then, that many pirates sally forth from this kingdom, and cruise about the sea, doing much harm to traders. And I assure you that it is by the will of their King, for he has made a covenant with the pirates, who have to give him all the horses they capture. And you must know that they capture them often enough, for, as I have told you before, there is a great trade in horses all over India, as the merchants take great numbers of them there to sell, so that few ships go to India without carrying some. For this reason, then, the King has covenanted with the pirates that they are to give him all the horses they capture; all other goods, including gold, silver, and precious stones, fall to the pirates' share. Now this is an evil practice, and not worthy of a King.

Now we have told you of the kingdom of Tana; we will therefore quit it, and tell you of the kingdom of Canbaet.

Here is told of the kingdom of Canbaet

Canbaet is a large kingdom lying to the west. They have a King of their own, and a language of their own, and pay tribute to no one. They are Idolaters.

From this kingdom the North Star is still more visible, for you must know that the more one proceeds to the west, the more visible is the North Star.

In this kingdom there is much trade, and plenty of excellent indigo. There are great quantities of buckrams and cotton, which are distributed from this kingdom over many other kingdoms and provinces. There is also much trade in tanned and dressed hides; it is very considerable because they dress hides here quite as well as in any other country. I will add that they have many other commodities that I will not mention in this book, for it would make too long a tale.

When merchants come hither with their wares loaded on their many ships, they bring above all gold, silver, copper, and *tutia*. They bring the products of their own countries, and carry away those of the kingdom, such as they think will give them the greatest profit and gain.

And you must know that in this kingdom there are no pirates. They live by trade and handicrafts, and are good people.

There is nothing else worth mentioning, and so we will leave this place and go on telling you of other places, namely of the kingdom of Semenat.

Here is told of the kingdom of Semenat

Semenat is a large kingdom lying towards the west. They are Idolaters, have a King and language of their own, and pay tribute to no one. There are no pirates. They live by trade and handicrafts, as good people should do.

You must know that this is a kingdom where a great deal of trade is carried on. Merchants go there from many lands, bringing with them much merchandise of different kinds. They sell there what they have brought with them, and take away the products of the kingdom.

I will add that they are exceedingly cruel and fierce Idolaters.

There is nothing else worth mentioning, and so we will leave the place; and go on to tell you of another kingdom, called Kesmacoran.

Here is told of the kingdom of Kesmacoran

Kesmacoran is a kingdom that has a King and a language of its own. Some of the people are Idolaters, but the majority are Saracens. They live by trade and handicrafts. They have abundance of rice and wheat. Their principal food-stuffs are rice, meat, and milk. Great numbers of traders flock thither both by sea and by land with wares of divers kinds; they take away with them the products of this kingdom. There is nothing else worth mentioning.

I will add that this is the last province of India to one going towards the west and north-west, for you must know that all the country from Maabar to this place—that is to say all the kingdoms and provinces of which I have spoken from Maabar onward—is part of Greater India, the best of the Indies. And you must also know that we have only told you of the provinces and cities of this Greater India that lie along the coast; of those that lie inland we have not spoken, for indeed it would make too long a tale.

We will hence leave this province, and tell you of certain islands, which also belong to India. We will begin with two islands called Male and Female.

Here is told of the islands called Male and Female

The island called the Male Island lies out in the sea, quite 500 miles to the south, when one leaves Kesmacoran. They are baptised Christians and follow the faith and customs of the Old Testament. For I assure you that when a woman is with child, the husband will not touch her until she is delivered, and, once she is delivered, he does not touch her for 40 more days. After the fortieth day, however, he approaches her at will. But I must add that neither the wives nor any other women live in this island; they all live in another island; called the Female Island. You must know that the men go from their own island to this island of the women, and stay there three months, namely March, April, and May. For these three months the men go to the other island to live with their wives, and during that period they take their pleasure with them. At the end of the three months, they return to their own island, and look after their business for the next nine months.

And you must know that in this island there is

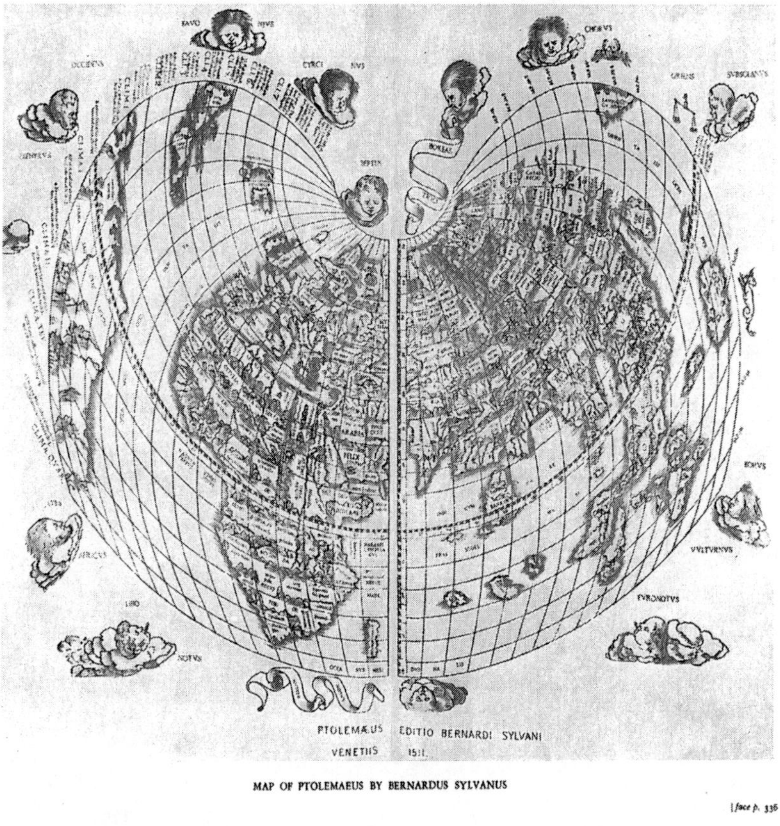

MAP OF PTOLEMAEUS BY BERNARDUS SYLVANUS

[face p. 336

abundance of very fine ambergris, of excellent quality and great beauty; this is due to the great number of whales captured in those seas.

They live on rice, milk, and meat. They are excellent fishermen. You must know, in fact, that quantities of excellent big fish are taken in the sea round the island. They take so much, indeed, that they dry it in great quantities, so that they have enough to eat all the year round, and can spare some to sell to others.

They have no Lord, except a Bishop, who is dependent upon the Archbishop of Scotra. They have a language of their own.

And you must know that from this island to that where their wives live, there is a distance of some thirty miles.

They say that they do not live all the year around with their wives, because if they did, they would not have enough to live on. The children that are born are brought up by the mothers in their island. As soon, however, as a male child reaches the age of twelve, the mother sends it to the father on the Male Island.

Such, then, as you have heard, are the customs on these two islands.

I will add, however, that during the three months that the husbands pass in the women's island, they sow corn, which the women then tend and reap. The women also gather the many kinds of fruit that grow on the island. Their principal occupation, however, is that of bringing up their children. The men provide them with all they need.

Now we have told you all about this; as there is nothing else worth mentioning, we will leave these two islands, and tell you of the island of Scotra.

Here is told of the island of Scotra

On leaving these two islands, and voyaging some 500 miles to the south, one finds the island of Scotra, which is very large and wealthy. And you must know that the inhabitants of this island are baptized Christians, and have an Archbishop.

In this island are gathered great quantities of ambergris; it is found in the belly of whales and cachalots, which are the biggest kinds of fish in the sea.

We will tell you how they catch whales in those parts. They have a great deal of tunny-fish, but they only catch it for the purpose we shall presently tell you. The tunny is a fish containing a great deal of fat; they cut it up into pieces, which they put into large vases or tubs; then they put salt on it, making abundance of brine. When this has been done, the whale-hunters, some sixteen of them, take a small boat, and, loading this fish on it with all the brine, namely the salt sauce it has produced, set out to sea. They have bundles of rags—old bits of cloth and other such waste—that they soak in this brine, which, as we said, is very fat; these they throw into the water, after tying them to the boat by means of a rope. Then they set up their sails, and cruise about all day on the sea. Wherever they go, the fat in the brine leaves as it were a trail on the water, which is visible just because it is produced by the fat. If the boat chances to pass over a spot where there is a whale, or if anyway a whale smells the fat of the tunny, say by crossing a spot where the boat has passed, it will follow the scent up for a hundred miles, if that be the distance from the boat where the tunny is; this it does on account of its greedy desire to get at the tunny. When it approaches the boat, so that the men on board see it, they throw out two or three pieces of tunny. The moment the whale has swallowed them, it becomes drunk, just like a man with wine. Then some of the men climb on to it. They have an iron rod, barbed at one end in such wise that, once it has been driven in, it cannot be pulled out again on account of the barbs. One of the hunters holds the rod over the whale's head, while another, armed with a wooden mallet, strikes the rod, straightway driving it all into the whale's head. For, on account of its being drunk, the whale hardly notices the men on its back, so that they can do what they will. To the upper end of the rod is tied a thick rope, quite 300 paces long, and every fifty paces along the rope, a little cask and a plank are lashed. This plank is fixed to the cask in the manner of a mast; on the bottom of the cask is a counterweight, to prevent the cask overturning, or, if you like, to keep the mast straight. The end of the rope is tied to a little boat they have with them, and in which some of them remain. Thus, when the whale, feeling itself wounded, turns to flee, those who were on its back to drive the rod in, keep afloat, and, swimming to the boat, get into it. Then one of the little casks with the mast is thrown into the water, and so 50 paces of rope are paid out. When the whale dives and flees, it hauls along the boat to which the rope is tied. If it looks as if the whale were getting the best of it, dragging the boat down, then another cask is thrown out, with its mast, for the whale cannot drag these casks with it beneath the surface. Thus it so tires itself out pulling these casks after it, that at last, exhausted by its wounds, it dies. Meanwhile the men in the boat have kept following it, guided by the casks, and, once the whale is dead, they haul it up near the boat, to tow it to their own or to some other neighbouring island, where they sell it. And out of one whale they will get as much as a thousand pounds. In the belly they find the ambergris. From the head they get several casks of oil. In this way, then, do they take whales.

They have splendid cotton cloths, and a great amount of other goods. Above all, they have great quantities of salt fish, both big and good. They live on rice, meat, and milk. They have no corn except rice. They go about all naked, after the fashion of the Indians, namely the idolatrous ones.

I will add that many ships call at this island, with

many merchants, who bring with them quantities of wares that they sell there. They take away with them the products of the island, and obtain great profit thereby. And you must know that all the ships and merchants bound for Aden touch at this island.

The Archbishop has nothing to do with the Pope of Rome, for he depends upon an Archbishop who lives at Baudac, called, as we have said before, Jatolic. It is this Jatolic of Baudac who sends the Archbishop to the island. He also sends prelates to many other parts of the world, just as the Pope of Rome does. And all these prelates obey not the Roman Church, but this great prelate of Baudac, whom they consider their Pope.

And I will add that many pirates come to this island with their ships, when they have finished their cruise. Here they encamp, and sell what they have got by plundering. And I assure you that they sell it very well, for the Christians in the island know that all these things have been stolen from idolaters and Saracens, and not from other Christians; and so they buy them.

You must also know that when the Archbishop of Scotra dies, his successor must come from Baudac; otherwise, if the people of the island elect him, the Jatolic must confirm him.

I will further add, that the Christians in this island are the cleverest enchanters in the world. True it is that the Archbishop does not wish them to practise sorcery, and warns and admonishes them. But in vain; they say that their fathers followed these practices of old, and so they wish to follow them too. The Archbishop can do nothing, as they will have it so; he suffers it, because he cannot do otherwise. Thus the Christians in this island practise their sorcery as they will.

I will tell you something about these sorceries. You must know in very truth that these enchanters do many strange things, almost anything they want. Thus, I assure you that, if a pirate ship has done some harm to the islanders, they can, by means of their charms, detain it, and prevent it leaving the island until complete restitution has been made. If it be a sailing-ship, and the wind be favourable, they raise a contrary wind, and make the ship turn back. For they can make any wind blow that they please. When they will, they can make a calm; and again, when they please, they raise great storms and winds at sea. They can perform many wonderful enchantments, which it is not well to dwell upon in this book, for they are of such a kind that who should hear them would be aghast with wonder. So we will leave this subject, and tell you no more about it.

There is nought else in this island worth mentioning; we will hence quit it, and tell you no more about it.

Here is told of the island of Mogdasio

Mogdasio is the name of an island lying to the south about 1000 miles from Scotra. They are Saracens, worshipping Mahomet. They have four Sheiks, that is to say four "old men." These four elders have the lordship of the whole island. And you must know that this is one of the noblest and largest islands in the whole world, for I assure you it has a compass of some 3000 miles.

They live by trade and handicrafts. I will add, too, that more elephants are born in this island than in any other country; and truly not in the whole world are so many elephants' tusks bought and sold, as are bought and sold in this island, and in that of Zanghibar.

You must know that in this island hardly any other flesh is eaten than that of camels, and I assure you that such an immense number of camels is slaughtered there daily, that no one could believe it, without having witnessed it. They say that the flesh of camels is better and more wholesome than all others. And so they are wont to eat it every day in the year.

You must also know that in this island there are red sandal-trees, about as tall as the trees in our lands. These trees would be of great value in other countries, and they have whole forests of them, as we have forests of other wild trees. They have abundance of ambergris, since in those seas whales and cachalots are plentiful. As they take many of these whales and cachalots, they have great quantities of ambergris. For, as you know, the whale is the animal that produces ambergris. They have leopards and ounces, and an enormous number of lions. They have plenty, too, of other animals, such as deer, fallow-deer, roes, and so forth. They have quantities of feathered game of many different kinds. They have many very big ostriches. There are different birds, that is to say birds in no way similar to ours, so that it is truly a wonder. They have much merchandise. To this island come many ships with many wares, such as cloths of gold and of silk of different kinds, and many other things we will not mention here; and all these wares are sold and exchanged for the products of the island. The traders come with their ships fully laden, and they unload and sell everything; then they load their ships again with the products of the island, and, thus laden, depart. For I assure you that these merchants get no small profit and gain therefrom.

I will add that ships cannot sail further south to other islands, but only as far as this island and that of Zanghibar, for the sea-current there flows so violently southwards, that they could only return with the greatest difficulty. For this reason ships do not go there. I will tell you, too, that the ships from Maabar take twenty days in coming, but when they return to Maabar they have to toil along for three months. And this is due to the current that ever flows south. And this current is constant, for it always flows in the same direction.

You must also know that in the other islands, which are so numerous towards the south, and whither ships do not go willingly on account of the current, it is said that there are gryphons, and that these birds appear at certain seasons of the year. But you must know that they are not such as the people in our country believe, and as we draw them. We say, in fact, that they are half birds and half lions, but, according to what those who have seen them relate, it is not true that they are half birds and half lions; for those who have seen them, say that they are made just like an eagle, but they add that they are immeasurably big.

About this bird I will tell you what those who have seen it relate; then I will tell you what I myself have seen. They say, then, that it is so big and so strong that it can take up an elephant in its talons, lift it up into the air to a great height, and then let it fall down to the ground, so that it is dashed to pieces. Then the bird swoops down, and tears it with its beak, and eats it, feeding off it. Those who have seen it, also say that the span of its wings reaches 30 paces, and that the wing-feathers are 12 paces long, and proportionally thick. As for what I myself saw of it, I shall tell you in due course, for so is it necessary to do on account of the nature of our book.

I have told you what those who have seen the gryphon say about it. Well, you must now know that the Great Kaan sent an embassy to that island, in order to get information concerning those regions; he also sent it in order to obtain the release of another envoy of his who had been taken prisoner. Now, both the second envoy and the one who had been kept prisoner, told the Great Kaan many great wonders concerning those distant islands. And I assure you that those envoys brought the Great Kaan certain teeth of a wild boar, that were enormously big; indeed, the Great Kaan had one weighed, and it was 14 pounds. You may imagine the size of the wild boar that had such teeth! They told him that, there were wild boars as big as buffaloes, and also giraffes and wild asses in abundance;

in a word, their beasts and birds are so different from ours, that it is a marvel to hear of, and still more to see. But, to return to our gryphon, the envoy who had been kept prisoner, brought the Great Kaan one of its wing-feathers. And I, Marco Polo, measured it, and I found it to be 90 of my spans in length; and the compass of the quill end was twice my palm; truly it was a marvellous sight to see, and the Great Kaan received it with great joy.

The islanders call the bird *ruc*, and by no other name, and do not know what *gryphon* means. But we are sure, on account of the great size they say it reaches, that it is the gryphon.

Now we have told you many things concerning the island. There is nothing else worth mentioning, and so we will quit it, and tell you of the island of Zanghibar, even as you shall hear.

Here is told of the island of Zanghibar

Zanghibar is a very large and noble island. It has a compass of no less the 2000 miles. They are all Idolaters. They have a King and a language of their own. They owe allegiance to no one. The people are big and stout, but not as tall as they should be in proportion to their stoutness; for they are so stout and brawny that they seem giants. I assure you that they are enormously strong for they can carry as much as four other men. Nor is it a wonder, for truly they eat as much as five men. They are all black, and go about naked, except that they cover their middles. They have such frizzly hair, that even with water you could hardly straighten it out. Their mouths are so big, their noses so turned up, their lips and eyes so large, that they are the most horrible sight. If anyone saw them in another country, he would take them for devils.

Quantities of elephants are born there, and there is a

thriving trade in elephants' tusks. They also have lions, all black, and different from those of other countries. They have many ounces, too; and leopards, also, are born there. What more shall I tell you? All their animals are different from all the others in the world. Thus I assure you that all their sheep are of one kind and colour—white with black heads. In the whole island you would not find a sheep that was not as I have said.

There are also many giraffes, which are beautiful to look at. They are as I shall tell you. You must know that the body is short, and rather low in the croup, for the hind legs are short; but the forelegs and the neck are very long, so that the head is quite three paces above the ground. The head is small, and the animal is not dangerous. It is red and white all over, in small circles. It is really a beautiful animal to look at.

I will add another thing I had forgotten about the elephants. You must know that when a bull-elephant wishes to cover its mate, it digs a hole in the ground, so as to put the female in it on her back, like a woman; this is because their sexual organs are very far forward towards the belly; then the elephant covers her like a man.

I will add, too, that the women of the island are most hideous to look at, for they have large mouths, big eyes, and big noses. Their breasts are four times bigger than those of other women, so that if they threw them behind their shoulders, they would reach the bottom of their backs. They are truly hideous.

They live on rice, flesh, milk, and dates. They have no grape-wine, but they make a kind of wine with rice, sugar, and spices, that is excellent to drink, and makes you drunk quite as much as grape-wine. There is a great deal of trade. Many merchants come to this island with many ships, laden with divers kinds of wares, and they sell everything. They then take away with them quantities of the products of the island,

and especially great numbers of elephants' tusks, which are so plentiful there. There is a great deal of ambergris in the island, for they take considerable numbers of whales.

You must also know that the men of this island are excellent soldiers, and fight gallantly in battle, for they are brave, and have no fear of death. They have no horses, but fight on camels and elephants. They set towers on the elephants' backs, covering them very well with the skins of wild beasts; then as many as 16 or 20 men get in, with lances, swords and stones. And the fight waged from the elephants' backs is a fierce one. They have no armour except a shield of hide, and no weapons but a lance and a sword. But even so they kill one another right merrily. Another thing I will also add: when they wish to take their elephants out to fight, they give them plenty of their wine to drink. This they do because, after drinking that wine, the elephant becomes bolder and fiercer, and behaves much better in the struggle.

Now I have told you a great deal concerning these islands, of the people, of their animals, and of their trade. There is nothing else worth mentioning. And so we will quit this place, and tell you of the great province of Abash.

But, before that, we will say something else about India. You must know that, in telling you of the islands of India, we have merely spoken of the most important provinces, kingdoms, and islands in that part of the world, for there is no man alive who could tell the whole truth concerning all the islands of India. I have told of all the finest islands, the very flower of India. You must know that the greater number of all the other islands of India, of which I have made no mention, is dependent upon those that I have spoken of; their customs may be deduced from what we have said concerning the larger islands. And you must know that in the Sea of India there are 12,700 islands, counting inhabited and uninhabited ones, according to what is stated in the charts and books of the skilful mariners who are used to sailing in that sea.

Now we will leave Greater India, which stretches from Maabar to Kesmacoran, containing thirteen very large kingdoms, of ten of which we have told you. Lesser India stretches from Chanba to Mutfili, with eight large kingdoms; but you must understand that I allude only to the kingdoms on the mainland, without counting those in the islands, which come to an immense figure. Now we will tell you of Middle India, namely of the province of Abash.

Here is told of the province of Abash, namely of Middle India

You must know that Abash is a very large province and constitutes Middle India. You must also know that the chief King of all this province is a Christian. All the other Kings of the province are subject to him; they are six—three Christians and three Saracens.

The Christians of this province have three marks on their faces: one from the forehead to half-way down the nose, and the other two on either cheek. These marks they make when they are children, with a hot iron, and it is a baptism for them; for, after having been baptized with water, they make those marks; to them they are, as it were, a sign of nobility, and a completion of their baptism; they also think that it is good for the health.

I will add that there are also Jews in the province; they have only two marks, one on each cheek. The Saracens have one mark only, namely that from the forehead to half-way down the nose.

The chief King resides in the centre of the province; the Saracens live towards Aden.

In this province, St. Thomas the Apostle preached.

He had first preached in the kingdom of Nubia, and had converted it; then he came to Abash, and with his preaching and his miracles turned part of it to the Law of Christ. After thus converting part of these people, he proceeded to Maabar, where he was killed, and where his body lies, as we have already told you previously in this book.

And you must know that in the province of Abash, there are excellent soldiers, and many horsemen. They have great numbers of horses. And it is well for them that it is so, for you must know that they have to fight with the Sultan of Aden, with that of Nubia, and with many more besides. On account of this constant practice in arms, they are deemed the best soldiers of all the provinces of India.

And I will tell you a fine story concerning what happened in the year 1288 after Christ's Incarnation.

You must know that one day the King who was the supreme Lord of the province of Abash—and who was a Christian—said he would go on a pilgrimage to adore the Sepulchre of Christ at Jerusalem. His barons remarked that it would be too dangerous for him to go thither, and advised him to send a Bishop or other great prelate in his stead. And the King accepted the barons' advice. So he sent for a Bishop who was a man of very holy life, and told him that he wished him to go in his stead to Jerusalem, to adore the Sepulchre of Our Lord Jesus Christ. And the Bishop said that he would perform his bidding as befitted a liegeman. The King then told him to get ready, and to set out as quickly as he might.

What more shall I tell you? The Bishop went; having taken leave of the King, and made himself ready to set out on his way, after the manner of a pilgrim, and most honourably attended. And he journeyed on, both by land and by sea, until he arrived at Jerusalem. He went straight to the Sepulchre, and adored it, and paid it such honour and reverence as is due from a Christian to so exalted and noble a thing as this Sepulchre is. He also made many splendid offerings on behalf of the King who sent him. When the Bishop had duly and wisely performed all that he had been charged with, like the wise man he was, he set out again with all his following. And he journeyed on, until he came to Aden. Now, you must know that in this kingdom of Aden Christians are greatly hated. For the people will not look at them, but detest them as their mortal enemies. When the Sultan of Aden heard that this Bishop was a Christian, and that he was an envoy of the great King of Abash, he had him straightway taken, and asked him if he was a Christian. And the Bishop answered that truly he was a Christian. Then the Sultan said to him, that unless he turned to the Law of Mahomet, he would do him shame and dishonour. And the other answered that he would sooner let himself be killed than do so. When the Sultan heard the Bishop's answer, he was greatly incensed, and bade him be taken and circumcised. So the Bishop was taken hold of by many men, and circumcised after the Saracen fashion. After this had been done, the Sultan told him that he had him thus ignominiously treated in order to spite and put to shame the King his Lord. Having said this, he let him go. When the Bishop had thus been put to shame, he was sorely grieved; but he found consolation in one thought, for, said he, he had suffered this for the sake of the Law of Christ, and so the Lord God would reward his soul in the world to come.

But why should I make a long story of it? Know in very truth that when the Bishop had recovered, and could ride a horse, he set out on his way with all his company, and journeyed so long, by sea and by land, until he came to the King his Lord in Abash. When the King saw him, he welcomed him right joyfully, and asked him news of the Sepulchre. The Bishop told him all the truth, and the King listened with reverent faith, as to a most holy matter. When the Bishop had told the King all about the Sepulchre, he next told him how the Sultan of Aden had had him circumcised to his shame and dishonour. When the King heard that such an outrage had been committed upon the Bishop, out of spite towards himself, he was so grieved, that he almost died of sorrow. He exclaimed aloud, so that all those around heard him clearly, that he would no longer wear a crown or rule a land, if he did not exact such vengeance that the whole world should speak of it.

What more shall I say? You must know in very truth that the King mustered an immense force of horsemen and foot soldiers; and he also took with him a great number of elephants, with well-armed towers on their backs, each containing 12 to 13 men. True it is, that in each tower even 20 soldiers can find room, if it is not a question of going to fight; but when they go campaigning, there are only 12 in each tower, that their movements may be less hampered. When he was quite ready, with all his men, he set out, and marched on until he reached the kingdom of Aden. When the King of Aden heard of his approach, he summoned to his aid two great Saracen Kings who were his neighbours, and with a vast multitude of horsemen and foot-soldiers, went to wait for him at the fortified frontier passes, to defend his land, and prevent the enemy from invading it. Now, the King of Abash reached those passes with his host, and found the enemy there in great numbers. Then the cruellest and most terrible battle began. But it so came about that the three Saracen Kings could not hold out against the forces of the King of Abash, for he had many and excellent troops. For Christians are much better soldiers than Saracens. So the Saracens retreated, and the Christian King and his men entered into the kingdom of Aden. But you must know that at those passes very many Saracens were killed. What more shall I tell you? Know in truth that when the King of Abash and his men had entered the kingdom of Aden, in three or four places, the Saracens barred the way at certain fortified passes; but in vain did they try to defend them, for they were killed and slaughtered in great numbers. Now, when the Christian King had remained about a month in the land of the enemy, and had harried and devastated it, and put to death a great multitude of Saracens, he said that now the ignominy suffered by his Bishop had been well avenged, and that they could honourably return to their country. I will add, too, that he could not do much more damage to the enemy, for the passes he would still have to force were too strong, and dangerous, so that a handful of men might have inflicted great losses upon him. So they left the kingdom of Aden, and set out on their way. And they journeyed on, never resting until they reached Abash, their country.

Now you have heard how well and completely the Bishop was avenged upon those Saracen dogs. For truly the number of the killed was so great that it could not be counted, and many regions were also harried and devastated. Nor need this be wondered at, for it is not right that the Saracen dogs should have the better of Christians.

Now that we have told you about this, we will leave the subject, and pass on to other things concerning the same province of Abash. You must know that this province abounds in all the necessaries of life. They live on rice, wheat, flesh, milk, and sesame. They have elephants, but they are not born there, for they get them from the islands of Greater India. Giraffes, however, are born in the country, and they have plenty of them. Lions, leopards and ounces there are also in considerable numbers, and hosts of other animals, different from those in our countries. Many wild asses are also born there. They have many kinds of birds, different from all others. They have the finest poultry in the world. They have large ostriches, no smaller than wild asses. There are also many other varieties of animals, differing from ours, of which we shall say nothing, for it were too long a tale. Know, however, that they have abundance of game, both beasts and birds. They have many fine parrots. They have monkeys of different kinds. They have indeed such strange apes and baboons that some of them really almost look as if they had human faces. It is also a province abounding in gold, of which quantities are found there.

We will now say no more on this subject, but will proceed, and tell you of Aden. But, before that, there is yet something we wish to say of this province of Abash. You must know that in this province of Abash there are many cities and towns, and many merchants that live by trade. Quantities of beautiful cotton cloths and buckrams are made there. There are many other things, too, but it is not necessary to mention them in our book. So we will leave this country, and tell you of Aden.

Here is told of the kingdom of Aden

As we have told you of the province of Abash, we will also tell you of the province of Aden, as you shall hear.

You must know, then, that in this province of Aden, there is a sovereign called the Sultan of Aden. They are all Saracens, worshipping Mahomet, and they detest Christians. There are many cities and towns.

In this country is the port which all the ships of India call at, with their merchandise. And great numbers of merchants flock there. From this port, the merchants, transferring their wares into smaller boats, sail for some seven days up a river. At the end of the seven days, they unload their ships, and, placing their wares on camels, take them for some thirty days further. At the end of the thirty days, they reach the river of Alexandria, called the Nile, where the wares are loaded on small vessels, called *jerms*, which easily carry them to Babylon up the river, and thence, along a canal called Calizene, to Alexandria. In such wise, by way of Aden, the Saracens of Alexandria have pepper and spices and other precious wares; nor is there any other good short route by which they can reach Alexandria.

From this port of Aden, many ships carrying wares and traders, set sail for the islands of India. I will add that from this port merchants take to India many fine Arabian chargers of great value, and good horses capable of carrying two saddles; and they derive great profit therefrom. For I wish you to know that the merchants will sell a good horse in India for quite 100 silver marks, and more.

I assure you that the Sultan of Aden receives a great income and revenue from the heavy dues paid by the ships and merchants that come and go about his territory. And I will add that for this very reason I have given, namely the heavy dues he receives from the traders that come to his land, he is one of the wealthiest Kings in the world.

I will also tell you, concerning the Sultan, that he did a thing that was most harmful to Christians. You must know in very truth that, when the Sultan of Babylon attacked the city of Acre, on the occasion when it was taken, and there was such a slaughter of Christians, this Sultan of Aden aided the Sultan of Babylon with no less than 30,000 horsemen and 40,000 camels from his own army; and this was to the great advantage of the Saracens, and to the great injury of the Christians. And he did it rather out of hatred for the Christians, than for the good of the Sultan of Babylon, or any particular love he bore him.

We also wish you to know that the ships of Aden,

Cormos, Kisi and other countries, that sail on the Sea of India, are so frail, that they are often wrecked. If that sea were as wild and threatening, and as subject to storms, as the sea in our parts, not a ship of theirs would reach its destination, but would be wrecked on the way. But what do the merchants do, and those who sail in those ships? They take with them many leather skins, and when they perceive the weather and the sea become threatening, they fill these skins with pearls and precious stones, if they have any, and with their clothes and personal belongings, besides the food they think fit; then they tie all these skins together, so as to make a kind of raft. Thus, if it chance that the ship, caught by the tempest, should sink, they all remain on the raft. Then, according to the direction the storm is following, they are driven, day by day, towards land, however far out at sea they may have been, even 200 miles. All the time they are floating along on these rafts, if any of them wishes to eat or drink, he takes the necessary liquid or food from the leather skin, which he then swells out again by blowing into it. In this way they escape; but the ships, with the bulkier wares, are lost.

Now we will quit this subject, and tell you of a very large city that belongs to the Sultan of Aden, and has a petty Lord of its own. It lies towards the north-west, and is called Eshier.

Here is told of the city of Eshier

Eshier is a very large city lying towards the north-west, 400 miles from the port of Aden. It belongs to a Count who governs his land well; he possesses also many other cities and towns. You must note, however, that he is a vassal to the Sultan of Aden. They are Saracens, worshipping Mahomet.

This city has an excellent harbour; and many ships and many merchants go there from India, carrying much merchandise. From this city, too, the ships and merchants sail back to India with much merchandise. I will add, moreover, that from this city traders take to India many fine chargers, and many good horses capable of carrying two saddles. These are very valuable and costly, and the merchants get great gain and profit thereby.

This province produces a great quantity of good white frankincense. It also produces great abundance of dates. They have no corn, except a little rice and millet; and I will add that merchants bring corn there from other countries, and get great profit from it. They have plenty of fish, and especially fine big tunny; there is so much of it, that for a Venetian *grosso* you would get two big ones. They live on rice, meat, milk, and fish. They have no grape-wine, but make a kind of wine with sugar, rice, and dates; it is very good.

Another thing I will tell you, too. You must know that they have sheep without ears, or even the holes of the ears; where they should have ears, they have a little horn. They are small and pretty.

I will add yet another thing that cannot but seem marvellous to you. You must know in very truth that their cattle, namely their sheep, oxen, camels, and ponies, eat fish. That is their food, for the whole region and district is without grass, being the driest place in the world. You must also know that the fishes that these animals eat are very small, and are taken in the months of March, April, and May, in such enormous quantities, that it is truly a wonder. I will add that they dry them and store them, dealing them out to their cattle in the course of the year. But the animals will eat them alive, too, just as they are taken from the water.

They also have excellent big fish, in great abundance and cheap. And I will add that they make fish-biscuits. They cut the fish up into pieces, and, with a certain flour of theirs, they make a liquid that keeps these pieces together like paste; then they make cakes of them, perhaps weighing a pound each, and dry them in the sun; these they store away in their houses, eating them in the course of the year, like biscuits.

The frankincense I mentioned, which is so abundant in this region, is bought by the Lord of the city at ten golden bezants a measure, and then sold again to others, including foreign merchants, at forty bezants the measure. This, however, is done on behalf of the Sultan of Aden. He it is who has the incense bought all over his dominions at ten bezants, and then has it sold again at forty, as we have said. Hence he gets an enormous profit and revenue therefrom.

There is nothing else worth mentioning in this city, and so we will leave it, and tell you of another city called Dufar.

Here is told of the city of Dufar

Dufar is a large city, both great and noble, and stands some 500 miles from Eshier, to the north-west. They are also Saracens, worshipping Mahomet. They are ruled by a Count, also subject to the Sultan of Aden, for you are to understand that this city, too, belongs to the province of Aden.

The city stands on the sea-shore, and has an excellent harbour, at which many ships with many merchants call, carrying immense quantities of merchandise. And I will add that they take there many fine horses from Arabia and other countries, and the traders get great gain and profit from them.

You must further know that this city has many other cities and towns dependent upon it.

I will add that here, too, great quantities of excellent frankincense are produced. And I will tell you how. You must know that they are not very big trees; they are like small firs. Incisions are made with a knife in various parts of the tree, and, from these incisions, trickle drops that become hardened; this is the frankincense. Moreover, even without these incisions, certain gummy galls are formed on the trees on account of the great heat; and that is also frankincense. And there is great trade both in this incense, and in the horses which the merchants take to India.

There is nothing else worth mentioning, and so we will leave this place, and tell you of the gulf of Calatu.

Here is told of the city of Calatu

Calatu is a large city, situated on a gulf that is also called Calatu, and lying 600 miles to the north-west of Dufar. It is a noble city, on the seashore. They are Saracens, worshipping Mahomet. They are dependent upon Cormos, and every time the Melic of Cormos is at war with some one more powerful than himself, he takes refuge in this city, for it is so well fortified and so strongly situated, that, once there, he fears no one.

They have no corn of any kind, but import it from other lands, for the traders bring it to them on their ships.

The city has an excellent harbour, and you must know that many ships go there from India, with quantities of goods. These find a very good market, for from there, goods and species are carried to many cities and towns in the interior.

I will add that from this city many good horses are taken to India, and the merchants get great profits therefrom. Indeed, one can hardly believe the enormous quantities of fine horses that are taken to India from this province and from the others that I have previously mentioned.

The city stands at the very entrance and mouth of the gulf of Calatu, so that no ship can come in or go out except at the citizens' pleasure. As a result, the Melic of Cormos has many a time obtained excellent conditions from the Sultan of Kerman on whom he is dependent. For, when the Sultan wishes to impose on the

Melic of Cormos, or any of his brothers, a duty that they refuse to pay, and sends an army to force them, they straighway leave Cormos, and, embarking on ships, come to this city of Calatu. Here they remain, and let no ship pass, so that the Sultan of Kerman is greatly damaged. He is thus obliged to come to terms with the Melic of Cormos, and does not take from him as much money as he had at first demanded. I will add that this Melic of Cormos has a castle that is still stronger than the city, and has a better command of the gulf and of the sea.

You must also know that the people of this country live on dates and salt fish, of which they have great quantities. True it is, however, that many among them, the rich and the noble, also have other and better food, and eat better fare.

Now we have told you of the city of Calatu, of its gulf, and of other things concerning it. We will therefore leave it, and tell you of Cormos. For you must know that, on leaving the city of Calatu, and travelling 300 miles between north and north-west, one reaches the city of Cormos. Whereas, if one leaves Calatu and goes 500 miles between north-west and west, one reaches Kisi. But we will leave out Kisi, and tell you of Cormos.

Here is told of the city of Cormos

Cormos is a large and noble city, standing on the sea-shore. It is subject to the Sultan of Kerman. It has a Melic; it also has many cities and towns dependent upon it. They are Saracens, worshipping Mahomet.

The heat is very great. On account of this, their houses are built with wind-chimneys, in order to catch the wind; they place the wind-chimney on the side whence the wind comes, and so bring the wind into the house. This they do because they could not otherwise endure the great heat.

But we will add nothing more, because we have already told you previously in this book concerning this city, as also concerning Kisi and Kerman. But, though coming back by different routes, we have had to return to this place. And since, as I have said, we have already told you all about this country, we will leave it, and tell you of Great Turkey, as you shall clearly hear.

Here is told of Great Turkey

In Great Turkey, there is a King called Caidu, who is a nephew of the Great Kaan's, for he is a son of the son of Chagatai, who was own brother to the Great Kaan. He possesses many cities and towns, and is a great Lord. He is a Tartar, and his people are also Tartars.

They are excellent soldiers, nor is it any wonder, for they are accustomed to fighting. I will add that this Caidu has never been at peace with the Great Kaan, but, on the contrary, constantly at war.

And you must know that Great Turkey lies to the north-west of one coming from the city of Cormos, of which we have told you. It is beyond the river Jon, and stretches northward, as far as the Great Kaan's dominions.

I say, then, that this Caidu has already fought many a battle against the armies of the Great Kaan. And I will tell you the reasons of his quarrel with him. You must know in very truth that Caidu has constantly claimed from the Great Kaan a share of the lands conquered by the Tartars; above all, he asks for parts of the province of Cathay and of the province of Manji. And the Great Kaan has always answered him, that he was quite willing to give him his share, as to his other heirs, on condition, however, that, like the others, he should come to his court, and take part in his councils, every time he summoned him thither. Further, the Great Kaan wished Caidu to owe him allegiance like his other heirs and barons. On such terms as you have heard, then, did the Great Kaan declare himself willing to give Caidu a share of his conquests. But Caidu, who in no way trusted the Great Kaan his uncle, said he would not go to him; he would indeed owe him allegiance wherever he might happen to be, but for nothing in the world would he go to court, for he was afraid of being murdered.

This, then, was the quarrel between the Great Kaan and Caidu, and on account of it a fierce war had broken out between them, and many a great battle had been fought. Indeed, the Great Kaan constantly kept his armies all round the territories of Caidu, to prevent the latter doing damage to his lands and peoples; yet, notwithstanding all the Great Kaan's armies, King Caidu has frequently succeeded in penetrating into the Great Kaan's dominions, and many a time has fought against the armics that advanced against him.

And I will tell you in very truth that when king Caidu makes his greatest effort, he can lead quite 100,000 horsemen into the field, all of them valiant and experienced in war and battles. Moreover, he has with him many barons of the Imperial blood, namely of the blood of Chinghis Kaan. (If I say "of the blood of Chinghis Kaan" it is the same as saying "of the Blood Imperial," because Chinghis Kaan was the founder of the Empire, and the first to have the lordship, and to conquer a part of the world). But we will leave this, and tell you of certain battles that king Caidu fought against the armies of the Great Kaan.

First of all, however, we will tell you how the Tartars go to battle. You must know that it is each man's duty to take sixty arrows to battle; of these thirty are small, and used for transfixing the foe, and thirty are bigger, with large points; these are shot at close quarters, and strike the enemy in the face or in the arms, cut bow-strings, and do other such damage. Once they have shot all their arrows, they take their swords and maces, and exchange terrible blows with them. And now that we have told you how they go to battle, we will return to our subject.

You must know that in the year 1266 after Christ's Incarnation, this King Caidu, together with certain of his cousins, one of whom was called Jesudar, mustered an immense force, and attacked two barons of the Great Kaan's, also his cousins, but owing allegiance to the Great Kaan. One of these barons was called Cibai or Ciban. They were also sons of a son of Chagatai, who was a baptized Christian, and own brother to the Great Kaan Cublai. What more shall I tell you? Caidu and his men fought against these two cousins of his, who also disposed of an immense force, so that counting both sides there were some 100,000 horsemen on the field. They fought together very fiercely, and many were killed on either side. But King Caidu ended by being victorious, and made a great slaughter of the others. But you must know that the two brothers, who were Caidu's cousins, escaped unscathed, for they had excellent horses, that quickly carried them away.

Thus, then, did King Caidu win the battle. And thereby his arrogance and pride were increased. And when he had won the battle as you have heard, he returned to his own country, and lived two years in peace, without wars or battles. Nor did the Great Kaan wage war or open hostilities against him during all that time.

Now it came about that at the end of the two years, King Caidu assembled a mighty army, an immense multitude of horsemen. He knew that at Caracoron there was one of the Great Kaan's sons, Nomogan by name, and with him Giorge, the son of the son of

Prester John. These two barons also had an immense multitude of horsemen. What more shall I tell you? When King Caidu had mustered all his force, he left his kingdom with his entire army, and set out. They rode on, day after day, without meeting with any adventure worthy of mention, until they came near Caracoron, where those two barons were, with their mighty hosts. And when these two barons,—namely the son of the Great Kaan, and the son of the son of Prester John—heard that Caidu had come into their country with so large an army to make war upon them, they were in no way dismayed, but on the contrary gave proof of their daring and valour. They made careful preparations, both they and their men, who amounted to more than 60,000 horsemen. When they were all ready, they set out, and advanced against the enemy. What more shall I tell you? They rode on, until they were at about ten miles' distance from Caidu. And then they pitched their camp, well and properly. And you must know that King Caidu was encamped in that same plain with all that great host of his. Both sides rested, and prepared themselves as best they might for the battle.

But why should I make a long story of it? You must know in very truth that, on the third day after the arrival of the son of the Great Kaan and of the son of the son of Prester John, very early in the morning, both sides armed themselves, and prepared themselves as well as they might. Neither side had the advantage, for each had 60,000 men, well armed with bows, arrows, swords, maces, and shields. Each side divided into six groups; and in each group were ten thousand horsemen, under good leaders. So the two sides were drawn up and ready on the field, and only waited to hear the sound of the *naccars*. For the Tartars would never dare to begin a battle until their Lord's *naccar* has begun sounding: as soon as it sounds, the battle begins. The Tartars have also this custom:

when they are drawn up awaiting battle, they sing and play their two-stringed instruments very sweetly, until the *naccars* begin to sound. And so, singing and playing, and amusing themselves, they await the beginning of the battle. In accordance with their custom, then, those two armies, while they were drawn up awaiting the battle, and the sounding of the *naccars*, sang and played so well, that it was truly a wonder to hear them. Thus they remained some time, waiting for the *naccars* to sound, when at last the latter sounded on both sides. What more shall I tell you? When the *naccars* began to sound, they made no further delay: straightway they charged one against the other. They took their bows and drew them. Now might one have seen all the air filled with arrows, as if it were raining. Now might one have seen many a man and many a steed wounded to death. Now might one have heard such great crying and lamentations and so mighty a din, that God's thunder would not have been heard. Truly was it manifest that they were mortal enemies. But why should I make a long story of it? Know in very truth, that, as long as they had arrows, those that were whole and sound did not cease shooting them. For there were great numbers killed, or wounded to death, so that truly that battle was begun in an evil hour for both sides, so many were the slain. When all their arrows had been shot and let fly, they put their bows in their quivers, and, taking up their swords and maces, charged upon one another. And so they started dealing out mighty blows with these swords and maces. Thus began a fierce and most terrible struggle. Now could one have seen terrible blows given and received. Now could one have seen hands and arms being hacked off. Now could one have seen many a man fall dead to the ground. For in very truth the sword-play had barely begun, before the ground was strewn with men slain or wounded to death.

Truly King Caidu performed deeds of great valour. Had it not been for his presence, more than once his men had fled from the field, and been defeated. But he fought with such daring, and so comforted his people, that they held out most valiantly. On the other side, the son of the Great Kaan and the son of the son of Prester John fought equally well: they gave great proofs of their valour in the thickest of the melley, and they wielded their weapons so well, and so exhorted their men, that it was truly a wonder.

What more shall I tell you? Know in very truth that this was one of the fiercest battles that ever were between Tartars. So great were the din and the clash of swords and maces, that God's thunder would not have been heard. And I assure you that each side made every possible effort to overcome its foe; they both strove beyond measure. But it was all of no avail, for neither side could succeed in overcoming the other. But I tell you truly that the battle lasted till after vespers, without either side being able to drive the other off the field. And so many were the slain on either side, that it was heart-rending to see. Truly the battle was begun in an evil hour for both sides. For many a man died, and many a lady was left a widow, and many a child an orphan. And many more ladies remained in tears and mourning for the rest of their days: and these were the mothers and the sisters [?] of those who fell.

When the battle had lasted even as long as I have said, and the sun was already setting, and so many lay slain, then perforce the struggle had to cease. So they left the field, and each side returned to its tents, so tired and worn out, that there was not one of them but had greater need of repose than of battling. And all the night they rested gladly on account of the terrible exertions undergone on the day of that great and mortal battle.

When the morning came, King Caidu, who had

received warning that the Great Kaan was sending another large army, comprising a multitude of men, to fall upon him and to capture him, said to himself that it was ill for him to remain. So, as soon as day broke, he armed himself with all his men, and, mounting their horses, they all set out to return to their country. When the son of the Great Kaan and the grandson of Prester John saw that King Caidu and all his men were departing, they did not pursue them, being so tired and worn out, but let them go in peace. And King Caidu and his men rode on, day after day, and did not stop until they reached their kingdom, which is in Greater Turkey, namely at Samarcan. And here Caidu remained some time without waging war.

Certainly, terrible was the Great Kaan's wrath against this Caidu, who constantly did such damage to his lands and his peoples. And he said to himself that, were Caidu not his nephew, nothing would keep him from putting him to an evil death. But the ties of blood kept him from destroying him and his land. Thus, then, as I have told you, did King Caidu escape from the hands of the Great Kaan.

We will now leave this matter, and proceed to tell you of a great marvel concerning the daughter of King Caidu, even as you shall hear.

Here is told of the daughter of King Caidu, and of her strength and prowess

Now you must know that King Caidu had a daughter, called in the Tartar language Aijaruc, which, in our tongue means "Shining Moon." This maiden was so strong that in the whole kingdom there was no youth or squire who could overcome her. For truly, I tell you, she defeated them all.

The King her father wished to give her in marriage

to some baron. But she would not hear of it, and said that she would never take a husband until she found some nobleman who should surpass her in feats of strength. And the King her father had granted in writing that she might marry according to her desires.

For you must know that, among the Tartars, there is indeed no custom of paying attention to rank in connection with marriage, except only from the point of view of the woman. If a King or prince or any nobleman wishes to take a wife, he does not seek for a woman of noble birth or equal in rank to himself, but takes any woman, as long as she is beautiful and well-shaped, even though she be not noble. For they say that no family or lineage takes its name from the woman, but from the man; in fact, as we should say, a man is not "the son of Bertha or of Mary," but the "son of Peter or of Martin." And this is why, in choosing a wife, they pay no attention to her nobility.

When the King's daughter had had the consent and written deed of her father, whereby she could marry according to her will, she was overjoyed. She had it proclaimed in various parts of the world, that, if there were any noble youth who wished to try his strength against her, and should succeed in defeating her, she would accept him as husband. And when this news was spread through many lands and kingdoms, I assure you that many a nobleman came from divers parts to pit himself against her. And you must know that the test of strength was made as I shall tell you. The King, with a great following both of men and ladies, took his seat in the principal pavilion in the camp (for the Tartars are always encamped in their tents). Then the King's daughter came into the middle of the pavilion, clothed in a leather tunic, very richly adorned; after her came the young nobleman, also clothed in a leather tunic. The conditions were as follows: if the young squire succeeded in overcoming her by throwing her to the ground, he would receive her as wife, but if the King's daughter succeeded in overcoming the squire, the latter would lose 100 horses, which would pass to the maiden. In this way she had already won over 10,000 horses. For she could find no squire or other young noble whom she did not defeat. Nor was it any wonder, for not only was she most shapely in all her limbs, but she was also so tall and so muscular, that she almost seemed a giantess.

Now it came to pass that, about the 1280 after Christ's Incarnation, there came the son of a wealthy King, who was very handsome and young. He had set out with a splendid retinue, bringing with him 1000 very handsome horses, in order to try his strength against the maiden. When the King's son had arrived, he made his intention known. King Caidu was greatly pleased, for it was his desire that this young man should have his daughter to wife. For he knew that he was the son of the King of Pumar. So King Caidu had his daughter privately told that she should let herself be vanquished. But his daughter answered that, for nothing in the world, would she do aught that was not right and reasonable.

What more shall I tell you? You must know that one day the King and the Queen, and many other men and ladies, assembled in the great pavilion. And so they saw the King's daughter and the other King's son come in; and they were both so fair and so handsome, that it was truly a wonder to see them. And I assure you that he was so strong and powerful a youth, that he could find no one to match his strength. And when the maiden and the youth had come into the middle of the pavilion, in the presence of all those people I have mentioned, the conditions were proclaimed: namely, if the young man was victorious, he would have the King's daughter to wife, but if he was defeated, he would lose all the 1000 horses he had brought with him for this test. Once the conditions had been proclaimed, the damsel and the young man came to grips. And all those who looked on hoped in their hearts that the young man might win, in order that he should become the husband of the King's daughter. And the King and Queen wished it too. But why should I make a long story of it? You must know in very truth, that, once the young couple had gripped one another, they both wrestled this way and that; but it so came to pass that the King's daughter defeated the youth, and threw him to the ground. Thus the King's son was overcome, and lost the thousand horses. He straightway departed with his company, and returned quite shamefaced to his own land. And I assure you that there was no one in that pavilion but was grieved thereat.

I will add, too, that King Caidu took with him into many battles this daughter of his, who had defeated the King's son. Nor was there in the thick of the battle a knight more valiant than she. And I assure you that many a time this maiden went into the midst of the enemy, and, taking some knight by force, bore him to her people. And this chanced often enough.

We have told you the story of this daughter of King Caidu. We will now leave this matter, and proceed to inform you of other things. And first we will tell you of a great battle that took place between King Caidu and Argon, the son of Abaga, Lord of the Levant, even as you shall hear.

How Abaga sent his son Argon to war

You must know that Abaga, Lord of the Levant, possessed many provinces and many lands, and his dominions marched with those of King Caidu: this was in the direction of the Arbre Sol, which in the *Book of Alexander* is called Arbre Sec. And, lest King Caidu and his men should do damage to his lands and peoples, Abaga sent his son Argon, with a great host of horsemen, into the region of the Arbre Sol, as far as the river Jon. There Argon resided with his army, guarding the land, in order that the armies of King Caidu should do it no damage.

Argon, then, dwelt as you have heard in the plain of the Arbre Sol, and protected many a city and town that stood in that district. Now, it came to pass that King Caidu mustered a great force of horsemen, and placed them under the command of a brother of his, Barac by name, who was a very wise and prudent man. And Caidu told him that he wished him to go and wage war on Argon. Barac replied that he would carry out his commands, and do all that lay in his power to inflict damage upon Argon and his people. Thereupon, Barac set out with all his men, who were indeed a great multitude. They rode on for many a day, without meeting with any adventure worth mentioning, until they reached the river Jon, and found themselves at ten miles' distance from Argon.

What more shall I tell you? When Argon was informed that Barac had come with such a host, he duly made ready with all his men. Not more than three days passed before the two armies stood drawn up and ready on the field of battle: namely, Argon and Barac with their respective hosts. What more shall I tell you? When they were duly arrayed and ready, the *naccars* began to sound, and so they made no further delay: straightway they charged against one another. Now one could see arrows flying in all directions, so that the air was so full of them, that it seemed to be raining. And when both sides had shot all their arrows, and many a man and horse lay killed, they took to their swords and maces, and dashed one upon another; and a most cruel and fierce struggle began. They hacked off hands and arms. They cut down horses. They played havoc upon one another. The din and uproar were so great, that God's thunder would not have been heard. And I assure you that in but a brief time the ground was littered with men slain or wounded to death. But why should I use so many words? Know, in very truth, that Barac and his men could not withstand the might of Argon. And so he retreated with his men, and withdrew beyond the river. And Argon and his host pursued him for part of the way, and slaughtered many of his men.

Such as you have heard, was the result of the battle: Argon was victorious. And, as I have begun speaking of Argon, I will tell you in detail how he was taken, and how he had the lordship after the death of Abaga his father.

How Argon went to assume the lordship

You must know that not long after Argon had been victorious over Barac and the army of King Caidu, he received news that Abaga his father was dead. He was greatly distressed, and got ready with all his army, and so set out in order to return to court and take over the lordship. And he had to travel quite 40 days before he reached his destination.

Now it came about that a brother of Abaga's, whose name was Acomat Soldan, and who had turned Saracen, as soon as he heard that his brother Abaga was dead, thought he might become lord, since Argon was so far away. So he mustered a very large army, and, going straight to the court of Abaga his brother, took over the sovereignty, and made himself Lord. And I assure you that he found there such an immense treasure, that if one heard the value of it in figures, one could hardly believe it. And he distributed part of it to his barons and knights with amazing bounty. And so these barons and knights, when they saw that Acomat Soldan gave them such generous gifts, said that he was a good lord. And they all loved him, and cherished him, and said they would have no other Lord but him. Indeed Acomat Soldan ruled excellently well, and he pleased all. But I must tell you that he did a scandalous deed, which was reproved by many: he took all his brother Abaga's wives, and kept them for himself.

What more shall I tell you? Know that not long after he had assumed the sovereignty, he heard that Argon was approaching with an immense host. He lost no time, and in no way showed himself dismayed. Most resolutely he had his barons and men summoned. And I assure you that in a week's time he collected a mighty army of horsemen, who marched gladly against Argon, all declaring unanimously that they desired nothing so much as to slay Argon, or to capture him, and put him to an exemplary death.

How Acomat advanced with his army to fight against Argon

When Acomat Soldan had mustered quite 60,000 horsemen, he set out against Argon and his host. They rode on quite ten days without stopping, and at the end of the ten days they heard that Argon was approaching, and was then only five days distant: and his forces were no greater than their own. Then Acomat had his tents pitched in a very vast and fine plain, and said that he would wait there for Argon's arrival, as that was an excellent place for an encounter between two armies.

When his tents were all duly pitched, he held his parliament, and, summoning his men, spoke to them as follows: " Gentlemen, said he, ye know well how I am by right the Lord of all my brother Abaga possessed, because I was born of the same father as he, and have taken part in all the wars in the course of which we conquered the lands and provinces we hold. True it is that Argon is the son of Abaga my brother, and that some might be tempted to say that the sovereignty is due to him. But, by leave of those who should be tempted so to think, this were neither reasonable nor right. Since his father held the lordship for so long a time, as you know, it is but right that I should hold it, now that he is dead. For it would have been but right had I received half of it during his life-time, but I, out of my good nature, left it all to him. Now, since matters stand so, I beg you to defend our rights against Argon, so that the kingdom and the lordship may remain to all of us. For I protest that, for myself, I only desire the honour and the glory: yourselves may have all the profit, the wealth, and the authority over all our lands and provinces. I will add no more, for I know that ye are wise, and lovers of justice, and will bear yourselves in such a way as shall bring honour and advantage to all." Thereupon he was silent, and said no more.

And when the barons and knights and all the others who were there, had heard the words of Acomat, they all answered of one accord that they would not fail him, as long as they had breath in their bodies; they would help him against any man in the world, and above all against Argon. They said he was to have no fear, for they would take Argon, and place him in his hands.

Thus, then, as you have heard, did Acomat speak to his men, and learn their intentions. They desired nothing better than that Argon and his host should come up and engage them.

Here we shall leave Acomat and his men, and return to Argon and his host.

How Argon took counsel with his barons about attacking Acomat

You must know then that, when Argon heard for certain that Acomat was awaiting him in his camp with such a large host, he was greatly afflicted. Still, he saw that it might do him great harm if he let himself look sad, and betrayed fear of his enemies, for this would lessen the courage of his men, So he said to himself that he must needs make a show of daring and courage. He summoned all his barons and wise men. And when a host of them had assembled in his pavilion —for he had placed his camp in a very fine spot— he spoke, and said as follows: "My good brothers and friends, said he, ye know well how tenderly my father loved you. As long as he lived, he held you as brothers and sons. Ye know, too, how ye have been with him in many great battles, and how ye helped him to conquer the lands he held. And ye know that I am the son of him who loved you so. I, too, love you as much as myself. And so, as this is the truth, it is right and reasonable that ye should help me against this man, who is bearing upon me contrary to all right and reason, and who would fain do us even so great an injury as that of depriving us of the heritage of our lands. And ye know, too, in very truth, that he does not believe in our Law; he has abandoned it, turning Saracen and worshipping Mahomet. Ye see how worthy it were, forsooth, should Saracens gain the sovereignty over Tartars! Now, my good brothers and friends, as there are all these reasons, your courage should increase on this account, as also your will to do all that is needful to prevent this coming about. Hence, I beg each one of you to be valiant, and to make every effort, to the utmost limit of his powers and beyond, in order to fight in such a way that we may win the battle, and that the sovereignty may remain with us, and not with the Saracens. And, in truth, everyone must have faith that we shall indeed win the battle, for we are in the right, and our enemies in the wrong. I will say no more about this, I only beg each one of you to see to it that he bear himself well."

Then he was silent, and said no more.

How the barons answered Argon

When the barons and knights who were present, heard the words that Argon had said wisely and nobly, each said to himself that he would rather die than not do all he could to win the battle. And while all remained silent and still, a great baron rose, and uttered these words: "Our beloved Lord Argon," said he, "we know well and clearly that the truth is even as you say. And so I shall answer in the name of all your men who are about to engage in this battle together with you; I say, then, that we will not fail you, as long as we have breath in our bodies. Rather will we all die, than not win this battle. And that we shall win it, we must needs be sure, for all the right is on our side, and all the wrong on the enemy's. So I propose and counsel that we shall advance as soon as possible in order to meet the foe. And this I beg of all my comrades, that we so bear ourselves in this battle, that the whole world shall speak of us." Thereupon the valiant man was silent, and added no other word.

What more shall I tell you? After him, no one wished to say aught. But all agreed with him. Indeed, none desired anything better than to come to grips with the foe.

When the morrow came, Argon and his men rose very early in the morning, and set out, longing to work havoc upon the enemy. They rode on until they reached the plain where the enemy were encamped. They pitched their tents well and wisely at ten miles' distance from those of Acomat.

Once they were encamped, Argon took two of his men, whom he greatly trusted, and sent them to his uncle, with the message that you shall hear.

How Argon sent envoys to Acomat

When these two wise men, who were much advanced in years, had received their commission from the Lord

Argon, and had been dismissed, they lost no time, but at once set out on two horses. They went straight to the enemy's camp, and dismounted outside Acomat's pavilion. And they found him with a large retinue of barons. Acomat and they knew one another very well. They greeted him very courteously. And Acomat, with a kind countenance, bade them be welcome, and made them sit before him in his pavilion. After they had remained silent some time, one of the two envoys rose up, and spoke as follows: "Fair Lord, said he, your nephew Argon marvels greatly at what you have done; for you have deprived him of his sovereignty, and, moreover, are advancing against him to fight him in a mortal battle. Truly it is not a good action, nor have you acted as a good uncle should act towards his nephew. So he sends word to you by means of us, that he earnestly begs you, as his uncle and his father (for he considers you as such), to give up your intentions, so that there may be neither a battle nor slaughter between you. And he assures you that he is willing to consider you as his elder and his father, and let you be the greatest Lord in all his lands. This is the prayer and the message your nephew sends you by us." Thereupon he was silent and added no other word.

How Acomat answered Argon's envoys

When Acomat Soldan had heard his nephew Argon's message, he answered as follows: "Gentlemen, said he, what my nephew says is without sense; for this land is mine, not his, as I conquered it quite as much as his father did. Therefore, do ye tell my nephew that, if he is willing, I will make him a great Lord; I will give him many lands, and he shall be as my son, and the greatest of all the barons after me. And if he is not willing, he may be sure that I will do all that lies in my power to put him to death. Such are my intentions concerning my nephew; nought else, no other condition shall you have from me." Thereupon Acomat was silent, and said no more. When the envoys had heard what the Soldan had said, they replied: "Shall we truly not be able to have aught else from you?" "Nought else," answered he, "shall you obtain, as long as I live."

When they heard this, the messengers tarried no longer, but set out on their way. And they rode on, until they reached the camp of their Lord. They entered his pavilion, and told him what answer they had had from his uncle. When Argon heard his uncle's message, he was sore afflicted, and exclaimed aloud, so that all those around heard him: "Since such a wrong, such an outrage, has been done me by my uncle, may I live no longer, may I no longer possess a realm, if I do not exact such great vengeance as the whole world shall speak of it!" After these words, he said to his barons and knights: "There may be no further delay. Let us try to set out as soon as possible, to put that disloyal traitor to death. It is my will that we attack them to-morrow, and do our utmost to destroy them."

What more shall I tell you? During the whole of that night they made ready all that was necessary for a battle on the open field. And Acomat Soldan, too, who had learnt from his spies that Argon was to attack him on the morrow, also made himself ready in every way, and exhorted his men to bear themselves valiantly and be brave.

Here is told of the great battle that took place between Argon and Acomat

When the morrow came, Argon armed himself, together with all his men, and drew up and ordered his battalions very wisely and well. With much sweetness he exhorted his men to bear themselves well. And, when everything was duly prepared, they set out towards the enemy.

The Soldan Acomat had done as much: he too had arrayed and drawn up his men. But he did not wait for Argon to come up to his camp, but wisely set out with all his host.

They had not gone far before they met Argon and his army. When the two hosts saw one another face to face, so great was their desire to come to blows, that they did not tarry. Straightway they charged, one against the other. Now could you have seen arrows being shot. Now could you have seen them flying in all directions, so thickly that it seemed as if the rain were falling from the sky. A most cruel and savage battle began. Now you could have seen horsemen fall and crash to the ground. Now you could have heard the cries, and the lamentations, and the great wailing of those who had fallen to the ground wounded to death. And when they had shot all their arrows, they took to their swords and their maces; and they fell fiercely upon one another. They exchanged terrible blows with their sharp swords. Now could you have seen hands, and arms, and bodies and heads hacked to pieces. The din and uproar were such that one could not have heard God's thunder. For you must know that this battle was begun in an evil hour for both sides. For truly many a good man died, and many a good lady was doomed thenceforward to tears and mourning.

But why should I make a long story of it? Know in very truth that Argon bore himself very well that day: he performed deeds of great prowess, and was a great example to his men. But it was all of no avail: for fortune and chance were against him, so that he was worsted and defeated. For, when his men saw that they could no longer hold out, they broke and fled as fast as they could. And Acomat and his men pursued them, and killed many of them, working great havoc among them. And during the pursuit Argon was captured.

As soon as Argon had been taken, they gave up the pursuit, and returned to their tents joyful and exultant. Acomat had his nephew Argon put in chains, and watched very closely.

Then Acomat, who was a most lascivious man, decided to return to his court and take his pleasure with many beautiful women he had there. He left a great Melic in command of the army, and entrusted him with the care of Argon, enjoining upon him to guard him as carefully as if he were his own person. He also ordered the Melic to come to court in short stages, so as not to tire out the soldiers. The Melic assured him that his orders would be carefully executed. So Acomat departed with a large following, and set out on his way to court.

Thus, then, as I have said, Acomat left his army, handing over the command to this Melic, of whom I have spoken. And Argon remained a prisoner in chains, and so sad that he would fain have died.

How the barons plotted to free Argon

Now it came to pass that a certain great Tartar baron, who was much advanced in years, felt great pity for Argon, and said to himself that they were doing a very wicked deed, and a disloyal one, in keeping their Lord prisoner. He said that he would do all that lay in his power in order to free him. So he lost no time, but straightway went to certain other barons, and told them that they were doing a wicked deed in keeping their rightful Lord prisoner, and that it would be an excellent action if they freed him, and made him sovereign, as was his right. And these other barons, when they heard what he proposed, knowing him to be one of the wisest men that ever were, and also realizing that what he said was true, all assented to his words, declaring that they were favourable to his design. When they were thus all agreed in this, Boga—namely he who had made the proposal—and his companions, Elchidai, Togan, Tegana, Tagachar, Oulatai and Samagar, went to the tent where Argon was kept prisoner. When they arrived there, Boga, who was the most important, and the ringleader, was the first to speak, and said as follows: "Our good Lord, said he, we openly admit that we have done ill in taking you, and so we are come to tell you that we wish to return to righteousness and justice; namely, we wish to free you, and desire you to be our liege Lord, even as you are by right." Thereupon Boga was silent and said no more.

How Argon was set free

When Argon heard what Boga said, he doubted not but that it was done in mockery, and answered in great sorrow and affliction: "Gentlemen," said he, "you do ill in mocking me. Surely it ought to suffice you that you have done me so great a wrong, in that, whereas you should regard me as your Lord, you have taken me, and keep me in chains. Certainly you are well aware that you are committing a most evil deed and a sin. Therefore I beg you to go your ways, and not make a mock of me." "Our good Lord," replied Boga, "know in very truth that this is no mockery; indeed it is the truth, and we swear it by our Law." Then all the barons swore that they would regard him as their Lord. And Argon, too, swore that he would not repay them with evil for having made him prisoner; nay, that he would treat them with as much love and affection as his father Abaga had done. After these oaths had been exchanged, even as you have heard, they freed Argon from his chains, and recognized him as their Lord. And Argon, pointing to the tent where was Acomat's Melic, ordered: "Let arrows be shot into that tent, that the Melic who held me prisoner and commanded this army, be killed." These words were followed by no delay, but straightway so many arrows were shot into the pavilion, that the Melic was killed.

When this was done, Argon took over the sovereignty, and issued what commands he thought fit as Lord, and was obeyed by all. And you must know that he whom we have called the Melic, and who was slain, was called [Alinac] Soldan, and he was the most powerful lord after Acomat.

Thus, even as you have heard, did Argon recover the sovereignty.

How Argon had his uncle Acomat put to death

When Argon saw that he was truly Lord, he gave orders to march towards the court. And so, without delay, they set out on the way thither.

Now it happened one day, when Acomat was at court in his palace, feasting gaily, that a messenger arrived and said to him: "Sire, I bring you news; not however such as I should wish, but truly evil news. Know that the barons have set Argon free and have recognized him as their Lord. They have slain Alinac Soldan, our dear friend. And I tell you that they are coming hither as fast as they may, to take you and kill you. Hence, do what you think is best for you." Thereupon he was silent, and said no more. When Acomat had heard what the messenger told him—and he knew that he was a trusty servant—he was so dismayed and affrighted, that he knew not what to do or say. Yet, like the brave and valiant man he was, he told the messenger not to mention a word of this news to any living soul. And the messenger said his commands should be obeyed.

Straightway Acomat mounted his horse, and together with those whom he most trusted, set out on his way to the court of the Soldan of Babylon, where he thought he would be safe. And no one knew whither he was going, except those that were with him.

When he had journeyed six days, he reached a pass through which he had perforce to go, for other way there was none. He who guarded the pass recognized Acomat, and understood that he was fleeing. So he decided to capture him, and this was easy for him, as Acomat had very few people with him. And you must know that this man did even as he had determined: he captured him straightway. Acomat cried for mercy, begged him to let him go, and promised to give him a great treasure. But the other, who was much attached to Argon, said that all this was useless, that he would not take any treasure at all, but would hand him over to Argon, his rightful Lord. What more shall I tell you? He who guarded the pass lost no time after capturing Acomat: he straightway made ready with a large escort, and set out towards the court. He took Acomat with him, and ever kept such good watch over him, that he could not escape. They rode on, without stopping, until they reached the court, where they found Argon, who had arrived only three days previously, and was greatly afflicted because he thought that Acomat had escaped.

When the guard of the pass came into his presence, leading Acomat, his joy was so great, that it could not have been greater. He bade his uncle be " ill-come " instead of welcome, and said that he would do to him what was just. Thereupon he commanded him to be removed from his presence. And, without taking anyone's advice, he ordered him to be slain and made away with. And he whom Argon had bidden do this, took Acomat, and brought him to some place whence he was never seen to return. Nor was it a wonder, for he had him killed, and his body cast in such a place that it has never again been seen.

Such, then, as you have heard, was this encounter between Argon and Acomat his uncle.

How the barons paid homage to Argon

When Argon had accomplished all that I have told you, and was settled in his royal palace in secure possession of the lordship, then from all the countries that had been subject to Abaga his father, the barons came to pay the homage that was due to him as their Lord. And all obeyed him, as they were in duty bound.

And, once he was securely in possession of the lordship, he sent his son Casan with quite 30,000 men into the district of the Arbre Sol, in order to guard and protect his territory and his people.

Thus, then, as you have heard, did Argon recover the sovereignty. And you must know that this came about in the year 1286 after Christ's Incarnation. Acomat Soldan had held the lordship two years, and Argon reigned six years. At the end of the six years, Argon died of disease—but it was also said that he died of poison.

How Kiacatu assumed the lordship after the death of Argon

As soon as Argon was dead, an uncle of his, called Kiacatu, who was own brother to Argon's father Abaga, took possession of the lordship. This he was easily able to do, because Casan was far away, in the region of the Arbre Sol. True it is, however, that Casan got to know that his father was dead, and that Kiacatu had taken possession of the lordship. He was greatly afflicted by his father's death, and still more so by the fact that his father's uncle had taken possession of the lordship. But he could not leave those parts for fear of a hostile invasion. He said to himself, however, that he would go at the proper moment, and exact a terrible vengeance, even as his father had done to Acomat.

What more shall I tell you? Kiacatu held the

sovereignty, and all obeyed him, excepting only those who were with Casan. He took the wife of Argon his nephew, and kept her for himself. He took great pleasure in the company of women, for he was a most lascivious man.

What more shall I tell you? Kiacatu held the lordship two years, at the end of which he died; for you must know that he was poisoned.

How Baidu assumed the lordship after the death of Kiacatu

On the death of Kiacatu, Baidu, who was his uncle and a Christian took possession of the lordship. This was in the year 1284 after Christ's Incarnation. Baidu held the lordship, and all were obedient to him, except Casan and his army.

When Casan heard that Kiacatu was dead, and that Baidu had taken the lordship, he was greatly afflicted by Kiacatu's death, for he could no longer exact vengeance upon him; as for Baidu, Casan said that he would wreak such vengeance upon him, that all the world should speak of it. So he decided to tarry no longer, but straightway to march against Baidu, and put him to death. He therefore got ready with all his men, and set out on his return, with the intention of assuming the lordship.

When Baidu knew for certain that Casan was bearing down upon him, he mustered a large host, and, after making all due preparations, set out to meet him, marching on for ten days; at the end of the ten days, he pitched his camp, and awaited Casan and his host, to give them battle. And he urgently entreated and exhorted his men to bear themselves well.

But why should I make a long story of it? Know, in very truth, that he had not been there two days before Casan arrived with all his army. And on the very day of their arrival, they began the fiercest and most terrible battle. But no effort of Baidu's could greatly prolong his resistance, for, once the battle had begun, many of those who were with him passed over to Casan, and fought against Baidu. For this reason Baidu was defeated; indeed, he was killed. So Casan won the battle, and became Lord and master of all.

Once he had won the battle and killed Baidu, he returned to the court, and assumed the lordship. And all the barons paid him homage, and obeyed him as their liege Lord.

And these things—namely Casan's accession to the throne and his recovery of the sovereignty—came about in the year 1294 after Christ's Incarnation.

Such as you have heard, then, were the events from the days of Abaga to those of Casan. And you must also know that Alau, who conquered Baudac, and was the brother of the Great Kaan Cublai, was the first of the line to which belonged all the kings we have mentioned. For he was the father of Abaga, and Abaga of Argon, and Argon of Casan, who now reigns.

Now that we have told you about these Tartars of the Levant, we will leave this subject, and go back to tell you of Great Turkey, even as you shall hear.

It is true, however, that we have already told you all about Great Turkey, and that Caidu is its King. So we have nothing more to tell.

We will therefore leave it, and tell you of certain lands and peoples situated to the north.

Here is told of King Canchi, who lives towards the north

You must know, then, that, towards the north, there lives a King called Canchi. He is a Tartar, and all his subjects are Tartars. They follow the real Law of the Tartars, which is very savage, but they follow it as Chinghis Kaan and the other real Tartars did. I will tell you something about it.

You must know that they make a certain god of theirs out of felt, and they call him Natigai. They also make his wife. Of these two divinities, namely Natigai and his wife, they say that they are divinities of the earth, and protect cattle, crops, and earthly possessions. They worship them. And when they happen to eat some good food, they smear the mouths of these two divinities.

Truly they live like beasts.

King Canchi is no one's vassal. He belongs, however, to the lineage of Chinghis Kaan, that is, to the Imperial line, and is a near kinsman to the Great Kaan.

This King possesses neither cities nor towns. His subjects always live in the open, moving about great plains, and mountains, and valleys. They live on the flesh and milk of their cattle. They have no corn. They are very numerous, yet their King does not wage warfare on anyone, but keeps them at peace. They have great quantities of cattle: camels, horses, oxen, sheep, and other animals. They have very big bears, white all over and more than twenty palms long. They have foxes that are all black, and quite large. They have wild asses. They have quantities of sables, namely of those animals which furnish the precious fur I have told you of, as being worth 1000 bezants when made into a man's coat. They have also abundance of vairs. There are great numbers of Pharaoh's rats. These are very big, and the people live on them during the whole summer. They have plenty of all kinds of game, as those regions are wild and trackless.

You must also know that this King possesses a certain country where no horse can go, for it is a country full of lakes and springs, and so there is such a quantity of ice and mud and mire, that no horse can get about. This evil region extends to the space of thirteen days' journey. At the end of each day's journey, there is a post-house, where lodge the messengers who travel about the country. At each of these post-houses, there are some 40 big dogs, little less than a donkey in size, and these dogs take the messengers from one post-house to another, namely a day's journey. I will tell you how. You must know then, that, as I said, there is a tract of thirteen days' journey over which no horse can go, on account of the ice and mire—and this is in a great valley, that one traverses during all that time, between two mountains, on account of which there is all that ice and mire. So, since, as I said, horses cannot go there, nor any kind of wheeled vehicle, because the wheels would sink into the mud, and skid on the ice, they use sledges, which have no wheels, and are made in such a way that they can travel on ice, as also on mud and mire, without sinking in too much. There are many of these sledges in our countries, too, namely those on which we carry hay and straw in winter, when there is a great deal of rain and mud. On the sledge, they spread a bear's skin, upon which the messenger sits. Six of the big dogs I mentioned, draw one of these sledges. These dogs are not guided by anyone, but make straight for the next post-house, drawing the sledge splendidly over ice and mud. Thus they go from one post-house to another. True it is that the keeper of the post-house also gets on a sledge, drawn by dogs, which he drives along the shortest and best way. When they reach the next stage, they find other dogs and sledges ready to carry them farther on; the sledges and dogs that have taken them so far, then turn back. Thus they do during all those days. Every day they are drawn by dogs.

I will add, too, that those who inhabit the valleys and mountains in this tract of land, that extends for thirteen days' journey, are great hunters. They obtain large profits and gains by catching animals of great value, such as sables, ermines, vairs, *erculins*, black foxes, and many other valuable animals, with which costly and precious furs are made. They have certain traps of theirs, thanks to which none of these animals escape. I must add, however, that, on account of the great cold, all their dwellings are underground, and underground they always live.

They are by no means handsome people.

There is nothing else worth mentioning, and so we will leave this country, and tell you of another, where there is everlasting darkness.

Here is told of the province of Darkness

You must know that much further on, far away to the north of the kingdom, there is a province called Darkness, because there is it constantly dark; the sun, the moon, and the stars never appear there, but it is always as dark as with us in the twilight. The people live like beasts. They have no Lord of their own. Nor do they owe allegiance to any foreign Lord. True it is, however, that the Tartars sometimes penetrate into the province, and I will tell you how.

The Tartars go there on mares that have foals, and these foals they leave on the confines of this land; in this way the mares return to their foals, being better able to find their way than men. Thus, then, do the Tartars go into this land on such mares as I have told you of, leaving their foals behind. They carry off with them all they can lay hands on. When they have collected their booty, they leave their mares free to return to their foals: and they find their way remarkably well.

These people have enormous quantities of very

precious furs. They have sables—that are so costly, as I have said—and they have ermines, and *erculins*, and vairs, and black foxes; and many more precious furs they have, too. They are all hunters, and collect such numbers of these skins that it is truly a wonder. The people who live on their borders, in the land where there is Light, buy all these furs off them. These people of the land of Darkness carry the furs into the Light, and sell them to the others. And I assure you that the merchants who buy these skins, obtain immense profit and gain from them.

I will add that these people are very tall, and shapely, but they are also pale and colourless.

I will add, too, that Great Russia borders upon this land.

There is nothing else worth mentioning, and so we will leave this place and proceed. And first of all we will tell you of the province of Russia.

Here is told of the great province of Russia, and of its inhabitants

Russia is a very large province, lying to the north. They are Christians, and follow the Greek rite. They have many Kings, and a language of their own. They are a very simple people, but are quite handsome, both the men and the women, for they are all white and fair. There are many strong defiles, both on the borders and in the interior. They pay tribute to no one, except a section of them, who give something to a King of the Ponent, who is a Tartar, and whose name is Toctai. To him they do pay tribute, but it is very little.

It is not a land of trade. True it is, however, that they have quantities of precious and costly furs, such as sables, ermines, vairs, *erculins*, and foxes, among the best and most valuable in the world. Moreover, they have many silver-mines, from which they extract quantities of silver.

There is nothing else worth mentioning, and so we will leave Russia, and tell you of the Great Sea, of the lands surrounding it, and of their inhabitants, as you shall hear in detail. And we will begin with Constantinople.

First of all, however, we will speak of a province lying between north and north-west. Know, then, that in this direction there is a province called Lac, which borders on Russia. They have a King of their own and are partly Christians and partly Saracens. They have plenty of good furs, which are carried by merchants into other countries. They live by trade and handicrafts. There is nothing else worth mentioning, and so we will leave this place, and speak of other subjects.

I wish, however, to tell you, first, certain other things I had forgotten concerning Russia. You must know that in Russia the cold is greater than anywhere else, so that it can hardly be borne. Such great cold as reigns there, is not to be found in any other part of the world, and, were it not for the many "stoves" they have, the inhabitants could not but die of the extreme cold. These stoves, however, are very numerous, and the noble and powerful have them built as a deed of charity, as in our countries they build hospitals. To such stoves anyone can always repair when the need arises. For, at times, the cold is so intense that when a man, going about a town, or else going home, or anyhow proceeding from one place to another on his business, leaves one of these stoves, he is almost frozen to death before reaching the next one; and this happens in spite of the fact that these stoves are so numerous and close to one another; for, indeed, one may say that there is one every 60 paces. Yet, as I have said, if a man comes out warm from one of these stoves, he is frozen before he reaches the next. On reaching it, he at once goes in and warms himself, and when he is warm, he leaves it, and proceeds to another, where he again warms himself. So he goes on, until he reaches his house, or whatever the place is that he is making for. Moreover, they always run, in order to pass more quickly from one stove to another, and feel the cold less. And it happens often enough that a man, who has not enough clothes on, or who, on account of advanced age, or because he is of a weaker constitution than the others, cannot walk fast, or again whose house is too far off, will fall to the ground, frozen by the excessive cold, in passing from one stove to the other. And there he would remain, did not other passers-by straightway take him up, and, after carrying him to a stove, strip him. As he gets warm, he recovers his senses, and returns to life.

And you must know that these stoves are made as follows. They consist of big beams, placed squarely one above the other, and so fitted together that no light passes between them; the cracks are so well filled up with mortar and other things, that the cold and the wind cannot find an entrance anywhere. On the roof above, there is a window, through which the smoke passes when they light the fire to warm them. Inside, in fact, they keep a great store of fuel, of which the people place a large quantity on the fire, making a fine blaze. As long as the logs burn and produce smoke, the window on the top is kept open, to let the smoke go out; when there is no more smoke, the window is closed with a very thick piece of felt. There remains a fine heap of ashes, that keep the stove exceedingly warm. Lower down, that is, in the wall of the stove, there is another window, closed with a thick piece of excellent felt. This window is opened when light is required in the stove, and the wind is not blowing; if, however, they want light when the wind is blowing, they open the window on the roof. The door leading into the stove is also made of felt.

Thus are these stoves made. The nobles and the rich, however, have their own stoves. The houses, too, are very well protected against the cold.

We will now tell you of a custom that they have. They make an excellent wine with honey and panic, which is called *cervisia*, or ale; they have great drinking-bouts of this, as you shall hear. They frequently assemble in companies of men and women, especially noblemen and magnates, 30, 40, or even 50 people together, husbands taking their wives and children with them. Each company elects a king or leader, and fixes rules, as for example, that if some one utters an improper word, or somehow breaks the rules, he is to be punished by the king the company has elected. Now, there are certain men, like our taverners, who keep that ale for sale. The companies go to these taverns, and pass the whole day drinking. These drinking-bouts they call *straviza*. In the evening, the taverners make up the reckoning of the ale drunk, and each person pays his share, and that of his wife and children, if they have been present. At these *straviza* or drinking-bouts it happens that they take money on loan, giving their children as pledges, from foreign merchants, say of Gazaria or Soldaia or of other neighbouring lands: they spend their money on drink, and so sell their children. The ladies who have to remain all day at these drinking-bouts do not leave the room when they have need to pass water; their handmaidens bring certain large sponges, and place them so delicately beneath them, that the rest of the company does not notice anything. For, while one lady pretends to be conversing with another, the maid places the sponge beneath her, and so the lady passes water, as she sits, into the sponge; the maid then takes the swollen sponge away. Thus they pass water every time they need.

Now we will tell you an episode that once occurred there. One evening, a certain man was going home from one of these drinking-bouts together with his wife, when the lady crouched down to pass water; on account of the great cold, the hairs of her thighs froze, and stuck to the grass, so that the woman, unable to move on account of the pain she felt, cried out. Then the husband, who was exceedingly drunk, felt pity for his wife, and, bending over her, began blowing, hoping to melt the ice with his warm breath. As he blew, however, the moisture of his breath froze, and so the hairs of his beard were caught with those of his wife's thighs, and he too was unable to move on account of the great pain; and so he crouched there. Hence, in order that they might get away, they had to wait for some one to pass by, and break the ice.

The currency of these people consists of gold bars, a span long, and of the value of some *5 grossi* each; their small change consists of martens' heads.

This province is so vast that it stretches as far as the Ocean Sea. I will add that there are many islands in that sea, in which gerfalcons and peregrine falcons breed in such quantities, that they are taken into many parts of the world.

I will add, too, that from Russia to Noroech the journey is not long; indeed, were it not for the great cold, one could go there in a very short time. The cold, however, is so severe, that it is no simple matter to go there.

We will now leave this subject; and tell you of the Great Sea, as I said before. True it is that there are many merchants and other people who know it, but those who do not, are still more numerous. For these, then, it is well to write about it. And so we will do, beginning with the entrance to it, namely the straits of Constantinople.

Here is told of the entrance to the Great Sea

At the very beginning of the western entrance to the Great Sea, there is a mountain called the Faro. . . .

But after beginning to tell you of the Great Sea, we have changed our mind about putting it into writing, because many people are acquainted with it. We will therefore leave the subject, and proceed to speak of other things. And we will tell you of the Tartars of the Ponent, and of the Kings who have reigned there.

Here is told of the Lords of the Tartars of the Ponent

The first Lord of the Tartars of the Ponent was Sain, a very great and powerful King. This King Sain conquered Russia, Comania, Alania, Lac, Menjar, Zic, Gothia and Gazaria. All these provinces did King Sain conquer.

Before he conquered them, they were all subject to the Comanians; but the latter did not hold together, nor was there any unity among them. This is why they lost their lands, and were scattered all over the world. And those who were not so scattered, but remained, were all enslaved by this King Sain.

After King Sain, reigned King Patu; after Patu, King Barca; after King Barca, King Mongutemur; after Mongutemur, King Totamangu; and after him, Toctai, who now reigns.

Now we have told you of the Kings of the Tartars of the Ponent. We will next tell you of a great battle that took place between Alau, King of the Levant, and Barca, King of the Ponent. We will also state the reason why this battle took place, and how it went.

Here is told of the war that broke out between Alau and Barca, and of the battle that they fought

You must know that in the year 1261 after Christ's Incarnation, there arose great discord between Alau, Lord of the Tartars of the Levant, and Barca, Lord of the Tartars of the Ponent. This came about on account of a province that marched with the territories of both. Each of them wished to possess it, and neither of the two would let the other have it, for both thought that they had a true and valid right to it. They challenged one another, and each sent word to the other that he would go and take it, and that he would fain see who would dare to oppose him. When they had thus challenged one another, each summoned all his men, and made the greatest preparations that had been seen for many a year. For you may be sure in very truth that both were determined to make the very greatest effort in order to force a decision.

And you must know that not six months after they had challenged one another, each had already mustered quite 300,000 horsemen, all excellently fitted out with everything that was necessary for a battle according to their manner of fighting.

When they were duly prepared, Alau, Lord of the Levant, set out with all his host. They rode on for many days without meeting with any adventure worth mentioning, until they reached a vast plain lying between the Iron Gates and the Sea of Sarai. In this plain Alau pitched his camp in due order. And I assure you there was many a rich pavilion, and many a rich tent. One could well see that it was the camp of wealthy men. Alau said that he would remain there to see whether Barca and his men would come. And so they did remain, and awaited the enemy. And you must know that this place, where they encamped, was on the very borders between the two kingdoms.

But here we will leave Alau and his men, and return to Barca and his host.

How Barca and his men advanced against Alau

Know, then, that when Barca had completed his preparations, and assembled all his men, on hearing that Alau had set out with his entire host, said that he would brook no further delay. So he tarried no longer, and set out. They marched, day after day, until they reached the great plain where the enemy were. And so Barca pitched his camp in due order at ten miles' distance from that of Alau. And I assure you that his camp was quite as gorgeous and rich as Alau's. For in truth, one who saw the pavilions of cloth of gold and the rich tents, might well have said that a more gorgeous and a richer camp had never been seen for many a long year. Further, Barca had more troops than Alau. For you must know—and it is no lie—that Barca had quite 350,000 horsemen. And when they were encamped, they rested two days.

On the third day, Barca summoned all his men to a parliament, and spoke as follows: " Good my lords, said he, ye know well that, ever since I came to the throne, I have loved you as brothers and sons; and ye know, too, that many of you have been with me in many a great battle, and that the greater part of the lands that we now possess, have been conquered with your aid. And, again, ye know that all that I have is as much yours as mine. So, as this is the truth, each of you must now make his very greatest effort in order to uphold our honour. Up till now, indeed, we have not failed to do so. Ye know that now this Alau, a great and powerful man, forsooth, wishes to fight against us, and that he is in the wrong. And as the simple truth is that he is in the wrong, and we are in the right, each one of you cannot but have faith in our victory. Moreover, our faith must be strengthened by the fact that we are more numerous than they. For we know for certain that they have only 300,000 men, while we have 350,000, as good as theirs, and better. Well, then, my good lords, for all these reasons that I have stated, ye see very clearly that we shall be victors in this battle. Hence, as we have come hither from such a great distance only to fight this battle, I desire that we should fight it three days hence. And let us fight it with such prudence and discipline, that our success be ensured. And I beg each one of you, as warmly as I can, that he be valiant; and let us bear ourselves in such a way that all the world shall fear us. I will say no more, except that I beg all of you to be ready on the day I have stated, and determined to bear yourselves well, and be valiant." Thereupon Barca was silent, and said no more.

We will now cease speaking of Barca and his men, for we have told you something about them. We will tell now of Alau and his army, and of what they did when they knew that Barca and his men had arrived in the neighbourhood.

How Alau addressed his men

History tells, then, that when Alau knew for certain that Barca had arrived with such a large host, he also summoned his wise men to a parliament. When he saw that they were all assembled, he spoke and addressed them as follows: "Good brothers, and sons, and friends, said he, ye know that, during the whole of my life, ye have been my strength and my support. Up to this day, ye have helped me to win many a battle, nor were ye ever in any battle, but we were victorious. This is, then, sufficient reason for our coming here to fight against this Barca—a great man, forsooth. I know well, and it is true, that he has as many troops as we, and more, but they are not so good. Indeed, I assure you that, were they twice as many, we should put them to flight, and defeat them with the good soldiers we have. As we know from our spies that they will attack us three days hence—and indeed I am glad of it—I beg all of you to be duly prepared for that day, and determined to bear yourselves as you are wont to do. One thing alone I will further remind you of: it is better to die on the field upholding one's honour, if it may not be otherwise, than bear the ignominy of defeat. Let everyone therefore so bear himself that our honour be safe, and our enemies defeated and slain." Thereupon Alau was silent.

Thus, even as you have heard, did these two powerful Lords hold their parliaments. And they waited for the day appointed for the battle to come round. And both sides, as best as they might, made all the preparations that they knew were necessary.

Here is told of the great battle between Alau and Barca

When the day appointed for the battle came round, Alau rose very early in the morning, and made all his men arm themselves. He set out, and drew up his troops to the best of his ability: and he did so prudently, wisely and well, for he was a wise man. And you must know that he formed thirty battalions. In each, he put 10,000 horsemen. For you must know that as I have already told you, he disposed of about 300,000 horsemen. To each battalion he assigned a good leader and captain. When he had ordered and arranged everything wisely and well, he commanded his host to advance towards the enemy. And his troops carried out his orders: they at once set out at a slow pace, and went as far as half-way between the two camps. Then they halted, and waited for the enemy to come to battle.

They were, then, waiting there, as I have said. On the other side, Barca had also risen early that same morning with all his men; and they armed and prepared themselves. Barca arrayed his troops well and in due order, like a good captain, who knows how to draw his men up wisely and well. He formed 35 battalions, for, like Alau, he put 10,000 horsemen in each, under good leaders and captains. When all this had been done, Barca commanded his troops to advance. And so they did, well and wisely. They marched on at a slow pace, until they were at half a mile's distance from the enemy. Then they halted, and rested somewhat. After that, they resumed their advance towards the enemy.

What more shall I tell you? When the two armies were at no more than two arrow-flights from one another, they both halted, and all the troops drew up for battle where they had halted. The plain was the most beautiful and the largest to be found, near or far, so that those two immense hosts of cavalry could come to grips there. And truly it was necessary that the plain should be beautiful and vast, for so many soldiers as these were, had not fought in a single field for many a long year. For you must know that it is no lie to say that they amounted to not less than 650,000 horsemen. For Alau and Barca were among the most powerful men in the world. And you must know that they were near kinsmen, for they both belonged to the Imperial lineage of Chinghis Kaan.

Of the same battle between Alau and Barca

The two Kings and their armies had not long been facing one another at the distance I have stated, and were only anxiously awaiting to hear the signal of the *naccars* when, without great delay, the *naccars* did indeed begin to sound on both sides. And as soon as they heard the *naccars* sound, they made no further delay: straightway one side charged against the other. They took up their bows, and drew them, and each man shot his arrows at the enemy. Now you could have seen arrows flying on both sides, so that in a short time the air was so full of them that one could no longer see the sky. Now you could have seen many a man, and many a horse, too, fall dead to the ground. And truly it could not be otherwise, since so many arrows were shot all together. But why should I make a long story of it? Know, in truth, that they never ceased shooting arrows, as long as there were any left in their quivers, so that all the ground was covered with men dead or dying. And when they had shot all their arrows, they took up their swords and their maces; and they fell one upon another, and exchanged savage blows. So they began so cruel and terrible a struggle, that it was a heart-rending spectacle. Now could one see hands and arms and heads hacked off. Now could one see dead men and horses crashing to the ground. So many were killed, that truly the battle had begun in an evil hour. Many a long year had passed since so many men had fallen on a single field of battle. The din and the uproar were so great that one could not have heard God's thunder. And I tell you in truth that one could not walk except on the bodies of the slain, for the ground was all covered with them, and red with blood. For I verily assure you that for many a year there had not been in the world a battle in which such a multitude of men was assembled as in this one. So great were the cries and lamentations of those who fell from their horses, wounded to death and unable to rise, that it was indeed a heart-rending spectacle. Truly this battle was begun in an evil hour for both sides, for many a lady was destined to be a widow thereafter, and many a child an orphan. Well indeed did they show this time that there was no love between them, but only mortal hatred.

King Alau, who was very valiant and mighty in arms, bore himself so well in that battle, that he clearly proved himself worthy of possessing a kingdom, and wearing a crown. He performed in person great deeds of prowess, and also strenuously exhorted his men. And when the latter saw that their Lord was bearing himself so well and gallantly, they were filled with courage and emboldened to do great deeds. And truly it was a great military marvel, so that all who saw it, both friends and enemies, were amazed. For Alau did not seem a man, but a thunderbolt, a whirlwind.

Thus, as you have heard, did Alau bear himself in the battle.

How Barca bore himself valiantly

As for King Barca, I will tell you how he too bore himself. You must know, then, that he truly did great things, and bore himself valiantly. Indeed, he behaved so well, that he deserved the praise of the whole world. Yet his prowess was all of no avail on that day, for so many of his men were slain, and so many fell mortally wounded to the ground, that they could hold out no longer. So, when the battle had lasted till evening, King Barca and his men could hold out no longer: they were obliged to abandon the field.

What more shall I tell you? When they saw they could hold out no longer, they turned and fled as fast as their horses could carry them. And when Alau and his men saw that the enemy had turned and fled, they pursued them, and chased them, hewing them down, and slaying them. They made such havoc of them, that it was a heart-rending spectacle. When they had gone on chasing them some time, they put an end to the pursuit, and returned to their tents. They laid down their weapons. Those that were wounded, had their gashes bathed and dressed. They were so tired and worn out, that there was not one of them but had greater need of repose than of fighting. And that night they rested, tired and exhausted. When the morrow came, Alau ordered all the dead bodies to be burnt, both of their friends and of the enemy. And his order was straightway carried out.

Once all this had been done, Alau returned to his own country, together with all those of his men who had survived the battle. For you must know that, though they were victorious, many a one of them had been slain. Yet truly many more of the enemy were killed. Indeed so great was the number of the slain in this battle, that anyone who should hear tell of it, would hardly believe it.

Such, then, even as you have heard, was the result of this battle. Alau was the victor.

But now we will cease speaking of Alau and the whole of this subject, and we will tell you of a battle that took place among the Tartars of the Ponent, even as you shall now hear in detail.

How Totamangu became Lord of the Tartars of the Ponent

You must know that when the Lord of the Tartars of the Ponent, Mongutemur by name, died, the sovereignty belonged by right to Tolobuga, who was still a youth. But Totamangu, who was a very powerful man, killed Tolobuga with the help of another king of the Tartars called Nogai. Thus, then, with the help of Nogai, Totamangu obtained the sovereignty.

Totamangu then began reigning, but after no long time he died, and Toctai, who was a very wise and valiant man, obtained the sovereignty, being chosen King.

So Toctai reigned and held the sovereignty that had belonged to Totamangu. Now, it happened that, in the meantime, two sons of the Tolobuga who had been killed, had grown up, and had become men capable of bearing arms. They were also wise and prudent. These two brothers, namely these sons of Tolobuga, got ready with a splendid retinue, and set out. They went to Toctai's court. On reaching it, they entered his presence, and greeted him most courteously. And they remained kneeling before him. Toctai bade them be most welcome, and made them rise. When the two brothers had risen, the elder spoke, and said as follows: " Beloved Lord Toctai, I will tell you as well as I can, why we have come before you. As you know, we are the sons of Tolobuga, whom Totamangu and Nogai slew. Of Totamangu I may say nothing, for he is dead; but against Nogai we demand justice, and we pray you, like the just Lord you are, that you will make him answer to us for that he killed our father. Namely, we beg you to summon him before you, and make him render account to us for the death of our father. For this reason we have come to your court, and this is our prayer."

Thereupon the young man was silent, and said no more.

How Toctai summoned Nogai to render account of the death of Tolobuga

When he heard the young man's words, Toctai knew that they were true. So he answered and said: " Fair friend, said he, most willingly will I do what thou askest of me, namely render thee justice as regards Nogai. We will summon him to our presence, and deal with him as reason demands."

So Toctai sent two envoys to Nogai, summoning him to his court in order to render account to the sons of Tolobuga of their father's death. But when the envoys had stated this message to Nogai, he laughed at it, and said that he would not go. When the envoys had received Nogai's answer, they departed, and went on their way.

They rode on and on, until they reached their Lord's court. They told him that Nogai sent him word, that he would not come for anything in the world. When Toctai heard Nogai's message, he took it as a great affront. And he said aloud, so that all could hear him: " So God help me, said he, either Nogai shall come to my presence, and render account to the sons of Tolobuga, or I shall fall upon him with all my men, and destroy him."

Thereupon he tarried not, but straightway sent him two more envoys, with such a message as you shall hear.

How Toctai sent his envoys to Nogai

The two envoys whom Toctai had entrusted with this task, set out, and rode on, until they reached the court of Nogai. They entered into his presence, and greeted him well and courteously. And Nogai bade them be welcome. Thereupon one of the envoys spoke, and said: "Good my Lord, said he, Toctai sends you word that if you do not come to his court to render account to the sons of Tolobuga, he will fall upon you with all his men, and will do you all the injury he can, both to your person and to your possessions. Consider, then, what you intend to do in this matter, and what answer you will send him through us."

When Nogai had heard Toctai's message, he took it as a great affront. And he answered the envoys as follows: "Envoys, said he, return now to your Lord and tell him that I for my part have little fear of the war he threatens. Tell him, too, that, if he attacks me, I shall not wait for him to enter my lands; for I shall come half-way to meet him. This is my message and answer to your Lord." Thereupon he was silent, and said no more.

On hearing Nogai's words, the envoys tarried no longer, but straightway set out. And they rode on, until they came to their Lord, and told him all that Nogai had said, how he cared not a straw for the war Toctai threatened, and that he would go more than half-way to meet him.

When Toctai had heard all this, and saw that war could not be avoided, he made no delay, but at once sent messengers in every direction to all those who were subject to him, summoning them, and bidding them prepare themselves to attack king Nogai. What more shall I tell you? He made the greatest preparations in the world.

On the other side, when Nogai knew for certain that Toctai intended to attack him with so great a host, he also made great preparations. But they were not so great as Toctai's, for he had not so many men, nor was he so powerful. All the same, they were great and mighty.

How Toctai advanced against Nogai

When he had finished his preparations, Toctai set out on his way, together with all his men. And you must know in very truth that he took with him quite 200,000 horsemen. They rode on, day after day, without meeting with any adventure worth mentioning, until they reached the plain of Nerghi, which is very vast and beautiful. And there Toctai pitched his camp while waiting for Nogai. For he knew that he was coming to give battle, as quickly as he could. And you must know that with Toctai were the two sons of Tolobuga, with a very fine company of horsemen; they had come to avenge the death of their father.

But here we will leave Toctai and his men, and return to Nogai and his host. You must know, then, in very truth, that, on hearing that Toctai had set out, and was advancing against him, Nogai made no delay, but straightway set out with all his men. And you must know, too, that he had quite 150,000 horsemen, all excellent and valiant soldiers, much better, indeed, than those of Toctai. What more shall I tell you? Not two days after Toctai's arrival in that plain, Nogai was also there with all his men. And he pitched his camp in good order, at ten miles' distance from the enemy.

And when the camp was pitched, one could see many a fair pavilion of cloth of gold, and many a beautiful tent. Truly it was seen to be a wealthy King's camp. And Toctai's camp was no less beautiful and rich; indeed, it was more so. For he had such rich pavilions and such rich tents, that it was a wonder to see.

When these two Kings had come to the plain of Nerghi, they rested, in order to be fresh and reposed on the day of the battle.

How Toctai spoke to his troops

Toctai summoned his men to a great parliament, and spoke to them as follows: "Gentlemen, said he, we have come thus far to fight against King Nogai and his men. And truly we have good reason to do this. For you know that all this hatred and all this rancour have arisen, because Nogai has refused to come to render account to the sons of Tolobuga. And truly, since he has placed himself in the wrong, it cannot be but that we shall win this battle, and kill and destroy him. Hence, every one of you must be comforted, and have good hope of defeating the enemy. Anyway, I pray you all, as earnestly as I may and can, to be valiant, and to make every effort in order to inflict destruction and death on the enemy." Thereupon he was silent, and said no more.

On the other side, king Nogai also held his parliament, and spoke as you shall hear: "Dear brothers and friends, said he, ye know well in how many great battles, in how many great struggles, we have already been victorious, how we have had to deal with many an army better than this one, and how we have ever had the better of them. So, as this is the truth, as ye yourselves know, ye cannot but be certain of winning this battle. Moreover, we are in the right, and they are in the wrong. For well you know that he is not my sovereign Lord, to summon me before him in his court, in order to render account to others. Now I will add no more, except, that I beg each of you to see to it that he bear himself well, and that we so behave in this battle that the whole world shall speak of us, and that we and our heirs be feared to all eternity." Thereupon King Nogai was silent, and said no more.

After these two Kings had held their parliaments, they delayed no longer, and on the morrow they prepared themselves, and drew up in good order. King Toctai made 20 battalions, and over each he placed good leaders and captains. King Nogai made 15, for each was composed of 10,000 horsemen; and he too placed good leaders and captains over them. What more shall I tell you? When the two Kings had arrayed and drawn up their troops in due order, they both advanced, and rode on towards each other, until they were at the distance of an arrow's flight. There the two armies halted, and remained some time. But, shortly after, the *naccars* began to sound. And when the *naccars* had sounded, they charged upon one another, and let fly their arrows. Now one could see arrows flying on both sides. There was such a multitude of them, that it was a wonder to look upon, and it seemed as if it were raining. Now could one see horsemen and horses falling to the ground, dead or mortally wounded. There was an immense din and uproar. And when they had shot all their arrows, and had no more, they took up their swords and maces; and they fell upon one another, and exchanged terrible blows. Then began the cruellest and most savage struggle. They hacked at one another's hands, and arms, and bodies, and heads. Now could one see dead and dying horsemen falling to the ground. The lamentations, and the uproar, and the clashing of swords were so great, that one could not have heard God's thunder. The dead were so many, that hardly were there ever as many in any other battle. But, without doubt, more of Toctai's men were slain than of Nogai's. For Nogai's were much better soldiers than Toctai's. But I will add that the two sons of Tolobuga bore themselves very well in that battle, and performed deeds of great prowess. For they made every effort to avenge the death of their father. But it was in vain. It was too great a task for them to put King Nogai to death. What more shall I tell you? The battle was so cruel and savage, that truly it had been begun in an evil hour, for great numbers of men, who in the morning had been hale and sound, were killed, and many a married lady was left a widow on account of this battle. Nor was it a wonder, for this was truly a most savage battle.

King Toctai made every effort to encourage his men and uphold his honour. He performed great deeds of prowess. And certainly he bore himself in such a way as to deserve the praise of the whole world. He threw himself among the enemy as if he recked not at all of his own life. He struck to the right and to the left, he broke up the enemy's ranks, and scattered the serried groups of fighters. His valour was such that day, that it wrought great havoc both on friends and foes—on his foes, because he felled many with his own hand; on his friends, because, when they saw him perform such deeds, they were filled with courage, and emboldened to rush upon the enemy, and attempt such actions as cost them their lives.

How King Nogai bore himself valiantly

The same I may say of King Nogai. For you must know, in very truth, that he bore himself so valiantly that there was no other, on either side, who equalled him. Without doubt, the greatest praise for this battle was due to him. He threw himself among the enemy as gallantly as a lion among wild beasts. He felled and slew many of them; he wrought great havoc among them. He thrust himself wherever the melley was thickest. He broke up and scattered the enemy, as if they were flocks of small cattle. His men, seeing their Lord bear himself thus, made every effort, and charged upon the enemy with fury, working great havoc.

But why should I make a long story of it? Know, in very truth, that Toctai's men made every effort that lay in their power to uphold his honour. But in vain: they had too good and valiant an army to deal with. They had suffered so much, that they clearly saw that if they still tarried, they would all be killed. So, when they understood that they could resist no longer, they turned and fled, as fast as they could. And King Nogai and his men pursued and chased them, and made a great slaughter.

Thus, then, even as you have heard, did Nogai win the battle. And I will add that no less than 60,000 men were slain. But King Toctai himself and the sons of Tolobuga escaped.

But you must also know that King Toctai had not mustered for this enterprise as many men as he might have, for he had felt sure of overcoming Nogai merely with those he had assembled, since Nogai had come to battle with one quarter less men than he. But, as you have heard, since Nogai's troops were more valiant and better in war than those of Toctai, the latter was overcome and defeated in the battle. Later, however, King Toctai assembled all his forces, and once more made war on Nogai in a manly manner. And he defeated him and killed him and four of his sons, too, who were very brave and valiant. And so vengeance was taken for the death of Tolobuga.

ANNOTATED INDEX

LIST OF BOOKS QUOTED

BENEDETTO: *Marco Polo: Il Milione.* Prima edizione integrale, a cura di Luigi Foscolo Benedetto. Firenze, 1928.

BRETSCHNEIDER: *Mediæval Researches from Eastern Asiatic Sources*, by E. Bretschneider, 2 vols., London, 1910.

CHARIGNON: *Le Livre de Marco Polo* (being a translation into modern French of the text published by Pauthier in 1867 and annotated from the Chinese sources), by A. J. H. Charignon, 3 vols., Peking, 1924.

CHAU-JU-KUA. *His work on the Chinese and Arab Trade* . . . translated from the Chinese . . . by F. Hirth and W. W. Rockhill, St Petersburg, 1912.

CORDIER: *Ser Marco Polo.* Notes and Addenda to Sir Henry Yule's edition, containing the result of recent research and discovery. By Henri Cordier, London, 1920.

RAMUSIO: *Navigationi et Viaggi*, Vol. II, pp. 2–60, Venice, 1559.

RASHĪD: *Histoire des Mongols de Fadlallah Rashid ed-Din*, edité par E. Blochet, Tome II, Leyden and London, 1911. This contains the original Persian text of the history of the successors of Chingiz Khan.

STEIN: *Serindia.* Detailed report of explorations in Central Asia . . . by Aurel Stein, Oxford, 1921.

YULE: *The Book of Ser Marco Polo* . . . translated and edited with notes by Colonel Sir Henry Yule. Third edition revised . . . by Henri Cordier, 2 vols., London, 1903.

CONTRACTIONS

F = Paris MS.. fr. 1116 (*see* Introduction, p. x).

Z = Cardinal Zelada's Latin MS. of Marco Polo (*see* Introduction, p. x).

INDEX

ABACAN, probably a copyist's error for Alacan, *i.e. Alahan*, of the Chinese sources: Tartar general sent by Kubilai against Japan, 271. *See Benedetto*, pp. 163, 164

ABACO, SEA OF (Baku ?). *See* CASPIAN

ABAGA, Il-Khan of Persia (1265–1281), 10, 368; his death, 370, 382

ABASH, Abyssinia (Arabic *Habash*), 346; the people's horsemanship, 348; their soldiery, 348; pilgrimage of its bishop to the Holy Sepulchre, 348; its king's punishment of Sultan of Aden, 350

ACBALUC, Aq-baliq, "the white city", Chêng-ting fu, 169. *See Yule*, II, 14

ACBALUC MANJI, *i.e.* Aq-baliq in Manji, as distinguished from the Aq-baliq in Cathay. The construction is Persian. Marco Polo probably heard *Aq-baliq-i-Manji*, 176

ACMAT, Ahmad, the "Bailo," Kubilai's Muslim governor. His power, his murder, etc., 124 *seqq.*

ACOMAT SOLDAN, Ahmad Sultan (1281–1284); seizes throne of Il-Khans on the death of his father Abaga, 370; marches against Arghun, 371; ignores remonstrance from Arghun, 375; defeats and imprisons him, 377; his death, 381

ACRE, visited by the Polos, vii, 8 *seqq.*

ADAM, his supposed sepulchre on mountain (Adam's Peak) in Ceylon, 319, 322; his teeth, hair, and bowl, 322

ADEN, ships from, 323, 331, 340; its Sultan's treatment of Bishop of Abyssinia, 349; his defeat, 350; described, 352; Sultan of (Sultan of Yemen), 349, 353, 354, 356

AGUIL, Ajul, the father of Nayan (*q.v.*) and a distant cousin of Kubilai; sent to suppress rebellion of Li T'an, 211. Benedetto says the MS. may read Agiul, and this of course is the correct reading, and should have been adopted

AHMAD. *See* ACMAT

AHMAD SULTAN. *See* ACOMAT SOLDAN

AIJARUC (MS. Aigiaruc), Ay-yaruq = "The brightness of the moon" (Turkish), daughter of Qaidu, called by Rashid (p. 9) Qutulun Chaghan, 365; her great strength, 365 *seqq.* Pelliot (*T'oung Pao*, 1930, p. 272) points out that Marco Polo heard the name pronounced *Ay-jaruq* according to the Qirghiz dialect

ALAN COUNTRY, Alania, 393

ALANS, also called *As* or *Az*, a Caucasian people represented today by the Ossetians, some of whom were brought to China at

INDEX

Alans—*continued.*
the beginning of the thirteenth century. They were Christians and were employed in the Emperor's special guard. An Alan with the Polos, 227; massacred at Canju, 232 (the story as told by Marco Polo differs from that of the Chinese annals where it is stated that the Alans were made to drink by the Sung general who had pretended to submit. *See* Pelliot, *T'oung Pao*, 1914, p. 21)

Alaodin, 'Alā ud-Dīn Muhammad, son of Jalāl ud-Dīn Hasan, was grand master of the Assassins (1220–1255). *See* Old Man of the Mountain

Alau, Hulagu, Il-Khan of Persia (1256–1265); grandson of Chingiz Khan and brother of Kubilai. His wars with Bärkä Khan, 3, 4; conquest of Persia, 23; takes Baghdad and puts Caliph to death, 26, 27; suppresses 'Alā-ud-Dīn, 53; his descendants, 384; battle with Bärkä, 394 *seqq.*

'Alā ud-Dīn. *See* Alaodin

Alexander the Great. His building of the Iron Gate, 22; site of his battle with Darius, 49; allusion to his marriage with daughter of Darius in Balkh, 54; princes claiming descent from him, 56; his horse Bucephalus, 57

Alexandria, 264; trade with India, etc., 331, 353

Alinek Soldan, Alinaq Sultan, a Melik, and one of Ahmad Sultan's generals, 378, 379, 380

Alligators. *See* Serpents

Almanacs. *See* Tacuini

Almonds, wild, in Taliqan, 55

Aloes-Wood, Lign-aloes, or eagle-wood. Used by "devil-charmers" in Zardandān, 195; in Champa, 277 *seqq.*; in Sumatra, 281

Altai Mountains, burial-place of Khans, 83, 90

Alton, presumably scribe's error for *Allau*, xiv, 83. *See* Alau

Ambergris, in Male and Female Islands, 337; way in which the fish containing it are caught, 338; in Madagascar, 342

An-Ching. *See* Nankin

Angaman (Andaman) Islands, described, 289 *seqq.*

Aniu(?) Province, described, 205, 277

Apples of Paradise, kind of citron. In Rudbar, 41; in Nicobar Is., 289; in the Andaman Is., 290

Apusca, Turkish *abuchqa* = old man. One of Arghun's barons sent as envoy to the Great Kaan, 15

Aq-Baliq. *See* Acbaluc

Arabi, Arabs, 24

Arbre Sol, or Arbre Sec. A *Chinar*, or Oriental Plane. *See Yule*, I, 128 *seqq.*; the region of this tree is Khurāsān, vii, 17, 37, 382; tree described, 49; plain of, 368

Argon, Arghun, "King of Tartars of the Levant"; son of Abaga; Il-Khan of Persia (1284–1291). Sends envoy to Kubilai for a wife, viii, 15; has died when she arrives, ix, 17, 18; falcons brought to him, 18; his war with Qaidu, 369, 370; prepares for war against Ahmad, 372; sends remonstrance to Ahmad, 374; taken prisoner by Ahmad, 377; recovers throne, 380

INDEX

ARGONS, half-breeds. The descendants of 3000 Muslims who had been transported from Samarqand to P'ing-yang and T'ai-yüan in Shan-hsi during the reign of Ögödäi, 95. *See* Pelliot, *Journal Asiatique*, 1927, II, 265, 266

ARMENIA, GREATER, 19; described, 20 *seqq.* 42

ARMENIA, LESSER, or Cilician, 11; its king, 19; unhealthiness of climate, 19

ARMENIANS, 20, 21, 24, 32, 33

ARMOUR, made in Kerman, 39; used by the Tartars, 86; in Qarajang, 191

ARZINGAN, Arzinjan, 20, 21

ARZIRON, Erzerum (Arzan ar-Rūm), 21

ARZIZI, Arjish, 21

ASHAR, one of five brothers who were kings of Tinavelly, 323

ASIDIN SOLDAN, Ghiyās ud-Dīn Balban, Sultan of Delhi (1256–1286), 43

ASSASSINS (Isma'ilis). Their training by 'Alā ud-Dīn, 51, 52; their suppression (1262) by Hulagu, 53

ASSES, in Persia, 37, 39, 48; in Etzina, 77; in Madagascar, 343; in Abyssinia, 351; in the Far North, 385

ASTROLOGERS, their prophecy by means of canes, 82; at summer court of Kubilai, 99; in Tibet, 182; in Manji, 247; in Coilum, 327

AVA, Āva, on the road from Sāva to Qum, one of the cities of the Magi, 36

AVICI, possibly the Arabic *'afṣī* = falcon. *See* GOSHAWKS

AY-YARUQ. *See* AIJARUC.

AZURE (lapis lazuli). Mined in Badakhshan, 57; in Tenduc, 94; in Khan-baliq ("dust of lapis lazuli"), 120

BABYLON, Cairo or Egypt, 11, 353; Sultan of, 11, 353

BACSI, Bakhshi, title of a class of Lamas, formerly regarded as a corruption of the Sanskrit *Bhikshu*, but see Laufer, *T'oung-Pao*, 1916, 485–487; and Pelliot, *Journal Asiatique*, 1925, I, 254; their enchantments, 100, 101, 124, 162

BADAKHSHAN. *See* BALASHAN

BAGHDĀD. *See* BAUDAC

BAIAN, one of the keepers of Kubilai's hounds, 140

BAIAN CHINCSAN (Ch'ing hsiang = "Minister of State"). It is hard to believe that Marco Polo thought Chincsan meant 100 eyes. There is a well-known pun on the name Bayan and the Chinese *pai-yen* meaning 100 eyes. Kubilai's greatest general, 219 *seqq.*; his cruelty at Chên-ch'ao, 232

BAIDU KHAN, grandson of Hulagu. Seizes throne of Persia (1295), 383; is defeated and killed in battle by Ghazan, 384

BAILO. Title held by agents of Venetian and Genoese colonies in the Near East, but here probably a corruption of Arabic *Wāli*. Title given to Kubilai's Saracen Minister Ahmad, *q.v.*

BAKHSHI. *See* BACSI

BALAS RUBIES. Rubies of inferior quality found in Balaksh, *i.e.* Badakhshan, 57

BALASHAN, Badakhshan, vii, 42; its line of kings, supposed to be

INDEX

Balashan—*continued.* descended from Alexander the Great, 56; its mines, 57; healthy plateaus of, 58; its women's strange mode of dress, 59

Balc, Balkh, vii; place of Alexander's supposed marriage with daughter of Darius, 54

Baldwin II, de Courtenay, last Latin Emperor of Constantinople (1237–1261), 3

Bangala, Bengal, 196, 200; described, 203; king of, *see* Mien

Barac, Buraq, or more correctly Baraq Khan (1266–1270), great-grandson of Chaghatai Khan, ruler of Bukhārā (not brother of Qaidu as stated by Marco), 4; war with Argon, 369. Pelliot (*T'oung-Pao*, 1930, p. 339) has pointed out that the commonly accepted form *Buraq* is due to the Muslim historians.

Barca Khan, Bärkä Khan, brother of Batu, son of Juji, son of Chingiz, the first of this family to accept Islam. Ruler of Western Qipchaq (1256–1266), 3, 4, 393; his war with Hulagu, 3, 394 *seqq.*

Bargherlac (Turki—*baghirtaq*). Kasghari (Brockelmann, No. 28) has *baghirlaq*, Radloff, *baghirtlaq*. Sand-grouse, *Syrrhaptes Pallasii*. The Manchu Mirror says it walks awkwardly and its feet resemble those of a hare, 91. *See Mem. As. Soc. Bengal*, Vol. II, No. 9, p. 129

Bargu, plain of, near Lake Baikal, 78, 90

Bark, paper money made from, 148; used for making clothes, 206

Barley, huskless in Badakhshan, 58

Barsamo, Saint, monastery called after him near Tabriz, 34

Barscol (Turkish — *bars-köl*), "Leopard Lake," 109

Bartizan, wooden fortification used by Kubilai, 106. *See Yule*, I, p. 339

Basman, Pasai, in Sumatra, 282

Bastra, Basra, its date-groves, 25

Baths, from hot springs near Hormuz, 47; heated by coal stoves in Cathay, 160; public swimming-baths in Kinsai, 245

Batui Kaan, Batu Khan, son of Juji, son of Chingiz, Khan of Qipchaq (1224–1256), wrongly included by Marco Polo among the Great Kaans. Also known as Sain Khan or "the Good Khan," and Marco mistakenly takes Batu and Sain for two separate kings, xiv, 83; by a scribe's error called Patu, 393

Baudac, Baghdād, 24; the city, 25; pearls pierced in, 26; attacked by Hulagu (1258), 26; death of the Caliph, 27; story of the good cobbler, 28 *seqq.*; the miracle of the mountain, 32; Jatolic of, 340

Bears, white, in Siberia, 385

Belor, Balur or Bolur, *i.e.* Kafiristan, 62; *see Tarikh-i-Rashidi*, p. 385

Beltasar. *See* Magi

Bengal. *See* Bangala

Bettalar, Patlam, on coast of Ceylon, centre of pearl fisheries, 293

Beyamini, wild oxen in Tibet (possibly Tibetan *ba-men*, the gayal, but the form recalls the Arabic word for cattle, *bahā'im*), 183

INDEX

BOARS' TUSKS, enormous (probably tusks of hippopotami from Zanzibar), 343

BOCARA, Bukhārā, province and city of, vii, 4

BOGA, Buka, great Mongol baron in service of the Il-Khans, 378, 379

BOLGANA, Bulagan = "sable" (Mongolian), successively the wife of Abaga and of his son, Arghun, she died on 7th April 1286, viii, 3, 4, 15

BOLOR. *See* BELOR

BOMBAY DUCKS. *See under* FISH

BONDOCDAIRE, Bunduqdarī. This name was adopted by the Mamluk Sultan of Egypt, Malik Zāhir Rukn ud-Dīn Baibars (1259–1276) after the name of a certain Amir Ai-tegin Bunduqdar (the Arbalaster) who had purchased him as a slave, 11

BRAHMINS, in Kashmir, 60; fish-charmers in pearl industry, 293; their trustworthiness, 313; their characteristic sign, 314; their omens, 314, 315; their long life, 315

BRANDING of released prisoners, 166

BRAZIL-WOOD, sappan-wood, used for red and brown dyes, in Locac, 280; Sumatra, 281, 287; Nicobars, 289; Ceylon, 291; Coilum (wood called Coilumin), 326

BREAD, bitter, 47

BRETHREN OF HOLY GHOST, 34

BRIDGES, Pulisanghin, 167; Chêngtu, 178; Su-chou, 233; Kinsai, 235, 236; in Chien-ning fu, 257

BRIUS RIVER, Chin-sha Chiang = "River of Golden Sand," 187

BUCEPHALUS, Alexander's horse, breed of, in Badakhshan, 57

BUCKRAM. Made in Arzingan, 20; Meridin, 25; Tibet, 182; Mutfili, 309; Malabar, 331; Tana, 333; Cambay, 334; Abyssinia, 352

BUDDHA. *See* SAGAMONI BORCAN

BUDDHISM. *See* IDOLATERS

BUKHĀRĀ. *See* BOCARA

BULARGUCHI. The *nomen agentis* formed from *bulargu* which is fundamentally the same word as the *pu-lan-ch'i* of the Chinese texts, which however seems to be the transcription of an alternative form *buralqi* which we find in Muslim works as a proper name (Pelliot). "Keeper of Lost Property," 142

BULAGAN. *See* BOLGANA

BUNDUQDARI. *See* BONDOCDAIRE

BURAQ KHAN. *See* BARAC

BURMA. *See* MIEN

CAAJU, Castle of (Ho-chou in Ssŭ-ch'uan), where Chingiz Khan is said to have been mortally wounded, 82. *See Yule*, I, 245

CACHALOT. *See* WHALES

CACHANFU, Ho-chung fu, in Shanhsi, now P'u-chou fu, 170, 173

CACHANFU, Ho-chien fu, in Chihli, 208

CACHAR MODUN, perhaps Hach'a-mu-tuan, but Charignon suggests it is a contraction of *Ha-la-ch'in* and *T'u-mei-t'ê*, the names of two tribes who for long occupied this region, 143

CAESARIA, 20

CAICHU, Castle of "The Golden King," 170

CAIDU, Qaidu Khan, son of Qashi, son of Ögödäi (Marco Polo persistently calls him the grandson of Chaghatai), a claimant for

INDEX

Caidu—*continued*.
the Great Kaanship on the death of Möngkä in 1257. His plots with Naian, 104, 110; his constant war with Kubilai, 359, 360; war against Kubilai, 361–65; Kubilai's anger with him, 365; the great strength of his daughter, 365–68; sends Baraq against Arghun, 369

Caiju, on the Huang-Ho, 218

Caiju, Kua-Chou = "Island of gourds," on the Yang-tyü, 230

Cail, Kayal = Tinnevelly. Once famous port at mouth of Tamraparni river, 323

Cail, King of, 324; his mother's peace-making between him and his brothers, 324

Cala Ataperistan, Qal'a Atashparastan = "Town of Fire-worshippers," 34

Calachan, probably Ting-yüan-ying (Alashan), residence of Tangut kings, 94. *See Yule*, I, 282

Calatu, Qalhat, S. coast of Arabia, 357 *seqq.*

Calif (Caliph). Mosta'sim Billah Caliph of Baghdād, 25; captured by Hulagu (1258), 27; starved to death by him, 27; plot of former Caliph against Christians, 28; miracle of the mountain, 29–30; secretly converted to Christianity, 30

Caliph. *See* Calif

Calizene, Arabic *Khalij*, canals drawn from the full Nile, 353. *See Yule*, II, 439

Camadi, City of Dakianus, 41. *See Yule*, I, 113

Cambaluc, Khan-baliq or "City of the Khan," Mongol name for Chung-tu (Peking), 104, 110; Kubilai's palace, 117–121; new city (*see* Taidu), 122 *seqq.*; described, 146 *seqq.*; the mint, 147; palace of twelve barons, 151; roads from, 152; astrologers in, 162; canals to Manji, 230. *See also* Peking

Cambay. *See* Canbaet

Camels, in Persia, 37; flesh eaten in Madagascar, 341; in Aden, 353; in Siberia, 385

Camlets (*cammellotti*), material of silk and wool, in Calachan, 94

Camphor, in Fu-Chien, 263; in Sumatra, 287; Fansuri, 287; mixed with Betel for chewing, 325

Camu, Shagreen leather, 137

Camul, Kamul or Hami, province on the border of the Gobi, 71, 72

Cananore. *See* Eli

Canbaet, Cambay, 334

Canchi, according to Pelliot = qonichi, shepherd, "King of the Far North," 384; a prince of the house of Juji, eldest son of Chingiz Khan. *See Bretschneider*, II, 15; *Yule*, II, 481

Canes (Bamboo), used by astrologers for prophesying, 82; used to build Kubilai's summer palace, 98; burnt to frighten wild beasts, 179; in Chê-Chiang, 255

Canju, Chên-ch'ao, north of the Yang-tzŭ—not Ch'ang-chou on the south. *See* Pelliot, *T'oung Pao*, 1914, p. 21

Cannibalism in Tibet, 100; in Fu-chien, 257; in Japan, 276; Sumatra, 282, 286; Andaman Is., 290

Canosalmi, Kamasal, 43

Canpchu or Campchu, Kan-chou, 75, 91

Carachoco, Qara-Khoja or Qara-Qocho, xii, 72

INDEX

Caracoron, Qaraqorum. Pelliot (*Journal Asiatique*, 1925, I, 374), says it was adopted by the Mongols in 1220 as their capital; the walled city was built by Ögödäi in 1235, 77, 90, 361, 362; battle of, 363

Carajan, Qarajang. Province, Yün-nan, viii, 13, 187–192, 193; City, Ta-li fu, 188, 196

Caramania. District of Qaraman in Asia Minor (including Qonia), mentioned only in "Z." Other texts here read Conia, 20

Caramoran River, Kara-Müren = "Black River," Mongol name for Huang Ho, Yellow River of Chinese, 173, 218, 222

Caraunas, Karaunas, Mongol robber trib 42, 43. *See Yule*, I, 101–106

Carpets of Turcomania, 20

Carriages, for pleasure drives in Kinsai, 244

Carts of nomadic Mongols, 84

Casan, Ghazan Khan (1295–1304), son of Arghun, ix; marries Lady Kokachin, 17; his liking for the Polos, 18; sent by Arghun to district of Arbre Sol, 382, 383; battle with Baidu, 384; obtains throne, 384

Cascar, Kashghar, vii, 62, 66

Cashan, Kāshān, 36; F. and several other MSS. here read *castel* which in the light of Z. and two other MSS. seems to be a scribe's error for *Cashan*. *See Benedetto*, p. 25 *n*.

Caspian Sea, known as Sea of Ghelukelan, 23; or Sea of Abaco, 23; or Sea of Sarai, 394

Casvin, Qazwin, 37

Cathay. Northern China as distinguished from Manzi or Manji, Southern China. Cathay is a corruption of the name *Khatā*, *Khitā*, *Qitā*, or *Khitā'i* employed by the Muslim historians. This is in turn derived from *Ch'i-tan* (*K'i-tan*) the name of a Mongolian people who founded a dynasty, known also as the Liao dynasty, which ruled over certain detached Northern provinces of China for 200 years after the fall of the T'ang dynasty, vii, 24, 26, 66, 92, 95, 105, 117, 159; coal in, 160; describing the province of, 167 *seqq.*, 216, 282

Cathayans. Their rebellion against Ahmad, 124–128; their wine, 159; astrologers, 163; their learning and religion, 165; gambling, 166; good manners, 167

Caugigu, Chiao-chih-kuo, modern Tonkin. *See Yule*, II, 117, 119, *Cordier*, 90, 204, and *Chau-ju Kua*, 46 *n*.

Cauiu, Kao-yü, 223

Cauli, Corea, 109

Ceylon. *See* Seilan

Chagannor, Chaghan-Nor = "White Lake," possibly *Hsin-hua*, 96

Chagatai, Chaghatai, erroneously described by Marco Polo as "own brother" to Kubilai. He was the son of Chingiz Khan and uncle of Kubilai. He founded a dynasty which ruled over Transoxiana from 1227 to 1358, 42; becomes a Christian, 63; his death (1242), 63, 359, 361

Chalcedony and Jasper, jade stone found in Pem, 65, 66

Champa. *See* Chanba

Chanba, Champa. Part of Annam, viii, 277, 347; King of, 277, 278

INDEX

CH'ANG-CHOU. *See under* CANJU

CHANDU, Shang-tu (Xanadu), or K'ai-p'ing fu, founded by Kubilai in 1256, viii, 97, 99, 126, 155. *See* Pelliot, *Journal Asiatique*, 1927, II, 277

CHANGAN, 234

CHANGLI (Yule's Chinangli)—Chinan fu, 209

CHANGLU, Ch'ang-lu, the modern Ts'ang-chou, 209

CHANSHAN, Chang-shan, 225

CHARCHAN, 66, 67

CHARIGNON, A. J. H., his translation of Marco Polo, xv, 409

CHÊN-CH'AO. *See* CANJU

CHÊN-CHIANG FU. *See* CHINGHIANFU

CHÊN-CHIN, son of Kubilai. *See* CHINGHIS

CHÊN-CHOU. *See* SINJU

CHENCU (Ramusio — Cenchu). *Ch'ien-hu*, commander of 1000 men. Used by Marco Polo as a personal name. (*See* Moule, *J.N.C.B.R.A.S.*, Vol. LVIII, 1927.) Conspires with Vancu against Ahmad, 126–128

CHIEN-NING FU. *See* KENLINFU

CHIN, SEA OF, China Sea, 276

CHINA, vii, viii, ix, xvi. *See* CATHAY and MANJI

CHINA SEA. *See* CHIN

CHINESE DIALECTS, 266

CHINGHIANFU, Chên-chiangfu, 231

CHINGHIS KAAN, Chingiz Khan, actually never called *Khagan* or *Qa'an*, xiv; made king of Tartars, 79; requests daughter of Prester John in marriage, 79; angry at his reply, 80; prepares for war against him, 80; awaits him at Tenduc, 81; defeats and kills him, Chingiz himself is mortally wounded six years later at the siege of Caaju (1227), 82; his burial-place, 83; race of Horiats, 99

CHINGHIS, the son of Kubilai. As explained in the Introduction, pp. xiv, xv, his name was Chinkim, representing the pronunciation in the thirteenth century of the Chinese *Chên-chin* ("real gold"), Mongolian *Chingim*. Chinkim died in 1285 leaving a son Tämür (Öljäitü), who succeeded Kubilai in 1294, 116, 120, 126

CHINGINTALAS. *See* GHINGHINTALAS

CHINGIZ KHAN. *See* CHINGHIS KAAN

CHI-NING-CHOU. *See* SINJUMATU

CHINJU, two separate places thus called by Marco Polo (*a*) 217; (*b*) 224

CHINKIM, son of Kubilai. *See* CHINGHIS

CHIN-SHA-CHIANG. *See* BRIUS RIVER

CHIPANGU, Jih-pên-kuo = Japan, 270; gold found there, 270; Kubilai's expedition against, 271–275

CHOIACH, name of unlucky hours in Ma'bar; xiii, 301. *See Yule*, II, 368

CHOLA. *See* SOLI

CHONCHA, error for Fuju, 258. *See Benedetto*, p. 156

CHORCHA, Manchu country, 78, 109

CHRISTIANITY, Kubilai's interest in, and reverence for, 110, 111

CHRISTIANS, of Greek Church, Georgians, 22, and Russians, 388; Jacobites and Nestorians, at Mosul, 7; Tiflis, 24; Baghdād, 28; the miracle of the mountain, 28–32, 33; in Kash-

CHRISTIANS—*continued.* ghar, 63; in Samarqand, 63; miracle of the removed stone, 63, 64; in Yarkand, 64; Tangut, 68; Chinchintalas, 73; Su-chou, 75; Kan-chou, 75; in Chingiz's camp, 81, 82; in Erginul, 92; Silinju, 92; Egrigaia, 94; Tenduc, 94; Sindachu, 95; at Kubilai's court, 110; in Yün-nan, 187; Cachanfu, 174, 208; churches in Chên-chiang fu, 231; at Kinsai, 251; St Thomas's, 309 *seqq.*; Coilum, 326; Male and Female Islands, 336; Socotra, 338; Abyssinia, 347 *seqq.*; Lac, 389; Manichæans, mistaken for Christians, xiii, 261–263

CHRISTIAN LAW, 7, 24

CH'ÜAN-CHOU FU. *See* ZAITUN

CHUJU, Kuei-chou, 206

CHUGHI, Yogi, in Gujarat, 316; their special drink, 316; other customs, 317, 318, 319

CIBAI or CIBAN, one of Kubilai's barons. Some texts make two persons of Cibai and Ciban, 361

CINNAMON, in Tibet, 182; Gaindu, 186; Malabar, 331

CIRCASSIA. *See* ZIC

CLEMENT IV, Pope, vii, 8

CLOCKS on bridges at Kinsai, 242

CLOVES, in Java, 279; Nicobars, 289

COAL, "black stone" found in Cathay and used for heating baths, 160; in Kinsai, 253

COBBLER OF BAGHDĀD, AND THE MIRACLE OF THE MOUNTAIN, 30–32

COBINAN, Kuh-binān, 48

COCACHIN, Kokachin, Mongolian princess. She was a relative of Bulagan Khatun (Marco Polo's statement to this effect is confirmed by *Rashīd*, Vol. II, p. 4), wife of Arghun Khan, and was sent by Kubilai to Persia to marry Arghun after the death of Bulagan, but Arghun died (1291) before she reached Persia and she was ultimately given in marriage to Ghazan Khan (1295) and died in the following year, viii, ix, 15, 18

COGACHIN, Hūkāji or Ūkāji = "herdsman," son of Kubilai, governor of Qarajang, 188

COGATAI, commander of Kubilai's city guard, 127, 128

COGATAL, perhaps a clerical error for Cogatai; Tartar envoy to the Pope, 6

COIGANJU, Huai-an fu, 218, 220, 222

COILUM, 326, 327, 328, *see Yule*, II, 377

COJA (MSS. Coia), one of Arghun's barons sent as envoy to the Great Kaan, 15, 17

COMANIA, COMANIANS (Comans), 22, 393

COMARI, Kumari = "The Virgin," Cape Comarin, 328

CONDUR and SONDUR, two islands in group now known as Pulo Condore, viii, 280

CONIA, Qoniya, Iconium, 20

CONSTANTINOPLE, ix, 3, 4, 19; straits of, 392

CORDIER, HENRI. His edition of Yule's *Marco Polo*, xv, 409

COREA. *See* CAULI

CORMOS, Hormuz, vii, ix, 33, 37, 43; plain of, 44; King of, 44, 357, 358; unhealthiness of climate, 44; ships from, 45, 323; great heat and wind, 45, 46; route to Kerman, 47; hot baths, 47

INDEX

CORN, Kubilai's large stores of, 161
COROMANDEL COAST. *See* MAABAR
COTAN, Khotan, vii, 65, 66
COTTON, in Meridin, 25; Persia, 38; Kashghar, 62; Yarkand, 64; Khotan, 65; Gujarat, 332; Tana, 333; Cambay, 334
COWRIES, used for money in Qarajang, 188, 189; found in Locac, 280
CRAMOISY, *quermesis*. *See Yule*, I, 65. Material made in Baghdād, 25
CRANES, of five kinds, near Chaghan-Nor, 96. *See Yule*, I, 297, *and Mem. As. Soc. Bengal*, Vol. II, No. 9, p. 260
CRIMEA. *See* GOTHIA and GAZARIA
CROSS, THE, on Naian's standard, 108–109
CUBEBS. Cubeb pepper in Java, 279
CUBLAI, Kubilai, Persian—Qubilay, Chinese—Hu-pi-lieh. Great Kaan of the Mongols and first Yüan Emperor of China (1257–1294), son of Tuluy, son of Chingiz. An earlier Kubilai, a grand-uncle of Chingiz Khan, was one of the great national heroes of the Mongols, vii, viii, xiv, 4; receives Niccolò and Matteo Polo, 5; sends them as envoys to the Pope, 6; sends messengers to meet them, 11; receives them, 12; sends Marco Polo to Qarajang, 13; is delighted with him, 14; sends Polos to Persia to accompany Kokachin, 16; sends a napkin of asbestos to the Pope, 74; white mare's milk, 99, 131; his lineage, 103; revolt of Naian, 103; Naian defeated and put to death, 104–108; rebukes gibes at Christians, 109; returns to Khan-baliq, 110; his Easter ceremony, 110; rewards his captains, 112; his personal appearance, 114; his wives and ladies, 114–116; his sons, 116; his palace at Khan-baliq, 117–121; builds Ta-tu, 123; Ahmad's influence over him, 124; punishes leaders of rebellion, 125; orders Ahmad's body to be thrown to the dogs, 128; prohibits certain customs of the Muslims, 129; his body-guard, 129; his feasts, 130–133; his birthday, 133; presents robes to barons, 133, 137; New Year's feast, 134; his elephants, 135; his game laws, 138, 144; his wild animals for hunting, 139; the *Cuiuci*, 140; falconing, 141; how he travels when hunting, 142; his great tents at Cachar Modun, 143; his mint and money, 147, 148; buys jewels, etc., 149; his great barons, 150, 151; his posts and runners, 152, 157; taxes, 158; has trees planted, 159; his store of corn, 161; his charity, 158, 161; his astrologers, 163–165; prohibits gambling, 166; war against the king of Mien and Bangala, 196–200; Li T'an's plot, 210; sends Baian to invade Manji, 219; accepts Polo's mangonels, 227; appoints Mar Sarghis governor of Chên-chiang fu, 231; his city of Kinsai, 234–252; revenue from the city, 252; and from Zaitun, 264; his expedition against Japan, 271; sends army against Chanba, 278; sends to buy Ceylon ruby, 291; sends for relics of Buddha, 322; missions to Madagascar, 343; Qaidu's wars against him, 361–365

INDEX

Cui Kaan, Küyük Kaan, son of Ögödäi, third Great Kaan (1246-48), xiv, 83

Cuiuci. This reading has been adopted on the strength of Pelliot's excellent suggestion that in *Rashīd* text, p. 501, we should read *Bayan Küyükchi* for *Nayan Kübükchi*. *See Cordier*, p. 70, *and Pelliot*, *J.A.*, 1927, p. 267. "Keepers of the Mastiffs," 140

Cuju, 256

Cuncun, Han-chung, 175

Curdistan, Kurdistan, 37, 53

Curds, The, 25

Curzola, Island of, ix

Dagroian, kingdom of, in Sumatra, 285

Damascus, 53

Dancing-girls in Hindu temples of Ma'bar, 304

Darius, King. Battle with Alexander, 49; his daughter wedded to Alexander, 54, 56. *See note on the* Golden King

Date trees or fruit in Basra, 25, 39; Rudbar, 41, 44; Qalhat, 358

David Melik, King of Georgia, 22. *See Yule*, I, 53

Dead, disposal of the, in Tangut, 69; at Khan-baliq, 146; in Toloman, 206; in Dagroian, 286

Deer, in Madagascar, 342

Deserts, of Persia, 37; Lop (Gobi), 67, 68, 71

Devil-dancing, in Yün-nan, 195

Dhufar. *See* Dufar

Diamonds, in Mutfili (Golconda Mines), 307

Dilivar, province and town (Lahore ?). Ramusio here calls the province Malabar and the town Dely (Delhi), 43

Dinghies, used on merchant ships of Manji, 269, 270

Dogs, Kubilai's mastiffs, 140; in Tibet, 182; in Chuju, 207

Dog-sledges, in Far North (Siberia), 386

Doria, Lamba, Admiral of Genoese fleet, ix

Duels, in Cail, 325

Dufar, Dhufar, 356

Eagles, trained for hunting, 139

Easter, Kubilai's ceremony at, 110

Ebony, in Champa, 279; in Locac, 280; in Sumatra, 281

Egrigaia, Ning-hsia, in Kan-su, 93

Egypt. *See* Babylon

Elephants, Kubilai's, 106, 135; Burmese, in battle of Vochan, 196; in Caugigu, 204; Champa, 277, 278, 279; Locac, 280; Sumatra, 283; Madagascar, 341; Zanzibar, 344, 345; Abyssinia, 351

Eli, Kingdom of, 328. *See Yule*, II, 386

Embroidery, in silk by women of Kerman, 39; on leather in Gujarat, 332

England, Sea of, 276

Erculin, according to Pelliot = squirrel (écureuil) 387, 388. *See Yule*, II, 483

Erginul, Liang-chou. *See Benedetto*, p. 58 *n*. The correct reading is Erguiul (Pelliot) Province, 91; town, 92, 93

Ermine, 86; used for lining Kubilai's tents, 143; in Siberia, 387, 388

Esca, tinder, 73

Esentemur, Esen-Temür, grandson of Kubilai, 187, 196

Eshier, Esh-Shihr, province of S. Arabia, 354

INDEX

ETZINA, this town has now been identified with Qara-khoto, a ruined town on the Etsin-Gol, 77. *See Journ. Roy. Geog. Soc.*, Sept. 1928, pp. 300–302

EUNUCHS, from Bengal, 203

EUPHRATES, 23

FACFUR, Baghpur—"Son of Heaven," title of King of Manji, Arabicised form of Persian translation of *T'ien-tzŭ*, one of the Chinese titles for the Emperor, 18; his effeminacy, 219; his flight before Baian's army, 220; his generosity, 221; his death, 222; his palace at Kinsai, 248–250

FALCONERS, Kubilai's, 141, 144, 145

FALCONS, of Kerman, 40; peregrine, 91; Kubilai's 141. *See also* SAKER *and* LANNER falcons

FANSUR, kingdom of, in Sumatra, 287

FARO, a "mountain" at the western entrance of the Black Sea, 393

FEMALE ISLAND, an island in Malaya supposed to be inhabited solely by women, 336, 337. *See Chau-ju-kua*, p. 151

FERLEC, Parlak, kingdom of, 282. *See Cordier*, p. 108

FIRE-ALARMS, in Kinsai, 243

FISH, miracle of, in Georgia, 23; in Caspian Sea, 24; in Badakhshan, 58; large quantity at Kinsai, 236; in Esh-Shihr, 355; M. P. here describes the manner in which the people of Esh-Shihr dry fish and preserve them like biscuits exactly in the same way that the well-known *Bombay ducks* eaten with curry are prepared from the Bommelay fish. The earliest reference in *Hobson Jobson* dates from the beginning of the seventeenth century; in Qalhat, 358

FLAX, in Kashghar, 62

FOUR GOSPELS, Book of, Kubilai's ceremony with, 110

FOXES, black, 387, 388

FRANCE, King of, 16

FRANCOLIN, bird similar to black partridge, in Rudbar, 41; in plain of Hormuz, 44

FRANKINCENSE, in Tana, 333; in Esh-Shihr, 355; in Dhufar, 356

FU-CHIEN. *See* FUJU

FU-CHOU. *See* FUJU

FUJU (F. Fugiu). Province (Fu-chien), xiii, 256, 263; town (Fu-chou), 258

FURS, trapping in Siberia, 387

GAINDU, Chiung-tu, or Chiang-tu = Chien-ch'ang, region of E. Tibet, 183-186. *See Cordier*, 83. Other texts have Caindu

GALINGALE, spice similar to ginger, in Fu-chien, 256; in Java, 279

GAMBLING, Kubilai's suppression of, 166

GANFU, K'an-p'u, near Hangchou, port of Kinsai, 245

GASPAR, one of the Three Magi, 34, 35

GAT-PAUL. The *Codex Cumanicus* (an old vocabulary of the Comani Turks) includes *gati pàuli* among the fur-bearing animals, while Marco Polo seems to include them among monkeys. Monsieur Antoine Thomas (as I learn through Professor Pelliot), suggests that *paul* may be derived

FF

INDEX

GAT-PAUL—*continued.*
from the Latin *paludem*, "a swamp," and that *Gat-paul* may be the name of a wild cat afterwards adopted for some variety of monkey, but that one would have expected rather the form *paulgat*. Professor Pelliot suggests the survival of this form in the English "pole-cat," 328

GAVI, low caste Hindus, probably Pariahs, 298

GAZARIA, 393

GEESE, in Fu-chien, 260

GENOA, ix, 2, 19

GENOESE, fleet, ix; merchants on the Caspian, 23; and at Tabrîz, 33

GEORGE, PRINCE, wrongly regarded by Marco as a grandson of Prester John, 94, 361, *see* Pelliot, *T'oung-Pao*, 1914, I, pp. 9–11

GEORGIANA, Georgia, 21; king of, 22; people, impassable country, seas and rivers, etc., 22–23

GERFALCONS (*Shunqar*), 91, 97; Kubilai's 141, 142

GERMANS, their fondacos in Cambaluc, 123

GHAZAN KHAN. *See* CASAN

GHELLE, silk of the Gilan province, 23

GHELUKELAN SEA OF = Gil-u-Gilān. *See Yule*, I, 58; *see* Caspian, 23

GHINGHINTALAS, Chinchintalas, identified by Charignon (pp. 141 *seqq.*) with the Barkul district, 73, 74. Pelliot suggests that it extended more to the north-west towards Besh-baliq

GHIUJU (F. Ghiugiu), Ch'ü-chao, 254, 255. *See Yule*, II, 222

GILDS (Z. *frataleæ*) of consecrated damsels in Ma'bar, 304

GINGER, near Huang-Ho, 173; Shan-si, 176; in Gaindu, 186; Su-chou, 233; Fu-chien, 256; Coilum, 326; Eli, 329; Malabar, 331; Gujarat, 332

GIRAFFES, in Madagascar (an error, as giraffes do not exist there), 343; Zanzibar, 345; Abyssinia, 351

GIRDLES, of St Barsamo, 34

GOG and MAGOG (F. Gogo and Mogogo), Ung and Mungul, country of, 95

GOLD, dust in Tibet, 182; exchanged for salt in Gaindu, 185; Brius River, 187; in Qarajang, 188; in Yün-nan, 188; Caugigu, 204; Toloman, 206; Japan, 270; Islands in China-Sea, 276; in Ma'bar, 297; imported into Malabar, 331, and into Cambay, 334; in Abyssinia, 352

GOLDEN KING, Altun or Altan Khan, the king of the *Chin* or Golden Dynasty (known also as the *Niu-chens* or *Jüchens*) which in 1123 displaced the Khitan (*Liao*) Dynasty in the independent northern provinces of China. The French name *Roi Dor* led some translators to suppose that King Darius was intended, 170; with Prester John, 171–173

GOMUTI PALM. *See* WINE

GOSHAWKS, called *Avigi* (*q.v.*) 23, 84; Kubilai's, 141; black, 283, 304

GOTHIA, Crimea, 393

GOZURAT, Gujarat, 331, 332

GRAND CANAL, of China, 216, 217; its construction, 230

GRASS, poisonous, in Su-chou, 75

GREAT DESERT, The Gobi, 67, 68, 71

GREAT KAAN. *See* CUBLAI

INDEX

Greater Sea, Black Sea, 23, 392, 393
Green Hill, an artificial mound on the north side of the Palace at Khan-baliq (not to be identified with the present Mei-shan, or "Coal-hill"), 120
Grégoire, group of Polo MSS., xii
Gregory X, Pope. *See* Tebaldo Visconti
Gryphon, or Rukh, the fabulous bird of Madagascar, 343, 344
Gudderi (Mongol *kuderi*). *See* Musk-deer
Guglielmo of Tripoli, Fra, 10
Gujarat. *See* Gozurat

Ha-ch'a-mu-tuan. *See* Cachar Modun
Han-chung. *See* Cuncun
Hang-chou. *See* Kinsai
Hawks, in Georgia, 23; in Kerman, 40; Badakhshan, 58; Etzina, 77; among the Tartars, 84; on shores of Northern Sea, 91; at Chaghan-Nor, 96; at Chandu, 97; Kubilai's, 141, 142, 144; in Tibet, 183; Ma'bar, 304
Hemp, in Kashghar, 62
Hens, featherless in Fu-chien, 257
Hindus. *See* Idolaters
Ho-Chien Fu. *See* Cachanfu
Horiat tribe, Öirats, a Mongolian tribe who were allowed to drink milk of Kubilai's white mares, 99. *See Yule*, I, 308
Hormuz. *See* Cormos
Horses, Turkish, 20; Persian, 37; sold to dealers for importation to India, 37, 45; of Badakhshan, 57; sacrificed, 83; Tartar, 88; owned by Kubilai, 99; presented to him on New Year's Day, 135; in Ma'bar, 296; in Tana, 334; in Abyssinia, 348; shipped to India, 353, 357
Hounds, Kubilai's mastiffs, 140; keepers of, called *Cuiuci* (*Küyükchi*), *q.v.*, 140
Huai-an fu. *See* Coiganju
Huang Ho. *See* Caramoran
Hukaji. *See* Cogachin
Hulagu Khan. *See* Alau
Hun-ho. *See* Pulisanghin
Hsi-an fu. *See* Kenjanfu
Hsiang-yang fu. *See* Sanianfu
Hsi-hsia. *See* Tangut

Iaci. *See* Yachi
Ianb. *See* Yanb
I-ching Hsien. *See* Sinju
Icoguristan, Uighuristan, xii, 72
Iconium. *See* Conia
Idifu, 96
Idolaters—Buddhists in Burma, Central Asia, China and Tibet—Buddhists or Hindus in India and Malaya
Idolaters—Brahmins, *q.v.*
Idolaters—Yogis. *See* Chughi
Idols, Tartar, 85, 166, 385; in Tangut, 68, 69, 75; very large, 75; Chinese, 213–215; of the Lamas, or Bacsi, 100–101; of the Sensin, 102; in general, 275; in India, 304, 305
Il-Khans, Mongol rulers of Persia. *See* Levant
India, 1, 15, 24, 26, 33; horses imported into, 37; trade with Manji or China, 236, 334; no horses bred there, 296, 353; trade with Persia and Arabia, 323; islands of, 346; division of, 347; trade with Aden and Egypt, 353; with Arabian ports, 354, 357
India, The Greater. *See* Maabar
India, The Lesser, 347

INDEX

INDIA, Middle (Abyssinia), 347
INDIA, Sea of, 16, 25, 37, 45
INDIGO, manufactured at Coilum, 326; in Gujarat, 332; Cambay, 334
IRON GATE, Pass of Derbend, 22, 394
ISFAAN, Ispahan, 37, 40

JACOBITE Christians, at Mosul, 24, 28; at Tabrīz, 33
JAPAN. *See* CHIPANGU
JASPER. *See* CHALCEDONY
JATOLIC, Katholikos, title borne by the Patriarch of the Nestorians, and by the Metropolitan of the Jacobites, 24, 337
JAVA, probably only touched by Marco Polo on one of his expeditions, viii, 16, 279, 280, 289, 328
JAVA, the Lesser (Sumatra), 281, 282
JERBOA. *See* PHARAOH'S RATS
JERMS (MS. VB. *cerme*: Ramusio, *zerme*), Arabic, *jarm*, pl. *jurūm*. Large barges on the Nile, 353
JERUSALEM, 7, 9
JESUDAR, Yesudar, Mongol baron, a cousin of Qaidu Khan, 361
JEWS, in Tabrīz, 24, 110; in Coilum, 326; in Abyssinia, 347
JIHUN RIVER. *See* JON
JON RIVER, Jihun, or Oxus, 23, 359
JONJU (F. Giongiu). Cho-chou, 168, 169, 208
JUJUBE, fruits, 217
JUGGLERS and TUMBLERS, at Kubilai's feasts, 132; conquer Mien, 202

KAAN, Qa'an, title applied to the Great Lord of all the Mongols, first assumed by Ögödäi. *See* CUBLAI
K'AI-P'ING FU. *See* CHANDU *and* KEMENFU
KAMASAL. *See* CANOSALMI
KAN-CHOU. *See* CANPCHU
KARAUNAS. *See* CARAUNAS
KARIPPU KAL, xiv
KASHGHAR. *See* CASCAR
KASHMIR. *See* KESHIMUR
KAYAL. *See* CAIL
KEINAN, Gulf of, 277
KEMENFU, 11, K'aip'ing fu, called by Rashid *Kaiminfu*. *See* CHANDU
KENLINFU, Chien-ning fu, 257
KENJANFU, province, Shan-hsi, 174, 175; city, Hsi-anfu, 174
KERMAN, vii; armour made there, 39; embroidery, 39; route to Hormuz from, 40; king of, 40, 45, 357, 359
KESHIMUR, Kashmir, 42; Buddhism in, 59; women, 60
KESITAN (Keshikten, pl. of *Keshiktü*, derived from *Keshik*—one who guards by turns), Kubilai's guard of 12,000 horse, 129, 137. *See* Pelliot, *T'oung Pao*, 1930, pp. 27–29. *Rashīd*, p. 457, reads *Kezik*
KESMACORON, Kij-Makran, 335, 347
KESMUR (F. Quesmur), Kashmir, race of idolaters, accused of cannibalism, 100
KHALIF. *See* CALIF
KHAN-BALIQ. *See* CAMBALUC
KHOTAN. *See* COTAN
KHURASAN. *See* ARBRE SOL
KIACATU (F. Chiacatu), Kaikhatu, who succeeded his brother Arghun as Il-Khan of Persia (1291–1295). Gives gold tablets to Polos, ix, 17, 18, 19; takes possession of throne, 382; his death, 383

KIAN, river, Yang-tzŭ-chiang, 228

KIANSUI, river, Yang-tzŭ-chiang, 177

KIJ-MAKRAN. *See* KESMACORAN

KINSAI (Rashīd—Khing-say), Hang-chou, capital of Manji. Called by Marco Polo "City of Heaven." Its topography, 234–236; its market, 236; baths, 237; guilds, 238; lake, 239; pleasure-barges, 240; character of people, 242; the guards, 242; fire-alarms, 253; paved streets, 244; carriages, 244; swimming baths, 245; revenue from, 252; ships from, 276

KISI, Ghez, or Kem, island in Persian Gulf, 25, 37; ships from, 323, 359

KISHM. *See* SCASEM

KOKACHIN. *See* COCACHIN

KUBILAI. *See* CUBLAI

KUEI-CHOU. *See* CHUJU

KUH-BINĀN. *See* COBINAN

KUMIS. *See* MARE'S MILK

KURDISTAN. *See* CURDISTAN

KURDS. *See* CURDS

KÜYÜK. *See* CUI KAAN

LAC, the Lezghians of the Caucasus, 389, 393. *See* G. I. Bratianu, *Recherches sur le Commerce Genois dans la Mer Noire au* XIII° *Siècle*, p. 295

LAHORE. *See* DILIVAR

LAIAS, Ayas, a port in the Gulf of Alexandretta, 8, 9, 10, 11, 19

LANBRI, kingdom of, on N.W. coast of Sumatra, 286, 287

LANGUAGES, Turkish and Tartar, 6

LANNER FALCONS, similar to saker falcons, *q.v.*; in Badakhshan, 58; in Tangut, 77; in Tibet, 183

LAPIZ LAZULI. *See* AZURE

LAR, Lar-desha or Lat-desha. Early name for Gujarat. *See Yule*, II, 367. Province of S.W. India whence the Brahmins come, 313

LEATHER, tanned in Gujarat, 332; goods made from, 332; in Tana, 333; in Cambay, 334

LEOPARDS, in Coilum, 328; Madagascar, 342; Zanzibar, 345; Abyssinia, 351; Cheetas, used by Kubilai for hunting, 98, 139

LEVANT, kingdom of Il-Khans of Persia, 4, 20; summer residence in Armenia, 21, 38, 54, 91; trade with Coilum, 327, 368, 384, 394

LEZGHIANS. *See* LAC

LINJIN, Lin-ch'ing (Yule has Lingiu), 216

LIONS, black, in Coilum, 327; near Balkh, 55; actually tigers, kept by Kubilai for hunting, 139; hunted with dogs in Kuei-chou, 207; in Chê-kiang, 255; in Fu-chien, 256; method of trapping, 259; in Comari, 328; Madagascar, 342; Zanzibar, 345; Abyssinia, 351

LITAN SANGON, Li T'an, hsiang-chün = general of division, one of Kubilai's barons. Raises a rebellion (in Shan-tung) against his master (in favour of the Sungs). Marco Polo gives the date as 1272. This should be 1262; 210, 211

LOCAC, province in Malay Peninsular. *See Cordier*, p. 104; 280

LOMBARDS, 123

LOP, city. *See Cordier*, p. 47. Stein says it must have occupied the site of the present Charklik, 67

LOP, desert, Gobi, 67, 68, 71

LOP NOR, vii

LYNX, used by Kubilai for hunting, 139; in Cuncun, 175

INDEX

MAABAR, Ma'bar = Coromandel Coast, 291; pearl fisheries, 292; horses, 296; suicide of criminals, 297; worship of oxen, 298; cleanliness of citizens, 299; arrest for debt, 300; their superstitions, 301; training of sons, 303; the monasteries, 304; customs in sleeping, 306; ships from, 342, 347

MADAGASCAR. *See* MOGDASIO

MAGI, The Three—Beltasar, Gaspar and Melchior, 34; story of, 35–36

MAHOMET, Muhammad, Law of, 38; worshippers of, *see* SARACENS

MAIMODI ACOMAT (Mahmūd-i-Ahmad ?), king of Hormuz, tributary to King of Kerman, 47

MAJAR. *See* MENJAR

MAKRAN, ix

MALABAR. *See* MELIBAR

MALACCA, Straits of, viii

MALAIUR, Malay Peninsula, 281

MALE ISLAND (fabulous), 336, 337

MANGALAI (Sanskrit, *Mangala*), third son of Kubilai, 174–175

MANGONELS, large slings said to have been made by the Polos for use in siege of Hsiang-yang fu (*q.v.*), 226. *See Yule*, II, 161

MÄNGÜ TÄMÜR. *See* MONGUTEMUR

MANICHÆANS. *See* under CHRISTIANS, xiii. Hamdulla Mustawfi writing in 1340 says the inhabitants of Manji (S. China) for the most part worshipped idols of the sect of Māni the Painter, *Nuzhat ul-Qulūb*, *Trans.*, p. 250

MANJI, or Manzi, name applied to Southern China (the far older name for S. China—Mahāchīn—was converted by Muslim writers into *Māchīn* as distinguished from *Chīn*. *Rashīd*, p. 371, says Manji is *Māchīn*). King of, 18. *See* FACFUR. Province, 105, 154, 169, 182, 216, 217; entrance to, 218, 223; conquest of, 219–222, 226, 232; the people, 233, 242, 248; streets and roads of, 244; nine provinces of, and their governors, 245, 266; its cities and guards, 245, 256; astrologers and superstitions, 247; form of "census," 251; revenue from, 253; Manichæans, 261–263; called Chin, 276; trade with Java, 280; trade with Coilum, 327; and with Eli, 329

MANJI, Queen of, 220, 222; her report on Kinsai, 234 *seqq.*

MARDIN. *See* MERIDIN

MARE'S MILK, *Kumis*, 84; at Kubilai's feasts, 99, 131

MARRIAGE, customs in Khotan, 65; moral laxity, 65; in Kan-chou, 76; of the Tartars, 85–86; after death, 89; in Thibet, 180, 181

MARSARKIS, Mar Sarghis—Dominus Sergius, 231

MARSDEN, his translation of Marco Polo, xv

MASTER OF THE TEMPLE, 11

MECRIT, Mekrit or Merkit, a Tartar tribe, 90

MELCHIOR. *See* MAGI

MELIBAR, Malabar, ix, xiii, 330, 331

MELIC OF CORMOS. *See* CORMOS

MELONS, dried, in Sapurgan, 54

MENJAR (Majar ?), 393

MERIDIN, Mardin, 21, 25

MESSENGERS, foot-runners, in relays of three miles each, 154; on horseback, 156

INDEX

Mien, Burma, combined by Marco Polo with Bengal. *See Yule*, II, 99; viii, 196, 200; gold and silver towers of, 201; king of, and Bangala, 196, 200

Milione, name given both to Marco and to his father Niccolò Polo. Title also given to this book, by which it is best known in Italy, 1. *See Benedetto*, pp. 245, 256

Mingan, one of the keepers of Kubilai's hounds, 140

Mogdasio, Madagascar, 431

Monasteries, Buddhist, 60, 75, 101, 229, 231, 304

Money, paper, made from bark of mulberry-tree, 148; cowries used for, *see* Cowries

Mongatai, one of Kubilai's barons sent to suppress rebellion of Li T'an, 211

Mongu Kaan, the elder brother of Kubilai who reigned as Great Kaan from 1251 to 1259. The Mongolian form of this name is *Möngkä*, meaning "immortal." Early Muslim historians and early European travellers heard the Turkish form *Mängü*, which has the same meaning, xiv, 26, 72, 83, 178

Mongutemur, Mängü Tämür, ruler of Qipchaq (1266–1280), xiv, 393, 401

Monkeys, in Sumatra, 283; made to resemble pygmies, 283, 284; in Comari, 328; in Abyssinia, 352

Moses, 110

Moslems, Muslims, 187

Mosul, 21, 24, 28, 33

Mosulin, muslin, 25

Motupallé. *See* Mutfili

Moule, The Rev. A. C., xiii, xv, xvii

Mountain of Noah's Ark, 21

Mount D'Ely. *See* Eli

Muhammad. *See* Mahomet

Muhammadans. *See* Saracens

Mulberry-trees, paper made from, 148; silk-worms fed on leaves, 169

Mus, Mush, in Armenia, 21, 25

Musk-deer, method of obtaining musk from, 92

Muslims. *See* Saracens

Mutfili, Motupallé, for Telingana, 307; diamond mines there, 307, 347

Nac (*nakh*), kind of brocade, 25. *See* Pelliot, *T'oung Pao*, 1930, p. 203

Naccars (naqqāra), kettledrums used as signal for battle, 107, 362, 369, 399

Naian, Nayan, second cousin of Kubilai, not his uncle as stated by Marco Polo; rebels against Kubilai, 103; Kubilai marches against him, 104, 105, 106; battle with Kubilai, 107; his death, 108, 109

Nankin, Nan-ching—An-Ch'ing, capital of An-huei, 225

Nasich, Arabic *nasīj*, Persian *nasich*, a kind of brocade, 25. *See* Pelliot, *Journal Asiatique*, 1927, p. 271

Natigai, Tartar god, 85; in Cathay, 166; in Far North, 385. *See Yule*, I, 258; Pelliot, *T'oung Pao*, 1929, p. 219, identifies this name with that of the Mongolian Goddess of the Earth Ätügän or Itügän. Plan Carpin has Ytogo.

Necuveran, Nicobar Islands, viii, 289

Negropont, ix, 8, 19

Nerghi, Plain of, scene of battle between Nogai and Toqtu, 404, 405

INDEX

NESCRADDIN, Nasr ud-Dīn, governor of Yün-nan, 197
NESTORIANS. *See* CHRISTIANS
NICCOLO OF VICENZA, FRA, 10
NICOBAR. *See* NECUVERAN
NILE, THE, 353
NOAH'S ARK, 21
NOGAI KHAN, great-great-grandson of Chinghiz Khan, 401; battle against Toqtu, 403, *seqq.* *See Yule*, II, 497
NOGODAR, Nigudar, King of Caraunas, 42, 43
NOMOGAN, son of Kubilai, 361
NONE, nona, one of the Canonical hours of prayer, 301. *See Yule*, II, 369
NONE, Noyan, a Mongolian title equivalent to our Count, 61
NOROECH, probably Norway, 392
NORTH, THE FAR, 384–387; king of, *see* CANCHI
NORTH STAR, Pole-star, invisible from Sumatra, 282; seen from Comari, 328; from Malabar, 330; from Gujarat, 332; and from Cambay, 334
NUBIA, 312
NUTMEGS, in Java, 279
NUTS, Indian, sometimes called by Marco Polo "Pharaoh's nuts," coconuts, in Sumatra, 285; in Nicobar Is., 289; Andaman Is., 290; Ma'bar, 309; Malabar, 331

OCEAN SEA, 44, 91, 167, 173, 177, 187, 220, 224, 245, 270, 276, 392
ÖGÖDÄI, xiv
OIL, holy, from the Sepulchre, 7, 9, 12; in Armenia (Baku), 22; made from sesame, 58, 291, 312; from walnuts, 58; from sperm whale, 339
OLD MAN OF THE MOUNTAIN, 'Ala ud-Dīn, 49–53; his "Paradise," 50; training of his Assassins, 51; his chiefs, 53; his son Rukn ud-Dīn submits to Hulagu (1256), 53. *See also* ALAODIN
ÖLJÄITÜ. *See* TEMUR
OMENS, importance of, in Ma'bar, 301; of the Brahmins, 314, 315
ONDANIQUE, fine kind of steel, in Kerman, 39; in Kuh-binān, 48; in Ghinghintalas, 73
OSTRICHES, in Madagascar, 342; in Abyssinia, 352
OULATAI, one of Arghun's barons, sent as envoy to the Great Kaan, 15, 379
OUNCE (*felis uncia*), feline carnivore similar to leopard, with lighter, longer fur and very broad skull, in Comari, 328; in Madagascar, 342; in Abyssinia, 351
OVIS POLI, this variety of sheep found in the Pamirs has been called after Marco Polo, although it had actually been seen and described by William Rubruk nearly fifty years earlier, 61
OXEN, in Rudbar, 41; in Tangut (yaks—*see Yule*, I, 277), 92; wild (Beyamini) in Tibet, 183; in Burma, 203; in Bengal, 203; Aniu, 205; worshipped in Ma'bar, 298; and by Brahmins, 316
OXUS. *See* JON

PAIPURTH, Baiburt, 21
PAIZAH. *See* TABLETS OF AUTHORITY
PAMIER, Pamir, Plain of, 61; large-horned sheep on, 61

INDEX

PAO-YING-HSIEN. *See* PAUKIN

PAPIONI, animals similar to foxes, in Fu-Chien, 260

PARIS GEOGRAPHIC TEXT, x, xi, xii

PARROTS, in plain of Hormuz, 44; in Coilum, 327; in Abyssinia, 352

PARTRIDGES, in Yezd, 39

PASAI. *See* BASMAN

PATARINS, heretics, 102. *See Yule*, I, 321

PATLAM. *See* BETTALAN

PATU, *sic*, for Batu, 393. *See under* BATU

"PAUCA, PAUCA, PACAUCA," prayer used by the King of Ma'bar, probably a corruption of *Bhagava* = "Oh! Lord," 294

PAUKIN (F. Pauchin), Pao-ying-Hsien, 222, 223

PAUTHIER, M. G., his translation of Marco Polo, xv

PAVING, in streets of Manji, 224

PEACOCKS, in Ma'bar, 311; in Coilum, 327

PEARLS, pierced in Baghdad, 25; in salt lake of Gaindu, 183; rose, in Japan, 271; fisheries off Ma'bar, 292

PEI-CHOU. *See* PINJU

PEKING. The town spoken of by Marco Polo as *Taidu* or *Cambaluc* corresponds more or less with the Tartar city of modern *Peking*. Kubilai succeeded his brother Möngkä as Great Kaan in 1260. In 1264 he transferred his headquarters to the old capital of the Chin Emperors, known as Yen-ching or Chung-tu, which had been captured and destroyed by Chingiz Khan in 1215, and built a new town near the old one, and in 1271 gave it the name of *Ta-tu* (Taidu). It was also known by the Turkish name of *Khanbaliq* (Cambaluc). Under the first Chin Emperors it had been called *Nanching* or Southern Capital. In 1151 the fourth Chin Emperor changed its name to *Chung-tu* or Middle Capital. It was the Ming Emperor Yung-lo who in 1421 gave it the name of *Pei-p'ing* or Northern Tranquility, which later became *Pei-ching*, or Northern Capital. The Republic has reverted to *Pei-p'ing*. *See* CAMBALUC and TAIDU

PELLIOT, Professor Paul, xiii, xv, xvii, *et passim* in Index

PEM, 65, 66. *See Cordier*, pp. 45–47

PENTAN, Island of, 281. *See Yule*, II, p. 280

PENZER, N. M., his edition of Marco Polo, xii

PEPPER, at Kinsai, 238; in Fu-chien, 264; white in Japan, 276; in Java, 279; Coilum, 326; Mount Eli, 329; Malabar, 331; Gujarat, 332; Tana, 333

PERSIA, viii, xvi, 1, 17, 33; its eight kingdoms, 37; cruelty of people, 38, 40

PERSIAN GULF, vii, ix

PHARAOH'S NUTS. *See* NUTS

PHARAOH'S RATS, Jerboa, 84, 385

PHEASANTS, in Rudbar, 41; "Reeve's Pheasant." *See Yule*, I, p. 280. In Tangut, 93, 223

PIANFU, P'ing-yang fu, 170

PINE-WOODS, in the Mongolian desert, 77

PINJU (Yule has *Piju*), Pei-chou, 217

PIRATES, in Malabar, 330; in Gujarat, 332; in Tana, 333; in Socotra, 340

INDEX

Pistachios, 41, 55

Pleasure-barges, in Kinsai, 240

Polo, Marco, vii–xvii, tells his story, 1, 2; leaves Venice with Matteo and Niccolò, 9; his journey with them to Kubilai, 9–11; welcomed by Great Kaan, 12; sent as envoy to Qarajang, 13; pleases Kubilai with his story, 13; given title of Messer, 14; his mission to India, 15; leaves with Matteo and Niccolò for Venice, 16–19; questions about Magi, 34; escapes from Karaunas, 43; hears of breed of Bucephalus, 58; is cured from illness in hill climate, 58; is told by Zurficar about the salamander, 73; at Kan-chou, 77; brings home hair of yak, 92; and head and feet of musk-deer, 93; sees events connected with Ahmad Bailo's death, 129; his good opinion of Chinese, 165; sent by Kubilai to western provinces, 167; "holds the government" of Yang-chou, 225; helps to construct mangonels for siege of Hsiang-yang fu (*q.v.*), 226; on Kinsai, 234; hears about the amount of pepper consumed there, 238; on the revenue from Kinsai, 253; with Matteo discovers the Manichæans, 261; 262; his great experience, 267; in Champa, 279; five months in Sumatra, 284; brings brazil-seed to Venice, 287; eats sago, 288; sees arrest of debtors in Ma'bar, 300

Polo, Matteo, uncle of Marco, and Niccolò, his father, vii–ix; set out from Constantinople, 3; received by Bärkä Khan, 3; reach Bukhara, 4; journey to Kubilai, 5; sent as envoys to Pope, 6; given golden Tablet of Authority, 7; reach Ayas, 8; reach Acre, 8; visit Venice, and find Marco

Polo, Marco, Matteo, and Niccolò, vii–ix; leave Venice and go to Acre, 9; fetch oil from Holy Sepulchre at Jerusalem, 9; return to Acre, and decide to return to China, 9; are recalled by newly elected Pope, 10; set out again from Acre with Pope's letters, gifts, and two friars, 11; arrive at K'ai-ping fu, 11; welcomed by Kubilai, 12; Kubilai refuses them permission to return home, 14; are allowed to go as escort to Kokachin, 15, 16; Kubilai gives them Tablets of Authority, 16; deliver Kokachin to Kaikhatu, 17; receive golden tablets from Kaikhatu, 17; the Great Kaan's trust in them, 18; reach Trebizond, Constantinople, Negropont, and Venice, 19; their year in Kan-chou, 77; their supposed part in siege of Hsiang-yang fu, 226, 227

Ponent, Qipchaq, Southern Russia, 393, 394, 401

Ponent, Tartars of, the Khans of Qipchaq, 393, 394, 401

Ponte, Messer, the Venetian Podesta of Constantinople, 3

Pope. *See* Tebaldo Visconti

Prester John. Mainly owing to a forged letter addressed in the first instance to Manuel I, Emperor of Byzantium about 1165, and purporting to come from Prester John himself, the legend of a fabulously rich and

PRESTER JOHN—*continued.* powerful Christian potentate, residing in "India" was widely circulated in Europe. The story probably originated in conection with the King of Abyssinia, which was at one time known as Middle India. But before the circulation of the forged letter, news had reached Europe of the victory which the Gur-Khan of the Qara-Khitais had gained over the Seljuk Sultan Sanjar in 1141. Some of the Turkish tribes fighting under the Gur-Khan were Christians, and on this account somebody invented a story that the Gur-Khan was a Nestorian king residing in the far East, by name Johannes Presbyter. No attempt was, however, made to enter into relations with this Christian king.

After the withdrawal of the invading Mongols from Central Europe in 1241 the Christian powers in the West were anxious to discover who these Mongols who had spread alarm throughout Europe might be, and certain learned priests were sent to the unknown East to see what they could learn about this mysterious people. These priests in their travels were naturally always on the look-out for the descendants of Prester John and each formed his own theory. Now there was a certain king of the Christian tribe of the Keraits who had the tautological title of *Ong* (or *Wang*) Khan, and had been engaged in warfare with Chingiz Khan. Marco Polo took *Ong Khan* to be a corruption of *Yohanna*, or John, and decided this must be the great Prester John. He further imagined that a prince named George, belonging, as Pelliot has pointed out, to another Christian tribe, the Öngüts, who ruled over Tenduc, was a grandson of Prester John. *See* Pelliot, *T'oung Pao*, 1914, p. 13. His great power, 78; Chingiz requests his daughter in marriage, 79; sends insolent message to Chingiz, 80; prepares for war against him, 80; marches to plain of Tenduc, 81; is killed in battle, 82; and the Golden King, 171–173

PULISANGHIN, commonly regarded as the Persian *pul-i-sangin*, or "stone bridge," but more probably stands for the bridge over the *San-kan* river; the river in question is known as the *Hun-ho* or *San-kan*. *Rashīd* (text, p. 463) calls it the river *Sangin*, which may have been the popular pronunciation in Marco Polo's day, 167. *See Yule*, II, pp. 5–8

PULO CONDORE. *See* SONDUR *and* CONDUR

PUMAR, King of, his son wrestles with daughter of Qaidu, 367. (Benedetto, p. 221, note, says this name is found only in the group TA, i.e. the Della Crusca recension.)

PYGMIES, really monkeys, in Sumatra, 285

QAIDU. *See* CAIDU

QALHAT. *See* CALATU

QARAJANG. *See* CARAJAN

QARA-KHOJA, or Qara-Qocho. *See* CARACHOCO

QARA-KHOTO. *See* ETZINA

INDEX

QARAQORUM. *See* CARACORON
QAZWIN. *See* CASVIN
QIPCHAQ. *See* PONENT
QONIYA. *See* CONIA
QUAILS, in Yazd, 39; in Chaghan-Nor, 96; in Ma'bar, 304
QUBILAI QA'AN. *See* CUBLAI
QUICKSILVER and SULPHUR, mixed together and drunk by Yogis, 316
QUILON. *See* COILUM
QUILTING, with cotton, in Gujarat, 332
QUNGURAT. *See* UNGRAT

RAGU KALAM, xiii
RAMUSIO, ix, x, xi, xv, 409
REOBAR, Rudbar, 41, 43, 46
RHUBARB, protective from effects of the heat, in Su-chou, 75, 233, *see Yule*, I, 218
RHINOCEROS. *See* UNICORN
RICE, used for making wine in Cathay, 159; in Qarajang, 187
ROCHELLE, Sea of, 276
ROME, 74
RUBIES, mined in Badakhshan, 57; in Ceylon, 291
RUC, *Rukh*, name given to gryphons in Madagascar, 344. *See also* GRYPHONS
RUDBAR. *See* REOBAR
RUKN UD-DĪN, grand master of the Assassins (1255–56). *See* OLD MAN OF THE MOUNTAIN
RUSSIA, xiv; the people, their furs, 388; silver mines, 389; the great cold, 389; stoves, 390; taverns, 391; the currency, 392, 393
RUSTICHELLO OF PISA, fellow prisoner in Genoa to whom Marco dictated his narrative, x, 2

SABLE, used to line Kubilai's great tents, 143; in Siberia, 385, 387; Russia, 388
SACHIU, Sha-chou, *i.e.* Tun-huang, site of the famous caves of the Thousand Buddhas, 68
SAGAMONI BORCAN (F. reads Sergamoni and Sergamuni), Sakya-Muni Burkhan—Buddha. The Chinese character now pronounced in Mandarin *fo* represents the word Buddha, and was once pronounced *but*. When the Soghdians translated the Chinese Buddhist scriptures the contemporary and local pronunciation was *bur*. *Bur* and *Khan* may have given *Burkhan*, Marco Polo's *Borcan*. Gold-covered figures of, 75; Kubilai's reverence for, 110; his sepulchre on Adam's Peak, 319; story of, 319 *seqq.*
SAGGIO, a Venice weight: $\frac{1}{6}$ oz.; coins in gold or silver, 193
ST JOHN THE BAPTIST, Church of, in Samarqand, 63
ST LEONARD'S MONASTERY, in Georgia, miracle of fish, 63
ST THOMAS THE APOSTLE, the descendants of his murderers, 298 (*see* GAVI); his shrine, 309; miracle of the rice, 311; in Abyssinia, 347
SAKER FALCONS, white and very swift falcon found in Badakhshan, 58; in Tangut, 77; in Tibet, 183
SAKYA-MUNI BURKHAN. *See* SAGAMONI BORCAN
SALAMANDER, asbestos; *see Yule*, I, 216; 73
SALMON, in Caspian Sea, 24
SALT, "mountains" in Badakhshan, 55; used for currency in Tibet, 182; and in Gaindu, 185; in Qarajang, 188; manufactured in Ch'ang-lu, 209; Coiganju, 222; Kinsai, 252

SAMARCAN, Samarqand, miracle at, 63; Qaidu's capital, 365
SAMAGAR, Mongol baron, 379
SAMARQAND. *See* SAMARCAN
SAMATRA, Sumatra, city and kingdom of, 284
SANDS, singing: strange noises heard in Lop Desert. *See Yule*, I, 212, *and Cordier*, 49, 50; 68
SANDALWOOD, in Nicobar Islands, 289; in Madagascar, 342
SANIANFU, Hsiang-yang fu, 226; siege of, by Kubilai, 226–28
The siege began in the winter of 1268 and the town finally capitulated in March 1273. It is therefore impossible that any of the Polos could have been present. *See* Moule, *Journal of the North China Branch of the Royal Asiatic Society*, Vol. LVIII, 1927
SAIN KHAN, or the Good Khan, a name by which Batu Khan (*q.v.*) was also known, 393
SANKAN-HO. *See* PUL-I-SANGIN
SAPPHIRES, mined in Badakhshan, 57
SAPURGAN, Shaburqān, 53, 54
SARACENS, Muslims, "worshippers of Mahomet," in Armenia, 20; in Georgia, 24; Baghdād, 25, 28, and the miracle of the mountain, 31, 32; at Tabrīz, 33; hypocrisy about wine, at Yazd, 39; dislike of turtle-doves as food, 41; Hormuz, 45; Kuhbinān, 48; Tunocain, 49; Shaburqan, 54; Balkh, 54; Taliqan, 55,; Badakhshan, 56; Kashmir, 60; Yarkand, 64; Khotan, 65; Pem, 65; Charchan, 66; Lop, 67; Qara-Khoja, 72; Ghinghintalas, 73; Kan-chou, 75, 91; Tenduc, 95; their gibes at Christians, 109; in Yūn-nan, 187; Sumatra, 282; reverence for St Thomas, 309; in Ceylon, 319, 322; pilgrims to Adam's Sepulchre, 322; in Kesmacoran, 335; Madagascar, 341; in Abyssinia, 347; Aden, 347, 352; outrage by, 349 *seqq.*; at Esh-Shihr, 354; Dhufar, 356; Qalhat, 357; Hormuz, 358. *See* also ACOMAT SOLDAN
SARAI, capital of Qipchaq Khanate, founded by Batu Khan on the Volga (Chaucer's "Sarra in the land of Tartarie"), 3
SARAI, Sea of. *See* CASPIAN
SCASEM, this is the correct reading. *Casem*, adopted by Pauthier and Yule from the Grégoire text may be due, as Benedetto suggests, to a wrong division of the words "*apele scasem.*" Scasem stands for the old form *Ishkāshm*, a town on the left bank of the Panja in Wakhan. In the *T'ang-shu* it is transcribed *Saï-chia-shen* (old pronunciation *Sak-ka-sim*), *see* Chavannes, *Documents sur les Tou-kiue Occidentaux*, p. 165. Al-Biruni gives *Sakāshim* as the capital of Shighnān. *See also* Stein, *Serindia*, I, 61–62. 56
SCOTRA, Island of Socotra, 337, 338, 339, 340, 341; Christian Archbishop of, 338, 340
SEILAN, Ceylon, ix, 319; mountain of Adam's Sepulchre, 319; story of Sagamoni Borcan, 319–322
SEMENAT, Somnat, in Kathiawar, a Hindu place of pilgrimage, 335
SENDALS, silk material similar to taffetas (see Chaucer's *Doctor of Physic*: "In sanguin and in persë clad was allé, Linëd with taffata and with sendallé."), 168 178, 208, 233, 331

INDEX

SENDEMAN, king of Ceylon, 291

SENDER BANDI DEVAR, Sundara Pandi Devar, King in Ma'bar, 292; his jewels, 294; his wives, 295; his lieges, 296; his horses, 296, 310

SENSIN, Hsien-shêng = Taoists, ascetics living on bran, 101, 102, *see Yule*, I, pp. 321–327

SEPULCHRE, of Adam, 319, 322

SEPULCHRE, of Christ, 7, 9; oil from, 7, 9

SERAZI, Shīrāz, 37

SERPENTS, i.e. alligators, 189, 190, 307, 308

SESAME, plant from which an oil similar to olive oil is extracted and used for cooking, lubrication, and lighting, 58; in Ceylon, 291; used for anointing children in Ma'bar, 312; in Abyssinia, 351

SEVASTA, Sivas in Asia Minor, 20

SHABĀNKĀRA. *See* SONCARA

SHA-CHOU. *See* SACHIU

SHANGTU. *See* CHANDU

SHAN-HSI. *See* KENJANFU

SHEEP, fat-tailed in Kerman, 42; wild in Badakhshan, 58; *ovis poli* (*q.v.*) in Pamir, 61; large in India, 309; black-headed in Zanzibar, 345; four-horned in Esh-Shihr, 355

SHELLS. *See* COWRIES

SHIENG, Shêng. *Shieng* probably refers to the administrative council called *Chung shu shêng*. This name was abbreviated to *shêng*. The provincial counterpart of this metropolitan council was called *Hsing chung shu shêng*—a name abbreviated to *Hsing shêng*. Perhaps the word *sing* which occurs in some texts refers to the *hsing* which was used as a prefix to mark the provincial counterparts of the governing bodies in the capital (Perceval Yetts), 152. *See also* THAI

SHIGNAN. *See* SIGHINAN

SHIPS, of the Great Khan, 16; of Hormuz, 45, 46; of Sinjumatu, 216; of Manji, 267–270; of Aden, 353

SHIRAZ. *See* SERAZI

SHULISTAN. *See* SULISTAN

SIGHINAN, Shignan, ruby mines, 57

SIKINTINJIN (F. Sichintingin). Some texts have Sikintinju. Not identified, 109. *See Yule*, I, 345

SILINJU, Hsi-ning-fu, formerly called Hsi-ning-chou, 95. *See Yule*, I, 276. Some texts have Sinju

SILK, in Turcomania, 20; Georgia, 23, 24; Tabrīz, 33; Yazd, 39; Kerman, 39; Tenduc province, 95; Khanbaliq, 147; Kuei-chou, 207; Taiuanfu, 169; Kenjanfu, 174; Cuncun, 175; Cachanfu, 208; Changli, 210; Pinju, 217; Pao-ying-hsien, 223; An-Ch'ing, 225; Chên-chiang fu, 231; Chên-ch'ao, 232; Su-chou, 233; Vughin, 233; Kinsai, 241, 249; Chio-chao, 255; Chien-ning fu, 257

SILVER, mines in Armenia, 21; in Badakhshan, 57; in Idifu, 96; imported into Malabar, 331; and into Cambay, 334; mines in Russia, 389

SINDACHU, Hsüan-hua fu, formerly called Hsüan-tê-chou, 95

SINDUFU, Ch'êng-tu fu, 177, 208. *See Cordier*, 79

SINGAPORE, Straits of, viii

SINJU, Chên-chou, now I-ching-hsien, 228 *seqq*. *See also under* SILINJU

INDEX

SINJUMATU, Hsin-chou-ma-t'ou, *i.e.* Ch'i-ning-chou, 215, 216. *See* Moule, *T'oung Pao*, July 1912, pp. 431–3

SIVAS. *See* SEVASTA

SOCOTRA. *See* SCOTRA

SOGATU, Sotu of the Chinese Annals, military governor of Canton districts, 278

SOLDAIA, Sudaq on S.E. coast of Crimea where the Mongol Khans of Qipchaq had authorised the establishment of a Venetian colony, 3

SOLI, Chola, *i.e.* Tanjore, kingdom of, 314

SOMNAT. *See* SEMENAT

SONCARA, Shabānkāra, province of Persia, 37

SONDUR. *See* CONDUR

SORCERERS, in Pashai, 59; Kashmir, 59; Dagroian, 286; Socotra, 340, 341

SPAIN, King of, 16

SPIKENARD, in Bengal, 203; in Java, 279; in Malabar, 331

SPITTOONS, pocket, used by Chinese in Kubilai's presence, 167

SPODIUM, residuum of ashes resulting from the smelting of copper or from the burning of vegetable matter or bones, 48, *see Yule*, I, 126

STEEL, in Kerman, 39; Kuh-Binan, 48; Ghinghintalas, 73

STEIN, Sir Aurel, xv, 409

STONE PILLARS, planted each side of the roads in Kubilai's kingdom where it was impossible to plant trees, 159

STOVES, stoked with coal for baths, 160

STURGEON, in Caspian Sea, 24

SU-CH'IEN. *See* CHINJU

SU-CHOU. *See* SUCHU and SUJU

SUCHU, Sukchur, Su-chou, province and city, 74, 75

SUDAQ. *See* SOLDAIA

SUGAR, in Bengal, 203; in Kinsai, 253; in Unken, 258; Fu-chien, 260

SUICIDE, in place of capital punishment, 297

SUJU, Su-chou. *Rashīd*, p. 488, has *Shak-ju*. Marco Polo is incorrect in giving the meaning of the name as "Earth," 232–233

SULISTAN (F. Çielstan = Çul(i)stan), Shulistan, province of Persia, 37

SUMATRA. *See* JAVA THE LESSER, and SAMATRA

SUNDARA PANDI DEVAR. *See* SENDER BANDI

TABLETS OF AUTHORITY, Paīzah, presented to the Polos by Kubilai, 7; by Kaikhatu, 17; presented for valour to captains, 112, 113; given to governors of provinces of Persia, 151

TABRIZ. *See* TORIS

TACUINI, occurs only in Z; probably clerical error for *tacuim*, Ar. *taqwīm*, almanacs, 163

TAGACHAR, Mongol baron in service of Arghun, 379

TAICAN, Tāliqān, 55

TAI-CHOU. *See* TINJU

TAIDU, Ta-tu, Kubilai's new city of Khan-baliq, 122, 138. *See under* PEKING

TAILED MEN, in Sumatra, 287

TAIUANFU, T'ai-yüan fu, 169, 170

TĀLIQĀN. *See* TAICAN

TALLY-STICKS, in Zardandān, 193

TAMBUR (Pers. *Tembul*, Sans. *Tambula*, betel-nut, 324

INDEX

TANA, near the modern Bombay. The capital of Konkan, 333, *see Yule*, II, 396
TANDINFU, probably Yen-chou, 210
TANGUT, originally the name of a people living on the north-west frontier of China, and known to the Chinese as *T'ang-hsiang* and to the Mongols as *Tăng* of which *Tăngŭt* is the plural. In 1032 they founded a dynasty which they called *Hsi-hsia*, or Western Hsia, which endured down to its overthrow by Chingiz Khan in 1227, who divided it into the various provinces described by Marco Polo. The whole country was first called *Kan-su* from the names of its two chief cities *Kan-chou* and *Su-chou*. It was known to the Mongols as *Qashin* (Ho-hsi = "West of the Yellow River"). As Marco Polo tells us, they had a language of their own; they also had a curious script which has the appearance of the Chinese but is totally different. Many coins and documents of the Hsi-hsia have been found, 68, 75, 91
TANJORE. *See* SOLI
TANPINJU, probably Shao-hsing fu, 254. *See Yule*, II, p. 220
TARANTULAS, 302, 306, 315
TARTAR, Great, Hulagu, *see* ALAU, 23
TARTARS, *i.e.* Mongols, 1, 4; tributary to Prester John, 78; Chingiz their king, 79; his successors, 83; their customs and religion, 84, 85; their drink, 85; dress, 86; clothes, 86; arms and customs of war, 86–88, 360; degeneracy, 88; administration of justice, and laws, 89
TARTARS, of the Levant. *See* LEVANT
TARTARS, of the Ponent. *See* PONENT
TARTARY, 1, 4
TATTOOING, in Zardandān, 192; in Caugigu, 204; in Fu-chien, 265
TAURIS. *See* TORIS
TEBALDO VISCONTI OF PIACENZA, Roman legate in Acre, afterwards Pope Gregory X, vii, 8, 9, 10
TEBET, Tibet, Province, 178; canes burnt to frighten wild beasts, 179; marriage customs of, 180, 181; dogs of, 182, 183; sorcery, 182
TEBET, a race of idolaters accused of cannibalism, 100
TEGANA, Mongol baron, 379
TELINGANA. *See* MUTFILI
TEMUR, Kaan, also called Öljäitu, third son of Chên-chin, son of Kubilai, reigned from 1295–1307, 116
TENDUC, plain of, T'ien-tê. (*See* Pelliot, *T'oung Pao*, December 1914, pp. 10 *seqq.*), 81, 94; city of, 94
THAI, *T'ai*, Kubilai's council of twelve barons. Probably refers to the Censurate *Yü-chih-t'ai*; if so, the apparent contradiction in calling each of two different bodies supreme is explained since the censors had the power of overriding all except the Great Kaan. There appears to be no authority in the *Yüan-Shih* for the statement made on p. 152 that the T'ai is the court to which the care of the armies is committed. The name of the council which controlled military affairs

THAI—*continued.*
was *Shu mi yüan* (Perceval Yetts), 151, 152. (*See also* SHIENG)
TIBET. *See* TEBET
T'IEN-TÊ. *See* TENDUC
TIFLIS, 24
TIGRIS RIVER, Volga, 4; at Baghdād, 23
TINJU, Tai-chou, 224
TINNEVELLY. *See* CAIL
TIUNJU, 264; porcelain manufactured there, 265
TOCTAI KHAN, son of Mängü Tämür, Lord of the Ponent, 401; war against Nogai, 403 *seqq.*
TOGAN, Mongol baron, 379
TOLEDO, Latin text of Marco Polo in, xi
TOLOBUGA, Tula-bugha, great-grandson of Batu, 401
TOLOMAN (part of Kwei-chou?), 205, 277
TOMAN, *tümän*, 10,000 (men), word of ancient origin used in Turkish and Mongolian, 87, 250
TORIS, Tabrīz, the capital of the Il-Khans of Persia, 21, 27; described, 32, 33; monastery of St Barsamo, 34
TORISINS, inhabitants of Tabrīz, 33
TOSCAOR, *tosqaul*, watchmen for Kubilai's falcons, 141
TOTAMANGU, Tuda Mängü, Khan of the Golden Horde (1280–1287), grandson of Batu, Lord of the Ponent, 393, 401
TRANSMIGRATION OF SOULS, 165, 321
TRAVANCORE. *See* COILUM
TREBIZOND, ix, 19, 21
TREE-FLOUR, sago, in Sumatra, 288
TREES, planted each side of Kubilai's roads to show the way, 159; producing camphor, 263; flour from, *see* TREE-FLOUR
TUC, *tugh*, yak's tail banner, 100,000 (men), 87. *See also* TOMAN.
TUDA-MÄNGÜ. *See* TOTAMANGU
TUGH. *See* TUC
TUMBLERS. *See* JUGGLERS
TUN-HUANG. *See* SACHIU
TUNNYFISH, 44, 338, 355
TUNOCAIN, *i.e.* *Tūn* and *Qa'in*. Both these Persian towns exist today and send representatives to the Majlis but under the Pahlavi régime the name of *Tūn* has been changed to *Firdaus*, the reason being that *Tūn* had a bad meaning. *Tūn* means the stove of a public bath (*hammām*), and in common parlance to tell a man "to go to *tūn*" is tantamount to telling him to go to Hades. *Firdaus*, the new name, means Paradise, 37, 49
TURAKINA, the Lady, xiv
TURBITH (*Radex Turpethi*), a spice, 331
TURCOMANIA, Anatolian Turkey, 20
TURCOMANS, 20
TURKEY, GREAT, Turkestan, 66, 359, 365, 384
TURQUOISE, in Kerman, 39; in Gaindu, 184
TURTLE-DOVES, in Rudbar, 41
TUTIA, oxide of zinc used as coryllium for the eyes, in Kuh-Binan, 48; Cambay, 334

UCACA, town on Volga, 4
UIGHURS, xii
UMBRELLA, used by commanders of Kubilai's army to show their rank, 113
UNC KAN, Wang Khan, Prester John (*q.v.*)

INDEX

UNG and MUNGUL. *See* GOG AND MAGOG
UNG, *Öng*, plural *öngüt*, name of Mongol Christian tribe, 95
UNGRAT, Qungurat, a Tartar tribe, 114
UNICORN, rhinoceros, in Sumatra, 283, 287. *See Yule*, II, 290
UNKEN, a town fifteen miles from Fu-chou, 258. *See Yule*, II, 230

VAIR, animal and its fur, 86, 387, 388
VANCU (Ramusio: Vanchu), probably not Wang-chu, but the title *Wan-hu* = commander of 10,000, used by Marco Polo as a personal name. *See* Moule, *J.N.C.B.R.A.S.*, 126, 127, 128, Vol. LVIII, 1927
VENICE, vii, ix, x, 1, 8, 9; Polos return to, 19; Marco brings articles from the East to, 92, 93, 287
VENTILATORS (*bād-gīr*), on houses in Hormuz, 358
VOCAN, Wakhan, 61
VOCHAN, Yung-ch'ang fu, in Yün-nan, 192; battle of, in 1278, at which Marco Polo was present, 196–200
VONSANICHIN, Fan-wên-hu, the correct reading must be Vonsamchin (Pelliot). Chinese general sent against Japan, 271
VUGHIN, probably Wu-chiang in Chiang-su, 233
VUJU, probably Chin-hua fu, formerly called Wu-chou, in Kiang-nan, 233; in Chê-chiang, 254

WAKHAN. *See* VOCAN
WANG KHAN. *See* UNG KAN
WATER, bitter, 47, 48
WHALES, in Indian Sea, 338; Cacholot, or Sperm, 338; method of catching them, 338, 339, 342
WHEAT, in Persia, 38; bread made from it not eaten in Yachi, 187
WHITE FEAST, celebrated by Kubilai and his subjects on New Year's Day, 134
WINE, hypocrisy of Muslims about drinking, 38; at Kubilai's feasts, 131; at Taiuanfu, 169
WINE, from rice, spices, etc., in Gaindu, 186; Yachi, 187; Caugigu, 204; Toloman, 206; Kinsai, 236, 237, 240
WINE, from *Gomuti* palm, in Sumatra, 285, 287; in Ceylon, 291
WINE, from dates, 327, 345

XANADU. *See* CHANDU

YACHI (F. Iaci), Yün-nan fu, according to Rashid the capital of Qarajang (Yün-nan), 187
YAK. *See* OXEN
YANB (F. ianb), Turkish *yam*, horse-post stations, on routes from Khan-baliq, 152. *See Bretschneider*, I, 187
YANJU, Yang-chou, a city in Manji governed by Marco Polo for three years, 224, 228
YANG-TZŬ-CHIANG river. *See* KIAN and KIANSUI
YARCAN, Yarkand, vii, 64
YASDI, Yazd, 38, 39
YAZD. *See* above
YEN-CHOU. *See* TANDINFU
YESUDAR. *See* JESUDAR
YETTS, W. Perceval, xvii

INDEX

YOGI. *See* CHUGHI

YRAC, Iraq, 32

YULE, Col. Henry, his edition of Marco Polo, xv, 409

YÜN-NAN. *See* CARAJAN

YÜN-NAN FU. *See* YACHI

ZAITUN or Zitūn, Arabic form of *Tzŭ-t'ung* (*see* FERRAND, *Textes relatifs à l'Extrême-Orient*, p. 455), famous seaport identified with Ch'üan-chou fu, east of Amoy, in Fu-chien, viii, 261, 263; revenue received from, 264, 276, 277, 280

ZANGHIBAR, Zanzibar, 341, 342; the people of, 344; their ugliness, 344; women, 345; methods of warfare, 346

ZARDANDAN (Persian *zar-dandān*; Chinese *Chin-ch'ih* = "gold-teeth"), Yung-ch'ang, in Yünnan. *See* VOCHAN, 192

ZELADA, Cardinal, his text of Marco Polo, x

ZIC, Circassia, 393

ZORZA, island Chorcha or Juchin, where Kubilai sent victims for torture and punishment, 274

ZULCARNEIN, Zu'l-qarnayn, "Lord of the two horns", Arabic epithet of Alexander the Great. Title held by kings of Badakhshan, 56

ZURFICAR, Zu'l-Fiqār, a Turkish friend of Marco Polo's, 73